ATLAS
of
MEDIEVAL
EUROPE

EDITED BY
ANGUS MACKAY WITH DAVID DITCHBURN

Routledge
Taylor & Francis Group

LONDON AND NEW YORK

1004111700

First published 1997
by Routledge
11 New Fetter Lane, London EC4P 4EE

Simultaneously published in the USA and Canada
by Routledge
29 West 35th Street, New York, NY 10001

First published in paperback 1997
Reprinted 1998, 1999, 2000, 2002, 2003

Routledge is an imprint of the Taylor & Francis Group

Introduction © 1997 Angus MacKay
Selection and editorial matter, bibliography
© 1997 Angus MacKay and David Ditchburn
Individual maps and texts © 1997 The contributors

Typeset in Garamond by Solidus (Bristol) Limited
Printed and bound in Great Britain by
TJ International Ltd, Padstow, Cornwall

British Library Cataloguing in Publication Data
A catalogue record for this book is available from the British
Library

Library of Congress Cataloging in Publication Data
A catalog record for this book is available from the Library of
Congress

ISBN 0–415–01923–0 (hbk)
ISBN 0–415–12231–7 (pbk)

CONTENTS

PREFACE

The preparation of an atlas of the history of Europe during the Middle Ages presents numerous and complex difficulties. In the first place the period to be covered stretches from the late fourth century down to the late fifteenth (or even early sixteenth) century. In addition, however, an atlas of this kind evidently cannot be confined to Western Europe: Byzantium and Eastern Europe have to be included, as indeed do such important matters as the exploits of crusading Europeans overseas, the impact of Muslims or Mongols, travel abroad, and the early voyages of discovery. In terms of social groupings equally formidable problems present themselves. Obviously the main political events from the fall of the Roman Empire down to the battles and treaties of the Hundred Years War have to be included, but so too do the activities of other protagonists; for example, popes and anti-popes, those who attended and participated in the great Church Councils or in parliamentary assemblies, Italian and Hanseatic merchants, tax collectors, women, colonists, peasants, shepherds (and their sheep), Jews and New Christians, heretics, writers and translators, troubadours, and architects and artists. Despite the difficulties inherent in such a task, however, the inclusion of such varied facets offers some positive advantages. For in addition to the emperors, kings, princes and great nobles, the artisans and peasants who participated in the French Jacquerie or the English revolt of 1381 left their mark on the period, as indeed did the humble Béguines and Beghards.

An atlas is an essential tool for the study of medieval history. This has long been recognized, but I believe that no adequate solution, specifically designed for this purpose, exists. When I was a student, which was admittedly a long time ago, we were advised to use a German atlas which was incredibly detailed and well nigh incomprehensible. The present atlas does not aim at minute detail compressed into a few cluttered maps. On the contrary, the main objective has been clarity, and each map is accompanied by an explanatory text.

Using nearly 140 maps, the atlas spans the entire medieval period. The actual selection of maps to be included was primarily determined by the years of undergraduate teaching experienced by the editor and contributors.

I am extremely grateful to all those colleagues who have helped in preparing this volume. Those who have contributed the maps, the accompanying texts and suggestions for further reading (contained in the bibliography) have suffered from my incessant demands, requests for clarification and advice, and all the delays inevitable in bringing such a co-operative enterprise to its conclusion. I owe a special debt to David Ditchburn whose efficiency and versatile talents have frequently made me ashamed of my own shortcomings.

It was Richard Stoneman who originally conceived of the project, and his constant encouragement and exemplary patience have been much appreciated. His successive assistants – Anita Roy, Jackie Dias, Kate Morrall and particularly Victoria Peters – have all displayed charitable forbearance when dealing with my absent-mindedness.

Finally, special thanks are due to the cartographer, Jayne Lewin, for her skill in converting rough drafts or even mere sketches into clear maps, dealing patiently with late changes, and in resolving contradictions implicit in some of the difficult instructions sent in by contributors.

I hope that university undergraduates, senior school pupils and professional historians will find the atlas useful and rewarding. I also imagine that enlightened tourists interested in the history and culture of the countries they are visiting may benefit from the maps and commentaries provided by the expert contributors.

Angus MacKay
Department of History
University of Edinburgh

CONTRIBUTORS

Frances Andrews, University of St Andrews
Michael J. Angold, University of Edinburgh
Malcolm C. Barber, University of Reading
Robert J. Bartlett, University of St Andrews
Ian Beavan, University of Aberdeen
Philip Bennett, University of Edinburgh
Louise M. Bourdua, University of Aberdeen
Thomas S. Brown, University of Edinburgh
Simon Coates, University of Edinburgh
Antonio Collantes de Terán, University of Seville
M. Gary Dickson, University of Edinburgh
David Ditchburn, University of Aberdeen
Marilyn Dunn, University of Glasgow
Robin Frame, University of Durham
Manuel González Jiménez, University of Seville
Anthony Goodman, University of Edinburgh
Alexander Grant, University of Lancaster
Philip Hersch, University of Edinburgh
John C. Higgitt, University of Edinburgh

Richard A. Hodges, University of Sheffield
Michael C. E. Jones, University of Nottingham
Derek Lomax, University of Birmingham
  (deceased)
Raymond McClusky, Glasgow
Martin McLaughlin, University of Oxford
Norman Macleod, University of Edinburgh
Malyn D. D. Newitt, University of Exeter
Richard Oram, University of Aberdeen
Richard Rose, University of Glasgow
Michael L. Ryder, University of Edinburgh
Ross Samson, Glasgow
Roger Tarr, University of Edinburgh
Alfred Thomas, Rutgers University
Elspeth M. Turner, University of Edinburgh
Ian Wei, University of Bristol
Christopher J. Wickham, University of
  Birmingham

PHYSICAL EUROPE

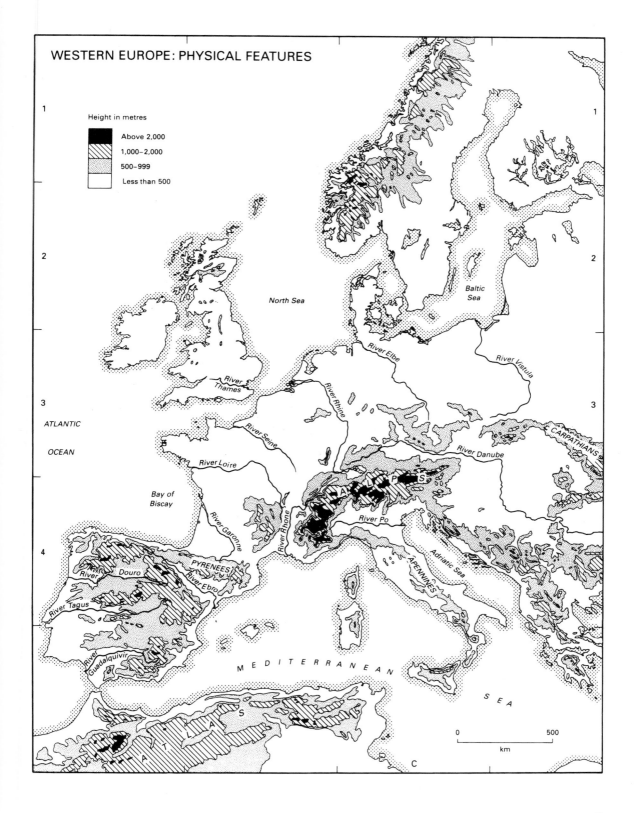

WESTERN EUROPE: PHYSICAL FEATURES

Height in metres

Above 2,000

1,000–2,000

500–999

Less than 500

ATLANTIC

OCEAN

North Sea

Baltic Sea

River Elbe

River Vistula

River Thames

River Rhine

River Seine

CARPATHIANS

River Loire

River Danube

Bay of Biscay

A L P S

River Garonne

River Rhône

River Po

PYRENEES

River Ebro

Adriatic Sea

River Douro

APENNINES

River Tagus

River Guadalquivir

M E D I T E R R A N E A N

S E A

A T L A S

0   500

km

THE EARLY MIDDLE AGES
(to *c.* 1100)

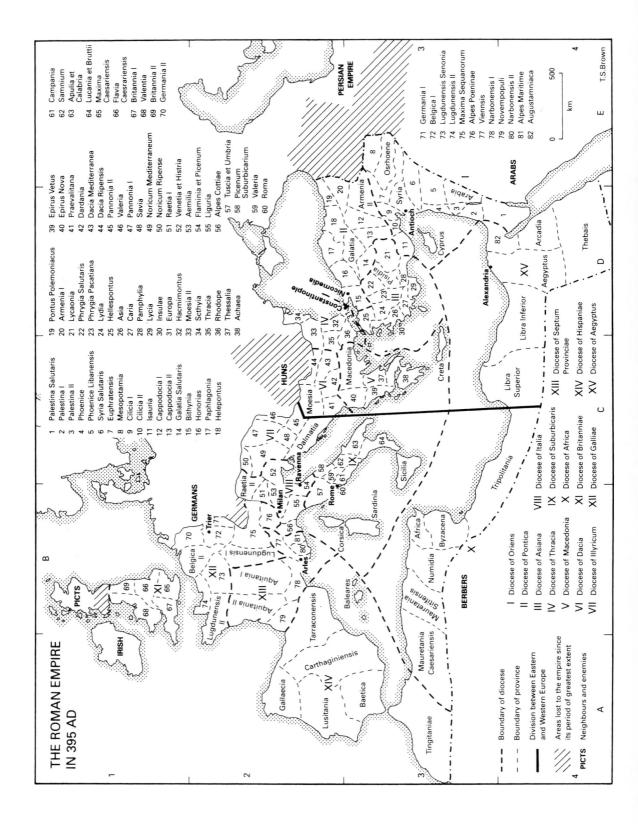

THE ROMAN EMPIRE IN 395 AD

1	Palestina Salutaris
2	Palestina I
3	Palestina II
4	Phoenice
5	Phoenice Libanensis
6	Syria Salutaris
7	Euphratensis
8	Mesopotamia
9	Cilicia I
10	Cilicia II
11	Isauria
12	Cappodocia I
13	Cappodocia II
14	Galatia Salutaris
15	Bithynia
16	Honorias
17	Paphlagonia
18	Helepontus

19	Pontus Polemoniacus
20	Armenia I
21	Lycaonia
22	Phrygia Salutaris
23	Phrygia Pacatiana
24	Lydia
25	Hellespontus
26	Asia
27	Caria
28	Pamphylia
29	Lycia
30	Insulae
31	Lycia
32	Hacmimontus
33	Moesia II
34	Scthyia
35	Thracia
36	Rhodope
37	Thessalia
38	Achaea

39	Epirus Vetus
40	Epirus Nova
41	Praevalitana
42	Dardania
43	Dacia Mediterranea
44	Dacia Ripensis
45	Pannonia II
46	Valeria
47	Pannonia I
48	Savia
49	Noricum Mediterraneum
50	Noricum Ripense
51	Raetia I
52	Venetia et Histria
53	Aemilia
54	Flaminia et Picenum
55	Liguria
56	Alpes Cottiae
57	Tuscia et Umbria
58	Picenum Suburbicarium
59	Valeria
60	Roma

61	Campania
62	Samnium
63	Apulia et Calabria
64	Lucania et Bruttii
65	Maxima Caesariensis
66	Flavia Caesariensis
67	Britannia I
68	Valentia
69	Britannia II
70	Germania II

71	Germania I
72	Belgica I
73	Lugdunensis Senonia
74	Lugdunensis II
75	Maxima Sequanorum
76	Alpes Poeninae
77	Viennsis
78	Narbonensis I
79	Novempopuli
80	Narbonensis II
81	Alpes Maritime
82	Augustamniaca

I	Diocese of Oriens
II	Diocese of Pontica
III	Diocese of Asiana
IV	Diocese of Thracia
V	Diocese of Macedonia
VI	Diocese of Dacia
VII	Diocese of Illyricum
VIII	Diocese of Italia
IX	Diocese of Suburbicaris
X	Diocese of Africa
XI	Diocese of Britanniae
XII	Diocese of Galliae
XIII	Diocese of Septum Provinciae
XIV	Diocese of Hispaniae
XV	Diocese of Aegyptus

- – – – Boundary of diocese
- – – – Boundary of province
- ▬▬▬ Division between Eastern and Western Europe
- Areas lost to the empire since its period of greatest extent
- PICTS Neighbours and enemies

km 0 500

T.S.Brown

POLITICS

The Roman Empire in 395 AD

By 395 AD the Roman Empire had changed considerably since the time of its first emperor Augustus (27 BC–14 AD). Increased external pressures, deteriorating economic conditions and political disorder aggravated by dynastic insecurity and the ambitions of generals led to the abandonment of outlying provinces and a period of prolonged upheaval in the third century. A major reorganization introduced by Diocletian (284–305) and continued by Constantine (306–37) saw the elevation of the emperor into a remote autocrat along Eastern lines, the creation of a large bureaucracy and a division of the army into a two-tier force consisting of elite mobile units and poorer quality local troops. In an attempt to improve local efficiency and to minimize the risk of revolt Diocletian doubled the number of provinces and grouped them into dioceses under *vicarii*, while Constantine established a separation of powers between civil governors and military commanders. After defeating his opponents at the Milvian Bridge (312), Constantine became a Christian and promoted what had been a minority faith by appointing Christians to key positions and endowing the Church with lands and buildings. Theological divisions remained acute, however, and pagan rites were not proscribed until the reign of Theodosius I (378–95). Constantine's transfer of the capital to the strategic site of Byzantium, re-named Constantinople in 330, reflected both his commitment to his new faith and the increasing importance of the East in the empire.

These changes produced a measure of political and economic stability although Constantine's dynasty was riven by family disputes and it died out after the death of the short-lived pagan emperor Julian fighting the Persians in 363. During the reigns of the succeeding emperors barbarian pressure on the frontiers increased, partly as a result of the arrival of the Hun nomads in Europe in the 370s. The Visigoths successfully requested asylum in the empire in 376, but ill-treatment led them to turn against the Romans and to wipe out a Roman army at the battle of Adrianople (378), in which the emperor Valens was killed. This defeat was a great blow to Roman prestige, but the direct effects were limited. The Goths were granted lands in the Balkans as *foederati* (allies) and order was restored by the staunchly Christian Spanish emperor Theodosius I.

Following Theodosius' death in 395 a critical stage in the transformation of the Roman world occurred with the division of the empire between his sons Honorius (West) and Arcadius (East). While the myth of imperial unity was maintained, tension grew between the two courts. The Eastern empire remained relatively powerful as a result of its greater wealth and population and its relative immunity from barbarian pressure and the dangerous influence which German mercenaries exercised in the West. Christianity became strongly entrenched, and, despite bitter christological controversies, served to reinforce imperial authority by treating the empire as an instrument of divine policy. In the West, however, fundamental economic and social weaknesses were aggravated by court intrigues, the self-interest of the senatorial elite and frequent revolts by usurpers. While Roman administration, society and culture remained resilient at the highest levels, the decentralization of the *pars occidentalis* was reflected in the growth of non-Roman cultures (as in Britain and North Africa) and the rise of local political allegiances (as in Gaul) even before the full effects of the barbarian migrations were felt in the fifth century.

T.S. Brown

7

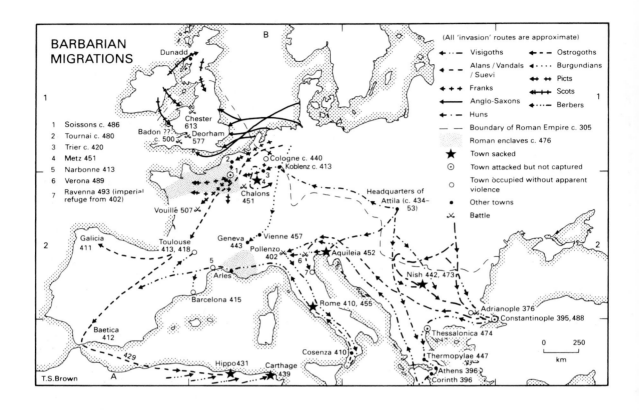

Barbarian Migrations of the Fourth and Fifth Centuries

The pressure from 'barbarians' (mostly Germans) which the Roman Empire had experienced from the late second century became more intense in the late fourth century. This *Volkerwanderung* (wandering of the peoples) involved unstable amalgams of diverse groups, many of whom settled gradually and relatively peacefully. The pressure of steppe nomads such as the Huns from *c.* 370 played a role, but probably more important were rivalries among the Germanic peoples, the formation of confederacies under aggressive military leaders from the third century and the opportunities presented to booty-hungry war-leaders and their retinues by Rome's political, military and financial weaknesses and the increasing alienation of Roman provincials from centralized rule.

The first serious case of Germanic penetra-

tion occurred after 376, as Visigothic and Ostrogothic tribes living beyond the Danube sought refuge as Roman allies (*foederati*) within the empire. Tension led to the battle of Adrianople in which a largely Visigothic force defeated a Roman army and killed the emperor Valens. Although a treaty was soon arranged the Visigoths continued to ravage Greece and Illyricum until, in 402, they entered Italy under the leadership of Alaric. A cat-and-mouse game took place while the imperial government in Ravenna prevaricated in the face of Gothic demands for land and gold. Finally Alaric's exasperation led to the sack of Rome in August 410 – an enormous blow to Roman morale. Alaric died soon afterwards and his brother-in-law Ataulf led the Goths to southern Gaul, where they were recognized as *foederati* by a treaty in 416. Under their kings

Theodoric I and II and Euric, they built up a powerful state based on Toulouse which had generally good relations with the Roman aristocracy and established overlordship in Spain.

The German peoples who had remained north of the Danube (Herules, Gepids, Rugi, Skiri and Ostrogoths) became subjects of the Huns, who built up a tributary empire under Attila (434–53). While launching regular attacks on the east Roman provinces in the Balkans, Attila remained friendly with Aetius, the dominant force in the west, until he was induced to launch inconclusive raids into Gaul (checked by his defeat at Chalons in 451) and northern Italy. The collapse of the Hun empire following Attila's death in 453 led to renewed pressure by Germanic bands (Ostrogoths, Rugi and others) on the Danube frontier.

Meanwhile northern Gaul had been thrown into confusion by the rupture of the Rhine frontier in late 406 by a mixed barbarian force dominated by Vandals, Suevi and Alans. While some Alans became Roman allies in Gaul, others joined the Vandal invasion of Spain in 409. The Suevi set up a robber kingdom based on Galicia which lasted until 585. In the face of Visigoth pressure the Vandals sailed to Africa in 429 and were granted the western provinces by a treaty of 435. Their able king, Geiseric, seized Carthage in 439, occupied the rest of Roman Africa and launched a series of lucrative naval raids, occupy-ing Sicily, Sardinia and Corsica and sacking Rome in 455. Following his death in 477 the aggressive and confiscatory policies towards the Roman aristocracy and the Catholic Church gave way to a generally more conciliatory and Romanizing regime.

The collapse of the Rhine frontier in 406/7 had wide repercussions. Britain saw its Roman garrison withdrawn and the assumption of power by rival British chieftains until the Anglo-Saxon invasions in the late 440s. The Burgundians were permitted to set up a kingdom on the upper Rhine in 413. Transferred as federates to the Jura/Lake Geneva area in 443, they built up a Romanized kingdom incorporating the Lyon and Vienne areas from 457. Along the middle and lower Rhine groups of Franks became powerful and attacked cities such as Cologne and Trier. In northern Gaul Roman rule was undermined by obscure rivalries between usurping generals, Bretons, peasant rebels (Bagaudae), Alans and the sub-Roman regimes of Aegidius and his son Syagrius based on Soissons (c. 456–86). The long-term beneficiary of this power vacuum was the Salian Frank dynasty of Childeric (d. 481) and his son Clovis, who gradually expanded from their original centre of Tournai by conquering or allying themselves with rival bands of Franks, including established *laeti* (soldier-farmers).

T.S. Brown

Barbarian Kingdoms in the First Half of the Sixth Century

By 500 the Roman Empire in the west had been replaced by powerful Germanic kingdoms. Prominent were the Frankish kingdom built up in northern Gaul by the Frankish rulers Childeric (d. 481) and his son Clovis (481–511) and the Ostrogothic kingdom established in Italy by Theoderic (489–526). Any semblance of stability in the west was, however, shattered over the next four decades. After his victory over the kingdom of Toulouse at Vouillé in 507 Clovis took over most of south-west Gaul and the Visigoths were compelled to transfer their political base to Spain, with their eventual capital at Toledo. The kingdom of their Ostrogothic cousins fell into decline on Theoderic's death as a result of dynastic uncertainties and tension between pro-Roman and traditionalist elements. Two of the initially powerful kingdoms were conquered in 533–4: the Burgundians' territories in south-east Gaul were incorporated by the Franks and Van-

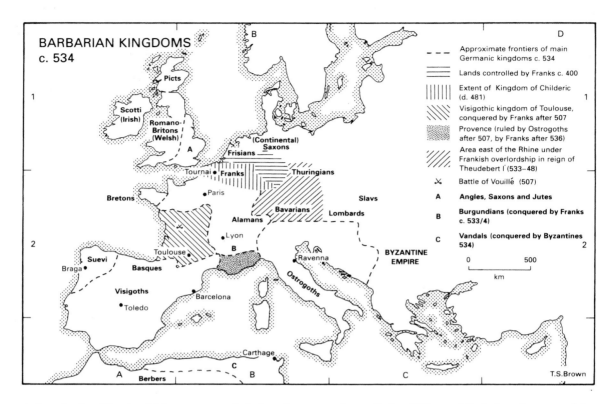

BARBARIAN KINGDOMS
c. 534

- - - Approximate frontiers of main Germanic kingdoms c. 534
≡ Lands controlled by Franks c. 400
||| Extent of Kingdom of Childeric (d. 481)
Visigothic kingdom of Toulouse, conquered by Franks after 507
Provence (ruled by Ostrogoths after 507, by Franks after 536)
Area east of the Rhine under Frankish overlordship in reign of Theudebert I (533–48)
✕ Battle of Vouillé (507)
A Angles, Saxons and Jutes
B Burgundians (conquered by Franks c. 533/4)
C Vandals (conquered by Byzantines 534)

0   500
km

Picts
Scotti (Irish)
Romano-Britons (Welsh)
(Continental) Saxons
Frisians
Thuringians
Tournai • Franks
• Paris
Bretons
Slavs
Bavarians
Alamans
Lombards
• Lyon
Toulouse •
Suevi
Braga •
Basques
BYZANTINE EMPIRE
• Ravenna
Ostrogoths
Visigoths
Barcelona •
• Toledo
Carthage •
Berbers
T.S.Brown

dal rule in North Africa was ended by the lightning campaign of the Byzantine general Belisarius. In 534 the Ostrogoths became the next target of the emperor Justinian's dream of restoring Roman power in the west and Belisarius' forces invaded Italy in 536. Despite fierce resistance by a Gothic army in the north led by Witigis, Belisarius occupied Ravenna in 540. In the 540s the tide turned, thanks to the divisions and corruption of the imperialists, and the able Gothic ruler Totila was able to claw back most of the peninsula. By 552, however, new forces dispatched from the east under Narses defeated the Ostrogothic army. Nevertheless, isolated pockets of Gothic resistance held out in the north until the 560s and Italy lay devastated by years of war. Justinian's attempted *reconquista* of the west went a step further in 551, when an enclave around Cartagena was seized from the Visigothic kingdom of Spain and remained Byzantine until the 620s. However, economic weaknesses and new pressure from the Avars, Slavs and Persians prevented Byzantium from consolidating its gains, and most of Italy was lost to the Lombards from 568. The dominant power in the west became, not the empire, but its nominal ally, the Catholic kingdom of the Franks.

T.S. Brown

Merovingian Gaul, *c.* 600

Although Clovis had extended the Merovingian kingdom over most of Gaul, for much of the sixth and seventh centuries it was beset by the strife vividly chronicled by the historian Gregory of Tours (d. 594). In 511 a complex division took place between Clovis' four sons, which ham-

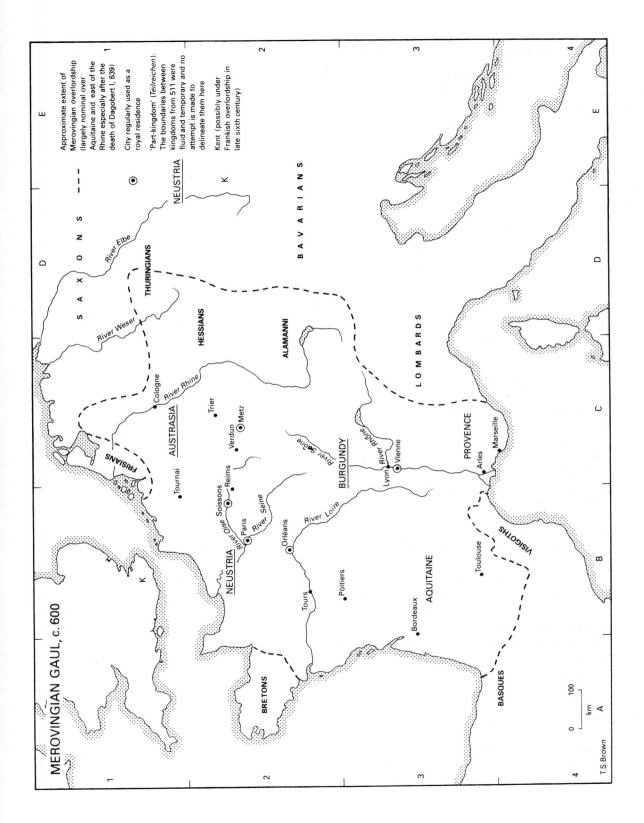

MEROVINGIAN GAUL, c. 600

Approximate extent of
Merovingian overlordship
(largely nominal over
Aquitaine and east of the
Rhine especially after the
death of Dagobert I, 639)

⊙ City regularly used as a
royal residence

K 'Part-kingdom' (*Teilreichen*).
The boundaries between
kingdoms from 511 were
fluid and temporary and no
attempt is made to
delineate them here

Kent (possibly under
Frankish overlordship in
late sixth century)

SAXONS

River Elbe

THURINGIANS

BAVARIANS

River Weser

HESSIANS

ALAMANNI

LOMBARDS

NEUSTRIA

River Rhine

Cologne

AUSTRASIA

Trier

Verdun ⊙ Metz

River Saône

FRISIANS

Tournai

Reims

Soissons

BURGUNDY

River Rhône

Lyon

River

Vienne

PROVENCE

Marseille

Arles

River Oise

Paris

River Seine

Orléans

River Loire

NEUSTRIA

BRETONS

Tours

Poitiers

AQUITAINE

Bordeaux

Toulouse

VISIGOTHS

BASQUES

100

km

0

T.S.Brown

pered efficient royal administration. The Burgundian kingdom was taken over in 534 and Provence in 536. Theudebert I (533–48) expanded his territory east of the Rhine and even beyond the Alps, but this overlordship collapsed after his death. The kingdom was then reunited under Clothar, but partition between his four sons on his death in 561 soon led to civil war and an increasing sense of identity within each *Teilreich* (part-kingdom).

The murder of King Sigibert of Austrasia in 575 provoked bitter conflict. For several decades the dominant force was Sigibert's widow, the Visigoth Brunhilda, but in 613 she was executed and the kingdom was reunited under Clothar II of Neustria (584–629). His son Dagobert I (623–38) proved the last effective Merovingian ruler, as royal power was undermined by the alienation of rights and estates, the loss of Byzantine subsidies and tribute from client peoples east of the Rhine and the growing power of counts and other territorial magnates. Subsequent Merovingian 'do-nothing kings' were incapable of ruling personally and power fell into the hands of aristocratic factions led by the mayors of the palace, such as the Arnulfings, the hereditary mayors of the palace of Austrasia. Under Pepin II this family capitalized on its powerful following in the north-east and its alliance with the Church to become the dominant force throughout the kingdom from 687. A serious revolt followed Pepin's death in 714 but effective power over Neustria and the Merovingian puppet-kings was restored by his illegitimate son Charles Martel (d. 741), who enhanced the power and prestige of his dynasty (the Carolingians) by his campaigns against Saxons, Alamans, Thuringians and Bavarians and most famously by his defeat of an Arab invading force at Poitiers in 733.

The conflicts of the Merovingian period should not obscure its achievements. The kingdom remained the most powerful force in the west as a result of its military strength, its relatively centralized structures, a number of centres of religious and cultural life, and the assimilation which occurred between a small Frankish elite and Gallo-Roman elements prepared to adopt Frankish laws and customs.

T.S. Brown

The Empire of Justinian, 527–65

When Justinian ascended the throne (527), the empire had reasonably well-defined frontiers: the Danube, the Euphrates, and the Arabian and Egyptian deserts. They were defended by powerful frontier fortresses, such as Singidunum, Dara and Edessa. Such threats as there were, the Sassanian Persians in the east, the Bulgars along the lower Danube, and the desert tribes, were more or less contained. Internally there were the rivalries of the circus factions, but religious divisions were more serious. The emperor and the Church at Constantinople were caught between those who valued ecclesiastical unity and the link with the papacy enshrined at the council of Chalcedon (451) and those who favoured an independent Byzantine Church. The latter had been in the ascendant since *c.* 484, when the Acacian schism separated the Churches of Rome and Constantinople. Even before coming to the throne Justinian worked for communion with Rome, which was achieved in 518. This reorientation implied an increased interest in the west, largely dominated by Germanic tribes which had adopted the Arian heresy. There was some discrimination against the native Catholic communities, and in North Africa under the Vandals outright persecution. Justinian saw himself as protector of the Catholic Church. In 533 he launched an expedition against the Vandals, and his commander, Belisarius, took Carthage, the Vandalic capital, and recovered the North African provinces. Next Justinian interfered in Ostrogothic Italy. In 535 Belisarius seized Sicily and invaded Italy. The key

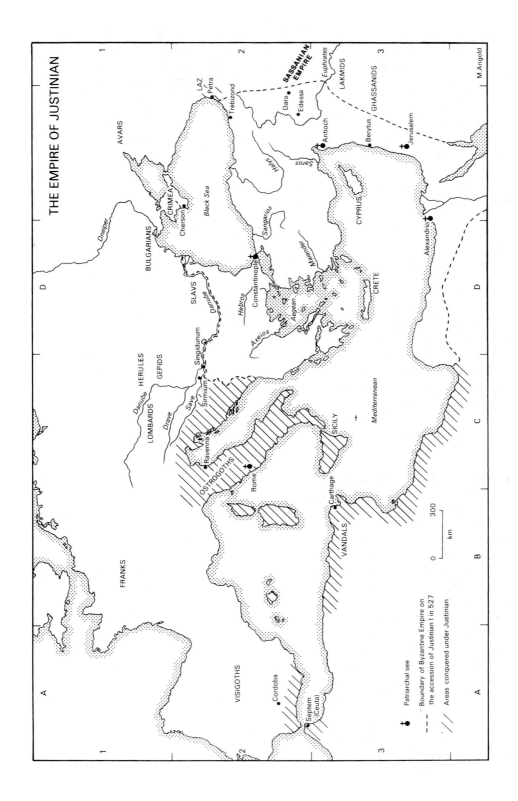

THE EMPIRE OF JUSTINIAN

M.Angold

Patriarchal see

Boundary of Byzantine Empire on
the accession of Justinian I in 527

Areas conquered under Justinian

FRANKS

VISIGOTHS

Cordoba

Septem
(Ceuta)

VANDALS

Carthage

OSTROGOTHS

Ravenna

Rome

SICILY

Mediterranean

0   300
km

LOMBARDS

HERULES

GEPIDS

Danube

Drave

Save

Sirmium

Singidunum

Drave

SLAVS

BULGARIANS

Danube

Hebros

Axeios

Constantinople

Aegean

Maiander

CRIMEA

Cherson

Black Sea

Sangarios

Halys

CRETE

CYPRUS

Dneiper

AVARS

LAZ

Petra

Trebizond

Saros

Dara

Edessa

SASSANIAN
EMPIRE

Euphrates

LAKMIDS

Antioch

Berytus

GHASSANIDS

Jerusalem

Alexandria

13

was Rome, which Belisarius took in 536. His successful defence of the city sapped Ostrogothic resistance, and he entered their capital of Ravenna in 540. The Ostrogoths were confined to the Po valley.

These relatively easy victories were to be tested over the next decade. The Sassanian king of kings, Chosroes I (531–79), sacked Antioch in 540, and his armies captured Petra which commanded access to the Black Sea and control of Lazica. In 544 the city of Edessa beat off a Persian attack and a truce was concluded. Both sides were suffering from the effects of the bubonic plague which had struck in 541/2. The loss of life at Constantinople was calamitous. The administration and the economy were paralysed. The Ostrogoths recovered most of Italy and the Slavs, massed along the Danube, raided deep into the European provinces of the empire. Justinian's government slowly began to recover its equilibrium. In 550 the European provinces were cleared of Slav raiders. In 552 Narses invaded Italy with an army depending heavily on contingents recruited beyond the Danube from the Herules, the Gepids and Lombards. The Ostrogoths were overwhelmed and Italy was restored to the empire. Meanwhile an expedition, despatched in 550, recovered southern Spain from the Visigoths, as well as the North African coast around Septem (Ceuta). Along the eastern frontier Petra was recovered from the Sassanians in 551 and with it control of Lazica. In the desert war the Ghassanids, an Arab tribe allied to the Byzantines, bested the Lakmids, who were clients of the Sassanians. In 562 a peace was concluded between Persia and Byzantium, designed to last for fifty years. Among other things it regulated cross-border trade, trade routes being an element in Byzantine–Sassanian rivalry. The Byzantines were dependent on these for raw silk to feed their industry which was centred on Berytus.

Thanks to heavy investment in fortifications the Danube frontier held, but there was intense pressure from the tribes, Slavs and others, who crowded along it. To counter this, Justinian turned to the Avars, recently arrived from central Asia and settled to the north of the Crimea. It was a miscalculation. After Justinian's death the Avars destroyed the Gepids in 567, pushed the Lombards into Italy, and intensified Slav raiding of Byzantine territories. It contributed to the eventual disintegration of Justinian's empire which was already apparent in the ecclesiastical field, where independent Churches were coming into being in Syria and Egypt. It has been said that 'Justinian's reign witnessed a belated attempt to unify a far-flung Empire that was gradually losing its cohesion'.

M. Angold

The Expansion of Islam in the Mediterranean Area (7th–9th Centuries)

Within ten years of Mohammad's death in 632 the armies of Islam stormed out of Arabia, overwhelmed the Sassanians of Persia, and wrested Syria, Palestine and Egypt from the Byzantine Empire. The Arabs were formidable because of their mobility. In 636 they concentrated at Yarmuk beyond the Jordan and completely defeated the Byzantine armies. The victory brought them Damascus, which became their headquarters. In 637/8 Jerusalem fell, followed quickly by Antioch and Edessa. The conquest of Palestine and Syria was completed in 642 when Caesarea was captured. Gaza had already fallen, and the conquest of Egypt was completed with the surrender of Alexandria (642).

The Byzantine Empire had to meet the challenge. It contained the Arabs in Anatolia by evolving the *theme* system of defence. Initially, this meant dividing Anatolia into three military commands: Opsikion, Anatolikon and Armeniakon. The Opsikion, originally the strategic reserve, was now quartered across the approaches

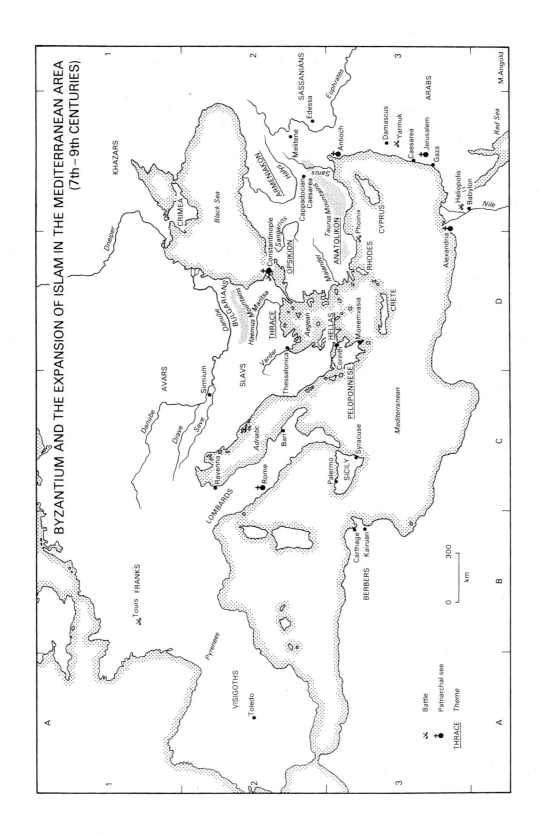

BYZANTIUM AND THE EXPANSION OF ISLAM IN THE MEDITERRANEAN AREA
(7th–9th CENTURIES)

M. Angold

15

to Constantinople. The Anatolikon was the old army of the East, but now withdrawn to defend south-eastern Anatolia. The Armeniakon was the army of Armenia, now established in northern Anatolia and covering the routes from Melitene and the middle Euphrates.

The threat from the Arabs was all the more formidable because they took to the sea. They occupied Cyprus (649–50) and destroyed the Byzantine fleet at Phoinix (655) off the coast of Anatolia. Constantinople was blockaded from 674 to 678, but this attack was beaten off with Greek fire. Another assault similarly failed in 718. From then on Constantinople and Anatolia were relatively secure, though there were intermittent raids down to the mid-ninth century, some penetrating to within striking distance of Constantinople.

The Byzantines were less successful in holding the Arabs in the Mediterranean. Carthage finally succumbed in 697, and from their new capital of Kairuan the Arabs converted the Berbers. This fuelled the Muslim advance into Spain. Toledo, the Visigothic capital, fell in 711 and by 718 the conquest of Spain was virtually complete. The Muslims advanced northwards across the Pyrenees, but their defeat in 732 by the Franks at the battle of Tours limited any further conquests in this area. Their efforts were concentrated in the Mediterranean. Crete fell in 824 and a start was made on the conquest of Sicily from the Byzantines. They established a base at Palermo, but it was not until 878 that the Byzantine provincial capital of Syracuse fell. In 840 Bari was captured and became the centre of an emirate which terrorized southern Italy and the Adriatic. It was recovered in 876 by the Byzantines and a degree of stability was restored in the central Mediterranean.

The Muslim advance stretched Byzantine resources to their limit, for it was also involved in the Balkans. In 582 Sirmium fell to the Avars, and their Slav tributaries swarmed into the Balkans. They settled on a permanent basis and penetrated as far south as the Peloponnese, where Monemvasia provided a refuge for the native population. In 679 the Bulgarians crossed the Danube and settled the lands to the south. Byzantine territories were now limited to Thrace and a few towns along the fringes of the Aegean, such as Thessalonica, which withstood a series of Slav sieges. To hold these areas the *themes* of Thrace and Hellas were established at the end of the seventh century. From the late eighth century a determined effort was made to strengthen the Byzantine hold in Europe. This culminated in the reoccupation of the Peloponnese and the creation (c. 805) of the *theme* of the Peloponnese with its headquarters at Corinth.

The Byzantine Empire survived the assaults and losses of territory which occurred from the seventh to the early ninth centuries. In many ways, it emerged all the stronger, thanks to its capital Constantinople and the evolution of the *theme* system.

M. Angold

Italy in the Eighth Century

The invasion launched by war-bands of Lombard and other peoples led by Alboin in 568 had a decisive effect on the map of Italy for centuries. Much of the north was rapidly conquered, including Milan in 569 and Pavia in 572. The inadequate Byzantine garrisons were thrown into disarray, Lombard raiding parties penetrated into Tuscany and the Rome area and semi-autonomous duchies were set up in the south at Spoleto and Benevento. Gradually the empire was able to put up more effective resistance by exploiting Lombard divisions, bribing the Franks to invade the Lombard kingdom, recruiting Lombard renegades as mercenaries and concentrating authority in the hands of one military governor, known by 584 as the exarch. By 603, when a truce was declared, the empire retained secure control of the Rome and Ravenna

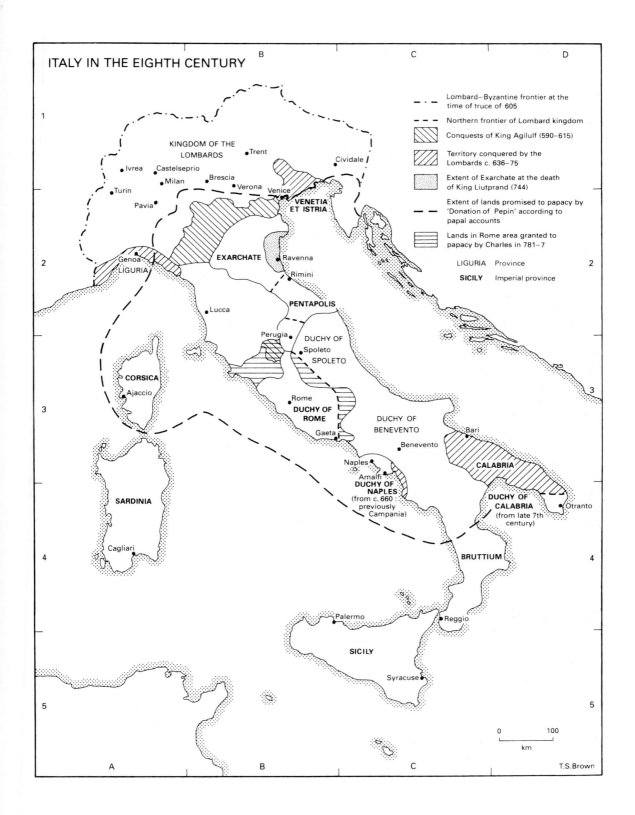

ITALY IN THE EIGHTH CENTURY

— · — Lombard–Byzantine frontier at the time of truce of 605

— — — Northern frontier of Lombard kingdom

Conquests of King Agilulf (590–615)

Territory conquered by the Lombards c. 636–75

Extent of Exarchate at the death of King Liutprand (744)

Extent of lands promised to papacy by 'Donation of Pepin' according to papal accounts

Lands in Rome area granted to papacy by Charles in 781–7

LIGURIA   Province

SICILY   Imperial province

KINGDOM OF THE LOMBARDS

Trent

Cividale

Ivrea   Castelseprio

Milan   Brescia

Turin   Verona

Pavia   Venice

VENETIA ET ISTRIA

Genoa   Ravenna

LIGURIA   EXARCHATE

Rimini

Lucca

PENTAPOLIS

Perugia   DUCHY OF Spoleto

CORSICA   SPOLETO

Ajaccio

Rome

DUCHY OF ROME

Gaeta   DUCHY OF BENEVENTO

Bari

Benevento

Naples

Amalfi   CALABRIA

DUCHY OF NAPLES (from c. 660 : previously Campania)

SARDINIA

DUCHY OF CALABRIA (from late 7th century)

Otranto

Cagliari

BRUTTIUM

Palermo   Reggio

SICILY

Syracuse

0   100
km

T.S.Brown

17

areas, together with a corridor following the line of the Via Amerina through Umbria, and coastal enclaves around Venice, Genoa, Naples and other southern cities.

For much of the seventh century the frontier remained static, broken by King Rothari's capture of Genoa in 643 and the defeat of the Emperor Constans' expedition against Benevento in 663/4. As the empire became increasingly endangered by threats in the east, more power within the Byzantine territories was exercised by the local military garrisons and their leaders, and in the case of Rome by the pope. In the Lombard kingdom dynastic instability did not prevent increasing prosperity and adoption of Roman institutions. By c. 680 the Lombards had dropped their Arian and pagan beliefs in favour of Catholic Christianity and secured recognition from the empire. Gradually their pressure on the imperial provinces increased, as the Romans became discontented with the religious and taxation policies of the eastern empire and King Liutprand (712–44) attempted to unite the peninsula under Lombard rule. Resistance to such a take-over was led by the popes, who remained essentially loyal to Byzantium, but they were unable to gain any substantial aid from their imperial 'protectors'. Following the Lombard Aistulf's capture of Ravenna in 751, and threats to Rome itself, Pope Stephen II obtained the intervention of the Frankish king Pepin III, who defeated Aistulf and recognized sweeping papal claims over much of central Italy (Donation of Pepin, 756). Threats were renewed by Aistulf's successor Desiderius against Pope Hadrian I, who called on Pepin's son Charles to intervene in 773. In 774 Charles captured Pavia and became king of the Lombards. The Lombard kingdom retained its distinctive social and governmental institutions and only gradually did an influx of Frankish officials and an increase in the wealth and power of the Church take place.

The political map of Italy remained confused in the late eighth century. Benevento (unlike its neighbour to the north, Spoleto) remained outside effective Frankish control and became a principality and a centre of traditional Lombard legitimacy under Desiderius' son-in-law Arichis, often allying itself with Byzantium to preserve its independence. The empire itself retained Sicily and its footholds in Calabria and Apulia, together with the nominal allegiance of the maritime cities of Amalfi, Gaeta, Naples and Venice. Its province of Istria fell to the Franks in the late eighth century. The papacy's claim to much of central Italy, including southern Tuscany, Spoleto, as well as the duchy of Rome and the old Exarchate, was zealously propagated by Lateran officials on the basis of the Donation of Constantine (a contemporary forgery) as well as the vague promises of the Frankish kings. In no sense, however, did it amount to a papal state. In many areas the papacy was more concerned with estates and rights than overall jurisdiction, while in others the Franks were induced by bribes or *Realpolitik* to leave power in the hands of local figures such as the archbishop of Ravenna. Even in the duchy of Rome, the papacy's authority was far from secure, as was shown by the revolt against Pope Leo III (795–816), which led to the latter's appeal to Charles for aid and the Frankish king's assumption of the imperial title in St Peter's on Christmas Day 800.

T.S. Brown

The Carolingian Empire under Charlemagne, 768–814

Charles Martel (mayor of the palace 717–41) and Pepin III (mayor 741–51, king 751–68) established the dominance of the Arnulfing/ Carolingian family in Francia by their military success against Arabs, Aquitanians, Frisians and various peoples east of the Rhine, by building networks of aristocratic support and by forging a close alliance with the Church. Following his

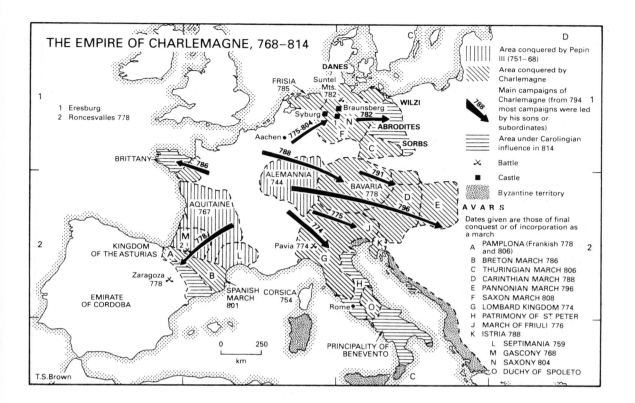

THE EMPIRE OF CHARLEMAGNE, 768–814

1 Eresburg
2 Roncesvalles 778

DANES

FRISIA
785

Suntel
Mts.
782

Syburg

Braunsberg 782

WILZI

ABRODITES

SORBS

Aachen • 775-804

BRITTANY

786

788

ALEMANNIA
744

BAVARIA
778

791

AQUITAINE
767

775

796

D

E

A V A R S

M
778

2

Pavia 774

774

796

J

K

KINGDOM
OF THE ASTURIAS

A

L

G

Zaragoza
778

B

H

EMIRATE
OF CORDOBA

SPANISH
MARCH
801

CORSICA
754

Rome

O

0   250
km

PRINCIPALITY OF
BENEVENTO

T.S.Brown

Area conquered by Pepin III (751–68)

Area conquered by Charlemagne

Main campaigns of Charlemagne (from 794 most campaigns were led by his sons or subordinates)

Area under Carolingian influence in 814

Battle

Castle

Byzantine territory

Dates given are those of final conquest or of incorporation as a march

A PAMPLONA (Frankish 778 and 806)
B BRETON MARCH 786
C THURINGIAN MARCH 806
D CARINTHIAN MARCH 788
E PANNONIAN MARCH 796
F SAXON MARCH 808
G LOMBARD KINGDOM 774
H PATRIMONY OF ST PETER
J MARCH OF FRIULI 776
K ISTRIA 788
L SEPTIMANIA 759
M GASCONY 768
N SAXONY 804
O DUCHY OF SPOLETO

election as king of the Franks with papal approval in 751, Pepin launched two expeditions against the Lombards and spent his last years campaigning against the Aquitanians and Saxons. On Pepin's death the kingdom was divided between his two sons, but on the death of the younger, Carloman, in 771, the elder, Charles 'the Great' (Charlemagne) became sole king. An energetic and charismatic war-leader, he exploited the superior numbers and technology of the Frankish army in campaigns against the Saxons (772, 775, 776), against the Lombards, whose kingdom he took over in 774, and against the Spanish Muslims, an unsuccessful expedition culminating in the massacre of his rearguard by Basques in 778. The 780s saw renewed campaigns against the Saxons (780, 782, 784, 785), visits to Italy to see his close ally the pope and intimidate the Lombard duchy of Benevento (781, 787), and the deposition of Duke Tassilo of Bavaria (788). In the 790s Charlemagne turned his attention to the powerful tributary empire of

the Avars, which he destroyed in a series of campaigns (791, 795 and 796).

Charles also became increasingly involved with non-military matters. He began to attract scholarly advisers to his court, such as the Englishman Alcuin in 782, he constructed a new palace complex at Aachen (his main winter residence from 794), expressed his theological views in the *Libri Carolini* (794) and developed diplomatic ties with the Caliphate of Baghdad and Byzantium (with whom marriage alliances were planned). The seizure of sole power by the Empress Irene in 797 and the blinding of Pope Leo III in 799 proved the catalysts for the most controversial event of his reign – his intervention in Rome in 800 and coronation as Roman emperor by the restored pope on Christmas Day.

The imperial title should be seen less as the culmination of Charles' policies or as a key stage in the formation of a distinct Western identity than as the product of particular, mainly local factors. The idea of a Christian Roman Empire clearly had an appeal to Charles' ecclesiastical advisers and an emphasis on imperial *renovatio* can be found in art, coins, charters, writings associated with the 'Carolingian Renaissance' and the issue of new more ambitious capitularies. In practice, however, the imperial title proved a hindrance to Charles, by tying his office too closely to the papacy and Rome and antagonizing Byzantium. Disenchantment is reflected in Charles' *divisio regnorum* between his three sons in 806, which makes no mention of an empire, and his personal coronation of Louis the Pious in 813. No serious attempt was made to create a new universal identity for Charles' subjects. Instead a clear ethnic distinction was stressed between Franks and other ethnic groups by the writing down of separate laws for each people ruled by Charles. The machinery for administering the 'empire' remained crude, with a minimal central bureaucracy and over-

dependence on powerful local counts. Innovations such as the use of capitularies, inspectors (*missi*) and legal advisers (*scabini*) were largely ineffective. Government depended more on success in war, with its consequent flow of land and booty, and personal ties such as oaths and grants of benefices to royal vassals and others.

Charles' less active later years were marked by feelings of decline, by concern about the succession and by external threats posed by the Danes, Arabs and Slavs. The fragility of his empire became evident during the reign of his conscientious but ill-advised son Louis (814–40). However, the fundamental structural weaknesses should not obscure the overriding commitment of Charles and his advisers to learning, justice and the reform of the Church, aspirations which were only realized in part but served as lasting ideals for later medieval rulers.

T.S. Brown

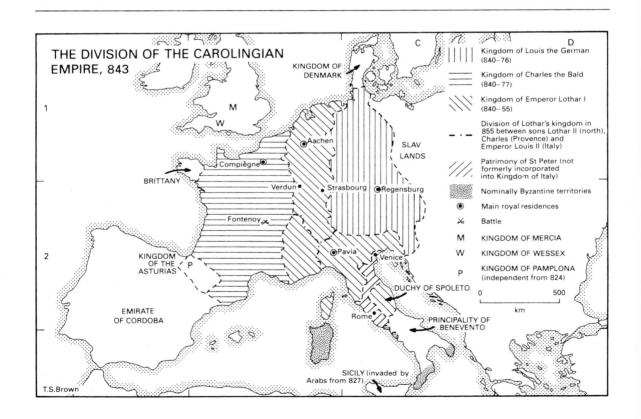

THE DIVISION OF THE CAROLINGIAN EMPIRE, 843

||| Kingdom of Louis the German (840–76)

= Kingdom of Charles the Bald (840–77)

\\\ Kingdom of Emperor Lothar I (840–55)

– · – Division of Lothar's kingdom in 855 between sons Lothar II (north), Charles (Provence) and Emperor Louis II (Italy)

/// Patrimony of St Peter (not formerly incorporated into Kingdom of Italy)

Nominally Byzantine territories

⊙ Main royal residences

✕ Battle

M KINGDOM OF MERCIA

W KINGDOM OF WESSEX

P KINGDOM OF PAMPLONA (independent from 824)

0   500
km

KINGDOM OF DENMARK

SLAV LANDS

Aachen

Compiègne

BRITTANY

Verdun •   • Strasbourg   ⊙ Regensburg

Fontenoy ✕

KINGDOM OF THE ASTURIAS   P

EMIRATE OF CORDOBA

⊙ Pavia

Venice

DUCHY OF SPOLETO

Rome

PRINCIPALITY OF BENEVENTO

SICILY (invaded by Arabs from 827)

T.S. Brown

Division of the Carolingian Empire, 843

The mismatch between administrative weaknesses and ideological aspirations in Charlemagne's empire gave rise to problems in the reign of his son Louis the Pious (814–40). Although his early rule was conscientious, personal and party conflicts provoked civil war between the king and his sons from 830. After Louis' death in 840 his eldest son, Lothar, whose power-base was Italy, sought to impose his power as emperor north of the Alps and deprive his half-brother Charles the Bald of his inheritance in west Francia. This encouraged Charles to make an alliance with his other half-brother, Louis the German, and together they defeated Lothar at Fontenoy in 841. The alliance was consolidated by oaths taken by each king's followers at Strasbourg in 842. Lothar was compelled at Verdun in 843 to agree to a division of the empire into three approximately equal parts. Lothar kept his imperial title and lands stretching from the North Sea to Italy, which incorporated the imperial centres of Aachen, Pavia and Rome, while Charles obtained the west Frankish lands and Louis those east of the Rhine. This arrangement was not envisaged as replacing the empire by nascent nation-states, but in practice centrifugal pressures were increased by rivalries between the rulers and the pressures of aristocratic supporters to regain offices and lands lost in the division.

Lothar's kingdom lacked viability and was divided in 855 among his three sons, none of whom had male heirs. As a result the kingdom of Lothar II (855–69) in the low countries was carved up between his uncles, Louis and Charles. In west Francia Charles fought manfully against Viking invaders and aristocratic separatism and succeeded in becoming emperor after the death of his nephew, Louis II, in 875. However, after his death (877) his descendants proved incompetent and short-lived. Louis the German proved the strongest king, but on his death (876) his kingdom was divided, and his sons died in rapid succession, apart from the youngest, Charles the Fat, who ruled a reunited empire fortuitously and ignominiously from 884 until his deposition in 887.

T.S. Brown

The Byzantine Empire under the Macedonian Dynasty (9th–11th Centuries)

From the mid-ninth century Byzantium took the offensive, responding to changes beyond its frontiers. After the battle of the Bishop's Meadow (863) the Arabs were never a real threat to Anatolia. Along the eastern frontier petty emirates emerged, not all of them in Muslim hands. Tephrike, for example, was held by the heretical Paulicians. Its capture in 878 brought the Byzantines within striking distance of the upper Euphrates. Care was taken to consolidate advances by creating new border *themes*, such as Mesopotamia and Lykandos (*c.* 900). Melitene, key to the middle Euphrates, fell in 934, and Theodosioupolis (Erzerum) in 949, allowing the Byzantines to exercise more influence in Armenian lands, where a policy of piecemeal annexation was pursued. In 968 the Armenian principality of Taron was annexed and turned into a *theme*. These advances were complemented by the conquest of Tarsus and of Cilicia (965). Antioch fell in 969 and the city of Aleppo was put under tribute. The eastern frontier thus advanced from the Taurus mountains and the Pontic Alps to northern Syria and the lands of the middle and upper Euphrates.

In the Mediterranean the Byzantines were still on the defensive in the early tenth century, but the Arab corsairs of Crete were driven out in

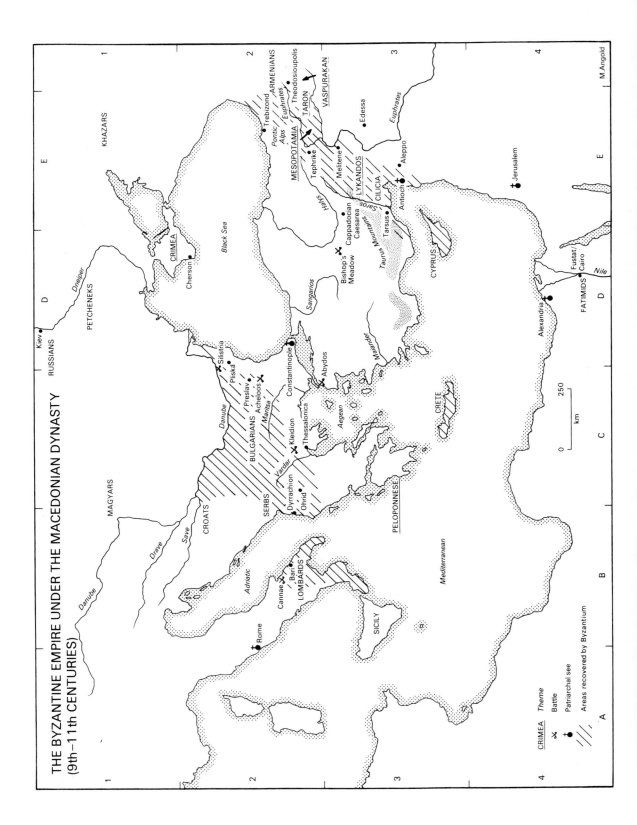

THE BYZANTINE EMPIRE UNDER THE MACEDONIAN DYNASTY
(9th–11th CENTURIES)

M.Angold

CRIMEA Theme
⚔ Battle
✝● Patriarchal see
▨ Areas recovered by Byzantium

0   250
km

960/61 and Cyprus was taken in 965. Further successes in the eastern Mediterranean were checked by the arrival of the Fatimids in Egypt (969). They quickly extended into Palestine and Syria.

Conditions had also changed rapidly to the north of the Black Sea. Ever since the seventh century Byzantium had relied on alliance with the Khazars. From the early ninth century, however, a new people appeared in the shape of the Russians, who controlled the rivers leading from the Baltic Sea and the Caspian. Byzantium reacted by creating a *theme* in the Crimea centred on Cherson (833). This did not prevent a Russian attack nearly taking Constantinople by surprise (860). Other Russian attacks followed in 907 and 941, but Byzantium countered by offering the Russians valuable trading concessions.

The Russians also had to contend with the Petcheneks, the dominant power on the steppes. Byzantium cultivated them – they could cut the Russian trade route down the Dnieper from Kiev, and they also threatened the Bulgarians across the Danube. The conversion of the latter to Orthodoxy in 865 promised to bring them within the Byzantine orbit, but the Bulgarian tsar, Symeon (*c.* 893–927), was a more able opponent than his pagan forebears. He won notable victories over the Byzantines, including the battle of Acheloos (917), and in 921, 922 and 924 advanced to the walls of Constantinople. He

mastered the Balkans and even penetrated the Peloponnese. He died in 927 and Byzantium hastened to make peace with his son Peter (927–69). Over the next forty years the balance of power swung towards the Byzantines. In 967 the Russian prince of Kiev, Svjatoslav, was called in against the Bulgarians, but he determined to conquer Bulgaria himself. The Russians were finally defeated by the Byzantines at Silistria on the Danube (971) and Bulgaria was annexed. The returning Russians were caught by the Petcheneks and Svjatoslav was killed. It was a text-book demonstration of Byzantine diplomacy. Svjatoslav's death prepared the way for the conversion of his son Vladimir to Christianity.

Vladimir helped the Emperor Basil II (976–1025) deal with a rebellion by the eastern *themes*, thus contributing to his victory at Abydos (989). These internal problems allowed the Bulgarians to establish a new state centred on Ohrid in Macedonia. Basil II concentrated on reducing the Bulgarians. Victory at Kleidion (1014) was decisive and by 1018 all resistance had collapsed. Basil II now extended Byzantine control in Armenia, annexing Vaspurakan (1021). He also strengthened Byzantium's hold in southern Italy, defeating the Lombards at Cannae (1018). It was an imposing achievement, but his successors found it hard to defend the new frontiers.

M. Angold

Vikings

Between 800 and 1100 the peoples of Scandinavia went from being an Iron Age to a fully medieval society. The profound social transformations are reflected in the changes in their adventurous expeditions and in their use of silver at home. Before 800 silver wealth was stored in jewellery, often huge arm rings or brooches. We assume many of these circulated as gifts, bride wealth, blood money and plunder. By the twelfth century kings had coins minted bearing their likeness and most silver, in the

shape of coins, was used in straightforward financial exchanges or the payment of rent or taxes or tithes. Whether silver was the motor of social change or simply an indispensable element of political and social competition in an increasingly hierarchical Scandinavian society, the Vikings burst out of their homeland dramatically and often terrifyingly in search of it.

In the ninth century they raided and traded for silver, but to call these early Vikings merchants is anachronistic. In Iceland's famous

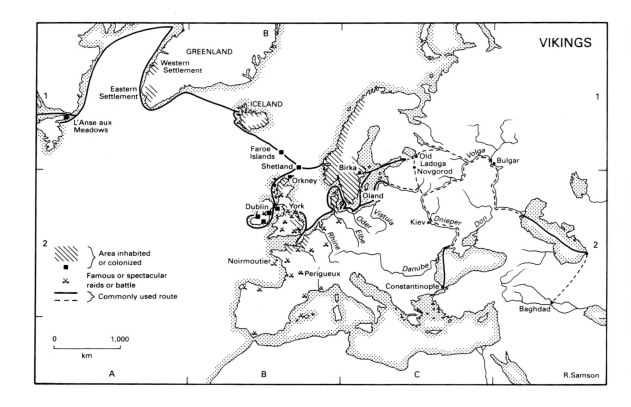

Njálssaga, a main character attempts to obtain hay from a neighbour, asking if he would sell it to him (denying any social relationship between them), next if he would give it to him as a gift (offering future friendship), and finally he had to threaten to take it (confirming their enmity).

In the east, Swedes travelled huge distances trading and swapping, buying and selling, gifting and stealing at entrepots and towns at Old Ladoga, Novgorod, Kiev and Bulgar. The major Russian rivers, the Dnieper, Don and Volga were their highways. At the end of these rivers lay Constantinople and the Byzantine Empire, but more importantly the caliphate of Baghdad and tons of Islamic silver. More than 85,000 Arabic coins have been found in Scandinavia. Although little appreciated today, contact with German and Slavic regions, along the coast and down the Oder and Vistula, was probably equally intense. More than 70,000 German coins have been discovered in Sweden.

While Vikings certainly traded around the British Isles, much silver was probably the fruit of violence. From the raid on the monastery at Lindisfarne in 793 or at Noirmoutier to the battle of Stamford Bridge in 1066, the violence grew from plundering raids of single boats to huge invasion armies. Even the big armies were interested primarily in silver, extracting tribute, the so-called Danegeld. Between 991 and 1014 they received more than 150,000lbs of silver officially, which is equal to 36 million coins!

The change from raids of small bands to huge armies reflects the changes in the Scandinavian societies at home. As political power became more centralized, economic and social organization in Scandinavia came to resemble that of other European nations. The final Scandinavian invasions resembled the wars of their neighbours; they aimed at conquest. Northmen would rule Normandy and give it their name; Danish law would run for much of eastern England (hence Danelaw); Canute would later be king of all England; and much of Ireland would be politically dominated by the Scandinavian kingdom based at Dublin until the battle of Clontarf in 1014.

Perhaps as the result of tensions in Scandinavia during this period of accelerated political centralization, many Norwegians left to settle lands in the North Atlantic: Shetland, Orkney, the Hebrides, Man, the Faroes, Greenland, and even North America. Certainly this is one of the mythical reasons the Icelandic sagas give for the original leaving of Norway. In these new lands the Norse may not have found identical climates and landscapes, but they were similar enough to allow old lifestyles to be perpetuated. Moreover, these islands were uninhabited or only sparsely inhabited.

The distances the Vikings travelled, their 'primitiveness' and their paganism impressed and frightened the peoples of more settled Europe of the ninth and tenth century. Their incomprehension has left us the Vikings of myth and legend.

R. Samson

Magyars

Where the Magyars came from we shall never know. Their language, of a Finno-Ugrian type, is said most closely to resemble that of some aboriginals of Siberia. The Hungarians (Magyar is their own name for themselves) first appeared in written sources only in 833 around the Sea of Azov when they attacked the Khazars. Thirty years later a raiding expedition had reached

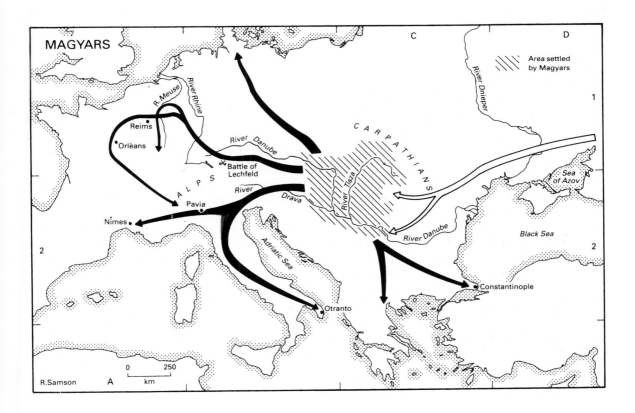

German borders. In 896 they entered the great Alföld basin, between the Danube and the Tisza, ringed by the Beskidy in the north, Carpathians in the east, Alps in the west, and Dinaric Alps in the south.

The plains here had been home to nomadic and semi-nomadic peoples since later prehistory. Like the Huns and the Avars before them, the Magyars, accomplished horsemen, plundered and pillaged far and wide. In 899 they attacked settlements along the Po river; in Italy they raided as far south as Otranto. In 900 they plundered Bavaria, and Germany was to bear the brunt of their unwanted attention. After 917 they regularly pillaged northern Gaul and in 924 they attacked the area of Nîmes.

Henry I of Germany had fortifications built against the Magyars, his son Otto I charged the frontier guardians with the duty of protecting the empire from their incursions. Little else was done to lessen the threat, nothing like Charle-magne's massive invasion of the Avar kingdom. In 955 Otto I defeated a band of marauders at Lechfeld as they returned home with booty.

The date more or less marked the end of the Magyar raids, which had lasted less than a century. Latterly they had become less frequent but the lost battle cannot have ended them. It seems inescapable that raids ended because of internal developments on the Alföld plain. The medieval Hungarian state was developing. The conversion to Christianity had begun with the work of Bishop Pilgrim of Passau (971–91). In 1001 Vaik, with the baptismal name of Stephen, took the title of king. By papal consent Hungary received its own metropolitan, thereby escaping the rival claims of Passau and the Greek Church, which had also sent missionaries.

When next Hungarians and Germans did battle, it was in wars between neighbouring kingdoms.

R. Samson

The East European States, *c.* 1000

Although there were few precise frontiers, by 1000 the political map of eastern Europe was becoming better defined. This was outwardly a matter of the conversion of the peoples of the region to Christianity and of the advance of dynastic claims at the expense of tribal loyalties. It also involved the question of political affiliation with the Byzantine and/or German empires. Bulgaria provides a precocious example. Caught between the two empires its ruler Boris finally accepted Christianity from Byzantium in 865 and with it Byzantine claims to overlordship. He concentrated on the conversion of his people, both the Bulgar elite and the Slav tributaries. It helped both to strengthen his dynastic authority and to unify his people. It was left to his son Symeon to challenge Byzantium. He assumed the imperial title and claimed patriarchal status for the Bulgarian Church. His ambitions led to war with Byzantium. His death in 927 temporarily ended hostilities, but Byzantium could not tolerate so potentially dangerous a competitor on its doorstep. The Byzantines finally destroyed all Bulgarian resistance in 1018 and annexed the country.

The Russians too were a threat, on occasion attacking Constantinople. They were originally Scandinavian freebooters who controlled the river routes from the Baltic to the Caspian and the Black Sea. They made Kiev their main centre and put the surrounding Slav tribes under tribute. Their warrior ethos militated against conversion to Christianity, which was delayed until the years 987–9, in the course of which Vladimir, the prince of Kiev, accepted Christianity from Byzantium. This he did on his own terms, because of the temporary weakness of the Byzantine emperor. He obtained the hand of the emperor's sister in marriage, which gave him enormous prestige. These circumstances meant that Byzantine political claims over Russia were always muted. It meant that there was no need for the

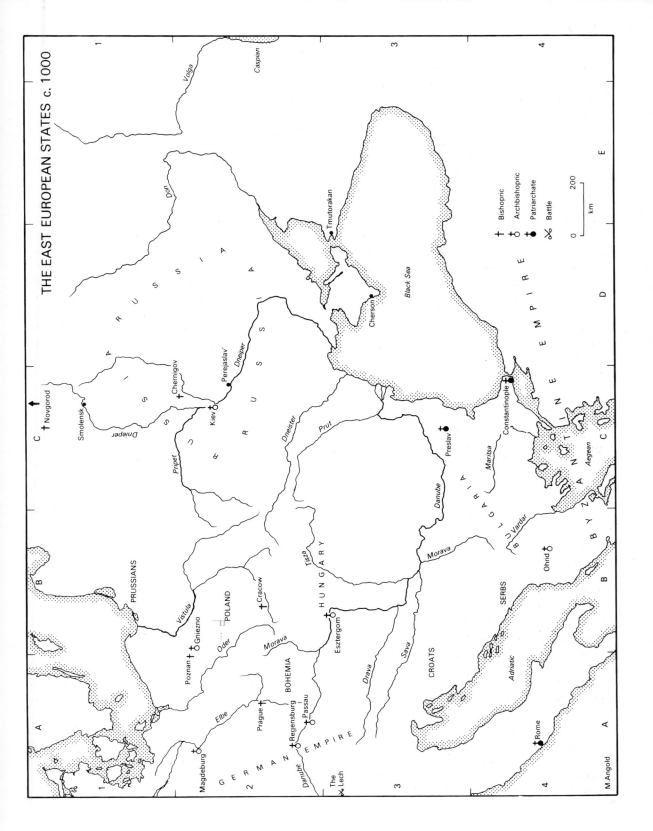

THE EAST EUROPEAN STATES c. 1000

Bishopric
Archbishopric
Patriarchate
Battle

0   200
km

M.Angold

Volga

Caspian

Don

Dnieper

R U S S I A

Smolensk
Novgorod
Chernigov
Perejaslav'
Kiev

Tmutorakan

Cherson

Black Sea

Pripet

Dnieper

Dniester

Prut

Danube

Preslav

B U L G A R I A

Maritsa

Constantinople

Vardar

Ohrid

SERBS

B Y Z A N T I N E   E M P I R E

Aegean

Adriatic

Rome

CROATS

Sava

Drava

Esztergom

H U N G A R Y

Tisza

Morava

PRUSSIANS

Vistula

Oder

Gniezno
Poznan

POLAND

Cracow

Morava

BOHEMIA

Prague

Elbe

Regensburg
Passau

Magdeburg

G E R M A N   E M P I R E

Danube

The
Lech

27

prince of Kiev to claim imperial status. Power remained in the hands of the ruling family. The Russian lands continued to be divided into a series of shifting principalities over which the prince of Kiev merely presided as senior member. At the head of the Russian Church was the metropolitan of Kiev. He may have been appointed from Constantinople, but there was a close identification of the Church with the ruling family: Vladimir was revered as its founder and his murdered sons Boris and Gleb were venerated as martyrs.

The Russians thus managed to solve the dilemma which led to the destruction of the Bulgarian Empire: how to avoid the political entanglements involved in conversion to Christianity. This dilemma was also apparent in the dealings of the western Slavs with the German Empire. Bohemia had to accept a large measure of German domination. In 973 its ruler recognized the suzerainty of the German emperor, Otto I, and the see of Prague was subordinated to Mainz, but the native Přemyslid dynasty continued in power thanks to the posthumous reputation of Duke Wenceslas, who was murdered in 929 and was soon revered as the national saint of Bohemia.

In the face of German encroachment the pagan Polish ruler tried to learn from the experience of Bohemia. He married a Bohemian princess and in 966 accepted Christianity voluntarily rather than have it forced upon him. Shortly before his death in 992 he made the 'Donation of Poland' to the papacy in order to block German claims over the Church in Poland. Under his brother Boleslav the independence of Poland was formally recognized by the German emperor, Otto III, in 1000, at a ceremony to inaugurate the Polish archbishopric of Gniezno, though no royal title was accorded.

The ceremony was solemnized by the translation of the relics of St Adalbert of Prague, recently martyred by the pagan Prussians. Adalbert came from a noble Bohemian family and was made bishop of Prague in 982. Most of his energies were devoted to evangelizing the lands to the east. He worked among the Poles and among the Hungarians, who had terrorized far and wide until their defeat in 955 by Otto I at the battle of the Lech. In 995 Adalbert baptized the Hungarian ruler Geza and his son, the future St Stephen, who in 1000 obtained a royal crown from the papacy. A Hungarian archbishopric was established at Esztergom. There are clear parallels between Hungary and Poland. Both turned to the papacy as a means of countering German domination. Boleslav of Poland would follow St Stephen's example and in 1025 obtained the royal crown denied him by the Germans from the papacy.

M. Angold

France and its Principalities, *c.* 1000

The political shape of France in the high Middle Ages was determined by the events of the tenth century. No king after 877 exercised the power wielded by Charles the Bald; mints and fiscal estates fell out of royal control and Carolingian methods of government such as *missi* and capitularies were abandoned. The kingdom remained threatened by Viking attack until the 920s and the crown oscillated between two families, the Carolingians (Charles the Simple 898–929, Louis IV 936–54, Lothar 954–86, Louis V 986–7) and the Robertian counts of Paris, who produced Odo (888–98), Robert I (922–30) and the latter's son-in-law Ralph of Burgundy (930–6). Although Louis IV and Lothar were energetic rulers they could not stop the Robertian Hugh the Great, 'duke of the Franks', from building up considerable authority over the counts of Neustria, and the coronation of his son Hugh Capet (987–96) established a lasting 'Capetian' dynasty.

In the tenth century the main beneficiaries of weakening royal power were the 'princes', dynamic personalities who accumulated power by various means: favourable marriages, obtain-

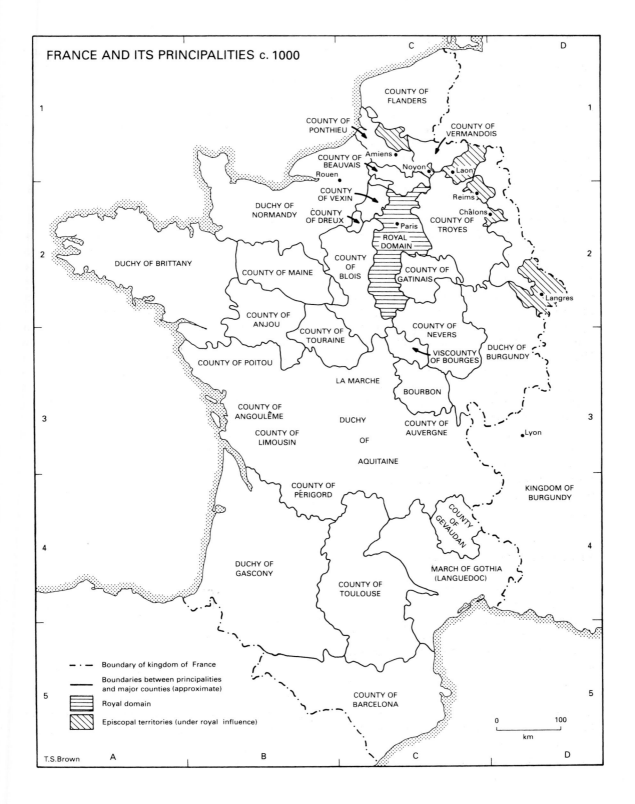

FRANCE AND ITS PRINCIPALITIES c. 1000

COUNTY OF FLANDERS

COUNTY OF PONTHIEU

COUNTY OF VERMANDOIS

COUNTY OF BEAUVAIS

Amiens

Noyon

Laon

Rouen

COUNTY OF VEXIN

Reims

DUCHY OF NORMANDY

COUNTY OF DREUX

Châlons

COUNTY OF TROYES

Paris

ROYAL DOMAIN

DUCHY OF BRITTANY

COUNTY OF MAINE

COUNTY OF BLOIS

COUNTY OF GATINAIS

Langres

COUNTY OF ANJOU

COUNTY OF TOURAINE

COUNTY OF NEVERS

VISCOUNTY OF BOURGES

DUCHY OF BURGUNDY

COUNTY OF POITOU

LA MARCHE

BOURBON

COUNTY OF ANGOULÊME

DUCHY

COUNTY OF AUVERGNE

Lyon

COUNTY OF LIMOUSIN

OF

AQUITAINE

COUNTY OF PÉRIGORD

KINGDOM OF BURGUNDY

COUNTY OF GEVAUDAN

DUCHY OF GASCONY

MARCH OF GOTHIA (LANGUEDOC)

COUNTY OF TOULOUSE

Boundary of kingdom of France

Boundaries between principalities and major counties (approximate)

Royal domain

Episcopal territories (under royal influence)

COUNTY OF BARCELONA

0   100
km

T.S.Brown

29

ing titles such as *dux*, amassing bundles of counties, establishing networks of *fideles*, assuming many of the financial and judicial functions of the *bannum* (Carolingian public authority) and exercising effective military leadership. Durable principalities included the duchy of Aquitaine, dominated by the counts of Poitou from *c.* 930; the duchy of Burgundy, built up by Richard the Justiciar (d. 921) but reduced by *c.* 960 to a rump ruled by a cadet branch of the Capetians; Flanders, whose counts capitalized on their military strength to build castles and exploit the vast economic potential of their county; and Toulouse, whose counts also ruled Gothia. Other principalities did not fit into such a clear-cut pattern. Some were weakened by a ruler's untimely death, such as the Vermandois block of counties in north-east France which collapsed after Herbert II's death in 943. The duchy of Brittany remained weak despite its distinctive identity and often fell under the overlordship of neighbouring rulers. Catalonia was a powerful unit under the counts of Barcelona but drifted out of the French orbit from *c.* 987, as did much of the duchy of Gascony. Normandy's origins as a Viking buffer state made it distinctive, but its dukes pursued familiar policies of reviving Carolingian-style administration, building up followings and co-operating with the Church.

In parts of Francia other types of polity existed, including largely independent bishoprics, such as Langres, Cahors, Reims and Laon, independent counties, such as the Rouergue, and areas which came under the weak rule of local counts and lords such as the Auvergne, Berry and Picardy.

In the eleventh century royal judicial and fiscal rights remained limited and the authority of kings such as Robert the Pious (996–1031) and Henry I (1031–60) was largely honorary. Although Carolingian lands around Laon and Reims were incorporated in the demesne, and the Church was a useful support, vassals such as the counts of Anjou and Blois became powerful figures and frequent rivals; Normandy proved an ally for a time but Duke William I's expansionist policies after 1047 provoked royal hostility.

The late tenth and early eleventh centuries also saw a number of socioeconomic changes, including a general recovery and a proliferation of castles. Often the latter resulted from the initiative of princes and counts, but some were built by lower aristocrats or 'new men' on allodial land and reflected a breakdown of the semipublic power of the counts. In many areas, such as Berry, the Auvergne and the Maconnais the castellans took over the public rights of the *bannum* and initiated a regime of oppression. This development was in part a reflection of the growing importance of mounted warriors (*milites* or knights), bound to their lords by feudal ties. Contrary to traditional views formal vassalage was not widespread or uniform among the aristocracy early on, but the wider use of the term fief in the eleventh century led to increased legal precision in relationships and ultimately enhanced the position of the king as feudal overlord.

T.S. Brown

England Before the Normans

The most detailed historical record illuminating the identities and activities of early English kingdoms is provided by Bede in the *Historia Ecclesiastica*, a work which, although valuable, is highly reflective of its author's own monastic concerns and milieu. Bede described how from the late fifth to the late seventh centuries, a series of kings held 'empire' over all the kingdoms south of the Humber. Three of them were Northumbrian and were thus overlords of all the English people. Alternative sources, such as the epic poem *Beowulf*, allow the thought world of this warrior nobility to be investigated. The hegemonies established by early English kings could fall as rapidly as they rose. Success depended on war, the acquisition of booty and reward-

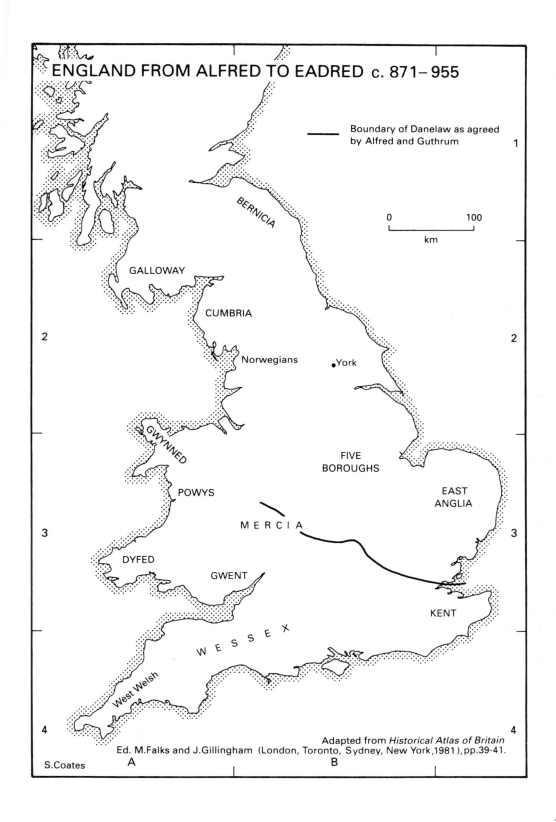

ENGLAND FROM ALFRED TO EADRED c. 871–955

Boundary of Danelaw as agreed
by Alfred and Guthrum

1

0   100
km

BERNICIA

GALLOWAY

CUMBRIA

2

Norwegians   •York

GWYNNED

FIVE
BOROUGHS

POWYS

EAST
ANGLIA

3

M E R C I A

DYFED

GWENT

KENT

W E S S E X

West Welsh

4

Adapted from *Historical Atlas of Britain*
Ed. M.Falks and J.Gillingham (London, Toronto, Sydney, New York,1981),pp.39-41.

S.Coates   A   B

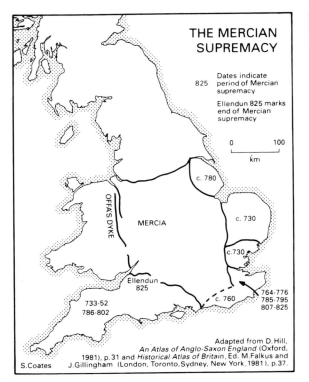

THE MERCIAN
SUPREMACY

825   Dates indicate
period of Mercian
supremacy

Ellendun 825 marks
end of Mercian
supremacy

0   100
km

c. 780

OFFA'S DYKE

MERCIA

c. 730

c.730

Ellendun
825

c. 760

764-776
785-795
807-825

733-52
786-802

Adapted from D. Hill,
An Atlas of Anglo-Saxon England (Oxford,
1981), p.31 and *Historical Atlas of Britain*, Ed. M.Falkus and
J.Gillingham (London, Toronto, Sydney, New York, 1981), p.37.

S.Coates

THE EARLY
KINGDOMS

DALRIADA

Picts

STRATHCLYDE

BERNICIA

NORTHUMBRIA

0   100
km

DEIRA

LINDSEY

POWYS

MAGONSAETE

Middle
Angles

East
Angles

MERCIA

HWICCE

East
Saxons

SURREY

KENT

West
Saxons

Jutish
Lands

South
Saxons

Adapted from D. Hill, *An Atlas of Anglo-Saxon
England* (Oxford, 1981), p.30 and B.Yorke, *Kings and
Kingdoms of Early Anglo-Saxon England* (London, 1990), p.12.

S.Coates

ing of followers. Feuds, assassinations and civil wars marked the early history of Northumbria, Wessex and Mercia. Successful kingdoms were those which were able to expand at the expense of their Celtic neighbours. By the eighth century the dominance previously held by Northumbria was on the wane and Mercia began to conquer all the kingdoms of the Midlands and the Southeast. The warlike Offa (757–96) was the first king to issue a royal coinage on a really significant scale and to profit from the commercial consciousness developing in southern England. He used monastic property to consolidate royal power in newly subordinated kingdoms holding a tight stranglehold over Kent and temporarily appointing an archbishop at Lichfield. However, the Mercians were to lose their hegemony with a defeat by the rising kingdom of Wessex at Ellendun in 825. The most enduring legacy left by Offa was the great dyke he built on the Welsh border which was less a negotiated frontier and more of a basis for future raids.

The ninth and tenth centuries were marked by the impact of Viking raids. In 865 the Great Army reduced a land that had once held several kingdoms to one where Wessex alone survived as a focus of English resistance under Alfred. Eastern England was marked by permanent Danish settlement. Vikings captured York in 867 and East Anglia in 869. In 874 the eastern part of Mercia became Danish territory. English fortunes revived when Alfred won a notable victory at Edington in 878 which was marked by King Guthrum's acceptance of Christianity and a treaty which created a frontier dividing England roughly along a diagonal line from Chester to London. This was to be a key area in the struggle for subsequent control of England under Alfred's descendants. By 924 Edward the Elder had overrun the five Danish boroughs of Lincoln, Derby, Nottingham, Stamford and Leicester. Athelstan (924–39), Edmund (939–46) and Eadred (946–55) eventually secured the submission of the north despite facing formidable opponents such as Eric Bloodaxe. By the end of his reign Eadred ruled a united England from within a vastly expanded Wessex. Separate regions were welded into a single political society through the use of ealdormen although the north remained much more independent than the old unit of Mercia.

S. Coates

The Spanish and Portuguese Reconquest to *c.* 1140

Although the peninsula, conquered by the Muslims in 711–15, was ruled after 756 by an independent Ummayad emir of Córdoba, his control over its regions varied enormously in different periods; and it was when central government was weak that its Christian enemies made their greatest advances.

These enemies first rose in Asturias (*c.* 718), where their leader, Pelayo, defeated a Muslim expedition at Covadonga (*c.* 722) and established an independent kingdom. His descendants annexed Cantabria and Galicia, and ravaged the area between the Cantabrian and Guadarrama mountains, turning it into a no-man's land behind which they could shelter from Muslim raids and build up their power. They claimed to descend from the Visigoths who had ruled in Toledo before 711 and to inherit from the whole peninsula; thus they proposed to liberate their country, that is, to 'reconquer' Spain.

Similar centres of resistance arose in Pamplona (740) and Aragon, though little is known of them. To the east, the Carolingians expelled the Muslims from Languedoc (751), took Gerona (785) and Barcelona (801), and organized Frankish Spain as an imperial March under the count of Barcelona. When their empire disintegrated, his descendants became hereditary rulers of the March, now called Catalonia, though they were unable to push the frontier much beyond Barcelona until 1120, when they captured Tarragona.

Meanwhile, inspired by the discovery of St James' alleged tomb at Santiago de Compostela (*c.* 810), the Asturians plundered in the emirate, and exploited its civil wars to resettle the Duero plains, including the towns of Oporto (868), Zamora (893) and León (856). The Duero became their new frontier, protected by fortresses and by villages settled with peasant-knights and organized often by the great abbeys such as Sahagún, Cardeña and Silos. It remained the frontier for a century, for Abd al-Rahman III (912–61) emerged as victor of the civil wars, with the title of caliph (929) and immense power; the Christian kings became his clients, and later the victims of continual raids by the military dictator, al-Mansur (976–1002). After 1031, however, the caliphate collapsed, leaving about thirty successor-states, the *taifa* kingdoms, which soon became clients of the Christians, paying tribute to the kings of León and to the Catalan counts.

Alfonso VI's conquest of Toledo (1085) ended this period of balance, and showed that León now had the strength and the strategic basis to conquer all Muslim Spain, unless it received help from outside. In desperation, the Spanish Muslims begged the Almoravid rulers of north-west Africa for such help; but after routing Alfonso at Sagrajas (1086), the Almoravids annexed the *taifa* kingdoms and turned them into mere provinces of their own Berber Empire. Henceforth the Spanish Muslims, too weak to defend themselves, relied on the Berber dynasties of Morocco for protection against the Christian reconquerors whilst chafing under their 'barbarous' African rule.

The Almoravids launched a holy war to recover the lands taken by the Christians. They met resistance from Rodrigo Díaz de Bivar, 'el Cid', who held Valencia (1094–9) and blocked their way up the east coast; and from thousands of French crusaders who came to defend Aragon, Navarre and Catalonia, and helped to reconquer Huesca (1096), Saragossa (1118) and the rest of the Ebro valley. As a result, a new state was formed in the north-east, Aragon-Catalonia,

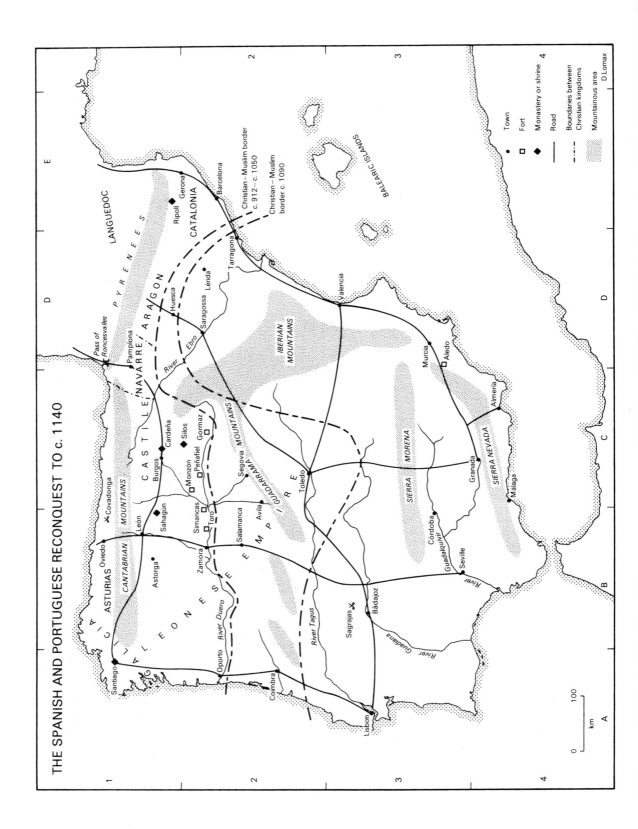

THE SPANISH AND PORTUGUESE RECONQUEST TO c. 1140

Town •
Fort ☐
Monastery or shrine ◆
Road ——
Boundaries between
Christian kingdoms —·—·—
Mountainous area
D.Lomax

Christian–Muslim border
c. 912–c. 1050
Christian–Muslim
border c. 1090

LANGUEDOC

PYRENEES

Pass of Roncesvalles

CANTABRIAN MOUNTAINS

ASTURIAS

Covadonga ✕

GALICIA

Santiago

Oviedo

León

Astorga

Sahagún ◆

Zamora

Toro

Simancas

Salamanca

Ávila

LEONESE EMPIRE

Oporto

River Duero

Coimbra

Lisbon

River Tagus

Sagrajas ✕

Bádajoz

River Guadiana

SIERRA MORENA

Córdoba

Guadalquivir

Seville

River

Granada

SIERRA NEVADA

Málaga

Almería

Murcia

Aledo

Valencia

IBERIAN MOUNTAINS

River Ebro

Saragossa

Huesca

Pamplona

NAVARRE / ARAGON

CASTILE

Burgos

Cardeña ◆

Silos ◆

Gormaz

Peñafiel

Monzón

SEGOVIA MOUNTAINS

GUADARRAMA MOUNTAINS

Segovia

Toledo

Lérida

Tarragona

Barcelona

Gerona

Ripoll ◆

CATALONIA

BALEARIC ISLANDS

km

0   100

34

which would rival León and ensure that the reconquest would continue to be a movement of divided, and sometimes conflicting, political forces. However, the fulcrum continued to be Toledo. There the Almoravids made their principal attacks in the period 1086–1139, and it was Toledo's resistance (plus the Almohad rising in Morocco) which finally broke their energies and their enthusiasm for the holy war. Meanwhile, the Christians had been building up their strengths in the area between the Duero and the Tagus, demographic, spiritual (with the influence of the papacy and a thoroughgoing Europeanization), military and political; and in 1140 were poised for further advances as the Almoravid Empire in its turn began to disintegrate.

D. Lomax

The Ottonian Empire, 962

With the virtual extinction of the Carolingian line, the dukes of the eastern, German kingdom chose one of their own number as king: Conrad of Franconia. He fought against them, but on his deathbed nominated another, Henry of Saxony, as his successor. The dukes of Swabia and Bavaria opposed Henry and it was not until the reign of his son, Otto, that both were pacified. Under the long reign of Otto (936–73), the German kingdom grew to be the most powerful political force in Europe.

Otto I was crowned emperor in 962 and is thus regularly compared to Charlemagne, crowned in 800. He was in many ways an inheritor of Charlemagne's political legacy, and the core of the Ottonian empire was built directly on the German portion of the subdivided Carolingian empire. However, Otto's German empire was far removed from the Frankish state of one and a half centuries earlier.

Following the subdivisions of Charlemagne's empire, the oldest portions, the French-speaking west, tended to fragment. The newest portions, the German-speaking east, on the other hand revealed stronger unifying tendencies. The differences cannot be ascribed to the problems caused by the Vikings. The Magyars proved to be a comparable nuisance to German kings, and political rivals were seen by late Carolingians of the French west and the new kings of the German east alike as greater threats. Indeed, this endemic violent political competition ensured that the simple vagaries of inheritance and succession could not be the sole cause of such different fates.

The suggestion that the western kingdoms fragmented as a result of the feudalization of society has more to recommend it. The German kingdom was more primitive. It was perhaps much like the Frankish kingdom inherited by Charlemagne. When Otto was crowned emperor, the last 200 years had seen the conversion to Christianity, the development of a diocesan organization that was incomplete at the borders of the empire, the foundation of abbeys, and the collection of tithes. The minting of coins east of the Rhine had not long been established. The exploitation of the countryside by ecclesiastics, lay magnates and the king based on land ownership and farming estates worked by servile peasants represented a departure from the more personal forms of authority and the renders of tribute that had gone before. Unlike Carolingian royal estates, some of which may even have gone back to Roman villas, Saxon royal villas (the densest concentration in the Harz hills, among them Tilleda, Goslar, Werla, Quedlinburg and Otto's 'new Rome' Magdeburg) were relatively new foundations. That Otto's Germany was not long out of the Iron Age with a society dominated by chieftains of small power is revealed by its subdivision based on tribal regions: Saxony, Friesland, Thuringia, Franconia, Swabia and Bavaria. Only Lorraine had a long history of developed complex political and social organization.

THE OTTONIAN EMPIRE, 962

Archbishopric
Bishopric
Abbey

Kingdoms, duchies
and Marches

Schleswig
Oldenburg

MARCH OF THE
BILLUNGS

Hamburg
Lüneburg
Bremen
Verden
Havelberg

NORTH
MARCH

FRIESLAND

Wildeshausen

SAXONY

SAXONY

Utrecht
Osnabrück
Minden
Braunschweig
Magdeburg
Brandenburg

Münster
Herford
Hildesheim
Nijmegen
Essen
Paderborn
Goslar
Halberstadt
MARCH OF
LAUSITZ

Antwerp
Werden
Corvey
Quedlinburg

Liège
Cologne
Memleben
Merseburg
Meissen

Aachen
Fritzlar
Naumburg
MARCH
OF
MEISSEN

Cambrai
Malmedy
Stablo
Koblenz
Hersfeld
Zeitz

Prüm
Fulda
FRANCONIA

Prague

Frankfurt
LORRAINE
Mainz
Bamberg
BOHEMIA

Trier
Würzburg
MORAVIA

Metz
Gorze
Worms
Lorsch
Speyer
Regensburg

Verdun
Weissenburg
Niederalteich

Toul
Eichstatt
Passau
MARCH OF

Strasbourg
Ulm
Augsburg
Freising
Vienna
AUSTRIA

Basel
SWABIA
Chiemsee
BAVARIA
Salzburg

Reichenau
Tegernsee
MARCH OF

Constance
St Gall
STYRIA

Chur
Brixen
CARINTHIA

MARCH OF
CARNIOLA

Lyon

KINGDOM
OF
BURGUNDY

Milan

KINGDOM OF ITALY

PAPAL STATE

0   100
km

R. Samson

36

Just as Charlemagne's empire was partly held together by eastward expansion against less developed German neighbours, Otto's empire in part maintained cohesion by attacking its barbarian Slavic neighbours. Frontier principalities, marches, were created in this process. From centres such as Brandenburg and Meissen these areas were brought under German political control and 'civilized'.

Unlike the great Frankish empire, the extension of centralized political power in the new German empire was largely achieved through the Church. By 951 Otto successfully declared eighty-five 'royal' monasteries and all the bishoprics exempt from all secular authority. They were 'immune' from ducal administration. Their lands could not be sub-enfeoffed without royal authority.

Rule of the Italian kingdom came when the pope invited the king to help drive out his political rival, Berengar. The campaign was quick and easy and Otto was made emperor by the pope, although Italy did not figure prominently in Otto's political programme, as it would in that of later German emperors.

R. Samson

RELIGION

Christianity and Paganism in the West, c. 350–750

Before and after the conversion of the Emperor Constantine (312–37) Christianity was less established in the West than the East. The problem of the strength of paganism was compounded by the less urban character of the West, lack of local pastoral institutions and of clear hierarchical organization, theological divisions in the church, and the increasing pressure from barbarian settlers, most of whom were either pagan or Arian (following the conversion of the Goths by Ulfila). The close alliance between Church and state in the East was not replicated in the West and the sack of Rome by the Visigoths in 410 led to a bitter debate between Christian and pagan apologists. Nevertheless, Christianity did much to strengthen its hold on the West from the late fourth century. The western emperor Theodosius I (379–95) took a firm line against Arianism and paganism, a formidable series of Latin theologians such as Ambrose (d. 397) and Augustine (d. 430) strengthened the Church's doctrinal position, and the conservative senatorial aristocracy finally abandoned paganism in the early fifth century. By the pontificate of Leo the Great (440–61) the see of Rome had built up a complex bureaucratic structure, emerged as the spokesman of the West in disputes with the East and on the basis of its petrine origins claimed special authority in the West including final ecclesiastical jurisdiction and the right to confirm appointments. The weakening of imperial institutions led to an enhanced political role for the bishops in Rome and other cities. Bishops took over social and charitable services in their cities, negotiated as the representatives of the Roman communities with barbarian leaders and reinforced their hold over their flocks by skilful manipulation of ceremonies and the cult of saints. The migration from the East of monastic

leaders such as Athanasius and John Cassian helped spread the phenomenon of monasticism. Although it differed in being more aristocratic and urban, individual monastic figures such as St Martin of Tours (d. 397) and St Severinus of Noricum (d. c. 470) played an important role in the leadership of their local communities and in evangelizing the countryside.

The collapse of the empire led to a general extension of the Church's power, but its position in particular areas in the sixth century varied according to political circumstances. Southern Britain was one of the few areas where an almost complete disruption of ecclesiastical structures is evident. In Africa, Spain and Italy the predominantly Arian regimes of the Vandals, Visigoths, Ostrogoths and Lombards restricted the Church's influence, although outright persecution was rare. In the Celtic north-west conversion of southern Scotland and of Ireland had been undertaken in the fifth century by the missionary bishops Ninian and Patrick, but in the sixth century the kin-based, non-urban nature of society promoted the emergence of an increasingly monastic form of church. On the continent new sees were founded, councils regularly convoked, and supervisory powers accorded to the heads of provinces (metropolitans or archbishops). With the spread of monastic rules such as that of St Benedict (d. 547) increasingly missionary work became the preserve of more disciplined and committed monks. Examples include the Irishman Columba, who initiated the conversion of the Picts from Iona c. 565, St Augustine, sent by the powerful Pope Gregory the Great to evangelize the English in 597 and Columbanus (d. 615) whose austere Irish foundations in Gaul and Italy extended the appeal of Christianity among Germanic aristocrats. The

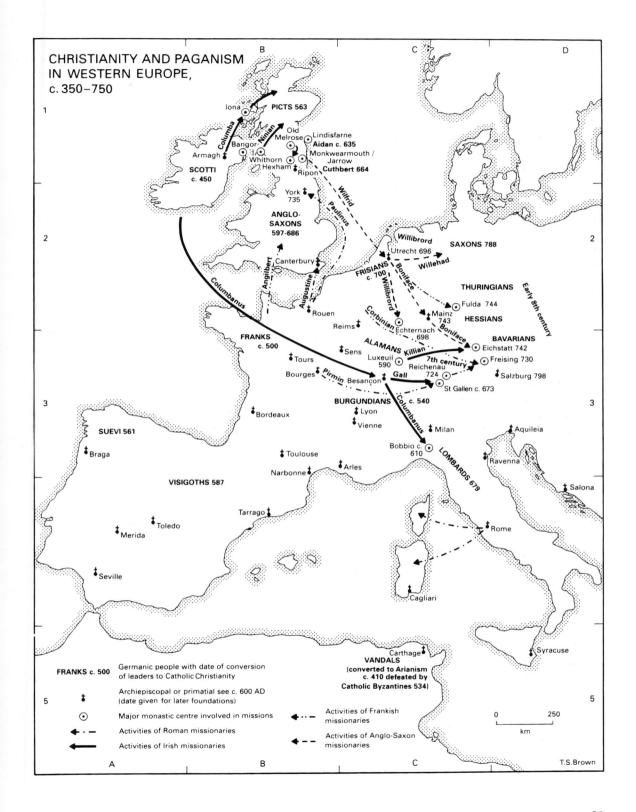

CHRISTIANITY AND PAGANISM
IN WESTERN EUROPE,
c. 350–750

PICTS 563

Iona

Columba

Ninian

Old
Melrose

Lindisfarne
Aidan c. 635

Bangor

Armagh

Whithorn

Hexham

Ripon

Monkwearmouth /
Jarrow
Cuthbert 664

SCOTTI
c. 450

York
735

Wilfrid

Paulinus

ANGLO-
SAXONS
597–686

Willibrord

SAXONS 788

Utrecht 696

Willehad

Angilbert

Canterbury

Columbanus

Augustine

Rouen

Reims

FRISIANS
c. 700

Willibrord

Boniface

THURINGIANS

Fulda 744

Mainz
743

HESSIANS

Boniface

Early 8th century

FRANKS
c. 500

Tours

Sens

Bourges

Pirmin

Besançon

Corbinian

Echternach
698

ALAMANS

Killian

Luxeuil
590

Gall

Reichenau
724

7th century

St Gallen c. 673

BAVARIANS

Eichstätt 742

Freising 730

Salzburg 798

Columbanus c. 540

BURGUNDIANS

Lyon

Vienne

Milan

Bobbio c.
610

LOMBARDS 679

Aquileia

Ravenna

SUEVI 561

Braga

Bordeaux

Toulouse

Arles

Narbonne

Salona

VISIGOTHS 587

Tarrago

Toledo

Merida

Seville

Rome

Cagliari

Carthage

Syracuse

0   250
km

T.S.Brown

39

extension and organization of the English Church was largely the work of monks, either Irish-inspired, such as Aidan at Lindisfarne, or Roman in allegiance such as Wilfrid at York. By the late seventh century Irish and Anglo-Saxon missionaries were winning converts and setting up sees east of the Rhine, the most prominent leaders being Willibrord and Boniface.

By 750 little headway had been made in converting pagans outside the old Roman Empire. Nominal Christians remained attached to traditional Germanic values and superstition remained widespread in the countryside, partly because local parish structures did not yet exist. However, by vastly improving its hierarchical organization, its writings and the quality of its trained personnel the Church had done much to spread its ideals.

T.S. Brown

Early Monasticism to 547

The recorded history of Christian monasticism begins in the Middle East in the late third or fourth century. Although not the first Christian solitary, the Copt Antony (?251–?356) is regarded as the father of Christian eremiticism (*eremos* = desert in Greek), spending many years in prayer and contemplation on the edge of the Egyptian desert and latterly retreating to his 'Inner Mountain'. By the mid-fourth century at Nitria, near the mouth of the Nile, at Scetis to the south and in the Thebaid in Upper Egypt colonies of several hundred hermits could be found: such a grouping was known as a *lavra* (from the Greek for a lane or passage). Its inhabitants lived in separate cells, but there were common buildings including a church where all gathered on Saturdays and Sundays for communal prayer and mass. The *lavra* spread to Syria and Palestine as did the cenobium (from the Greek *koinos bios* = common life), also Egyptian in origin, and founded by another Copt, Pachomius (*c.* 292–346). The first Pachomian community was at Tabennisi on the Upper Nile: such communities were very large, and the monks (or nuns) lived together in a number of houses and supported themselves by handicrafts. Cenobitism was spread to the eastern empire and was further refined by the intellectual and theologian Basil of Caesarea (329–79), who entered the monastic life at Annesi and who eventually achieved a more integrated community than that of Pachomius. He stressed the need for the monk to exercise Christian charity towards his fellows. It is generally held that the monastic movement in the western empire began its real evolution under the influence of the East although there already existed an independent tradition of Christian virginity and asceticism and it is possible that the description of the Antonian or *lavra*-style monasticism established at Ligugé and Marmoutier by the 'father' of Gallic monasticism, Martin of Tours (d. 397), stemmed from his hagiographer's knowledge of the East as much as Martin's own practice. The visits of the exiled Archbishop Athanasius of Alexandria to Trier and to Rome (335–7 and 339–46) may have inspired western monasticism, but possibly even more influential was the translation in the fourth century into Latin of his *Life of Antony* which would become a classic of hagiography and a model for the ascetic life and was the first of several works about the 'desert fathers' to reach the West. Augustine's conversion to a Christian life followed his introduction at Milan to the *Life*; he founded his own monastery at Tagaste in his native North Africa in 388 and wrote an eastern-influenced *Rule* for his sister's community of nuns. Eastern ascetic ideals were imported into the West by Jerome, who founded his own monastery in Bethlehem in 385 and by Honoratus who founded Lérins *c.* 410 on his return from travels in the East. About the same time, John Cassian, who had spent a considerable time in eastern monastic communities, and who com-

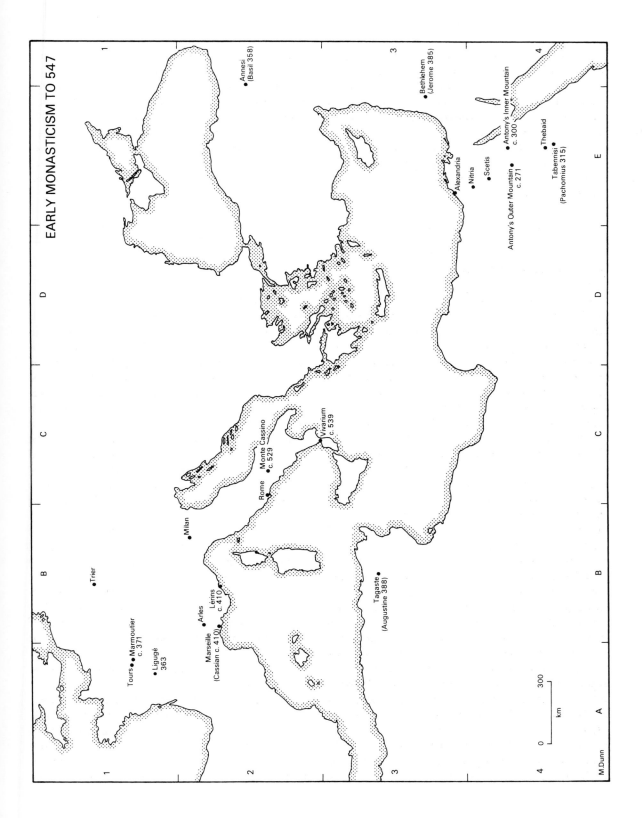

EARLY MONASTICISM TO 547

Annesi
(Basil 358)

Bethlehem
(Jerome 385)

Antony's Inner Mountain
c. 300

Thebaid

Alexandria
Nitria
Scetis

Antony's Outer Mountain
c. 271

Tabennisi
(Pachomius 315)

Vivarium
c. 539

Monte Cassino
c. 529
Rome

Milan

Trier

Tours Marmoutier
c. 371

Ligugé
363

Lérins
c. 410
Arles

Marseille
(Cassian c. 410)

Tagaste
(Augustine 388)

0   300
km

M.Dunn

41

piled the *Conferences* of the desert fathers, founded two cenobitic houses at Marseille. His *Institutes* represent the earliest surviving work of monastic instruction composed in western Europe which gave detailed descriptions of the practice of the East. In the sixth century, southern France and Italy produced a number of cenobitic *Rules* including those by bishops Caesarius (*c.* 470–542) and Aurelian (d. 552) of Arles and the (perhaps surviving) compilation of Eugippius of Lucullanum. More controversial is the *Rule of the Master* which is said to have influenced Benedict of Nursia, the founder of Monte Cassino (*c.* 480–*c.* 547). Benedict's *Rule* was not, in any case, an isolated work but reflects both contemporary practice and earlier teaching. It divided the day of the monk between worship (eight offices), reading (*lectio divina*) and work. At Vivarium, founded by Cassiodorus, monastic life was combined with a well-organized programme of studies.

M. Dunn

Northern European Monasticism

One of the disciples of Martin of Tours, Ninian (d. 432), began the evangelization of south-west Scotland from his monastery at Whithorn. Martin's monasticism was influential in western France, while the east was dominated by Lérins and Marseille. Radegund, wife of Chlothar I, founded the Convent of the Holy Cross in Poitiers which followed the *Rule* of Caesarius of Arles. Irish monasticism had begun its own development, supposedly influenced, directly or indirectly, by the East, and the mid-sixth century saw the foundation of a cluster of important monasteries, including Clonard (founded by Finian), Clonfert (Brendan), Bangor (Comgall) and Clonmacnoise (Ciaran). Columba (or Colmcille, *c.* 521–97) founded Durrow and Derry and in the 560s migrated to Iona, where he established a monastic centre which also undertook missions among the Scots and Picts. Irish-style monasticism also spread to Melrose and Lindisfarne. About 590, Columbanus travelled from Bangor in Ireland to the Continent, where he established Luxeuil under the patronage of the Merovingian court. His *Rule* and accompanying *Penitential* are the earliest surviving documents of this kind from an Irish background and despite the severity of his regime, both Luxeuil and his Italian foundation, Bobbio, attracted recruits. Parts of the *Rules* of Benedict, Columbanus, and of Caesarius of Arles appear in conjunction in Donatus' seventh-century *Rule* for nuns at Besançon. The use of 'mixed rules' apparently characterized other Frankish foundations, particularly those made in Neustria and Austrasia by some reforming bishops and by the Merovingians and their court – houses such as Rebais, St Wandrille, Jumièges, Pavilly, Fleury and Fécamp. Balthild, wife of Clovis II, founded Corbie with monks from Luxeuil and royal diplomas ensured that older houses such as St Martin, Tours, and St Denis, Paris, were free from episcopal financial exactions. Several renowned 'double houses' (i.e. foundations containing both a monastery and a convent) were established in this area and period: the best-known are Faremoutiers, Jouarre, and Balthild's own re-foundation of Chelles-sur-Cher. In England, continental monasticism arrived from Rome when Augustine and his companions landed in Kent in 597: traditional assumptions that they followed exclusively the *Rule* of St Benedict have been subject to criticism and revision and it is now generally assumed that they too used some sort of 'mixed rule'. In seventh-century England, several double houses on the Hiberno-Frankish model were founded, among them Whitby: its first abbess, Hild, presided over the Synod of Whitby (664). Wilfrid, abbot of Ripon and later bishop of York, sought to root out the Celtic practice debated between 'Romans' and 'Celts' at the synod, and instituted a more exclusively 'Roman' form of monasticism in his own houses, such as Hexham.

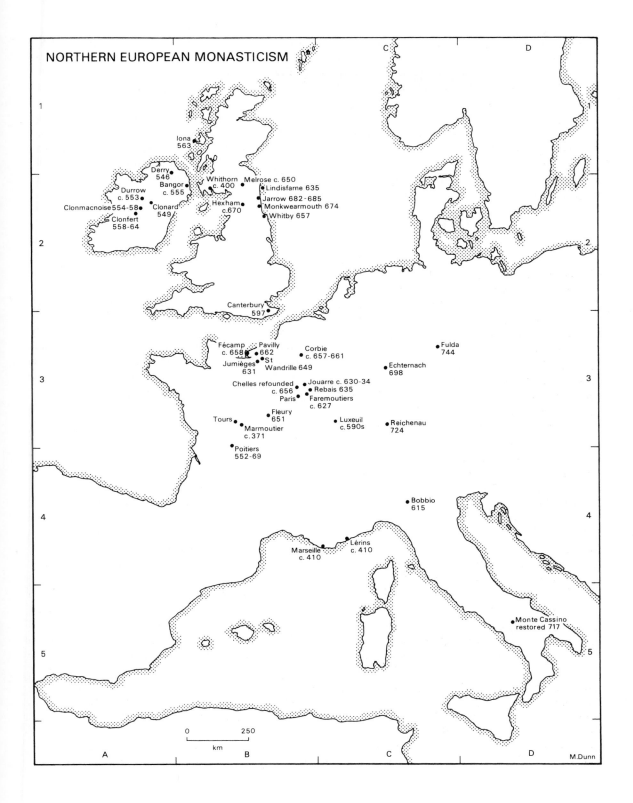

NORTHERN EUROPEAN MONASTICISM

Iona
563

Derry
546
Whithorn   Melrose c. 650
c. 400   Lindisfarne 635
Bangor   Jarrow 682-685
c. 555   Monkwearmouth 674
Durrow   Hexham   Whitby 657
c. 553   c.670
Clonmacnoise 554-58   Clonard
Clonfert   549
558-64

Canterbury
597

Fécamp   Pavilly   Corbie   Fulda
c. 658   662   c. 657-661   744
            St
Jumièges   Wandrille 649   Echternach
631   698

Chelles refounded   Jouarre c. 630-34
c. 656   Rebais 635
Paris   Faremoutiers
                 c. 627
Tours   Fleury   Luxeuil   Reichenau
            651   c.590s   724
Marmoutier
c. 371
Poitiers
552-69

Bobbio
615

Marseille   Lérins
c. 410   c. 410

Monte Cassino
restored 717

0   250
km

M.Dunn

43

At Monkwearmouth and Jarrow, founded by his friend and contemporary, Benedict Biscop, the customs were based on the Benedictine *Rule* and those of seventeen monasteries (including continental houses) which Benedict Biscop had visited. On the Continent, in the late seventh and eighth centuries, Frisia, Hesse and Thuringia were evangelized largely by English monks, in particular Willibrord and Boniface: foundations such as Echternach and Fulda showed increased Benedictine influence. So did Reichenau, established by the monk-missionary Pirmin, who may have come from either Ireland or Spain. At the Synod of Aachen of 817, Abbot Benedict of Aniane and the emperor, Louis the Pious, gave formal legislative backing to the Carolingian dynasty's previous promotion of the Benedictine *Rule*. However, despite Benedict of Aniane's encouragement of the use of a 'pure' version of the text of the *Rule*, he also tried to impose a customary with usages in liturgy and practice which often supplemented and surpassed the first Benedict's provisions.

M. Dunn

Byzantine Missions among the Slavs

The beginnings of this work are closely associated with the brothers Constantine and Methodius, the 'Apostles of the Slavs'. Their first joint mission was in 860 when they were sent to Byzantium's steppe-allies, the Khazars. Though primarily political, it provided them with experience in the mission field. They put the case for Christianity to the Khazars, who were converting to Judaism. They had limited success, but were the obvious choice, when in 862 the ruler of the

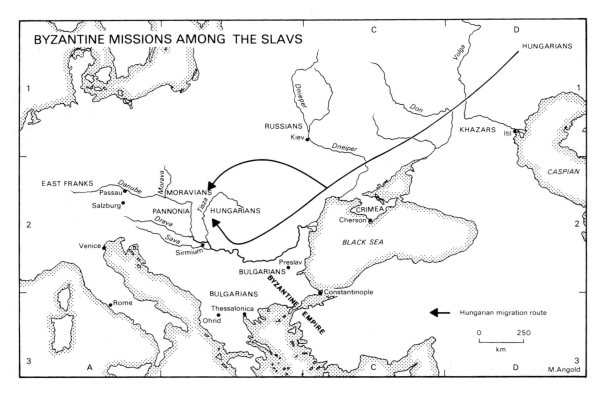

Moravians turned to Byzantium for missionaries to counter the Frankish priests working from Passau and Salzburg. Coming from Thessalonica, Constantine and Methodius had the great advantage of knowing the Slavonic language. Their first task was to translate the liturgy and parts of the gospels into Slavonic for use among the Moravians. This angered the Frankish clergy who insisted that there could be no addition to the number of sacred languages. Constantine and Methodius went to Rome to put their case and secured the support of the papacy. After Constantine's death in 869 Methodius was appointed to Pannonia and the see of Sirmium. The immediate results of his work were unpromising. He was hampered by Frankish hostility, and the Hungarian invasion of 895 left almost no trace of his work among the Moravians. After his death in 885 the remnants of his mission were welcomed by the Bulgarian ruler Boris, who was unhappy with the ascendancy of the Greek clergy following his forced conversion in 865 in the aftermath of a Byzantine invasion. Recourse to the papacy was not a success, but with the help of Methodius' followers, Clement and Naum, the Bulgarian Church became the main centre of Slavonic Christianity. Much of this achievement passed to the Russians after the baptism at Cherson in 989 of Vladimir, the prince of Kiev. The success of Byzantine missions to the Slavs owed much to the use of Slavonic. It also allowed Slavonic Christianity to develop independently of Byzantium.

M. Angold

Tenth- and Eleventh-Century Centres of Reform

The foundation of the abbey of Cluny in Burgundy in 910 by Abbot Berno and Duke William of Aquitaine was the first step in the creation of the congregation of Cluny. Cluny placed itself directly under the protection of the papacy and eventually became head of a grouping of several hundred monasteries following the Benedictine *Rule* and its own 'customs' (supplementary usages). Another important congregation, also Benedictine in basis, but with different emphases from Cluny was launched in 933 with the reform of Gorze. Brogne brought Benedictine observance to several Flemish monasteries. In England, between 940 and the 980s Dunstan, Ethelwold and Oswald, with the backing of the Wessex kings, began a reform at Abingdon and Glastonbury which was partly influenced by the Continent (Fleury, Ghent, Cluny and Gorze) and which led to the composition of the *Regularis Concordia*.

At the beginning of the eleventh century, Romuald of Ravenna became the father of an organized eremitical life; after spending time as a hermit in the area of Venice and travelling to the Benedictine house of Cuxa in the Pyrenees, he returned to north-eastern Italy and founded monasteries and hermitages. The most famous of these was Camaldoli, which combined a sort of *lavra* for hermits with a *cenobium* which acted as a buffer between the hermits and the world. A similar organization characterized Fonte Avellana, of which the reformer, Peter Damian, was prior. Around 1039, John Gualbert founded the house – later the congregation – of Vallombrosa, which adhered strictly to the *Rule* of St Benedict, and was grouped on federal lines. The foundation of the Grande Chartreuse by Bruno of Rheims in 1084 marked the beginning of an order which, by the early twelfth century, had both eremitic and cenobitic characteristics: the monks lived an austere contemplative life, keeping largely to individual cells which were ranged around a cloister. The idea of a common life for canons, hitherto strongest in the empire, gained fresh impetus in France and Italy with the foundation of the influential houses of St Ruf and St Frediano.

M. Dunn

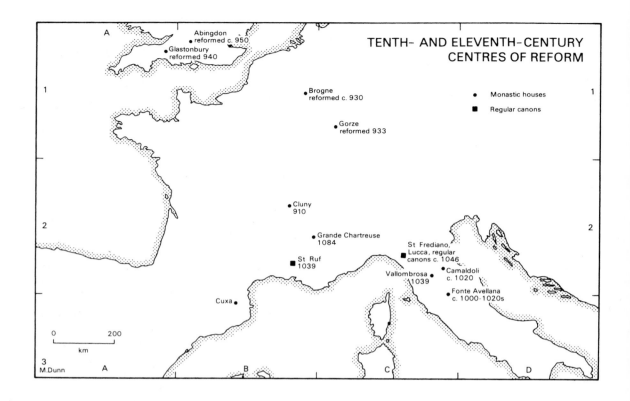

The map shows the following labeled points:

TENTH- AND ELEVENTH-CENTURY
CENTRES OF REFORM

- Monastic houses
■ Regular canons

Abingdon reformed c. 950
Glastonbury reformed 940
Brogne reformed c. 930
Gorze reformed 933
Cluny 910
Grande Chartreuse 1084
St Frediano, Lucca, regular canons c. 1046
St Ruf 1039
Camaldoli c. 1020
Vallombrosa 1039
Fonte Avellana c. 1000–1020s
Cuxa

0   200
km

M.Dunn

Episcopal Sees in Europe at the End of the Tenth Century

The martyrdom on the Baltic of Adalbert, bishop of Prague at the hands of the Prussians in 997 marked the drawing to a close of more than two centuries of sustained missionary activity, which gradually brought about the conversion of the pagans of northern and central Europe. The persistent threat that had hitherto been posed to Christian Europe by these pagans, Vikings and Slavs, with all the trouble they had brought on the Church, was coming to an end as their rulers chose to adopt Christianity. What was to follow was a period of consolidation and reform, at length led by the papacy, during which the process of Christianization was advanced throughout the territories inhabited by both the old and the new adherents of the Latin Church.

Politics and religion were closely intertwined on the frontiers of the German kingdom, as its rulers sought to dominate the nascent churches of neighbouring peoples. Missionaries were sent forth from the province of Hamburg-Bremen in the north to convert the Danes, which resulted in the creation of several new sees in the mid-tenth century. Otto I's pet project in this field was the archbishopric of Magdeburg, which was founded in 968 in the wake of the German settlement of the lands between the Elbe and the Oder, and a new see was erected in the heart of Polish territory at Poznan as a suffragan to it. But with the creation of the metropolitan see of Gniezno in 1000 Poland obtained a Church independent of German control, just as politically it remained outwith the bounds of the empire, though for a short time jurisdiction over Poznan was retained by the German archbishop. The Hungarian experience was similar. It was the Bavarian province of Salzburg that was most active in the evangelization of the Bohemians, Moravians and

46

Hungarians. The Bohemian diocese of Prague (973) was subjected to Mainz and remained so until the fourteenth century, but Hungary like Poland achieved an independent Church with the creation of the metropolitan see of Esztergom in 1001.

The eastern and western churches were in competition with one another for the allegiance of the Slavs, and while Rome had gained most of central Europe, the Byzantines had successfully established the Bulgarian and, more recently, the Russian Churches. Tension between Latins and Greeks, due to complex reasons of which theological differences were a part, was most evident in southern Italy. Here the Byzantines held sway over Apulia, Basilicata and Calabria, with a considerable Greek population in the extreme south, which belonged to the patriarchate of Constantinople. On the western side of the peninsula the Lombards of Campania observed the Latin rite. The German Ottonian emperors (962–1002) had ambitions to wrest the region from Byzantine control, which would have effected its union with the Roman or western patriarchate, but it was not until some years after the Norman conquest that the entire south was subordinated to Rome. By 1000 there were five southern Italian provinces in the Constantinopolitan obedience: Reggio di Calabria, St Severina, Otranto, Taranto and Brindisi-Oria. Apulia was an area of mixed population and technically pertained to Rome. Nevertheless, the metropolitans of the province of Bari-Canosa were as likely to recognize the authority of Constantinople as that of Rome, and from the mid-tenth century they frequently also held the archbishopric of Brindisi-Oria. Moreover, the decision to erect the archbishopric of Trani (by 987) was taken in Constantinople rather than Rome and may have been a reaction against Rome's creation of the province of Benevento in 969. Pope John XIII, at the request of Otto I, seems to have expressly established Benevento, with its many suffragans, as a Latin outpost. The same at least might be said of Salerno, if indeed its foundation cannot be described as an outright attempt to eat into the Greek patriarchate. In 989 John XV gave the new archbishop jurisdiction over Acerenza and the Calabrian sees of Bisignano, Malvito and Cosenza. Acerenza, although also technically belonging to Rome, had already been assigned with four other sees to the province of Otranto by Polyeuctes, patriarch of Constantinople in 968, and Bisignano, Malvito and Cosenza had at the beginning of the tenth century been listed among the suffragans of Reggio di Calabria. Continual confirmation of these sees to Salerno by successive popes casts some doubt on the ability of the archbishops to command the obedience of their occupants, and such difficulties probably lay behind the Norman Robert Guiscard's agreement with Nicholas II in 1059 to subject the churches of any territories he might conquer to Rome. In any event, Acerenza and Cosenza were erected into metropolitans by the mid-eleventh century, and Bisignano and Malvito were made immediately subject to Rome by the mid-twelfth.

From the early eighth century the chief threat to the Christian church in the Mediterranean was Islam. As well as the greater part of the Iberian peninsula and its outlying islands, the Arabs held Sicily, Sardinia and Corsica, and these were used as bases to harry the coasts of Europe. In the early eleventh century the Pisans and Genoese cleared them out of Sardinia and Corsica, and by the 1070s the Normans had taken control of Sicily. In Spain provincial organization had broken down as a result of the Muslim conquest. The surviving sees of Catalonia, which had formerly belonged to the province of Tarragona, were eventually attached to that of Narbonne across the Pyrenees, but elsewhere in the Christian north the bishops were not formally subjected to any metropolitan authority until the end of the eleventh century. Nevertheless, in the kingdom of Asturias-León the bishop whose see was to be found in the same place as the seat of royal power, first Lugo, then Oviedo and finally León, performed the functions of and was in all but name the metropolitan. Similarly, in the eleventh century the bishop of Jaca was known in official documents as bishop of Aragon, and the bishop of Burgos as bishop of Castile. These associations point clearly to the great degree of control the Spanish Christian rulers maintained

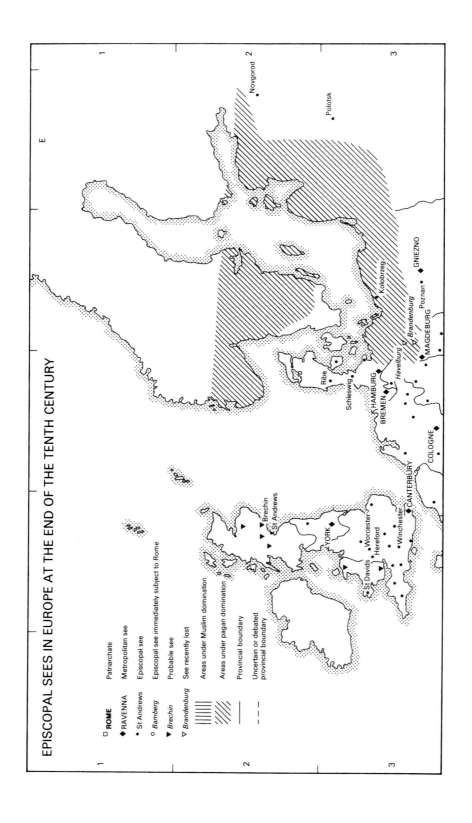

EPISCOPAL SEES IN EUROPE AT THE END OF THE TENTH CENTURY

□ ROME   Patriarchate
◆ RAVENNA   Metropolitan see
• St Andrews   Episcopal see
○ Bamberg   Episcopal see immediately subject to Rome
▼ Brechin   Probable see
▽ Brandenburg   See recently lost

Areas under Muslim domination

Areas under pagan domination

Provincial boundary

Uncertain or debated provincial boundary

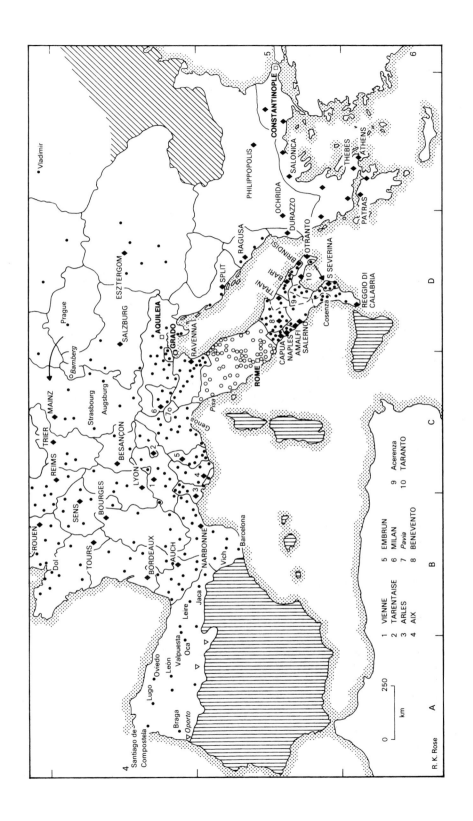

over ecclesiastical affairs. As the old centres of metropolitan authority were taken from the Muslims during the course of the *Reconquista*, provincial organization in the normal way was re-established: at Toledo in 1088, at Tarragona in 1091, and at Braga in 1104. In addition, the growing importance and prestige of Santiago de Compostela as a place of pilgrimage made it, too, a natural site for an archiepiscopal see (1120).

North of the Pyrenees the provincial boundaries that had come into being in the Frankish kingdoms by the early ninth century remained unaltered until the later Middle Ages. Under Charlemagne metropolitan authority was reaffirmed in 779, and he furthermore favoured metropolitan bishops' assumption of the honorific title of archbishop, which had earlier been accorded to the missionary Boniface by Pope Gregory III. Those sees that had been disrupted by the Viking invasions were by 1000 all restored. In England the two provinces of Canterbury and York established at the end of the sixth and seventh centuries remained, but the distribution of episcopal sees had been worse affected here with the permanent loss of several and was soon to be changed to some extent by the Normans. In Wales and Scotland a territorial episcopate had not yet completely emerged, and only at St Davids and St Andrews were there undoubtedly bishops' sees of this kind. Its full development took place in the eleventh and twelfth centuries under Norman influence. Similarly, the territorial division of Ireland into dioceses and provinces was not begun until the mid-twelfth century.

R.K. Rose

The Influx of Relics into Saxony

Between 772 and 804, in a long series of bloody campaigns, Charlemagne subjugated the pagan Saxons. A natural corollary to the conquest was a programme of missionary activity and the creation of an ecclesiastical establishment. The heart of Christianity, however, was not formal ecclesiastical structures, but rather the cult of the saints and their wonder-working bones. The conversion of the Saxons required the importation of relics, holy bones, from places where they existed in some abundance, such as the churches of northern Francia and, especially, Rome. New monasteries like Corvey and new sees like Hildesheim had to possess such relics as a focus for local devotion and a source of supernatural power. 'The populace can be turned from their superstitions most easily if the body of some famous saint be brought here', remarked one contemporary Saxon bishop. In 851 the Saxon noble Waltbraht brought the bones of St Alexander from Rome to his monastery at Wildeshausen. The conversion was obviously sending down roots, for Waltbraht was the grandson of Widukind, the hero of the Saxon opposition to Charlemagne.

R. Bartlett

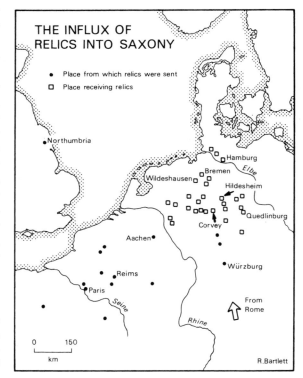

THE INFLUX OF RELICS INTO SAXONY

• Place from which relics were sent
□ Place receiving relics

Northumbria

Hamburg
Bremen
Wildeshausen
Hildesheim
Corvey
Quedlinburg

Aachen

Würzburg

Reims

Paris

From Rome

Elbe

Seine

Rhine

0   150
km

R. Bartlett

GOVERNMENT, SOCIETY AND ECONOMY

Royal Carolingian Residential Villas

Carolingian kings had many palaces, villas and estates, but they only resided at the more important. Even a partial picture of all the farming estates of Carolingian kings cannot be painted because records survive for only some of the farms given away to churches, whose own records, on rare occasion, do survive. We assume that most agricultural estates were not far distant from the places of residence, as transport of food overland was expensive. Exceptions were luxury products, such as wine, and vineyard estates might be far distant. With the increased use of coin in paying rents, distance became less problematic.

Royal estates, however, were more than sources of financial gain or places to sleep, they had a political nature too. The great royal Carolingian villas of Aachen, Compiègne, Frankfurt, Herstal, Ingelheim, Nijmegen, Paderborn, Quierzy and Thionville were effectively centres of government. Here charters were witnessed, ambassadors met, great assemblies and even church synods convened, laws enacted.

The concentration of estates along the Rhine and between the Meuse and Moselle reflects the homeland of the Carolingian family. Visits to estates east of the Rhine reflect political activity, such as the planning of campaigns against the

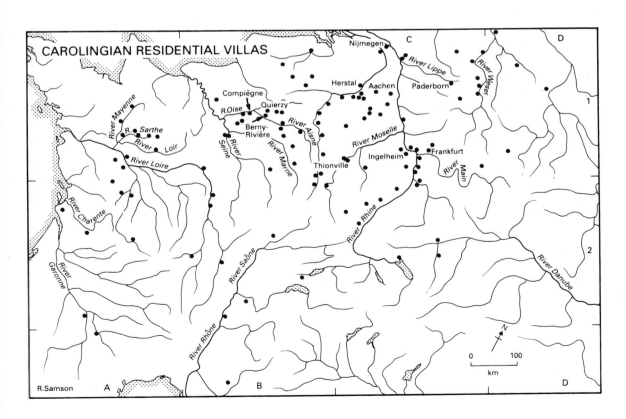

51

Saxons. The rarity of sojourns in southern France reveals a lack of personal wealth there but also an absence of important political threats or interests.

Where estates were left too long unvisited in the hands of officials, they were often usurped. Rarity of estates and weakness of political authority went hand in hand. The dissolution of the Carolingian fisc was the title given to the theory that Carolingian political power dwindled as estates were given away on a huge scale, but how much land was truly lost is not clear. As estates and palaces grew old, kings favoured newer ones. Thus the favourite royal Merovingian palaces, such as Berny-Rivière, while still owned by Carolingian kings, were rarely visited by them. Charlemagne and his son's most loved palaces, Aachen and Ingelheim, were those they had built anew.

R. Samson

Burhs and Mints in Late Anglo-Saxon England

Coinage provides a major source of insight into the administrative and organizational abilities of late Anglo-Saxon England. Maintenance of the integrity of the coinage was a factor of considerable importance to royal prestige. Mintage rights were completely regalian and counterfeiters were heavily punished. In the second quarter of the tenth century, Athelstan decreed that each burh should have a mint and attempted to limit the number of moneyers. A major reform of

BURHS AND MINTS IN LATE ANGLO-SAXON ENGLAND

- •   Existing mint
- ○   New mint of Edgar
- □   New mint of Edward the Martyr
- △   New mint of Aethelred II to 999
- ▽   New mint of Aethelred II from 1000
- ////   Area of strong Danish settlement marked by wapentakes

1 Salisbury
2 Wilton
3 Shaftesbury
4 Milbourne
5 Bruton
6 Cadbury
7 Ilchester
8 Langport
9 Bridgport
10 Dorchester

S.Coates

coinage took place under Edgar in 973 who decreed that 'there shall run one coinage throughout the realm'. Under Aethelred there was a tremendous increase in the output of mints, partly due to the need to pay off large sums of money demanded by the Danes. Great national mints existed at London, Lincoln, Winchester and York. Provincial centres were at Exeter, Stamford and Chester, and Oxford and Shrewsbury were shire centres.

Burhs were originally fortified, walled towns which had proliferated in Alfred's reign and served a military purpose. They were royal in nature and if the king so wished could be made into mints or markets. They became increasingly important as mercantile centres with the development of trade and had their own laws and administration. The extension of English author-ity into territories held for a generation or more by the Danes was heavily reliant on burhs. Hertford, Northampton, Huntingdon and Cambridge had been fortified headquarters of Danish armies.

Local administration was marked by the divisions known as shires which came under the charge of an 'ealdorman', later a shire reeve or sheriff. Shires were not systematically organized and did not settle into more permanent moulds until the reign of Edward the Confessor. They possessed their own courts and were further split into territorial divisions known as hundreds where courts were also held. In areas of strong Danish settlement these were known as wapentakes.

S. Coates

Royal Itineraries: Eleventh-Century France and Germany

Most medieval kings were itinerant. They did not reside for long periods in one place or govern from fixed capital cities, but journeyed continually from place to place. There were several reasons for this. Economically, it might be cheaper and more convenient to move the king, his retinue and their horses to the supplies of food, drink and fodder rather than vice versa. The itinerant court thus consumed the produce of royal manors or received 'hospitality' from bishops, abbots or others on whom the obligation lay, before moving on to its next source of sustenance. Obviously, as the European economy became more monetized and commercialized, such an economic rationale for itinerant kingship grew less pressing: market solutions were now available to meet the problem of supply. There were also political advantages to itineration, however. In an age of low rates of literacy, when local bureaucracies were rudimentary or non-existent, the physical presence of the king was the surest way of making royal authority a reality. Medieval government, it has been said, was 'a government of the roadside'.

The map shows the places visited during their long reigns by two contemporary rulers, Philip I of France (1060–1108) and Henry IV of Germany (1056–1106), as they are revealed by contemporary documents. Both kings were constantly on the move, but the patterns of their itineraries show significant variation. First, much more is known about the movements of Henry IV than Philip I, partly because the number of royal documents from the German king's reign is much greater than that from the French king's (491:171), partly because Henry was a controversial figure and excited the chroniclers' attention. Also clearly visible is the fact that the German kings of the eleventh century acted on a far vaster scale than their French contemporaries. Henry moved regularly throughout Germany, was deeply involved in Italy and campaigned south of Rome, east of Austria and north of the Meuse. The extreme limits of his journeyings produce an axis of around 1,500 km.

53

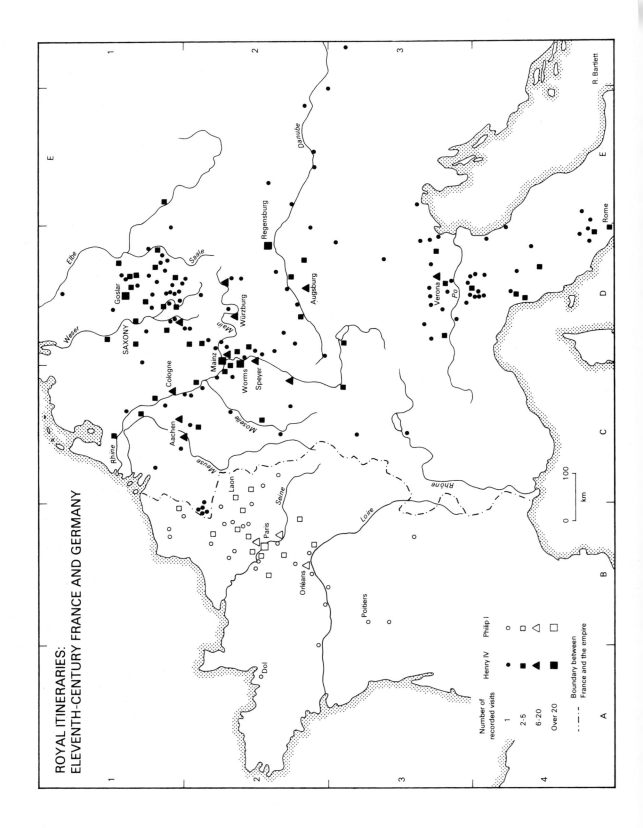

ROYAL ITINERARIES:
ELEVENTH-CENTURY FRANCE AND GERMANY

Number of recorded visits	Henry IV	Philip I
1	●	○
2–5	■	□
6–20	▲	△
Over 20	■	□

Boundary between
France and the empire

R. Bartlett

Not all of this was happy: the concentrations of activity in Saxony and north Italy represent prolonged attempts to subdue opposition. Nevertheless, the geographical range of Henry IV's activities indicate the ambitious scope of the German monarchy.

In contrast, the Capetian king was limited to a relatively small area, especially the zone between the three main royal centres of Orléans, Paris and Laon. Outside this region the king travelled almost as a foreign prince in his own kingdom. His visits to Poitiers and Dol, for example, which took place in 1076, were to seek a military alliance with the duke of Aquitaine and to relieve a castle besieged by William, duke of Normandy – he was treating with equals or enemies rather than subjects. The virtual autonomy of the great French princes in the eleventh century, com-pared with the relatively greater subordination of the German dukes to royal authority, is reflec-ted in the itineraries of the two kings.

The map demonstrates the basic geographical pattern of royal power in the two kingdoms: in France a royal demesne in the Ile-de-France which was the only real arena for Capetian power; in Germany a monarchy deeply embed-ded in the Rhine valley and south-east Saxony (the homelands, respectively, of the Salian dynasty and their predecessors, the Ottonians), but which sought also to maintain a hold over the Po valley and Rome. Within two centuries these patterns would be fundamentally altered as the Capetians extended their power beyond the Ile-de-France while the German monarchy saw its lands and powers disintegrate.

R. Bartlett

England under William I

The Norman Conquest was a momentous event in English history. England received a new royal dynasty, a new aristocracy, a new language, a new architecture and a virtually new Church. A tenur-ial revolution extinguished many noble English families leaving less than half a dozen Englishmen amongst the 180 tenants-in-chief when the Domesday Book was made in 1086. In theory all land was held directly from the king although in practice much of the land acquired by William's adherents was acquired privately.

Landed wealth and political power was concentrated in the hands of a small number of men such as Odo of Bayeux, Robert of Mortain and Hugh d'Avranches, who were bound to the king through close bonds of blood and personal loyalty. Military considerations led to substantial changes in patterns of land-holding in frontier areas. Unlike their Anglo-Saxon counterparts, the great Norman lords possessed their seats of power and a substantial portion of their land along the edges of the kingdom and not in the heart of England. The king demanded knight-service and financial aid from his tenants-in-chief and knight-service was also imposed on the Church.

Before the Conquest England possessed very few castles and these were built by Edward the Confessor's Norman or French favourites. The Normans were great castle builders. Castles were built at strategic points on roads and in centres of population. Early post-conquest castles where possible attempted to make use of existing for-tifications and were swiftly constructed of earth and timber. Often the castle was marked by the distinctive motte or mound and a surrounding bailey or enclosure. The Bayeux Tapestry depicts the speed of castle building showing the con-struction of a motte at Hastings although the army was only there for fifteen days. It was only after military urgencies had passed that the Normans constructed more elaborate castles.

S. Coates

ENGLAND UNDER WILLIAM I

- • Castle built by William I or with his sanction
- □ Prominent tenants placed near important sources of their terriorial wealth

Newcastle
Durham
Alan of Brittany
Hugh d'Avranches
William of Percy
Robert of Mortain
Ilbert de Lacy
York
Gilbert de Gand
William of Warenne
Alan of Brittany
Roger of Poitou
William Peverel
Roger de Busli
William of Percy
Chester
Lincoln
Hugh d'Avranches
Henry de Ferrers
Ivo Taillebois
Nottingham
William of Warenne
Robert of Stafford
Alan of Brittany
Shrewsbury
Stafford
Norwich
Roger de Montgomery
Thorkill of Arden
Rockingham
Countess Judith
Ely
Robert Malet
William
Urse d'Abitot
Peverel
Huntingdon
Cambridge
Roger Bigot
Worcester
Warwick
Alan of Brittany
Richard of Clare
Hereford
Roger d'Ivry
Colchester
William Fitzosbern
Oxford
Geoffrey of Mandeville
Aubrey de Vere
Gloucester
Henry de Ferrers
Eustace of Boulogne
Suen of Essex
London
Wallingford
Windsor
Odo, Bishop of Bayeux
Rochester
Edward of Salisbury
Hugh de Port
William
Robert Montfort
Hugh of Montfort
Canterbury
Geoffrey, Bishop of Coutances
Old Sarum
of Braose
Robert of Mortain
Richard of Clare
Dover
Baldwin the Sheriff
Winchester
Bramber
Lewes
Hastings
Robert of Mortain
Arundel
Pevensey
Exeter
Corfe
Robert of Mortain
Judhael of Totnes

0   100
km

S.Coates

56

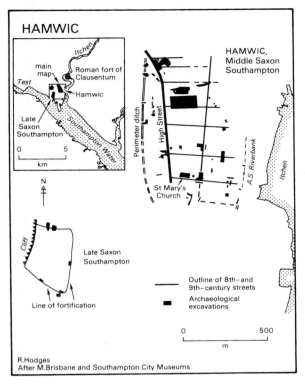

HAMWIC

HAMWIC,
Middle Saxon
Southampton

main map

Roman fort of Clausentum

Hamwic

Test

Late Saxon Southampton

0   5
km

N

Itchen

Southampton Water

Perimeter ditch

High Street

A.S. Riverbank

Itchen

St Mary's Church

Cliff

Late Saxon Southampton

Line of fortification

Outline of 8th- and 9th-century streets

Archaeological excavations

0   500
m

R.Hodges
After M.Brisbane and Southampton City Museums

Hamwic: Anglo-Saxon Southampton

Hamwic, Anglo-Saxon Southampton, has been discovered by a large number of archaeological excavations in the St Mary's district of Southampton. These show that the town covered an area of about 45 hectares within a deep perimeter ditch, and was laid out with a grid of streets. The principal or high street was nearly 15 m wide and may have served as a market place. Most of the many buildings were occupied by various kinds of artisans, but traces of Frankish merchants who may have visited the town have been found near the likely beaching places for boats alongside the river Itchen. Hamwic was probably founded about 690 by King Ine of Wessex, and flourished during the eighth and early ninth centuries before it was sacked by the Vikings in 842. In the late ninth century, if not before, the town was largely deserted in favour of the new fortified town of Southampton to the west, or King Alfred's capital at Winchester.

R. Hodges

Dorestad

The emporium of Dorestad is commonly mentioned by travellers in the seventh to ninth centuries. The site was identified in the nineteenth century by L.D.F. Janssen and substantially excavated first by J.H. Holwerda after the First World War, and then by W.A. Van Es between 1967 and 1976. The excavations show that this sprawling town covering in excess of 50 hectares lay at the confluence of the rivers Rhine and Lek, in which were constructed substantial timber docks. Behind the docks lay a row of commercial properties including warehouses, but the heart of the settlement was composed of many farms typical of this part of Frisia. The vast amount of Middle Rhenish trade goods indicate that Dorestad acted as an entrepot for trade around the North Sea between the later seventh and mid-ninth centuries. The town was abandoned after Viking raids and the silting up of the Rhine in the 860s. A museum in modern Wijk bij Duurstede displays the discoveries made in medieval Dorestad.

R. Hodges

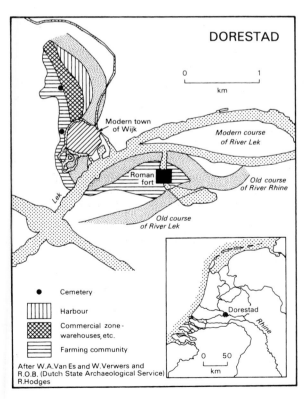

DORESTAD

0   1
km

Modern town of Wijk

Modern course of River Lek

Roman fort

Old course of River Rhine

Lek

Old course of River Lek

Cemetery

Harbour

Commercial zone - warehouses, etc.

Farming community

Dorestad

Rhine

0   50
km

After W.A.Van Es and W.Verwers and R.O.B. (Dutch State Archaeological Service) R.Hodges

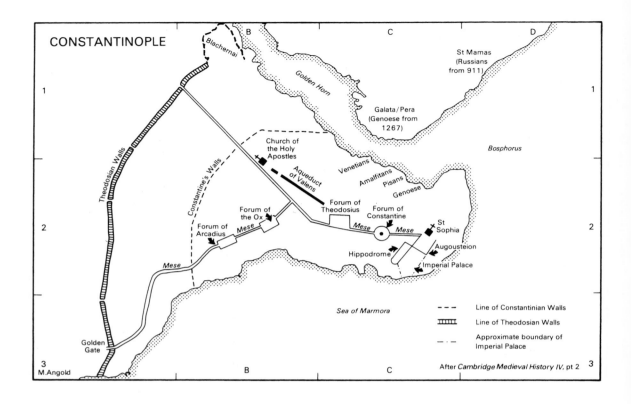

Constantinople

Constantinople was chosen in 324 by Constantine as the capital of the Roman Empire in the east. It stands on a peninsula at the meeting point of the Bosphorus, the Golden Horn and the Sea of Marmora, at the hub of the main routes connecting Europe and Asia. Though Constantine wanted his capital to conform schematically to Rome, with its seven hills, twelve regions and forums, its lay-out was radically different, even before the construction of the Theodosian Walls in 413. It was articulated around the *Mese*, the great avenue which proceeded from the Golden Gate, the ceremonial entrance to the city, through a series of forums to the Augousteion. This was the heart of the city, surrounded by the Imperial Palace, the cathedral of St Sophia, and the Hippodrome. It suffered extensive damage during the Nika riots of 532, but this allowed Justinian to reconstruct many public buildings, including St Sophia, thus setting his stamp on the city. Particular attention was paid to the water supply with its aqueducts and cisterns. This was a necessity with a population approaching half a million. Population declined rapidly from the seventh century, however, and only in the ninth century did the city recover some of its prosperity, a new feature being the foreign 'factories' established along the Golden Horn, which was the commercial centre of the city. Permanent decline set in after its fall to the fourth crusade in 1204.

M. Angold

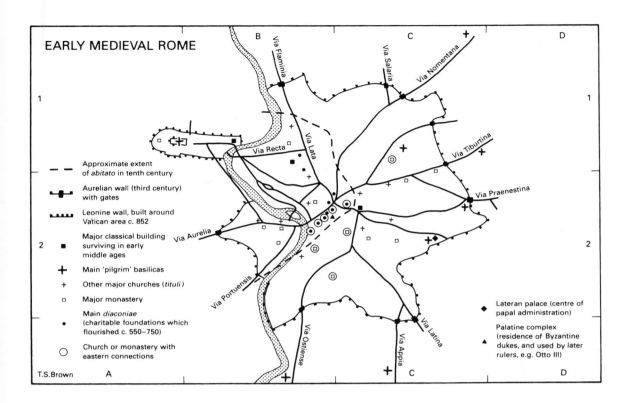

Map legend:

- – – – Approximate extent of *abitato* in tenth century
- Aurelian wall (third century) with gates
- Leonine wall, built around Vatican area c. 852
- ■ Major classical building surviving in early middle ages
- ✚ Main 'pilgrim' basilicas
- + Other major churches (*tituli*)
- ▫ Major monastery
- • Main *diaconiae* (charitable foundations which flourished c. 550–750)
- ◯ Church or monastery with eastern connections
- ◆ Lateran palace (centre of papal administration)
- ▲ Palatine complex (residence of Byzantine dukes, and used by later rulers, e.g. Otto III)

Early Medieval Rome

Although Rome ceased to be a regular imperial residence by the fourth century, it retained great prestige as the seat of the senate and the papacy. Numerous churches were built, including martyr-shrines, transformed houses of earlier private patrons (*tituli*), and major imperial foundations. Despite sacking by Visigoths and Vandals and Germanic rule after 476, its wealth, population and artistic production remained high until the mid-sixth century, when the Gothic War (535–54), the eclipse of the Senate and the Lombard invasion (568) led to precipitate decline. The city was capital of a Byzantine duchy *c.* 536–727 but the papacy exercised increasing control over the city from the pontificate of Gregory I (590–604). Although habitation was largely confined to the river banks beneath the Palatine, it remained culturally important because of the many Greek monasteries manned by eastern refugees and churches which continued to be built to serve as charitable complexes (*diaconiae*), or to cater for a growing number of relics and pilgrims.

Following conflicts with Byzantium over iconoclasm, taxation and the empire's inability to resist Lombard encroachments, the popes strove from *c.* 727 to set up an autonomous papal state. A close alliance was built up with the Franks, culminating in the imperial coronation of Charlemagne in St Peter's (Christmas Day 800). Although relations were often uneasy and Byzantine cultural and social influence remained strong, Rome's enhanced political and jurisdictional role led to increased wealth and building activity. This was reaffirmed (and the endemic problem of local noble violence was partly reduced) by the imperial coronation of the Saxon king, Otto I, in 962.

T.S. Brown

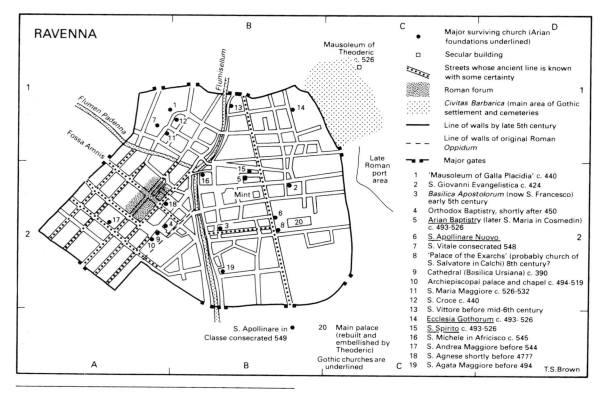

RAVENNA

- Major surviving church (Arian foundations underlined)
- Secular building
- Streets whose ancient line is known with some certainty
- Roman forum
- *Civitas Barbarica* (main area of Gothic settlement and cemeteries)
- Line of walls by late 5th century
- Line of walls of original Roman *Oppidum*
- Major gates

Mausoleum of Theoderic c. 526

Late Roman port area

Flumisellum

Flumen Padenna

Fossa Amnis

Mint

S. Apollinare in Classe consecrated 549

20 Main palace (rebuilt and embellished by Theoderic)

Gothic churches are underlined

1 'Mausoleum of Galla Placidia' c. 440
2 S. Giovanni Evangelistica c. 424
3 *Basilica Apostolorum* (now S. Francesco) early 5th century
4 Orthodox Baptistry, shortly after 450
5 Arian Baptistry (later S. Maria in Cosmedin) c. 493-526
6 S. Apollinare Nuovo
7 S. Vitale consecrated 548
8 'Palace of the Exarchs' (probably church of S. Salvatore in Calchi) 8th century?
9 Cathedral (Basilica Ursiana) c. 390
10 Archiepiscopal palace and chapel c. 494-519
11 S. Maria Maggiore c. 526-532
12 S. Croce c. 440
13 S. Vittore before mid-6th century
14 Ecclesia Gothorum c. 493- 526
15 S. Spirito c. 493-526
16 S. Michele in Africisco c. 545
17 S. Andrea Maggiore before 544
18 S. Agnese shortly before 477?
19 S. Agata Maggiore before 494

T.S.Brown

Ravenna

Roman Ravenna, with its port of Classe, was an important naval base. The security and good communications afforded by its surrounding marshes and canals encouraged the emperor Honorius to transfer the imperial capital there in 402 and the size of the city increased dramatically, during its 'first golden age' (lasting until the fall of the western empire in 476 and reflected in richly decorated buildings such as the Mausoleum of Galla Placidia and the Baptistry of the Orthodox).

Ravenna continued to flourish as the capital of the Italian kingdom under King Odoacer (476–93) and his Ostrogothic successors (493–540), whose commissions include the Arian baptistry, the Gothic cathedral, Theoderic's palace and its chapel (later renamed S. Apollinare Nuovo) and the same king's mausoleum. The city's status was matched by the power of its bishops, whose foundations include the octagonal S. Vitale and the basilica of S. Apollinare in Classe (only completed after the Byzantine conquest (540) when such decoration as the court mosaic of the emperor Justinian and his empress Thedora was added).

The city's affluence and artistic production declined after Justinian's death (565) because of the Lombard invasions, weakening links with the east and the silting up of its harbour. However it remained politically important as the residence of the exarch (first mentioned 584). This imperial garrison became a powerful force as it put down local roots, and led a number of revolts from the early seventh century. The patronage of external rulers and pious locals helped the archbishops to become de facto rulers of the Romagna and Marches after Ravenna's capture by the Lombards in 751 and subsequent incorporation in the papal state. For three or more centuries the city remained an important local capital, despite its commercial and cultural decline.

T.S. Brown

Trade Routes of the Carolingian Empire

The trade routes of the Carolingian Empire can only be reconstructed with some difficulty from the written sources of the period. As a result, before archaeological evidence was available, there was a good deal of debate about whether the Carolingians engaged in trade on any scale at all. In the past twenty years, however, archaeological investigations of the major trading towns at Dorestad (the Netherlands), Haithabu (Germany), Ribe (Denmark), Quentovic (France), Ipswich, London, Southampton (Hamwic) and York have made it possible to reconstruct the trading activities in which the Carolingians played a direct role. In addition, excavations of comparable settlements around the Baltic Sea reveal the far-flung influence of the empire, while current research in Italy begins to point to small-scale trade connections between the kingdom of Beneventum and the Aghlabid dynasty of the Maghreb.

The pattern of trade in this period is most conveniently described in terms of commercial networks embracing (a) the North Sea, (b) the English Channel, (c) the Baltic Sea and (d) the Mediterranean.

Archaeological evidence indicates that traders operated between the Austrasians (in the Rhineland), the Frisians, the Danes and the Anglo-Saxon kingdoms of Kent and East Anglia as early as the sixth century. This trade was probably on a small scale, involving prestige goods. But late in the seventh century a large Frisian trading community was founded at Dorestad, near the mouth of the Rhine, from where Rhenish manufactured goods were shipped to new ports as far as Ribe, London and Ipswich, serving the kingdoms of Denmark, Mercia and East Anglia respectively. By Charlemagne's time the commerce had grown and was of considerable political importance. At this time, Ribe was replaced by the new port at Haithabu, at which place the North Sea and Baltic trade networks intersected. After about 830, however, the North Sea network declined, and was not fully revived until the eleventh century.

Carolingian traders also maintained a largely separate trade network from northern France (the old kingdom of Neustria) to Kent and Wessex. The principal Carolingian port was Quentovic near Montreuil-sur-Mer, and Hamwic, Anglo-Saxon Southampton – a planned town spread out over 45 hectares – was the main port on the opposite side of the Channel. The history of this system ran parallel to the North Sea network, and it too went into decline after c. 830.

Trade across the Baltic Sea existed on a small scale between the later Roman period and c. 790, when Scandinavians made contact with the Abbasid caliphate. At this point small trading towns, handling oriental silver and prestige goods, as well as Scandinavian slaves and furs, were founded in several territories around the Baltic of which Staraja Ladoga (Russia), Birka (Sweden), Vastergarn on Gotland and Kaupang (Norway) are the best-known. It is likely that several distinct trade networks embraced this large region, linking merchants who plied the rivers of western Russia in the east to those who operated out of Haithabu and dealt with North Sea and west Scandinavian traders. This pattern of trade continued intermittently until the later tenth century.

Little evidence exists for trade across the Mediterranean between the late seventh century and the early eleventh century. However, the Abbasid caliph, Harun al' Rashid gave Charlemagne an elephant which he sent by ship from Egypt to Pisa late in the eighth century, which may indicate the path of small-scale connections at this time. Certainly, a number of Carolingian written sources point to a trade route from Sousse and other North African ports to Gaeta, Naples and Salerno in the Kingdom of Beneventum. This may explain the source of the large amounts of gold and silver that the Kingdom of Beneventum was obliged to pay as tribute to the Carolingians. The connection, though, was short-lived, and faltered once the empire disintegrated. The demise of this trade route in the 830s may have spurred the Arabs to raid for what previously they had traded, much as their counterparts, the Vikings, were doing in the North Sea.

R. Hodges

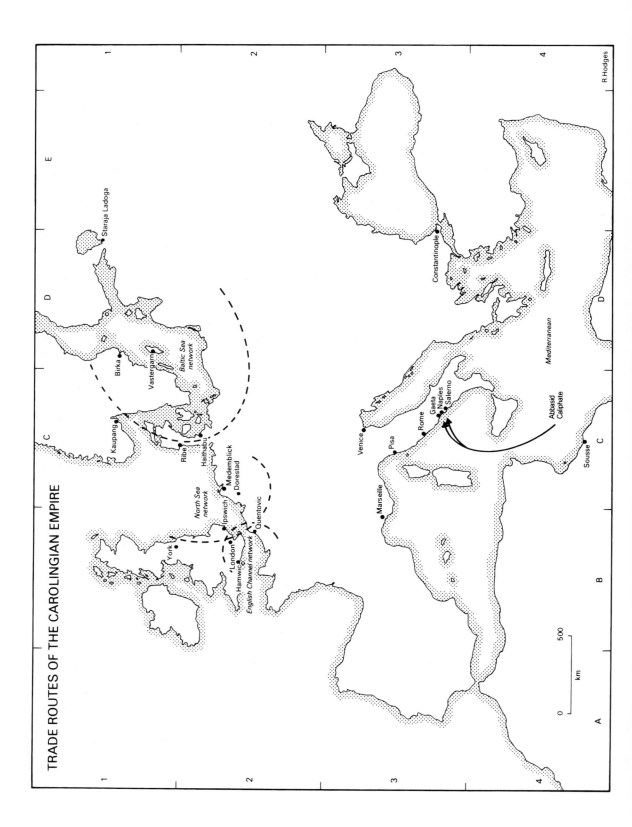

TRADE ROUTES OF THE CAROLINGIAN EMPIRE

R.Hodges

Staraja Ladoga

Birka
Vastergarn
Baltic Sea network

Kaupang
Ribe
Haithabu
Medemblick
Dorestad
North Sea network
Ipswich
York
Hamwic
London
English Channel network
Quentovic

Venice
Pisa
Marseille
Rome
Gaeta
Naples
Salerno

Constantinople

Mediterranean

Abbasid
Caliphate

Sousse

0   500

km

The Economy of San Vincenzo al Volturno

The Benedictine monastery of San Vincenzo was founded in *c.* 703 close to the source of the River Volturno on a plateau in the foothills of the Apennines. Its long and sometimes epic history can be reconstructed from a twelfth-century chronicle, *Chronicon Vulturnense,* and from archaeological excavations of part of the site. Like its close neighbour, Monte Cassino, its foundation seems to have been supported by the Lombard dukes of Beneventum. Up until *c.* 780 it was a small retreat, acquiring only a tract of land in the upper Volturno valley and a few minor estates in the high mountain zone (the Abruzzo) to the north. In 787, however, San Vincenzo came under Carolingian jurisdiction, and was granted privileges and immunities from taxation. At this time excavations show that new buildings were erected in the monastery, accommodating, as the chronicler Paul the Deacon notes, a large body of monks.

In 792 a Frank called Joshua was elected abbot and over the next twenty-five years was responsible for creating an ambitious new monastery, much larger than before, with a grand new abbey, new guest quarters, new churches and many other buildings. Up to 500 monks and a similar number of lay brethren lived here. Archaeological investigations, however, show that this Carolingian renaissance abbey depended upon labour and resources which were not to be found locally. The villages in its *terra* in the upper Volturno valley were apparently largely unaffected by the abbey's new-found affluence. Instead, San Vincenzo obtained many estates as gifts from the lower-ranking aristocracy of Beneventum in the heartland of the kingdom. These estates made it one of the richest landowners in Italy, and must have made its abbot a major political figure.

From these estates, it is proposed, San Vincenzo obtained a workforce to build the new monastery, and also younger sons of the aristocracy to be monks. The *Chronicon* records that the columns for the new abbey-church were taken from a Roman site in this region. Craftsmen, too, may have been lent to the abbey. In addition, whereas the villages of the *terra* contributed little or nothing to the abbey, some archaeological evidence points to the development of the estates in the heartlands where stock-breeding and cereal production was intensified.

San Vincenzo may have capitalized on its location at the foot of the mountains to obtain dairy products from the uplands for exchange with the cereals and animal products of the coastlands. The monastery's own industries may also have been used to obtain donations and gifts. Glass vessels and fine liturgical metalwork were made in its workshops, and may have been traded within the kingdom. When Joshua died in 817 San Vincenzo had become a great centre with a rich treasury and extensive land-holdings. In sum, its economy and power were based largely upon espousing the Carolingian ideological spirit, and its hold over the Beneventans.

San Vincenzo acquired a few more estates in the 820s, and then the number of donations waned. The Beneventan civil war in the 840s contributed to its decline, and then on 10 October 881, the monastery was sacked by an Arab war-band. The monks returned in *c.* 916, but did little to repair the ruined buildings before the turn of the millennium. Instead, between *c.* 940–1000 the monastery sponsored the development of villages (*incastellamento*) in its *terra,* creating a network modelled on those known from the ninth century in the heartlands of the kingdom. The leases granted to these villages indicate that settlers were attracted to the *terra* to help clear the woodland and develop a mixed farming regime. Evidently, rents from these villages as well as a revival of popular support for monasticism helped San Vincenzo to rebuild its abbey-church and cloisters, and to obtain new estates in the mountains and coastal littoral. Now, though, in economic terms, it was a prosperous magnate, having to compete in the incipient market economy of this region with other ecclesiastical and secular magnates.

R. Hodges

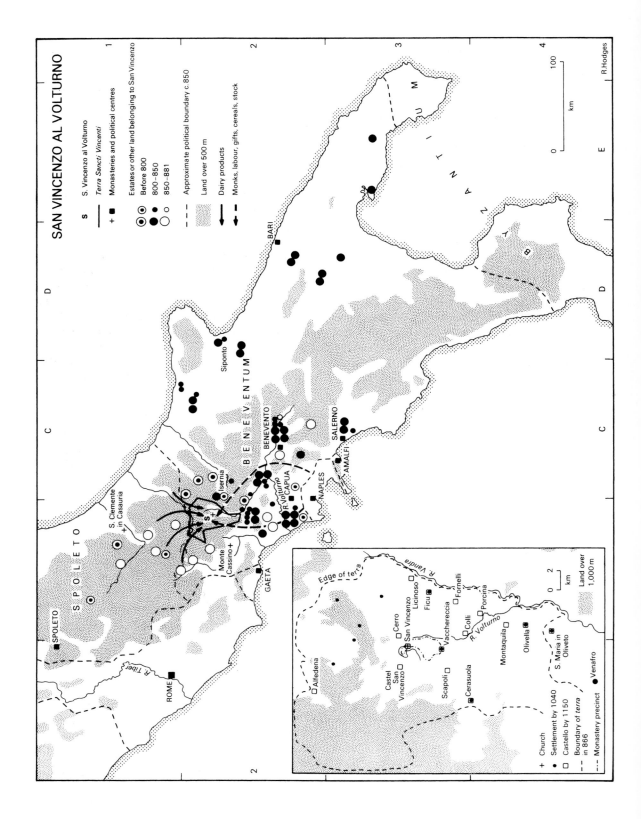

SAN VINCENZO AL VOLTURNO

s S. Vincenzo al Volturno

Terra Sancti Vincenti

■ Monasteries and political centres

Estates or other land belonging to San Vincenzo

⊙ Before 800
● 800–850
○ 850–881

- - - Approximate political boundary c. 850

Land over 500 m

↓ Dairy products

↓ Monks, labour, gifts, cereals, stock

SPOLETO

ROME

R. Tiber

SPOLETO

S. Clemente
in Casauria +

Monte
Cassino +

GAETA

Isernia

BENEVENTUM

BENEVENTO

R. Volturno
CAPUA
R. Volturno

NAPLES

AMALFI
SALERNO

Siponto

BARI

A P U L I A

B

km

0   100

E

R. Hodges

Inset map:

+ Church
● Settlement by 1040
□ Castello by 1150
- - - Boundary of *terra* in 866
-·-· Monastery precinct

Land over 1,000 m

km
0   2

Edge of *terra*

R. Vandra

Alfedena

Castel
San
Vincenzo

Cerro

San Vincenzo

Licinoso

Ficu

Vacchereccia

Fornelli

Porcina

R. Volturno

Colli

Scapoli

Montaquila

Cerasuola

S. Maria in
Oliveto

Olivella

Venafro

CULTURE

Irish and Anglo-Saxon Centres on the Continent in the Early Middle Ages

The conversion of the Irish and Anglo-Saxons inevitably involved contact with the Christian Continent. Direct contacts with Gaul and Italy became frequent after Augustine's mission to Kent (597). A few years earlier there began the Irish Christian custom of undertaking voluntary, penitential exile, which led to the establishment of monasteries abroad. Thus, following Columba's foundation of Iona, Columbanus founded Annegray and Luxeuil in Gaul and Bobbio in Italy. Other important foundations followed at St Gall and Péronne.

From the late seventh century the Anglo-Saxons, whose conversion owed much to the Irish, followed the Irish lead on the Continent, being, however, primarily concerned with the conversion of their fellow Germans in Frisia and Germany. Amongst the best known of these missionaries are Wilfrid, Willibrord, founder of the monastery of Echternach, Boniface, martyred in 754 and buried at Fulda, and Lull, archbishop of Mainz. The cathedral of Würzburg, an Anglo-Saxon foundation and Irish pilgrimage centre, exemplifies Anglo-Irish contacts. The strongly papal outlook of the Anglo-Saxons could lead to such difficulties as

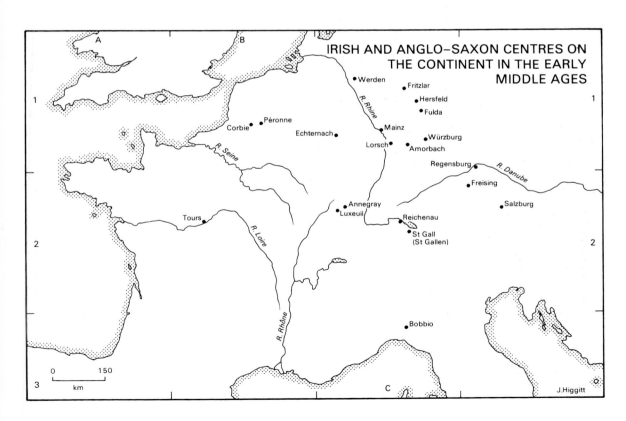

IRISH AND ANGLO-SAXON CENTRES ON THE CONTINENT IN THE EARLY MIDDLE AGES

J.Higgitt

65

the dispute between Boniface and the Irish Virgil of Salzburg.

Irish and Anglo-Saxon influences on Continental Christian culture appear in exegetical, grammatical and other literature and in the transmission of earlier Latin texts. Virgil of Salzburg, Johannes Scottus and Sedulius Scottus were among Irish scholars achieving fame on the Continent during the eighth and ninth centuries. Alcuin, a product of the Northumbrian school at York and one of the scholars called by Charlemagne to assist in his ecclesiastical and cultural reforms, worked during his last years at Tours.

The Irish and Anglo-Saxon presence is often indicated by the use in manuscripts of 'Insular' scripts and abbreviations. (A ninth-century book-list from St Gall groups such books under the heading *Libri Scottice Scripti.*) More spectacular are the manuscripts decorated in the Hiberno-Saxon style. Some like the Echternach Gospels or the Irish Gospel books at St Gall were perhaps imported. Others like the Cutbercht Gospels (written perhaps at Salzburg) were made on the Continent. The initials of such books were widely imitated in Carolingian manuscripts and in the ninth century the style became the basis for the decoration of the 'Franco-Saxon' group of manuscripts.

Such influences cannot easily be mapped. The places selected here are major Irish and Anglo-Saxon foundations and/or centres to which books with Insular characteristics have been plausibly attributed.

J. Higgitt

Bede's World

Bede (*c.* 672–735), biblical scholar and 'Father of English Church History', spent his entire life in the Northumbrian monastery of Wearmouth-Jarrow. His horizons, however, extended far beyond Northumbria. He was something of an armchair traveller. Through texts and travellers he was acquainted with the geography and culture of Europe and as a result Anglo-Saxon England was able to preserve and transmit the Christian culture of the Latin Mediterranean.

Bede described how books, relics, musicians, vestments and glaziers were procured by Benedict Biscop, abbot of Wearmouth who travelled to Rome six times and was well acquainted with monastic life in Gaul, having received the tonsure at Lerins. Ceolfrith left Wearmouth-Jarrow for Rome with a complete Latin Bible, the Codex Amiatinus, but died at Langres. Kings travelled to Rome and sent their daughters to monasteries in Gaul. The turbulent career of Bishop Wilfrid took him to Rome, Gaul and Frisia where the Northumbrian missionary Willibrord later established a bishopric.

Anglo-Saxon England became a notable centre of study through the establishment of schools. Theodore, a Greek monk originally from Tarsus, came to England from an Italian monastery with the African, Hadrian, to become archbishop of Canterbury. He established a school at Canterbury equipped with Greek texts. Foremost among its students was the scholar Aldhelm, who established a school of his own at Malmesbury. Boniface, the future apostle of Germany composed his *Ars grammatica* at a school at Nursling, and in Northumbria the bishopric and school at Lindisfarne produced an anonymous life of its famous bishop, Saint Cuthbert, and a series of lavishly written manuscripts, most notably the Lindisfarne Gospels.

Bede was also aware of the geography of the Holy Land as a result of the travels of the Frankish bishop, Arculf, which were recorded by the ninth abbot of Iona, Adomnan. Adomnan visited Northumbria and enabled Bede to compose his *De Locis Sanctis*. Bede's world was threatened by Arabs. He knew that they had invaded Sicily and that Charles Martel had defeated them at Poitiers in 732.

S. Coates

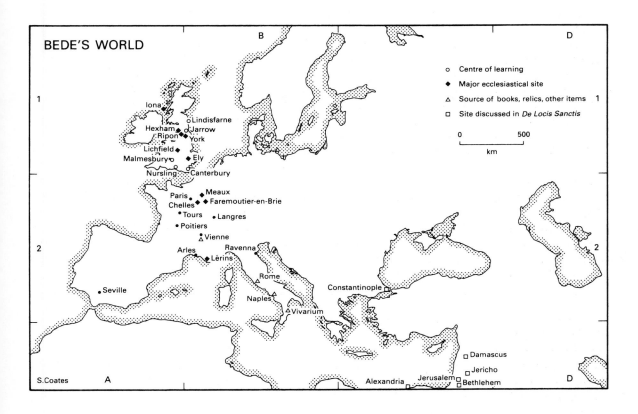

BEDE'S WORLD

○ Centre of learning
◆ Major ecclesiastical site
△ Source of books, relics, other items
□ Site discussed in *De Locis Sanctis*

0   500
km

Iona
Lindisfarne
Hexham Jarrow
Ripon York
Lichfield Ely
Malmesbury
Nursling Canterbury
Paris Meaux
Chelles Faremoutier-en-Brie
Tours Langres
Poitiers
Vienne
Arles Ravenna
Lérins
Rome
Seville
Naples
Vivarium
Constantinople
Damascus
Jericho
Alexandria Jerusalem Bethlehem

S.Coates

THE CENTRAL MIDDLE AGES
(*c.* 1100–*c.* 1300)

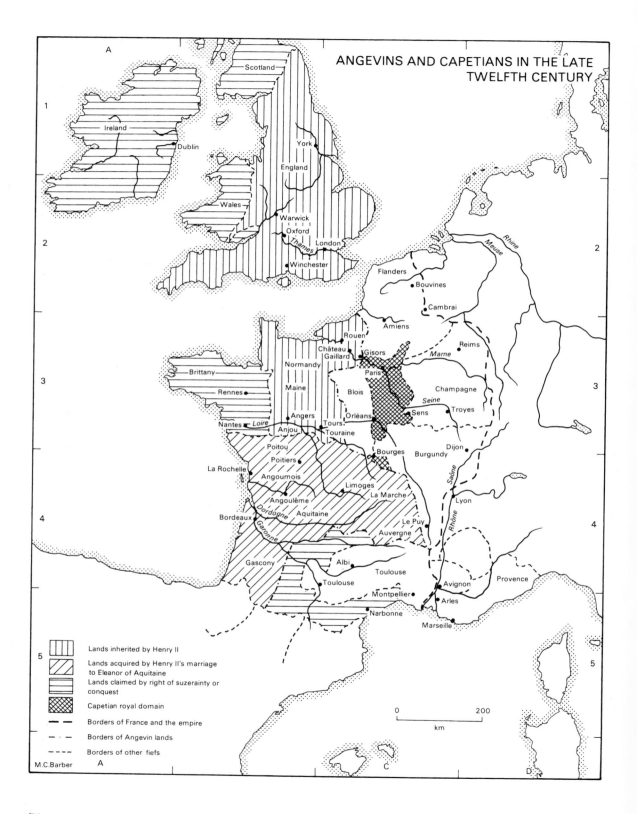

ANGEVINS AND CAPETIANS IN THE LATE TWELFTH CENTURY

Scotland
Ireland
Dublin
York
England
Wales
Warwick
Oxford
Thames
London
Winchester

Flanders
Bouvines
Cambrai
Amiens
Rouen
Château Gaillard
Gisors
Marne
Reims
Normandy
Paris
Champagne
Maine
Blois
Seine
Troyes
Brittany
Orléans
Sens
Rennes
Angers
Tours
Dijon
Nantes
Loire
Anjou
Touraine
Bourges
Burgundy
Poitou
Poitiers
Saône
La Rochelle
Angoumois
Limoges
Lyon
Angoulême
La Marche
Bordeaux
Dordogne
Aquitaine
Le Puy
Rhône
Garonne
Auvergne
Gascony
Albi
Toulouse
Avignon
Provence
Toulouse
Montpellier
Arles
Narbonne
Marseille

Rhine
Meuse

	Lands inherited by Henry II
	Lands acquired by Henry II's marriage to Eleanor of Aquitaine
	Lands claimed by right of suzerainty or conquest
	Capetian royal domain
— —	Borders of France and the empire
— · —	Borders of Angevin lands
– – –	Borders of other fiefs

M.C.Barber

0   200
km

A   C   D

POLITICS

Angevins and Capetians in the Late Twelfth Century

The relationship between the Angevins and the Capetians illustrates the ambiguities and tensions inherent in the changing feudal structure of the twelfth century. Although the Capetians had held the French throne since 987, by the early twelfth century they had not noticeably expanded their influence beyond their family lands in the Ile-de-France. The great lords who held the neighbouring fiefs, although nominally their vassals, were often just as politically influential and as economically powerful. Indeed, with the invasion of England in 1066, the duke of Normandy became a king in his own right, independent in matters involving his new realm.

The Norman Conquest demonstrates that the Capetians operated within a political kaleidoscope in which dynastic ambition and the wheel of fortune might suddenly produce such unexpected agglomerations of territory that the theoretical superiority of the king of France at the apex of the social hierarchy might bear little relationship to the realities of political power. In the 1150s such a change did indeed occur, for in 1154, following the death of King Stephen, Henry of Anjou was crowned king of England. He had already been accepted as duke of Normandy in 1150 and had inherited from his father, Geoffrey (d. 1151), the lands in western France centred on Anjou, Touraine and Vendôme. Moreover, his wife Eleanor, recently divorced from Louis VII of France, had brought him the duchy of Aquitaine on their marriage in 1152. Nor were these to be the limits of Henry's domains, for the king of Scotland was his vassal, he claimed authority over the Welsh princes and he had plans for the conquest of Ireland. When his brother Geoffrey died in 1158 he invaded Brittany, while, in 1173, he even received the homage of the count of Toulouse.

Under Henry II (d. 1189) and his son, Richard I (d. 1199), this collection of disparate territories was held together quite successfully, although at the cost of continuous vigilance and high expenditure. Despite their theoretical overlordship neither Louis VII (d. 1180) nor Philip II could make any substantial impact. However, the Angevin 'empire' was ultimately dependent on dynastic circumstances, especially when the lands concerned lacked any other real political coherence. Richard's early death left a succession disputed between his brother John and his nephew Arthur of Brittany, with John being accepted in England and Normandy, while Arthur gained adherence in Anjou, Touraine and Maine, forcing a wedge across the middle of the Angevin lands. Nevertheless, by 1200 a combination of energetic military action against Arthur and negotiations with King Philip had gained John recognition, which, although it left him in a relatively greater feudal subordination than that of his father or brother, did maintain most of the Angevin lands under his rule.

Yet by 1204 John had lost Normandy, and during the next two years Anjou, Touraine, northern Poitou and Brittany as well. In 1214 at the battle of Bouvines, ten years of strenuous fund-raising and careful alliance-building was brought to nothing, when Philip II defeated John's allies. John himself was not present, having been driven back to La Rochelle. Philip's shrewd exploitation of John's political and military errors had been enough to prise apart the lands which had been so fortuitously brought together, leaving him master of northern France with access to Norman resources and administrative expertise, a gain which lifted him into a different political league from that of Louis VII.

The limitations of a single map of these

changes are evident. Contemporaries did not think in terms of clearly defined borders or of national entities, nor was their authority evenly spread throughout the lands which theoretically owed them allegiance. The constant itinerary of these rulers underlines their awareness of this last point, and the larger the territory the greater the problems. The map can convey the broad geo-political structure, but it is misleading without an awareness of twelfth-century political attitudes.

M.C. Barber

Frederick Barbarossa and Germany, 1152–90

Characterized as belief in a rearguard action to curb aristocratic decentralizing tendencies, royal authority in Germany at the time of Frederick's election is seen traditionally as having declined continuously since 1077. This view is counterbalanced by conflicting evidence for maintenance and enhancement of that authority throughout the same period. At his death in 1190, Frederick had as firm a grip on Germany as any previous ruler, and had, indeed, expanded the limits of his personal rule. Nevertheless, elsewhere in Germany there was a decline in active royal intervention, often viewed as indicative of a surrender of powers to the greater nobles presaging the emergence of 'an estate of princes'.

Successful extension of his personal estates in south-western Germany was balanced by the need to court noble assistance for the Italian wars, thereby limiting opportunities to extend his political power. Forced, thus, to confirm the Welf Henry the Lion's inheritance of Bavaria and Saxony, Frederick created the duchy of Austria to counterbalance Welf power. In the jurisdictional sphere, however, Frederick made positive advances, using the German diets as platforms to stress the dependent relationship of nobleman to king, and to assert the principle that the prescription and application of law was a royal prerogative.

Frederick's success in establishing the supremacy of his jurisdiction was demonstrated by his triumph over the Welfs in 1179–80. Massive enlargement of Henry's possessions through conquest of Slav territory provided an opportunity to demonstrate co-operation between king and nobles. Frederick's concern over growing Welf power was matched by the jealousy of the nobility. Action against Henry, however, came through the collective judgement of the emperor and his great men rather than military intervention, for the duke was forfeited as a contumacious vassal. Political goodwill and future co-operation of the nobility was ensured by the redistribution of Welf land between them, strengthening royal authority and establishing Frederick's unchallenged supremacy.

R. Oram

Frederick Barbarossa and the Lombard League

Benefiting from a weakening of imperial authority in north Italy from the late eleventh century, by the time of Frederick's election as emperor in 1152 the Lombard cities had established considerable independence as urban republics. Civic powers had never been confirmed by formal grant, but by the early twelfth century towns had appropriated for their own uses various

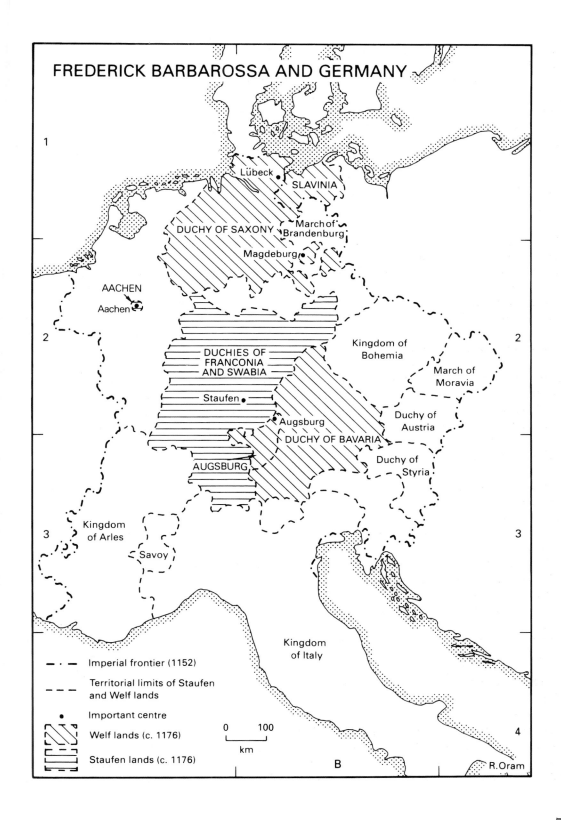

FREDERICK BARBAROSSA AND GERMANY

Lübeck
SLAVINIA

DUCHY OF SAXONY

March of
Brandenburg

Magdeburg

AACHEN
Aachen

Kingdom of
Bohemia

DUCHIES OF
FRANCONIA
AND SWABIA

March of
Moravia

Staufen

Duchy of
Austria

Augsburg
DUCHY OF BAVARIA

AUGSBURG

Duchy of
Styria

Kingdom
of Arles

Savoy

Kingdom
of Italy

Imperial frontier (1152)

Territorial limits of Staufen
and Welf lands

Important centre

Welf lands (c. 1176)

Staufen lands (c. 1176)

0   100

km

B

R. Oram

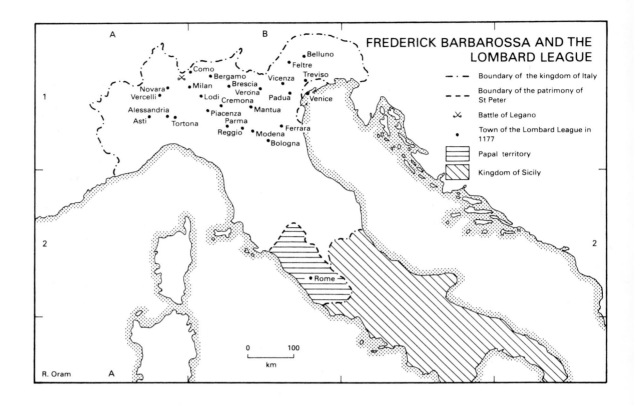

FREDERICK BARBAROSSA AND THE LOMBARD LEAGUE

- · - Boundary of the kingdom of Italy
- - - Boundary of the patrimony of St Peter
- ✕ Battle of Legano
- · Town of the Lombard League in 1177
- Papal territory
- Kingdom of Sicily

Belluno
Feltre
Como
Bergamo Vicenza Treviso
Milan Brescia Verona
Novara Lodi Cremona Padua Venice
Vercelli
Alessandria Piacenza Mantua
Asti Parma Ferrara
Tortona Reggio Modena
Bologna

Rome

0   100
km

R. Oram   A

imperial dues and services. Such control, it was felt, gave a customary entitlement to possession. Frederick's reassertion of imperial rights raised the prospect of greater domination than the cities were prepared to accept and drove Milan, followed by its neighbours, into collective resistance, formalized in 1167 in the Lombard League. Support from a papacy made anxious for itself by re-establishment of imperial power south of the Alps held the League together, and in 1176 at Legnano its forces crushed Frederick's army. Forced thus to recognize that plans for direct rule in Lombardy were unattainable, Frederick, in return for an annual tribute, reached in the 1183 Treaty of Constance a settlement which established the limits of imperial overlordship and effectively confirmed the independence of the cities.

The treaty recognized the status quo and gave the imperial sanction of legitimization to the League. Cities received the right to fortify themselves and renew their league, and a fiction of imperial approval was established for recognition of the consuls whom the cities elected for themselves. It was a face-saving arrangement for Frederick, but it could not disguise the fact that any chance of restoring an imperial north Italian power-base had been lost. More significantly, it granted the power of custom, legislation and the weight of royal authority to the urban republics, ensuring the future spread of civic independence throughout north and central Italy.

R. Oram

The Empire of the Comneni, 1081–1185

Alexius I Comnenus (1081–1118) rescued the Byzantine Empire from a period of political difficulties which had meant the loss of southern Italy to the Normans, much of the Balkans to the Petcheneks, and Asia Minor to the Seljuq Turks following the battle of Mantzikert (1071). Alexius dealt with these threats one by one. After an initial set-back at Dyrrachion he defeated the Normans at Larissa (1083) and recovered Dyrrachion (1085). Though defeated by the Petcheneks at Dristra (1087), he won a decisive victory over them at Mount Levounion (1091) and restored the frontiers of the empire to the Danube. His plan to recover Asia Minor from the Seljuqs was complicated by the arrival of the first crusade at Constantinople in 1096. With crusader help he took Nicaea, the Seljuq capital, and then under the cover of the crusader victory at Dorylaion his forces were able to recover the coastlands of western Asia Minor. But involvement with the crusader states was to mean that neither he nor his successors were able to make any significant advances into the interior.

His grandson Manuel I Comnenus (1143–80) established close dynastic ties with the crusader states, but this involved him in a costly expedition against Damietta and the Fatimids (1169) and another against the Seljuq capital of Ikonion, which came to grief at the battle of Myriokephalon (1176). Manuel's attempt to recover southern Italy (1156–7) from the Normans was also a failure, but it did counter the serious Norman attacks (1147–9) which were directed against the Greek provinces. The Byzantines were more successful along the Danube. The victory over the Hungarians at Sirmium (1167) not only brought Hungary within the Byzantine orbit, but also pacified the Serbs. Only in Asia Minor did the territories controlled by the Comneni differ significantly from those held in the mid-eleventh century.

If the Comneni relied more heavily on the indirect exercise of authority than their predecessors, their empire enjoyed a period of great prosperity thanks to the stability they ensured for nearly a century. Agricultural wealth was more fully mobilized and there was a growth of towns. The Venetians had an important role to play. They had been exempted from the payment of customs duties (1082) in return for naval assistance against the Normans and had been given a factory at Constantinople. They contributed to the growth of internal trade, mostly in agricultural goods, within the empire. They were particularly active at Corinth and Halmyros, which were the main outlets for the agricultural wealth of Greece.

Their presence also produced friction which was largely political in origin. There was a conflict of interests in the Adriatic and the Venetians resented the favours shown to their commercial rivals, the Pisans and the Genoese. This led in 1171 to the arrest of all the Venetians in the Byzantine Empire and the confiscation of their goods. Despite all efforts relations never returned to normal. This contributed to the diversion of the fourth crusade and the fall of Constantinople (1204). There were many other factors involved in the collapse of the empire of the Comneni in the late twelfth century. Perhaps the most important was loss of control at the centre following the death of Manuel I Comnenus in 1180. The ascendancy of the Comneni, which was vital to the stability of the empire, was undermined in a series of coups and rebellions.

M. Angold

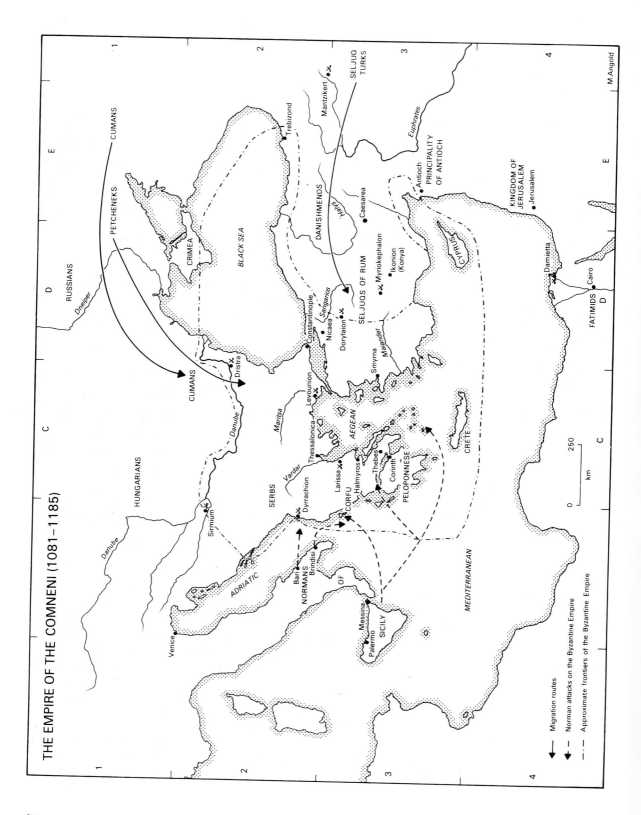

THE EMPIRE OF THE COMNENI (1081–1185)

RUSSIANS

CUMANS

PETCHENEKS

CUMANS

HUNGARIANS

Dneiper

Danube

CRIMEA

BLACK SEA

Trebizond

SELJUQ TURKS

Mantzikert

DANISHMENDS

Halys

Caesarea

Euphrates

Antioch

PRINCIPALITY OF ANTIOCH

KINGDOM OF JERUSALEM

Jerusalem

Constantinople

Nicaea
Dorylaion
Sangarios

SELJUQS OF RUM

Myriokephalon
Ikonion (Konya)

CYPRUS

Damietta

Cairo

FATIMIDS

Smyrna
Maiander

Drista

Danube

Sirmium

Maritsa

Levounion

Vardar

SERBS

Thessalonica

AEGEAN

Larissa
Halmyros
Thebes
Corinth
PELOPONNESE

CRETE

Dyrrachion

CORFU

Venice

ADRIATIC

Bari
NORMANS
Brindisi

OF

Messina
Palermo
SICILY

MEDITERRANEAN

250

km

0

C

M. Angold

→ Migration routes

▶ Norman attacks on the Byzantine Empire

–·–·– Approximate frontiers of the Byzantine Empire

Anglo-Norman Penetration of Wales and Ireland

Norman penetration of Wales began soon after the conquest of England (1066). William the Conqueror created strong earldoms along the Anglo-Welsh frontier, centred on Chester, Shrewsbury and Hereford, and gave them to trusted followers. These men and their retainers began encroachment into the lands west of Offa's Dyke, the traditional demarcation between England and Wales. By the 1090s the Normans had built castles along both the north and south coasts of Wales and established footholds as far west as Pembrokeshire and Anglesey, while simultaneously infiltrating the middle march around Brecon and Builth. Not all acquisitions were permanent. Sometimes, as in the case of the advance into the north-west, the Normans were decisively rebuffed by the native rulers. In other parts, especially the south-west, areas went repeatedly back and forth between native and Anglo-Norman rule. Thus, from the eleventh to the thirteenth centuries, Wales was divided between native principalities, of which Gwynedd, Powys and Deheubarth were the most important, and numerous lordships established by Anglo-Norman invaders. These latter gradually assumed a distinctive legal and constitutional identity as 'The March of Wales'.

The lords of the March established their power by building castles, exacting tribute and hostages, and encouraging the settlement of English, French and Flemish immigrants as farmers or as burgesses in the newly created towns. The evidence of place names and of late medieval surveys and rentals shows that these immigrants settled densely along the southern coastal plain and that areas such as southern Pembrokeshire, the Gower and southern Glamorgan underwent a cultural and ethnic transformation. In other parts, alien colonists existed in heavily fortified enclaves in the boroughs adjoining seigneurial castles.

Despite occasional royal expeditions, the penetration of Wales was largely the result of freelance baronial campaigns. A similar seigneurial expedition took the Anglo-Normans to Ireland. In 1169–70 Richard fitz Gilbert ('Strongbow'), lord of Chepstow and claimant to the earldom of Pembroke, led assorted Anglo-Normans, Welshmen and Flemings in an enterprise that began as a mercenary undertaking in support of the Irish king of Leinster and culminated in Strongbow himself becoming lord of Leinster. The English king, Henry II, could not allow a fractious member of his own aristocracy to set up in quasi-regal state so near to his domains and, in 1171–2, took an army to Ireland and received Strongbow's submission, along with that of the majority of the native Irish kings.

After 1171–2, the situation in Wales and Ireland showed some similarities. In both countries an aristocracy of Anglo-Norman descent had established control over substantial territories, where they built castles, established boroughs and encouraged immigration. But in both countries there survived native rulers, whose power was deep-rooted and might well recover. The English Crown claimed a position of ultimate superiority over both colonial lords and indigenous leaders.

The map shows the approximate distribution of power in 1200. In Wales, the dominant native principality, it was becoming clear, was Gwynedd. Powys and Deheubarth were weakened by divisions and encroachment. The latter, in particular, was hemmed in by the important royal centres of Cardigan and Carmarthen. At this time Glamorgan too was in royal hands. The Marshal earl of Pembroke, Strongbow's successor, and William de Braose, lord of Brecon, were the most important Marcher aristocrats.

In Ireland the situation was more fluid. The Anglo-Normans had only been establishing themselves for a single generation by 1200 and some areas, such as Connaught, were as yet virtually untouched by their expansion. The great lordships of Leinster and Meath were in the hands of the Marshals and de Lacys, well-rewarded servants of Henry II, while John de

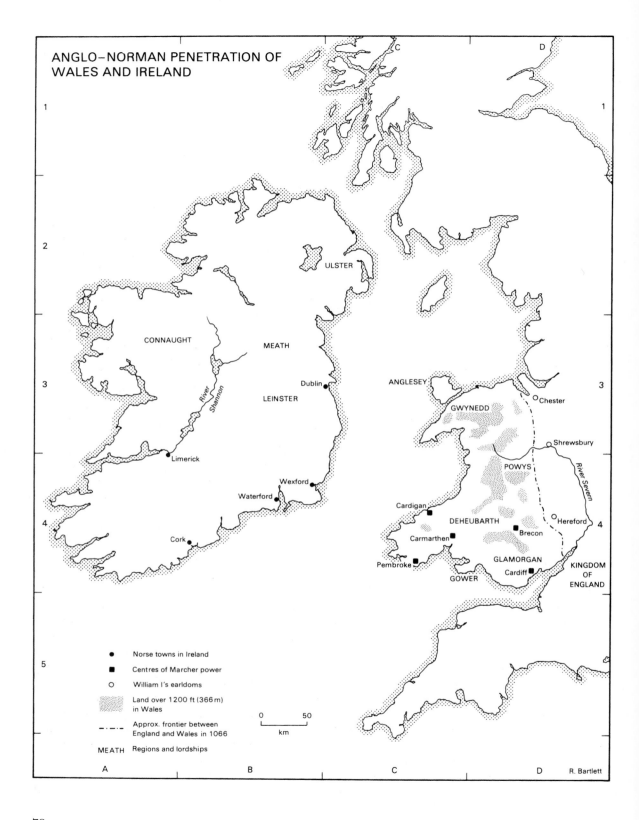

ANGLO–NORMAN PENETRATION OF
WALES AND IRELAND

●	Norse towns in Ireland
■	Centres of Marcher power
○	William I's earldoms
(stipple)	Land over 1200 ft (366 m) in Wales
–·–·–	Approx. frontier between England and Wales in 1066
MEATH	Regions and lordships

0   50
km

R. Bartlett

78

Courcy, the paradigm of the maverick *conquistador*, had created his base of power in Ulster. The Norse cities of the south, such as Waterford, Cork and Limerick, were also advanced bases of Anglo-Norman settlement and authority.

R. Bartlett

Scotland in the Central Middle Ages

Medieval Scotland grew out of Gaelic/Pictish Alba, whose core was in the Tay valley, Fife, and the north-east coastal plain (map A). Eleventh-century Alba was a collection of local provinces (which became 'provincial' earldoms) under 'mormaers' (later, earls); but the term *mormaer*, or 'great steward', implies some superior royal authority, and so does the network of thanages, which were royal estates run by crown agents ('thanes') (map A). From this core, the kingdom of Alba/Scotland expanded to the south, north and west. Southern expansion was at the expense of ancient Northumbria and Strathclyde/ Cumbria: Lothian and Strathclyde were gained at around the time of Malcolm II's victory over the Northumbrians at Carham in 1018; while the twelfth century saw the incorporation of Galloway and temporary conquests south of what was becoming the Anglo-Scottish border. In the north, the great province of Moray came directly under the Crown when its ruler, Macbeth, seized the throne in 1042, and it was later subjugated after 1130, when the mormaership/earldom was suppressed; further north, the Norse province of Caithness was also brought within the kingdom during the twelfth century. Pressure westwards came later, chiefly in the thirteenth century; after the Western Isles were surrendered by Norway in 1266 (following the battle of Largs, 1263), the West Highland and Island Gaelic magnates mostly came to accept royal overlordship (map A).

The expansion was partly military, both by external conquest and by defeating frequent internal rebellions, and partly seigniorial, by the installation of effective local agents. The essential basis was already present in the eleventh century, but the process was closely associated with the twelfth-century feudalization of Scotland; the best way for rulers to consolidate power was through subordinate feudal knights and castle-based lordships. Scotland's first feudal king was David I (1124–53) – who recruited many Anglo-Norman and English followers – and his example was followed by Malcolm IV (1153–65), William I (1165–1214), Alexander II (1214–49) and Alexander III (1249–86). Great new 'provincial' lordships were created for leading 'Normans' (map B); while individual knights' fees and other feudal tenancies, generally based on mottes and castles, were established throughout southern and eastern Scotland (map C). At the same time the new administrative structure of sheriffdoms was imposed (initially probably for the areas outside the 'provincial' earldoms and lordships, but eventually incorporating them); the burghs (trading towns) were created; and many monasteries were founded by both kings and magnates for the new reformed ecclesiastical orders (map D).

Thus Scotland was turned into a fairly typical twelfth/thirteenth-century feudal state. But the transformation of the pre-existing infrastructure was far from absolute. Even the burghs were not all entirely 'new'. In the Church, new foundations were made within an older ecclesiastical framework (many bishoprics dated to before 1100). And no earldoms were granted to incomers; they stayed with native families, only being 'Normanized' through the marriages of heiresses to 'Norman' lords (map B). Similarly, most thanages were held by native thanes during the twelfth and (often) the thirteenth centuries (map A). Thus much native (mostly Gaelic) lordship survived in 'feudal Scotland'. During the central Middle Ages, in fact, Scotland was a hybrid kingdom, in which Gaelic, Anglo-Saxon, Norman and Flemish elements all coalesced, under the leadersip of its 'Normanized' but nevertheless native line of kings. Despite clashes and rebellions (Map A), the result was a remarkably successful small kingdom.

A. Grant

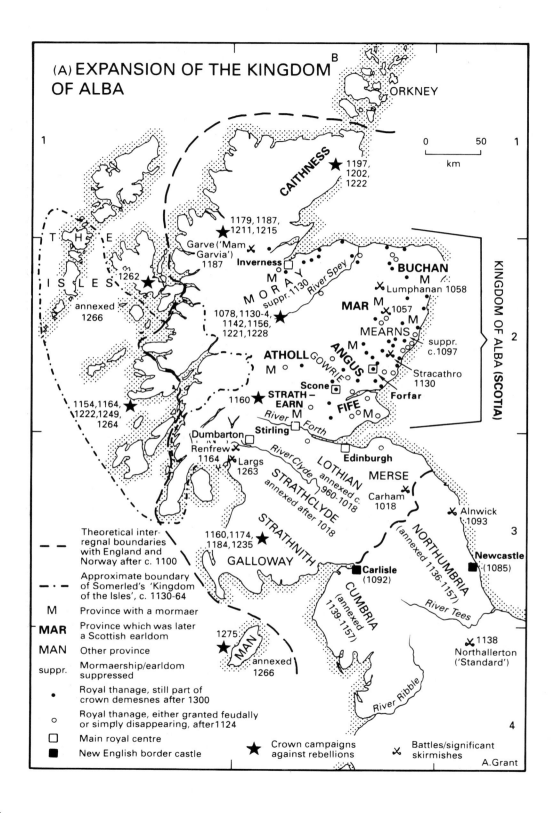

(A) EXPANSION OF THE KINGDOM OF ALBA

ORKNEY

CAITHNESS 1197, 1202, 1222

1179, 1187, 1211, 1215

Garve ('Mam Garvia') 1187

Inverness

M O R A Y suppr. 1130

River Spey

BUCHAN M

Lumphanan 1058

MAR M 1057

MEARNS M

suppr. c.1097

Stracathro 1130

ATHOLL M

GOWRIE

ANGUS M

1262

annexed 1266

1078, 1130-4, 1142, 1156, 1221, 1228

THE ISLES

Scone

STRATH-EARN 1160

FIFE M M

Forfar

River Forth

1154, 1164, 1222, 1249, 1264

Stirling

Dumbarton
Renfrew 1164

Largs 1263

River Clyde

STRATHCLYDE annexed after 1018

Edinburgh

LOTHIAN annexed c. 960-1018

MERSE

Carham 1018

Alnwick 1093

NORTHUMBRIA (annexed 1136-1157)

Newcastle (1085)

1160, 1174, 1184, 1235

STRATHNITH

STRATH

GALLOWAY

Carlisle (1092)

CUMBRIA (annexed 1139-1157)

River Tees

KINGDOM OF ALBA (SCOTIA)

1275

MAN

annexed 1266

1138 Northallerton ('Standard')

River Ribble

Theoretical inter-regnal boundaries with England and Norway after c. 1100

Approximate boundary of Somerled's 'Kingdom of the Isles', c. 1130-64

M   Province with a mormaer

MAR Province which was later a Scottish earldom

MAN Other province

suppr. Mormaership/earldom suppressed

•   Royal thanage, still part of crown demesnes after 1300

○   Royal thanage, either granted feudally or simply disappearing, after 1124

☐   Main royal centre

■   New English border castle

★   Crown campaigns against rebellions

⚔   Battles/significant skirmishes

A. Grant

0   50 km

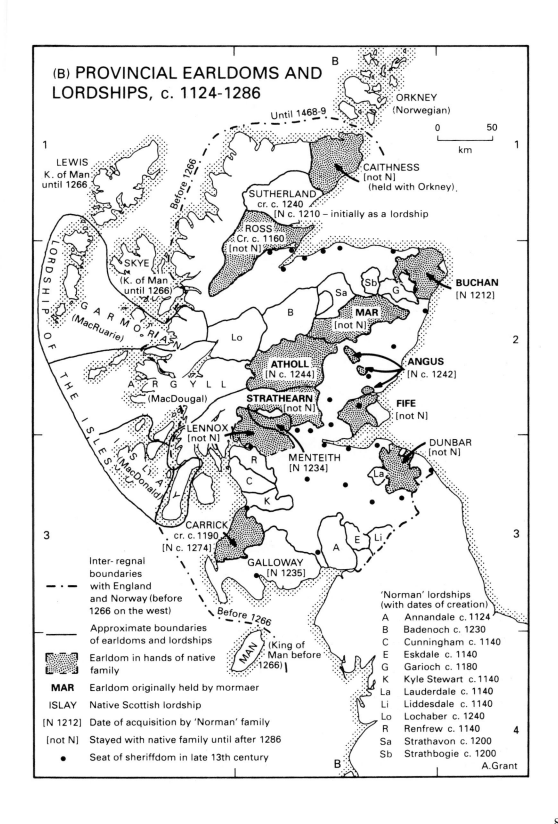

(B) PROVINCIAL EARLDOMS AND LORDSHIPS, c. 1124-1286

ORKNEY
(Norwegian)

Until 1468-9

0   50
km

1

LEWIS
K. of Man
until 1266

CAITHNESS
[not N]
(held with Orkney)

SUTHERLAND
cr. c. 1240
[N c. 1210 – initially as a lordship

SKYE
(K. of Man
until 1266)

ROSS
Cr. c. 1160
[not N]

BUCHAN
[N 1212]

Sa   Sb   G

MAR
[not N]

B

Lo

ATHOLL
[N c. 1244]

ANGUS
[N c. 1242]

STRATHEARN
[not N]

FIFE
[not N]

LENNOX
[not N]

R

MENTEITH
[N 1234]

DUNBAR
[not N]

La

C

K

A   E   Li

CARRICK
cr. c. 1190
[N c. 1274]

GALLOWAY
[N 1235]

A

Inter- regnal
boundaries
with England
and Norway (before
1266 on the west)

Before 1266

MAN
(King of
Man before
1266)

Approximate boundaries
of earldoms and lordships

Earldom in hands of native
family

MAR   Earldom originally held by mormaer

ISLAY   Native Scottish lordship

[N 1212]   Date of acquisition by 'Norman' family

[not N]   Stayed with native family until after 1286

•   Seat of sheriffdom in late 13th century

'Norman' lordships
(with dates of creation)

A   Annandale c. 1124
B   Badenoch c. 1230
C   Cunningham c. 1140
E   Eskdale c. 1140
G   Garioch c. 1180
K   Kyle Stewart c. 1140
La   Lauderdale c. 1140
Li   Liddesdale c. 1140
Lo   Lochaber c. 1240
R   Renfrew c. 1140
Sa   Strathavon c. 1200
Sb   Strathbogie c. 1200

A.Grant

LORDSHIP OF THE ISLES

GARMORAN
(MacRuarie)

ARGYLL
(MacDougal)

ISLAY
(MacDonald)

Before 1266

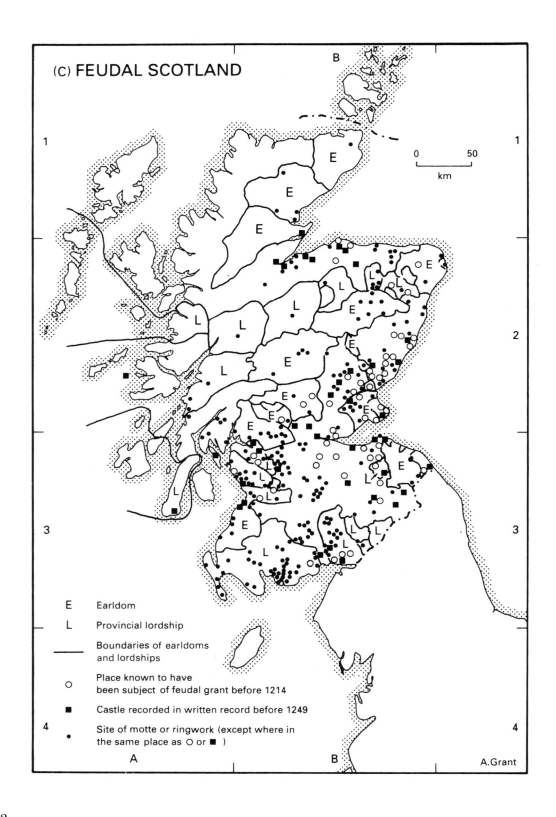

(C) FEUDAL SCOTLAND

0   50
km

E   Earldom

L   Provincial lordship

────   Boundaries of earldoms
        and lordships

○   Place known to have
     been subject of feudal grant before 1214

■   Castle recorded in written record before 1249

•   Site of motte or ringwork (except where in
     the same place as ○ or ■)

A.Grant

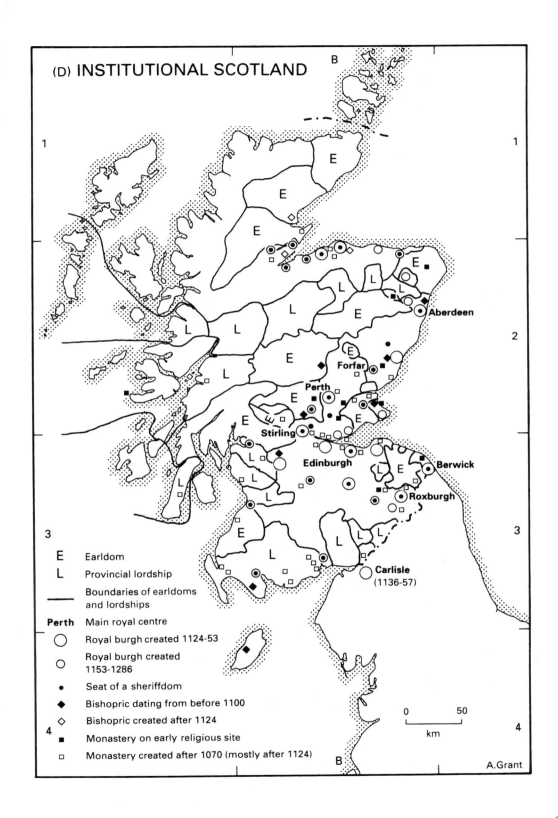

(D) INSTITUTIONAL SCOTLAND

E   Earldom

L   Provincial lordship

——   Boundaries of earldoms and lordships

Perth   Main royal centre

◯   Royal burgh created 1124-53

○   Royal burgh created 1153-1286

•   Seat of a sheriffdom

◆   Bishopric dating from before 1100

◇   Bishopric created after 1124

■   Monastery on early religious site

□   Monastery created after 1070 (mostly after 1124)

Aberdeen

Forfar

Perth

Stirling

Edinburgh

Berwick

Roxburgh

Carlisle (1136-57)

0   50 km

A.Grant

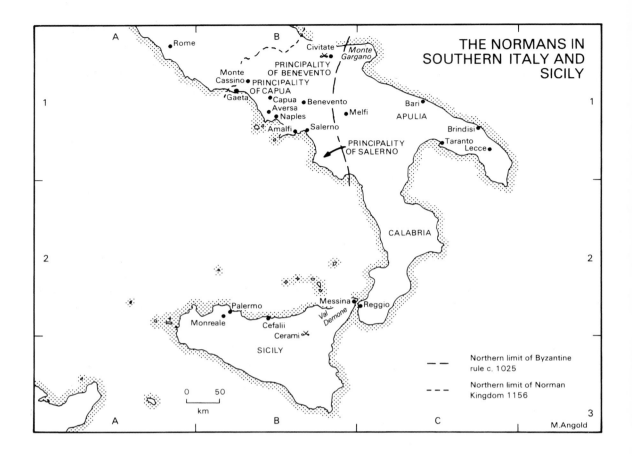

Rome

Civitate ✂ / Monte Gargano

PRINCIPALITY OF BENEVENTO

Monte Cassino

PRINCIPALITY OF CAPUA

Gaeta

Capua
Aversa
Naples
Amalfi
Salerno
Benevento
Melfi

Bari

APULIA

Brindisi

Taranto
Lecce

PRINCIPALITY OF SALERNO

CALABRIA

Palermo
Monreale
Cefalù
Cerami ✂
Messina
Reggio
Val Demone

SICILY

0   50
km

Northern limit of Byzantine
rule c. 1025

Northern limit of Norman
Kingdom 1156

M. Angold

The Normans in Southern Italy and Sicily

From *c.* 1000 the struggles of the Lombard princes of Benevento, Capua and Salerno, both against Byzantine hegemony and among themselves, provided opportunities for military service which attracted the Normans to southern Italy; but they only established a permanent presence with the acquisition of Aversa in 1030. They went on to seize Melfi in 1041, from where they began the conquest of Apulia and Calabria from the Byzantines, who turned to the papacy for help. The turning point came in 1053 at the battle of Civitate, where Pope Leo IX was defeated and captured by the Normans. This produced a realignment of forces, culminating in 1059 with the Investiture of Melfi, whereby

Pope Nicholas II invested Richard of Aversa with Capua and another Norman leader Robert Guiscard with Calabria, Apulia and Sicily. Calabria fell in 1060 with the capture of Reggio, but the conquest of Apulia was delayed until 1071, when Bari, the Byzantine capital, surrendered. Guiscard left the conquest of Sicily from the Muslims to his brother Roger, who in 1061 established a bridgehead at Messina. Victory at Cerami (1063) brought him control of the Val Demone, from which he threatened the capital of Palermo. It capitulated in 1072, though Muslim resistance continued until 1091. After Guiscard's death in 1085 Sicily increasingly became the centre of Norman power, which reached its height under

Roger II. He assumed the royal title in 1130 and extended his authority over all the Norman territories in southern Italy. This was at first opposed by the papacy, but later accepted in 1156 at the treaty of Benevento. The Norman kings were great patrons of the arts. Their achievement is still visible in their churches and palaces at Palermo and in the cathedrals of Monreale and Cefalii. The Norman kingdom passed to the Hohenstaufen in 1194 following a disputed succession.

M. Angold

Where Did the Crusaders Come From? Major Areas of Recruitment to the Crusade in the Near East From the Latin West, 1095–1271

The problem of crusade motivation must be put into its geographical context. As one might have expected, there was a strong correlation between the leadership of individual crusades and the regions of crusade recruitment. The first crusade, preached by Pope Urban II at the Council of Clermont in 1095, attracted recruits from virtually all over Christendom. Englishmen, Scots, Scandinavians, Italian merchant-seamen, even Tuscan monks (who were forbidden to go) and Spanish knights (who were told to stay and fight the Moors at home) sought to take the cross. But from the major areas of recruitment came the great feudal nobles, bringing their vassals, and assuming leadership positions. The most prominent amongst them were Robert of

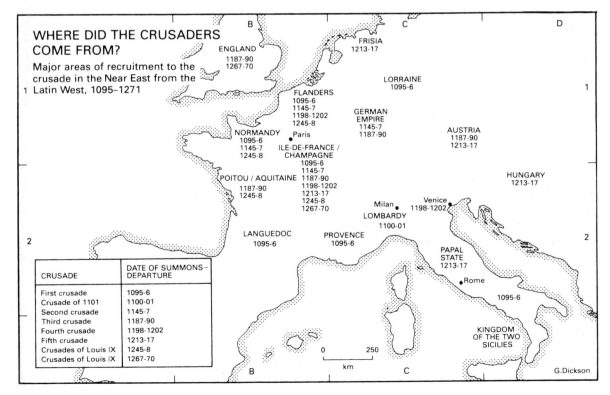

WHERE DID THE CRUSADERS COME FROM?

Major areas of recruitment to the crusade in the Near East from the Latin West, 1095–1271

CRUSADE	DATE OF SUMMONS – DEPARTURE
First crusade	1095-6
Crusade of 1101	1100-01
Second crusade	1145-7
Third crusade	1187-90
Fourth crusade	1198-1202
Fifth crusade	1213-17
Crusades of Louis IX	1245-8
Crusades of Louis IX	1267-70

G.Dickson

Normandy, Robert of Flanders, Hugh of Vermandois, Godfrey of Bouillon, Baldwin of Boulogne, Bohemund of Taranto, Adhemar of Le Puy (the papal legate) and Raymond of Toulouse. The crusade of 1101 drew a large army of Lombards under Archbishop Anselm of Milan, as well as first-crusaders who had failed to honour their original vow, along with some others. In the second crusade, led by Louis VII of France and Conrad III of Germany, kings and kingdoms became involved for the first time. The champions of the third crusade were Emperor Frederick I, King Richard Lionheart of England (who also brought his troops from Poitou) and King Philip II Augustus of France. The fourth crusade saw the Venetians join great barons from northern and central France and Flanders, while the fifth crusade – after the first, perhaps the most truly 'international' crusade – aroused Frisians, Rhinelanders, Frenchmen, Italians from the papal state, Austrians, Hungarians and other contingents, too. The crusading armies of King Louis IX of France (St Louis) were overwhelmingly composed of Frenchmen, although his latter expedition attracted far less support than his first. Prince Edward of England's crusading army, which arrived in Tunis after Louis had already died there, must still be counted as part of Louis' crusade. The geography of crusade recruitment may be an essential clue to the psychology of crusade motivation.

G. Dickson

The Routes of the First Crusade

Following Pope Urban II's appeal at Clermont in November 1095 the crusaders set out over the next summer for Constantinople. They followed two main routes. The first was through Hungary to the Byzantine frontier post at Belgrade and then along the military road across the Balkans. This was taken by Peter the Hermit and by Godfrey of Bouillon, duke of Lower Lorraine. Other leaders, such as Robert of Normandy, Robert of Flanders and Stephen of Blois, travelled through Italy and crossed over to Dyrrachion, whence the *Via Egnatia* led to Constantinople. Variants of this route were followed by Bohemund of Taranto and by Raymond of Toulouse, who were the last to arrive at Constantinople (April 1097). The next stage was across Asia Minor which was controlled by the Seljuq Turks. The crusaders captured Nicaea, the Seljuq capital, and then on 1 July 1097 defeated the Turks at Dorylaion. This victory opened up the routes across the Anatolian plateau to Edessa, which was occupied in March 1098, and to Antioch, which finally capitulated on 28 June 1098. The crusaders set out in January 1099 on their last stage to Jerusalem, which fell after a month's siege on 15 July. Their successes were made possible by help from the Genoese, who dispatched a fleet in July 1097. News of these triumphs prompted the departure of two more crusading expeditions. Both were cut to pieces by the Turks in the summer of 1101. These defeats were decisive. They meant that Anatolia would remain Turkish and that the crusaders' hold in Syria would always be tenuous.

M. Angold

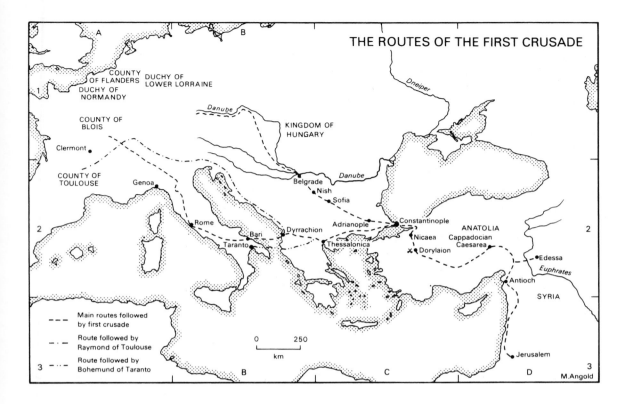

THE ROUTES OF THE FIRST CRUSADE

The Second and Third Crusades

The second crusade was in response to the fall of Edessa in 1144. Its inspiration was St Bernard who in 1146 persuaded both Louis VII of France and the German Emperor Conrad III to participate. The route chosen was through Hungary and across the Balkans. The Germans reached Constantinople in September 1147 and the French arrived in October. The Germans were turned back by the Turks near Dorylaion and joined up with the French who were marching down the west coast of Asia Minor. Conrad fell ill and returned to Constantinople, where he took ship to Palestine. Louis fought his way to Attaleia, whence he was ferried by the Byzantines to Antioch. Damascus was chosen as the goal of the crusade. A brief siege (24–28 July 1148) broke up in confusion. As a participant observed, 'if it brought no worldly success, it was good for the salvation of many souls'. Associated with this

crusade were an English expedition which captured Lisbon from the Muslims (October 1147) and a Saxon campaign across the Elbe against the Slavic Wends.

The third crusade aimed to recover Jerusalem which had fallen to Saladin on 2 October 1187. The Germans under Frederick Barbarossa set out in May 1189 and followed the traditional route across the Balkans and Anatolia, but Frederick died *en route*. The English and French went by sea, wintering at Messina. The French under Philip Augustus arrived before Acre in April 1191; the English under Richard I not until June, having secured Cyprus on the way. Acre fell on 12 July. Philip Augustus then returned home. Richard stayed for another year. Despite his victory over Saladin at Arsuf Jerusalem eluded him. He only secured a foothold along the coast.

M. Angold

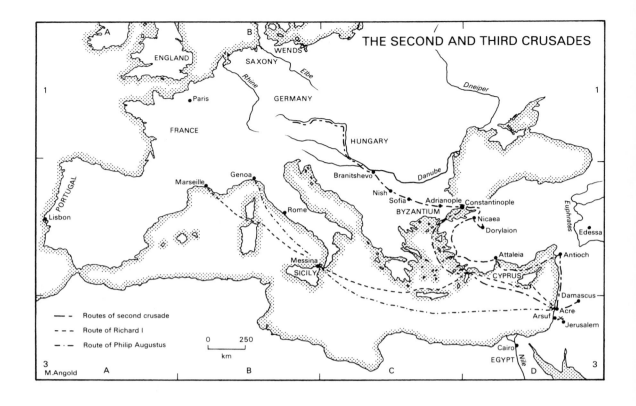

THE SECOND AND THIRD CRUSADES

Routes of second crusade
Route of Richard I
Route of Philip Augustus

0   250
km

M. Angold

The Crusades of the Emperor Frederick II and St Louis

As king of Sicily the Emperor Frederick II was well-informed about the Muslim world. He realized that the rivalry between the Muslim rulers of Egypt and Syria could be exploited to recover Jerusalem. Even before he set off on crusade in 1228 he was negotiating with the sultan of Egypt, who in February 1229 agreed to the return of Jerusalem. Frederick entered the city and crowned himself king on 18 March. This propaganda coup turned sour, as he found himself condemned. The manner of his recovery of Jerusalem was an affront to the crusading ideal, while the terms left it isolated. It fell in 1244 to the first serious Muslim attack.

This produced a wave of crusading fervour centring on Louis IX of France. In 1249 from his base on Cyprus he launched an attack on Egypt – seen as the key to Jerusalem. Damietta fell in June, but Louis delayed his advance against Cairo until the autumn. He won a victory at Mansourah, but then found himself cut off. On 6 April 1250 he surrendered. He was released after paying a ransom of 800,000 bezants. To atone for his failure he stayed in the Holy Land until 1254, strengthening its defences. In 1270 he launched another crusade; this time against Tunis. Its ruler was thought to be ready to convert to Christianity. Louis fell ill outside the city and died on 25 August.

St Louis was an idealist who brought meticulous planning to his crusades – down to the construction of the port of Aigues-Mortes. His utter failure did more harm to the cause of the crusade than Frederick's blatant opportunism.

M. Angold

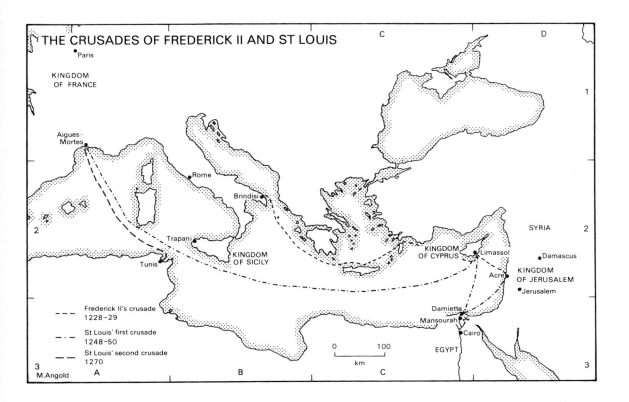

THE CRUSADES OF FREDERICK II AND ST LOUIS

Paris

KINGDOM
OF FRANCE

Aigues-
Mortes

Rome

Brindisi

Trapani

KINGDOM
OF SICILY

Tunis

SYRIA

KINGDOM
OF CYPRUS   Limassol

Damascus

Acre   KINGDOM
OF JERUSALEM

Jerusalem

Damietta
Mansourah

Cairo

EGYPT

— — — Frederick II's crusade
1228–29

— · — St Louis' first crusade
1248–50

— — St Louis' second crusade
1270

0   100
km

M.Angold   A   B   C   C

The Crusader States

Of the four states the first to be established (1098) and the first to fall to the Muslims (1144) was the county of Edessa. Its position athwart the middle Euphrates left it exposed, but provided cover for Antioch, while its crusader princes tried and failed to take Aleppo which blocked expansion inland. After the defeat at the Field of Blood (1119) they were more or less restricted to the coastal plain. To the south the county of Tripoli was similarly confined to the coast, where the plain known as La Bloquée opened up a route inland, but it was blocked by Homs. Krak des Chevaliers was built in 1142 to defend the frontier.

This pattern of going onto the defensive after failing to break out into the interior was repeated by the kingdom of Jerusalem, but with differences. While a frontier was quickly established along the Jordan from Galilee to the Dead Sea and then in 1115–16 extended as far south as the Gulf of Aila (Aqaba), the coast took much longer to secure. Tyre only fell in 1125; Ascalon not until 1153. The kingdom of Jerusalem thus drove a wedge between the Muslim powers of Egypt and Syria. It threatened both Cairo and Damascus, but once these were united by Saladin in 1174, the crusaders were forced on the defensive. Though the kingdom of Jerusalem prospered – Acre was becoming the entrepot of the trade of the eastern Mediterranean – the costs of defence, particularly the construction and maintenance of fortresses, were crippling. The strain contributed to the collapse of the kingdom after Saladin's victory at Hattin in 1187. Though reconstituted by the third crusade, it was virtually limited to the coast; Jerusalem was only briefly recovered (1229–44). The kingdom survived thanks to the commercial interest of the Italians

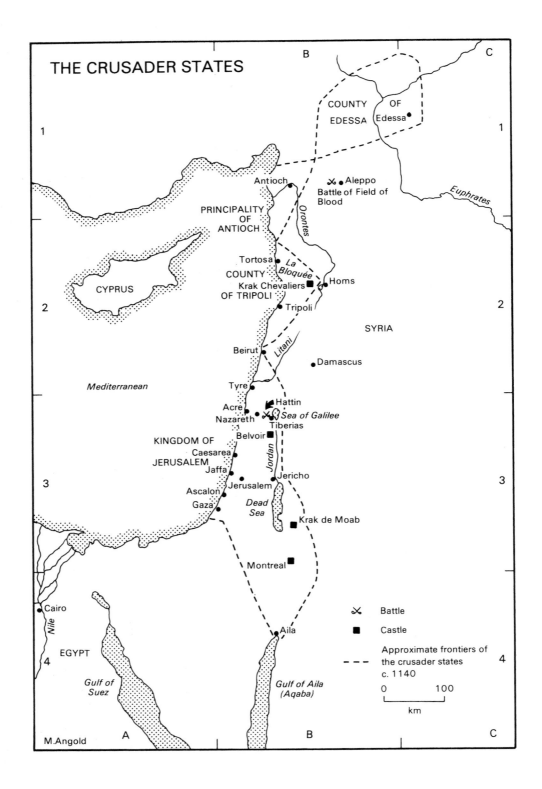

THE CRUSADER STATES

COUNTY OF EDESSA
Edessa

Euphrates

Antioch
Aleppo
Battle of Field of Blood

PRINCIPALITY OF ANTIOCH

Orontes

CYPRUS

Tortosa
La Bloquée
COUNTY
Krak Chevaliers
OF TRIPOLI
Homs

Tripoli

SYRIA

Beirut
Litani

Damascus

Mediterranean

Tyre

Acre
Nazareth

Hattin
Sea of Galilee
Tiberias

Belvoir

KINGDOM OF
Caesarea
JERUSALEM
Jaffa

Jericho

Ascalon
Jerusalem
Gaza
Dead Sea

Jordan

Krak de Moab

Montreal

Cairo
Nile

EGYPT

Aila

Gulf of Suez

Gulf of Aila (Aqaba)

✗ Battle

■ Castle

- - - Approximate frontiers of the crusader states c. 1140

0   100
km

M. Angold

90

and divisions among Saladin's successors. Once Egypt passed to the Mamluks (1250), who were dedicated to the revival of the holy war, it was only a matter of time for the crusader states, with Acre finally falling in 1291.

M. Angold

The Templar Network

The Templars were founded in 1119 with the limited aim of protecting the pilgrim routes between Jaffa and Jerusalem and the adjacent holy sites. At first they attracted little attention, but papal confirmation granted at the Council of Troyes in 1128, followed by a vigorous recruiting drive in the West, set in motion an expansion which, during the twelfth century, transformed them from a small charitable association into an international corporation, possessing estates in all the Christian lands. According to the Rule of the Order their possessions were divided into ten provinces, each governed by a hierarchy of commanders ultimately responsible to the Grand Master. By this means new members were recruited and a set proportion of income sent to the East in the form of responsions. The need to make large sums of money available in the various different parts of Christendom soon led to the development of a complementary banking structure. This vast organization was geared to the protection of the crusader lands in the

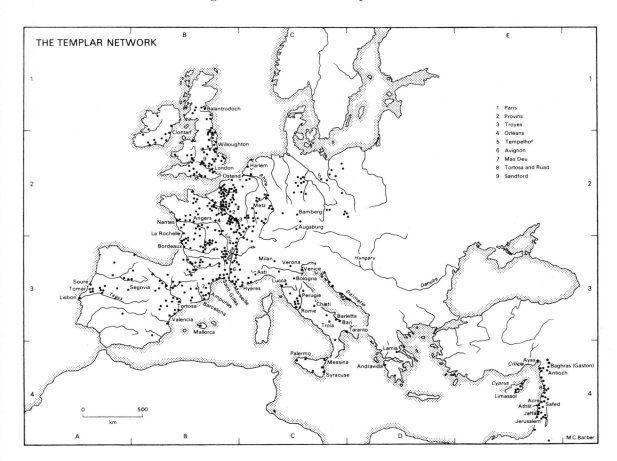

THE TEMPLAR NETWORK

1 Paris
2 Provins
3 Troyes
4 Orléans
5 Tempelhof
6 Avignon
7 Mas Deu
8 Tortosa and Ruad
9 Sandford

M.C.Barber

East where, at various times the Order was responsible for at least fifty-three fortified places, ranging from massive castles like Athlit and Safed to small watch-towers in which pilgrims could take refuge. By the 1180s it could muster over 600 knights and 2000 sergeants in Outremer.

This network was therefore a complex back-up organization for the front-line. Since these possessions originally derived from the generosity of pious benefactors, there was inevitably a certain random element in the pattern, but the map shows the effects of shrewd management unrestricted by the desire for isolation that affected the distribution of Cistercian houses. The Order had houses in the major Atlantic and Mediterranean ports, while its inland possessions cluster around the main trade and pilgrim routes to and from northern Europe: in the east through Champagne, along the Rhône and into Provence and Italy, and in the west through Normandy, Anjou and the Charente into Languedoc and Iberia. Indeed, the expansion of the reconquest in Spain created a second front for the Order, where it became well-established in Aragon and, later, Portugal, although the Castilian rulers relied much more upon local military orders. The Templars were least important along Christendom's eastern frontier, dominated first by the Hospital and, from the early thirteenth century, by the Teutonic Knights.

Nevertheless, one of the provinces listed by the Rule was that of Hungary which in this period incorporated Dalmatia, a region in which it seems likely that the Templars held many more houses than can at the moment be shown with any certainty on a map. The Order's shipping maintained regular links with Outremer, where the Templars had their own quays and warehouses in all the main ports of the Palestinian and Syrian mainland and, in the thirteenth century, in Cyprus and Cilicia as well. In 1307 the Templars were arrested in France, accused of heretical and immoral activity by the government of Philip IV, and during the next two years they were similarly seized in other countries as well. Although there was little substance in the charges the Order was suppressed by the papacy in 1312 and its lands transferred to the Hospitallers.

At its height the membership is unlikely to have been fewer than 5,000, excluding dependants of various kinds, nor to have had fewer than 800 houses, ranging from great complexes like the Paris Temple to remote rural preceptories administered by perhaps two brothers. A map of this kind should therefore be used with caution, for it cannot mark every single establishment, nor show their relative importance. Moreover, the situation was never static; a more dynamic picture would require several maps.

M.C. Barber

Crusader Jerusalem

In 1099 the crusaders took over the Muslim city more or less intact. The outer walls were later repaired and the citadel in the Tower of David strengthened. The need was for colonists. At first, the crusaders only occupied a single quarter around the Holy Sepulchre, the Muslims and the Jews having been either massacred or expelled. A partial solution was the settlement in 1116 of Christian Syrians from Transjordan, probably in the old Jewish quarter. Repopulation accelerated with the organization of the pilgrim trade. This was largely the work of the Hospital and the Temple, which took over the Dome of the Rock and the al-Aqsa mosque. There was much rebuilding. Notable were the enlargement of the church of the Holy Sepulchre, rededicated in 1149, and the construction of the church of St Anne (1140). The covered market was partially reconstructed in 1152. The Muslims were much impressed by the city which fell to them in 1187. The city briefly returned to the crusaders from 1229–44.

M. Angold

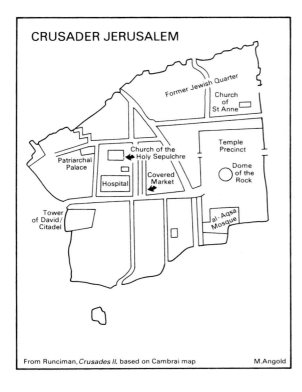

CRUSADER JERUSALEM

Former Jewish Quarter

Church of St Anne

Church of the Holy Sepulchre

Temple Precinct

Patriarchal Palace

Covered Market

Dome of the Rock

Hospital

Tower of David/ Citadel

al-Aqsa Mosque

From Runciman, *Crusades II*, based on Cambrai map   M.Angold

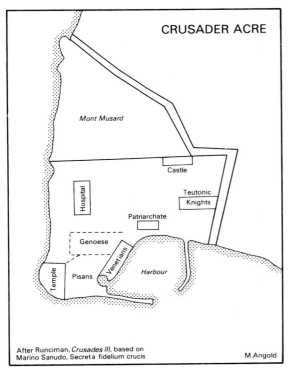

CRUSADER ACRE

Mont Musard

Castle

Hospital

Teutonic Knights

Patriarchate

Genoese

Temple

Pisans

Venetians

Harbour

After Runciman, *Crusades III*, based on Marino Sanudo, *Secreta fidelium crucis*   M.Angold

Crusader Acre

Acre was captured by the crusaders with Genoese help in 1104. It developed into the major port of the kingdom of Jerusalem. Though the Italians enjoyed concessions it remained within the royal demesne. It fell to Saladin in 1187. Its recovery in 1191 was the main achievement of the third crusade. Its single line of walls was now strengthened with a moat and an outer wall, incorporating the rapidly developing suburb of Mont Musard. Nominally the capital of the restored kingdom of Jerusalem, Acre increasingly passed into the hands of the Temple, the Hospital and the Italians after a commune had been created in 1232 to defy the vestiges of royal authority. Trade flourished. It was organized through the *cour de la chaine*, which dealt with seaborne trade, and the *cour de la fonde*, responsible for the market. The latter comprised two Franks and four Syrians, who were increasingly important. The topography of the city on the eve of its fall in 1291 is known through a map left by Marino Sanudo.

M. Angold

Frederick II, the Papacy and Italy

Elected emperor in 1211, Frederick found his imperial inheritance threatened by growing noble power. Secure only in his maternal inheritance in Sicily, in 1216 he recognized it as a papal fief. This provided a strong base throughout his reign, offering both material assistance and intellectual inspiration in his imperial schemes. Strong in Sicily but with ambitions in Germany, Frederick required full control of Italy before progressing north of the Alps. This threatened papal independence and the freedoms of the Lombard cities granted in 1183.

Schemes to separate papal and Lombardic interests failed. Frederick intended the 1226 diet at Cremona to be the occasion for re-establishing imperial authority in Lombardy, but provoked instead a hostile revival of the Lombard League. Papal support courted through promises of a crusade was lost since failure at Cremona made

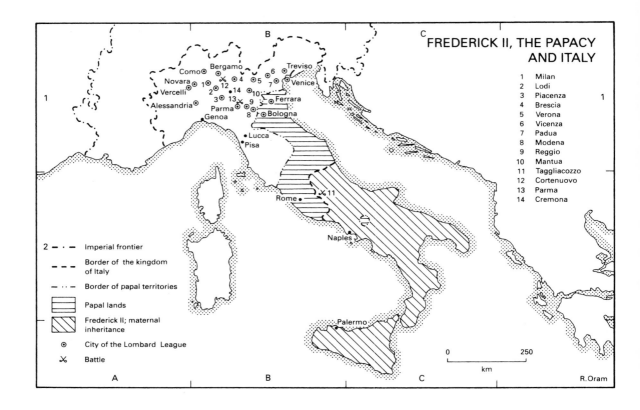

FREDERICK II, THE PAPACY AND ITALY

1 Milan
2 Lodi
3 Piacenza
4 Brescia
5 Verona
6 Vicenza
7 Padua
8 Modena
9 Reggio
10 Mantua
11 Taggliacozzo
12 Cortenuovo
13 Parma
14 Cremona

- — · · — Imperial frontier
- - - - Border of the kingdom of Italy
- — · · — Border of papal territories
▤ Papal lands
▨ Frederick II; maternal inheritance
⊙ City of the Lombard League
✗ Battle

0   250
km

R. Oram

Frederick unwilling to depart, but excommunication for breach of his vow forced his hand. Success on crusade failed to win desired Church support at home, and he returned in 1229 to repulse a papal attack on Naples. Reconciliation with Rome in 1230 was followed by moves to centralize the government of his territories, which served only to renew hostility.

At Mainz in 1235 Frederick annulled the 1183 treaty, effectively declaring war on Lombardy and, after a failed attempt at mediation, the pope joined Frederick's enemies. Victorious over the Milanese at Cortenuova in 1237, Frederick failed to capture Brescia in 1239 and his initiative faltered. Excommunicated in 1239, in 1240 the war against him gained crusading status, but only in 1245 did the papacy declare him deposed as emperor. Frederick fought on, despite defeat in 1248 at Parma, until his death at Florentino in 1250. Frederick left a crippling legacy of war to his family and the continued enmity of the papacy was to lead to the eventual destruction of the Hohenstaufens in 1268.

R. Oram

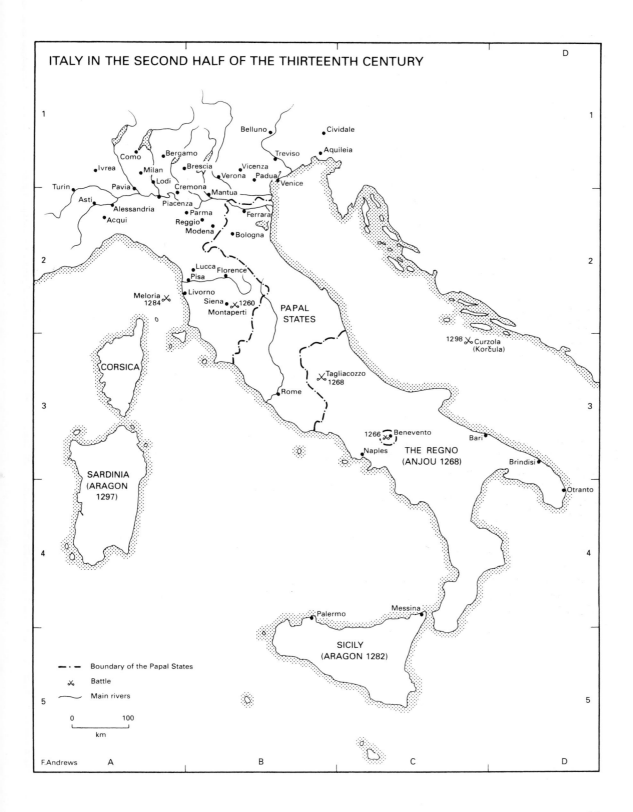

ITALY IN THE SECOND HALF OF THE THIRTEENTH CENTURY

Belluno
Cividale
Como
Bergamo
Treviso
Aquileia
Ivrea
Brescia
Vicenza
Milan
Verona
Padua
Lodi
Turin
Pavia
Cremona
Mantua
Venice
Asti
Piacenza
Alessandria
Parma
Ferrara
Acqui
Reggio
Modena
Bologna

Lucca
Florence
Pisa
Meloria 1284
Livorno
Siena 1260
Montaperti
PAPAL STATES

CORSICA

1298 Curzola (Korčula)

Tagliacozzo 1268

Rome

1266 Benevento
Bari
SARDINIA (ARAGON 1297)
Naples
THE REGNO (ANJOU 1268)
Brindisi
Otranto

Palermo
Messina

SICILY (ARAGON 1282)

— ·· — Boundary of the Papal States

Battle

Main rivers

0   100
km

F.Andrews

Italy in the Second Half of the Thirteenth Century

The Italian peninsula can be divided into three politically distinct regions. In the south the Hohenstaufen *regno* ('kingdom') collapsed after the battles of Benevento and Tagliacozzo and the death of the last Hohenstaufen heirs of Frederick II, his grandson Conradin and his illegitimate son Manfred. By 1268 the *regno* had passed to Charles of Anjou, the younger brother of Louis IX of France. Charles had been invited to intervene in the *regno* by the papacy and the 'Guelph' alliance between Charles and the papacy resulted in the cession of Benevento to the papacy after 1263. Once established in the south Charles sought to dominate the north too, by uniting Guelph factions in Lombardy and by assuming the lordship of several Tuscan towns. He also secured influence in Rome. His domination of Italy collapsed, however, following the massacre of French Angevins in Palermo and across the island of Sicily at Easter 1282, an event known as the Sicilian Vespers. The Angevin dynasty continued to hold sway in Naples until the fifteenth century but Sicily now passed to King Pere II of Aragon, whose wife Constance was the daughter of Manfred. The ensuing War of the Vespers between the Angevins and Aragonese was to last for ninety years. Pere's son Jaume later also acquired Sardinia and Corsica from the papacy.

In central Italy the papacy had emerged as the leading political force and Ferrara, Bologna and the towns of the Romagna were formally ceded to the papal states by the emperor-elect Rudolph of Habsburg in 1278. A series of short pontificates, however, weakened papal authority in this region. In an attempt to retrieve the situation Boniface VIII (1294–1303) appointed Charles of Valois, brother of Philip IV of France, as vicar of the papal state but his success in reasserting papal authority was limited. Boniface also attempted, with greater success, to establish members of his Caetani family in the Roman hinterland as a basis for support. But this policy alienated others, notably the Colonna family, and in 1303 it joined the now hostile French in kidnapping the pope at Agnani. Unable to pacify the papal state, the papal court was transfered to Avignon in 1307.

In the north, meanwhile, commerce flourished but political factionalism was rife in the vacuum caused by the demise of imperial power. Ostensibly, at least, much of this conflict (both between and within towns) assumed the guise of a contest between 'Guelph' and 'Ghibelline' powers: the pro-papal Guelphs deriving their name from the old Welf opponents of the Hohenstaufen in Germany while the pro-imperial Ghibellines derived theirs from the Hohenstaufen castle of Waiblingen. In the 1250s the papacy led a crusade against Ezzelino da Romano and Oberto Pelavicini (Pallavicini), who, disguised as imperial vicars, between them controlled Cremona, Pavia, Piacenza, Vercelli, Verona, Vicenza and Padua. Ezzelino was killed but, by opportunely changing sides, Oberto built up an even stronger lordship, which briefly included Milan. Thereafter control of that city alternated between the Ghibelline della Torre (1263–81) and Guelph Visconti factions (1281–95). In Tuscany conflict polarized between traditionally Guelph Florence, defeated at Montaperti in 1260, and traditionally Ghibelline Siena. In reality attachment to these parties depended more on local rivalries than wider loyalties, but the parties did at least provide a measure of cohesion to a politically fragmented region. Elsewhere Pisa, Genoa and Venice fought to defend their trading interests: the Genoese defeated the Pisans at Meloria in 1284 and the Venetians at Curzola in 1298. In the north-west Gugliemo VII of Monferrato extended his power over Piedmont by acquiring authority in Alessandria, Asti, Turin and elsewhere, while in the north-east an alliance of 1262 between Verona, Padua, Treviso and Vicenza was designed to prevent the dominance of one person in any of these cities. Nonetheless, Verona and later Vicenza fell to the della Scala family, Treviso to the da Camino and Padua to the Carrara.

F. Andrews

The *Ostsiedlung*

Between 1100 and 1350 eastern Europe was transformed by a wave of German immigration (the *Ostsiedlung*), which moved the eastern boundaries of the German-speaking world hundreds of miles beyond its former limit on the rivers Elbe and Saale. In some areas, such as Brandenburg, this new settlement came in the wake of conquest by German lords and knights, but in many other regions, such as Pomerania and Silesia, it was local Slav princes who encouraged German settlement. National antagonism was not important. The new settlers wanted land and the local rulers were happy to grant it and to profit, directly or indirectly, from the taxes, rents and tithes flowing from the new villages.

The frontier of settlement began to move in the first half of the twelfth century when immigration was actively promoted by such vigorous border lords as Adolf of Holstein, Henry the Lion, duke of Saxony, and Albert the Bear, margrave of Brandenburg. They advertised the attractions of the eastern frontier among the overcrowded inhabitants of western Germany and the Low Countries and soon streams of colonists were arriving in east Holstein, Schwerin, Ratzeburg and Brandenburg. The pace quickened in the thirteenth century as planned and large-scale development was undertaken in Pomerania and the Polish lands.

Rural settlement often involved the lay-out of entirely new villages, composed of standard, rectilinear farms (*Hufen* or *mansi*). The recruitment and organization of the colonists was the task of a planning entrepreneur (*locator*), who received land and privileges in the new settlement as his reward. Slav peasants were not usually dispossessed (though there are some instances of this), since in general there was plenty of land, especially for those willing to drain marshes or fell forests.

Rural settlement was complemented by new urban foundations. German burgesses formed the core of most of the new chartered towns founded in eastern Europe in these centuries. They brought their language, culture and law with them. Places as significant for German civilization as Lübeck, Berlin and Leipzig were twelfth- or thirteenth-century foundations in previously Slav landscapes. German urban settlement spread far beyond the limits of German peasant settlement and up to the borders of Russia there were German burgesses, living according to German town law, in the midst of native rural populations.

In some regions German conquest and settlement coincided with conversion to Christianity. The Slavs who inhabited Mecklenburg and Brandenburg, for example, were pagan until the twelfth century. In most areas, however, Germans came to lands that were already Christian. But one German settlement was unique in being created and permanently maintained by holy war. This was the domain of the Teutonic Knights, Prussia and Livonia, where German crusaders brought forcible baptism to pagan Baltic peoples. By the fourteenth century, although the pagan Lithuanians were far from being defeated, a German population of landlords, churchmen, burgesses and (in Prussia) peasants had settled, from Danzig to the Gulf of Finland, under the rule of the crusading knights.

The end result of the *Ostsiedlung* was the Germanization of vast areas east of the Elbe and an increase in their economic productivity. Some of the political units created in the process, like Brandenburg and Prussia, were to have an important role in subsequent European history.

R. Bartlett

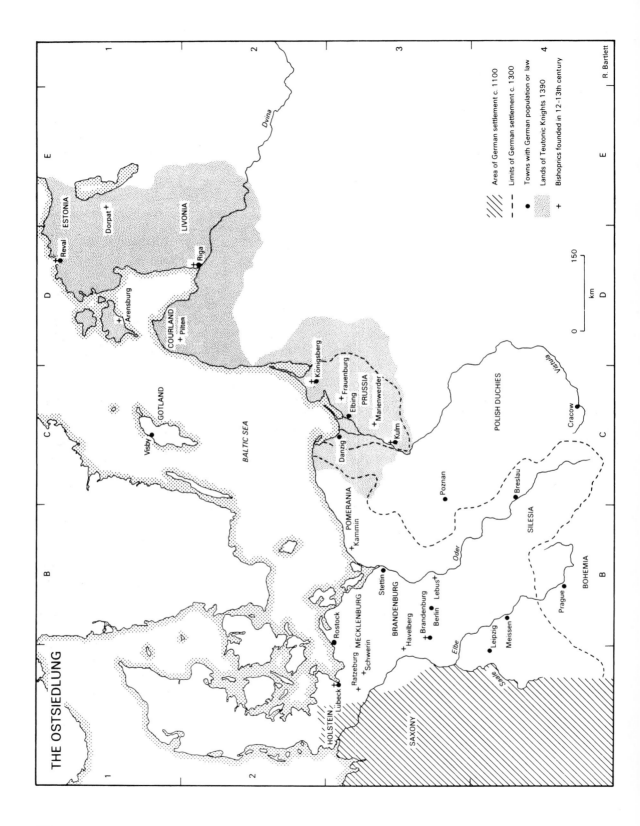

THE OSTSIEDLUNG

HOLSTEIN

Lübeck +

Ratzeburg +
Schwerin +
MECKLENBURG

Rostock ●

Stettin ●

Havelberg +
Brandenburg ●
Berlin ● Lebus +
BRANDENBURG

SAXONY

Leipzig ●
Meissen ●

Elbe

Saale

BOHEMIA

Prague ●

POMERANIA

Kammin +

Oder

POLISH DUCHIES

Poznan ●

Breslau ●
SILESIA

Cracow ●

Vistula

BALTIC SEA

Danzig ●
Kulm +
Marienwerder +
Elbing +
PRUSSIA
Frauenburg +
Königsberg +

GOTLAND

Visby ●

COURLAND
Pilten +

LIVONIA

Riga +

Dvina

ESTONIA
Reval ●
Dorpat +

Arensburg +

Area of German settlement c. 1100

Limits of German settlement c. 1300

● Towns with German population or law

Lands of Teutonic Knights 1390

+ Bishoprics founded in 12–13th century

0   150
         km

R. Bartlett

Scandinavia, the Germans and the Baltic

In parallel with the expansion of Latin Christendom in the Mediterranean, the two centuries after 1100 saw the spread of Christianity into the pagan lands beyond the Elbe and in the eastern Baltic. The mechanisms of expansion were varied: missions, military conquest and colonization, economic domination and cultural assimilation. By 1300, these lands were largely integrated into the political and religious framework of Christendom by the efforts of missionaries, knights, merchants and peasant colonists. The initiative was chiefly, but not solely, German, and driven as much by hunger for land as by religious zeal.

Earlier attempts to convert the pagan West Slavs ended with their revolt in 983, which forced abandonment of German sees and monasteries east of the Elbe. Only after the Polish conquest of Pomerania in the 1120s did missions resume under the direction of Bishop Otto of Bamberg, and in 1140 a separate Pomeranian bishopric was created. The advance quickened after the Wendish Crusade of 1147, when Albert, margrave of Brandenburg, and Henry, duke of Saxony, restored the territory between the Elbe and the Oder to German rule. Refoundation of bishoprics abandoned in 983 followed military conquest. It was the Danes, however, who in 1168 destroyed the focus of West Slav paganism at Arkona on the island of Rügen, and Danish and Swedish fleets joined the Germans in freeing the Baltic trade routes of Slav raiders. These successes prompted Pope Alexander III in 1171 to plan an abortive Danish-led crusade against Estonia, with a view to establishing a new bishopric there. It was, however, only in 1206 that the Danes began their conquest of Estonia.

In the eastern Baltic, the first foothold was not established by conquest but by missionaries arriving in the wake of German merchants. In 1186 a bishopric was created in Livonia and fixed in 1200 at the German trading colony of Riga. In 1251 it was raised to archiepiscopal status and given metropolitan authority over all the sees from Prussia eastwards. Many early missionary bishops were from reformed monastic orders, such as the Cistercians who directed the conversion of Prussia. Monasteries, however, played little part in the process of conversion, but were major agents in the colonization which followed. Cistercian abbeys, for example, not only cleared forest for their own needs, but introduced colonizing peasant tenants onto their estates. The need to defend the new Christian lands in Prussia and Livonia saw the establishment of two orders of military monks, the Knights of Dobrin and the Swordbrothers respectively, but by 1240 both had been absorbed into the older Teutonic Order. By the mid-thirteenth century, the Teutonic Knights ruled a territory which stretched from the Vistula to Estonia.

Trade and colonization were the chief factors which tightened the Christian grip on these new lands. Lübeck, founded as a German colony in east Holstein in 1143 by Count Adolf, was a bishopric by 1160 and the major trading centre for the Baltic. By 1161 German merchants were present at Visby on the Swedish island of Gotland, and in 1165 Westphalian traders were active from Denmark to Russia. In the eastern Baltic, German trade and settlement led to the creation of the new city of Riga, while in Estonia Reval was developed by the Danes. Urban and mercantile colonization was not alone, however, for in the wake of the military conquerors came the peasant settlers, drawn east from the overcrowded communities of Flanders, Holland and Westphalia. Through their efforts, by 1300 Brandenburg, the Neumark, Silesia and territories extending far into the former Slav lands had been reshaped in the mould of western European civilization.

R. Oram

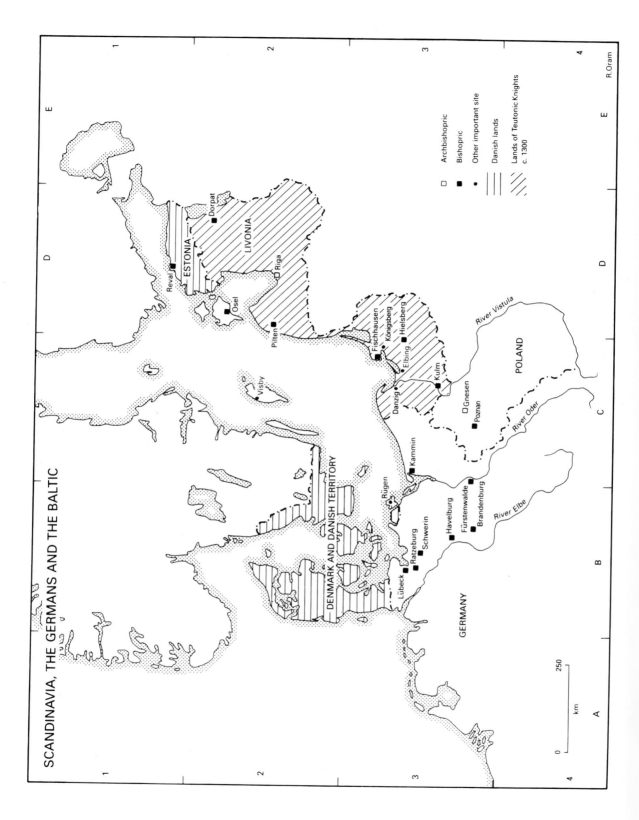

SCANDINAVIA, THE GERMANS AND THE BALTIC

R.Oram

A 1 2 3 4

Archbishopric
Bishopric
Other important site
Danish lands
Lands of Teutonic Knights
c. 1300

ESTONIA
Reval
Dorpat
LIVONIA
Osel
Riga
Piiten
Visby

Fischhausen
Königsberg
Hielsberg
Elbing
Kulm
Danzig
Gnesen
Poznan
River Vistula
POLAND
River Oder

Kammin
Rügen
Havelburg
Fürstenwalde
Brandenburg
River Elbe

Lübeck
Ratzeburg
Schwerin

DENMARK AND DANISH TERRITORY

GERMANY

km
0   250

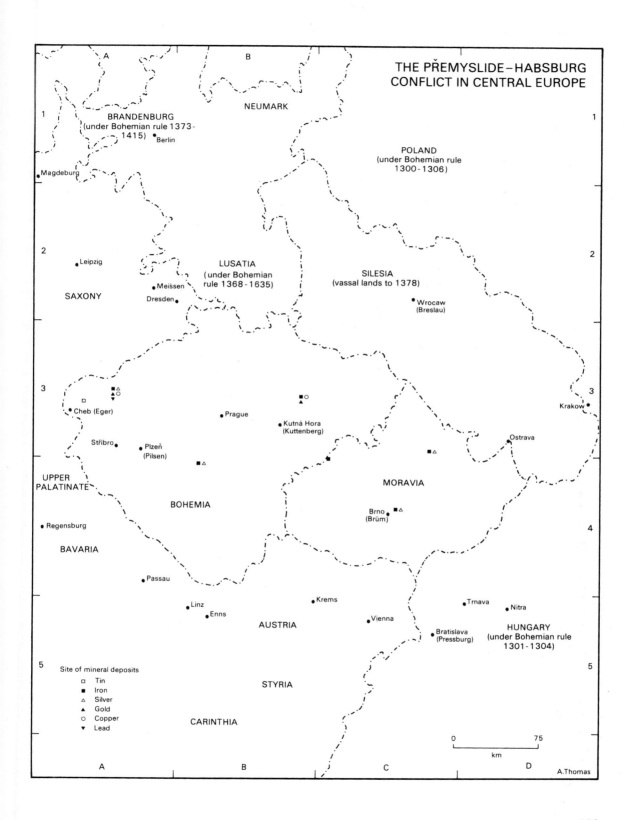

THE PŘEMYSLIDE–HABSBURG
CONFLICT IN CENTRAL EUROPE

NEUMARK

BRANDENBURG
(under Bohemian rule 1373–
1415) •Berlin

POLAND
(under Bohemian rule
1300–1306)

•Magdeburg

•Leipzig

LUSATIA
(under Bohemian
rule 1368–1635)

SILESIA
(vassal lands to 1378)

SAXONY

•Meissen

Dresden•

•Wrocaw
(Breslau)

•Krakow

Cheb (Eger)

•Prague

•Kutná Hora
(Kuttenberg)

Ostrava•

Stříbro•

•Plzeň
(Pilsen)

MORAVIA

UPPER
PALATINATE

BOHEMIA

Brno•
(Brüm)

•Regensburg

BAVARIA

•Passau

•Linz

Krems•

•Trnava

•Nitra

•Enns

AUSTRIA

Vienna•

Bratislava
(Pressburg)

HUNGARY
(under Bohemian rule
1301–1304)

Site of mineral deposits

□ Tin
■ Iron
△ Silver
▲ Gold
○ Copper
▼ Lead

STYRIA

CARINTHIA

0   75

km

A.Thomas

101

The Přemyslide–Habsburg Conflict in Central Europe

The history of Přemyslide Bohemia from its mythical origins under Přemysl the Ploughman to the extinction of the native dynasty in 1306 is one long struggle against the German hegemony to the west. The rulers of Germany availed themselves of every opportunity to interfere in the affairs of Bohemia while the Přemyslide dukes sought to advance their own interests at the expense of the empire. Successfully resisting the right of the emperor to nominate the holder of the crown, the Czech dukes gradually asserted a position of influence among the seven electors of the empire. By 1114 the ruler of Bohemia, as hereditary cup-bearer, was in a strong enough position to influence the election of the emperor himself.

The struggle between the Czech and German ruling houses was not racial in character; on the contrary, Czech princes married princesses from Saxony, Swabia and Meissen. Germans held high office within the Bohemian clergy and the Czech rulers, by now kings, invited large numbers of German colonists to Bohemia, granting them special privileges and laws quite separate from those of the indigenous population. This colonization, which reached its height in the second half of the thirteenth century, was in two stages: the first wave of immigrants were farmers contracted to cultivate the heavily wooded border region of the realm; the second wave consisted of skilled artisans, principally miners, who established their own towns such as Stříbro and Kutná Hora, east of Prague. This colonization was part of a larger economic and political policy to exploit the mineral resources of the kingdom while creating a middle-class wedge between the king and his traditional rivals for power, the nobility.

The first Přemyslide ruler to capitalize on dissensions within the empire was Přemysl Otakar I (1198–1230) who obtained from the emperor a Golden Bull (1212) which confirmed the royal title and renounced the imperial right to ratify each successor to the crown. The most powerful member of the dynasty was Přemysl Otakar II (1253–78). Already duke of Austria by the time of his accession, Otakar skilfully played off the rivals for the vacant imperial throne while furthering his own dynastic ambitions in Central Europe. By a series of brilliant military campaigns, Otakar added Styria, Carinthia, Carniola and Istria to his domains, so that at the height of his power he ruled from Silesia to the Adriatic, revealing as historical reality Shakespeare's claim that Bohemia was once in possession of a coastline.

Otakar's successes inevitably attracted the antagonism and resentment of the German princes who in 1273 elected Count Rudolph of Habsburg to the imperial office. In 1274 Otakar's rights to Austria, Styria and Carinthia were annulled by the diet of Regensburg. In 1276 Rudolph, supported by the Hungarians and Otakar's recalcitrant lords resentful of the king's pro-German policies, marched against Otakar. Deserted on all sides, Otakar appealed in the form of a letter to the dukes of Silesia and Poland, invoking an all-Slav resistance to the German threat. But Otakar's army was routed at the Battle of Dürnkrut on the Marchfeld and the king himself was slain. The Habsburg rule over Austria was established until its demise in this century. Although Bohemia was to prosper under the next king, Wenceslas II (1278–1305), and enjoyed a Golden Age under Charles IV, emperor and king of Bohemia, the real focus of power had shifted to the Habsburgs in the south. While the fortunes of Bohemia waxed and waned over the next three centuries, Habsburg Austria was destined to become one of the major European powers on the map of modern Europe.

A. Thomas

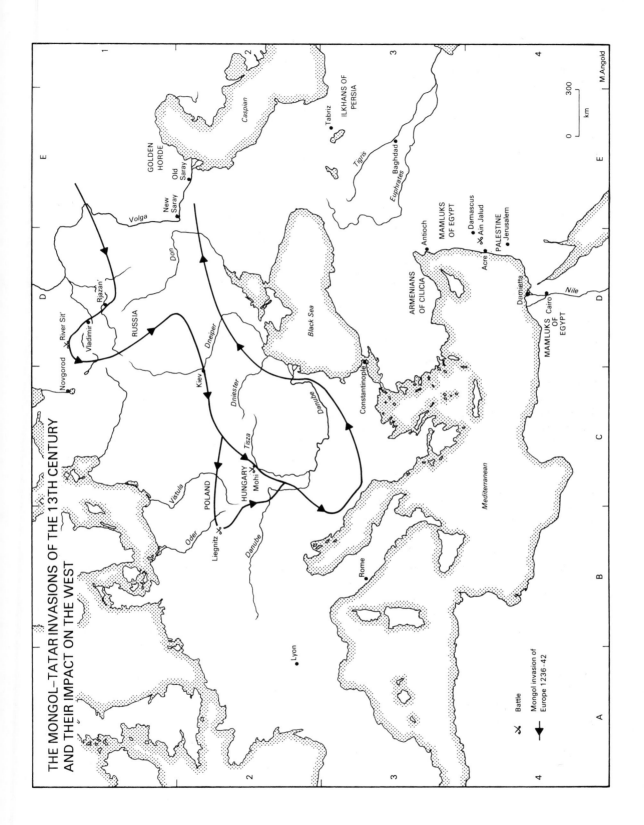

THE MONGOL–TATAR INVASIONS OF THE 13TH CENTURY
AND THEIR IMPACT ON THE WEST

M. Angold

Battle

Mongol invasion of
Europe 1236-42

GOLDEN
HORDE

ILKHANS OF
PERSIA

MAMLUKS
OF EGYPT

ARMENIANS
OF CILICIA

MAMLUKS
OF
EGYPT

PALESTINE

Old
Saray

New
Saray

Volga

Don

Dnieper

Dniester

Danube

Tisza

Danube

Oder

Vistula

Caspian

Black Sea

Mediterranean

Tabriz

Baghdad

Tigris

Euphrates

Antioch

Damascus
Ain Jalud
Jerusalem

Acre

Damietta

Cairo

Nile

Constantinople

Rome

Lyon

Novgorod

Vladimir

Rjazan'

River Sit'

RUSSIA

Kiev

POLAND

Liegnitz

HUNGARY

Mohi

km

0   300

103

The Mongol–Tatar Invasions of the Thirteenth Century and Their Impact on the West

Rumours of the conquests made by the Mongols under Ghingis Khan reached the crusader camp at Damietta in 1221, exciting only momentary interest. The Russians paid scarcely more attention, despite being defeated in 1223 by a Mongol reconnaissance force. They were unprepared for the Mongol assault launched in 1237 by Batu. The northern Russian principalities were the first to suffer. Rjazan' was sacked, then Vladimir. Its prince, Jury, died fighting the Mongols on the River Sit' (4 March 1238). The Mongols then turned south, their campaign culminating in December 1240 with the destruction of Kiev. A carefully organized sweep into the heart of Europe followed. While one army was destroying Polish resistance at Liegnitz (9 April 1241), another was crushing the Hungarians at Mohi (12 April 1241). The Mongols met up in Hungary, but the danger that they might settle permanently was averted when news came of the death of the Great Khan Ögedei. Batu evacuated his armies to their base north of the Caspian, the better to influence events at the Mongol capital of Karakorum. His withdrawal gave the new pope, Innocent IV, a chance to evaluate the Mongol threat. It came high on the agenda of the General Council he called at Lyon in 1245. He also dispatched the Dominican John of Pian Carpini to the new Great Khan Güyük to discover more about Mongol intentions and to sound out the possibilities of their conversion to Christianity. The reply brought back in 1247 was scarcely encouraging. The Great Khan claimed world dominion by mandate of the Sky God and demanded the pope's submission. The succession struggle following Güyük's death in 1248 forced the Mongol lieutenant in Persia to adopt a more conciliatory stance when confronted by St Louis' first crusade (1248–50). St Louis rejected his offer of an alliance, insisting that conversion to Christianity must come first. His caution was justified when his emissary returned with yet another demand from the Great Khan for submission.

Such demands explain why the West remained suspicious of Mongol overtures even when the Mongol Empire began to disintegrate. In Persia the Ilkhans made repeated requests for a western alliance. This Mongol successor state was founded by Hülegü, who favoured the Nestorian Christians and was hostile to Islam. In 1258 he sacked Baghdad and put the caliph to death. He had the support of the Armenian king of Cilicia and the crusader prince of Antioch, who rode in triumph into Damascus in 1260 with the Mongol army. This was almost immediately followed by the defeat of the Mongols at Ain Jalud by the Mamluks of Egypt. Thereafter the Ilkhans found their western flank along the Euphrates under threat from the Mamluks who in 1268 took Antioch. They turned to the West for an alliance, even sending emissaries in 1274 to the second council of Lyon, where a crusade was being mooted. Religion proved a stumbling block. The Ilkhans therefore sent the Nestorian Rabban Sauma in 1287 to impress the West with their devotion to Christianity. There was talk of the restoration of Jerusalem. The West remained aloof, but the Mamluks took the possibility of a western alliance with the Mongols seriously and countered it by occupying the remaining crusader places in Palestine, Acre falling in 1291. The Mongol impact on the West was muted. The *pax mongolica* briefly opened up the Orient to western merchants, the Ilkhan capital of Tabriz being a favourite destination. It also offered some scope for western missionaries, but this quickly reduced with the conversion of the Ilkhans to Islam from the turn of the thirteenth century. For the Russians it was a different matter. Until the fifteenth century they were tributaries of the Golden Horde – the Mongol successor state established by Batu and his descendants, with its capital at Saray. The Mongol yoke allowed Russia to develop in isolation from the West, while Mongol favour to the Orthodox Church enhanced its hold on Russian society.

M. Angold

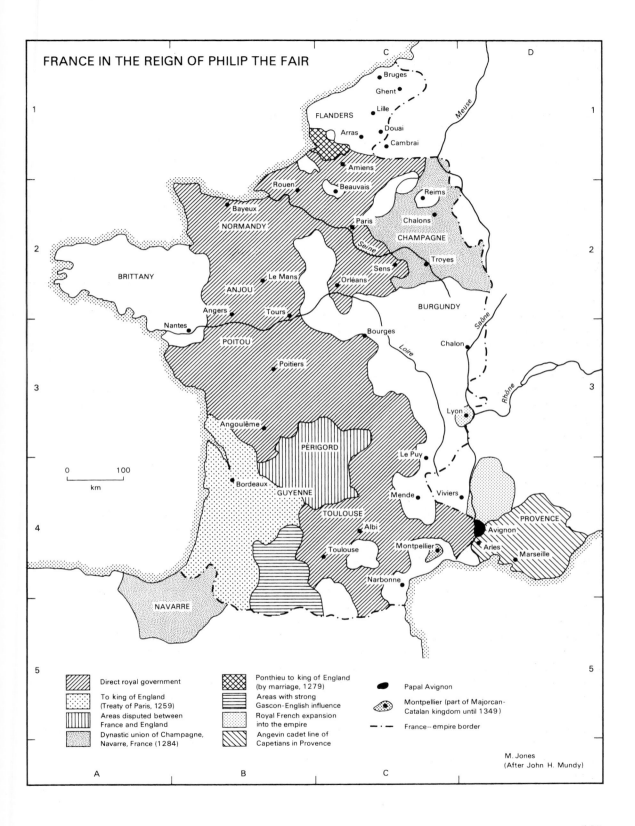

FRANCE IN THE REIGN OF PHILIP THE FAIR

Bruges
Ghent
Lille
Douai
FLANDERS
Arras
Cambrai
Amiens
Rouen
Beauvais
Bayeux
Reims
NORMANDY
Paris
Chalons
CHAMPAGNE
Sens
Troyes
BRITTANY
Le Mans
Orléans
ANJOU
BURGUNDY
Angers
Tours
Nantes
Bourges
POITOU
Chalon
Poitiers
Angoulême
Lyon
PÉRIGORD
Le Puy
Bordeaux
Mende
Viviers
GUYENNE
PROVENCE
TOULOUSE
Avignon
Albi
Arles
Toulouse
Montpellier
Marseille
Narbonne
NAVARRE

Meuse
Seine
Loire
Saône
Rhône

0   100
km

M. Jones
(After John H. Mundy)

	Direct royal government		Ponthieu to king of England (by marriage, 1279)		Papal Avignon
	To king of England (Treaty of Paris, 1259)		Areas with strong Gascon-English influence		Montpellier (part of Majorcan-Catalan kingdom until 1349)
	Areas disputed between France and England		Royal French expansion into the empire		France—empire border
	Dynastic union of Champagne, Navarre, France (1284)		Angevin cadet line of Capetians in Provence		

France in the Reign of Philip the Fair

The reign of Philip IV (1285–1314) saw the Capetian monarchy at the height of its powers. There were no spectacular conquests to rival those of Philip Augustus. But in conformity with recent royal policy, Philip consistently built up the royal *domaine* by more peaceful means such as marriage alliances, purchase, *paréage* agreements (obtaining shared jurisdiction with another lord, usually an ecclesiastic, prior to gaining outright control) and the clever manipulation of uncertainties in successoral law, backed up by the judicious but limited use of force. As a result the frontiers of the kingdom were extended, particularly towards the east, whilst the internal authority of the Crown was consolidated. Some acquisitions were permanent additions to the *domaine*. Others were used to endow cadets like Charles of Valois and Louis of Evreux, the king's brothers, or his sons, returning to the Crown for the most part in the next few generations.

By his marriage (1284) to Jeanne, heiress to the counties of Champagne and Brie as well as to the small kingdom of Navarre, Philip obtained extensive properties in eastern France bordering on imperial territory. The acquisition of Valenciennes (1292), recognition of his suzerainty by the count of Bar (1301) and by the archbishop of Lyon for the Lyonnais (1307), together with a *paréage* with the bishop of Viviers in the same year, helped to bring the frontiers of the realm close to those formerly established by the treaty of Verdun (843), with the Meuse and Rhône marking the extent of royal control. By arranging the marriage of the future Philip V with the heiress of the county of Burgundy, he was even able to carry this influence across the Saône. Other *paréages* were made with the bishop of Mende for the Gevaudan, the bishop of Le Puy for Velay and the bishop of Cahors for Cahors (all in 1307).

There remained four great feudatories enjoying extensive independent authority: the count of Flanders and the dukes of Guyenne, Brittany and Burgundy. The seizure of Guyenne (1294) and Flanders (1301) proved shortlived triumphs. Philip soon had to release them to their former rulers, gaining only the small Pyrenean *vicomté* of Soule (1306) and the castellanies of Lille, Douai and Béthune (eventually exchanged for Orchies in 1322) as more permanent additions to royal properties. But in all four principalities local power was coming to be circumscribed by the Crown and its agents. For in developing a royal doctrine of sovereignty in conformity with Roman law precepts, the *Parlement* of Paris now exercised the right to hear appeals from provincial courts, the king issued *ordonnances* for general application and royal officials kept a close eye on local princely governments, frequently intervening. Ties between the Crown and leading vassals were also often given more definite form. In 1297, for instance, the duke of Brittany was made a peer of France, emphasizing his prestige but also his liege status and carefully defining the services he owed.

An authoritarian streak marked many royal actions, especially in attacks on vulnerable minorities like the Jews and Lombard financiers. It was most spectacularly displayed in the persecution of the Order of the Temple whose members were, with few exceptions, seized in a remarkable country-wide operation on 13 October 1307. It is perhaps not surprising that Philip's death was followed by a widespread provincial reaction against the centralizing tendencies that had so strongly marked his policies and calling into question the Capetian achievement.

M. Jones

The Spanish and Portuguese Reconquest During the Twelfth and Thirteenth Centuries

In the 1140s the Almoravids were overthrown by the heretical sect of the Almohads, who replaced them as rulers of the Maghreb and of Muslim Spain. During the interregnum, however, various towns were taken by the Christians: Lisbon (1147) by the newly independent kingdom of Portugal; Tortosa (1148) and Lérida (1149) by the newly united realm of Aragón-Catalonia; and Almería (1147), temporarily, by León. Moreover, the Spanish Muslims tried to create their own independent kingdom, based on Murcia and Valencia; but it was absorbed by the Almohad Empire in 1172. Thenceforward, Portugal, León, Castile (independent from 1157), Navarre and Aragon-Catalonia were frequently the targets of the Almohad caliph's holy wars and were relieved only by his equally frequent need to suppress Muslim dissidents in Tunis and Majorca. To resist his attacks, the Templars and Hospitallers were sent to garrison fortresses on the highways leading north, and when they failed to do so Iberian military orders were created for the same purpose. Thus the Order of Calatrava (founded 1158) defended the approaches to Toledo at Calatrava and Zorita; that of Santiago (founded 1170) defended Toledo at Uclés and Mora, Lisbon at Palmela, and the Seville-León road at Cáceres; and other highways were defended by the friars of Evora (later Avis) and Alcántara. In contrast, no help was received from foreign crusaders, except for those sailing to the Holy Land who helped capture Lisbon, Silves (1189) and Alcácer (1217).

At Alarcos (1195) Alfonso VIII of Castile (1158–1214) suffered a great defeat, but at Las Navas de Tolosa (1212) he avenged it, routing the caliph and breaking Almohad morale. After 1224, as the Almohad Empire disintegrated in a war of succession for the caliphate complicated by religious, racial and tribal hatreds, the Spanish Muslims once more fought to set up their own state, independent of both Christians and Africans, and achieved this, though under nominal Castilian suzerainty, in the kingdom of Granada (1232–1492). The Christians profited by these Muslim dissensions to conquer almost all southern Spain, with papal help and encouragement. Alfonso IX of León (1188–1230) took Cáceres (1229) and Badajoz (1230). His son, St Ferdinand III of Castile (1217–52), inherited León (1230) and used the combined Leonese-Castilian forces to conquer all the Guadalquivir valley, including Córdoba (1236), Jaén (1246) and Seville (1248), and to make the Muslim successor states of Murcia (1243), Granada (1246) and Niebla his vassals. Alfonso X, 'the Learned', St Ferdinand's son (1252–84), annexed Murcia and Niebla, expelled almost all Muslims from Castilian Andalusia and replaced them with Christian settlers. Thus, when the next dynasty ruling Morocco, the Banu Marin, invaded Spain (1275–1340), they were unable to reconquer any territory because they were opposed by a solid mass of Christian peasant warriors, who would defend Castile against any Muslim irredentism until the Catholic Monarchs, Ferdinand V and Isabella I, led them to the final conquest of the last Muslim stronghold in the Peninsula, Granada (1492).

Meanwhile in Portugal the Palmela peninsula and Alcácer (1217) were captured by the military orders and Rhenish crusaders; but then King Sancho II (1223–48) reconquered all the area to the south, down to the Algarve coast, leaving only Faro (1250) to be taken by his successor, Afonso III (1248–79). With the exception of certain cities on the south coast, the rest of the territory was handed over to the military orders and developed mainly for cattle-ranching.

To the east, James I of Aragon, 'the Conqueror' (1213–76), captured the Balearic Islands (1229–35) and the city (1238) and kingdom of Valencia. In the latter kingdom he expelled the Muslims only from the cities, where he replaced them with Christian settlers; but he left the Muslim peasants in the countryside almost

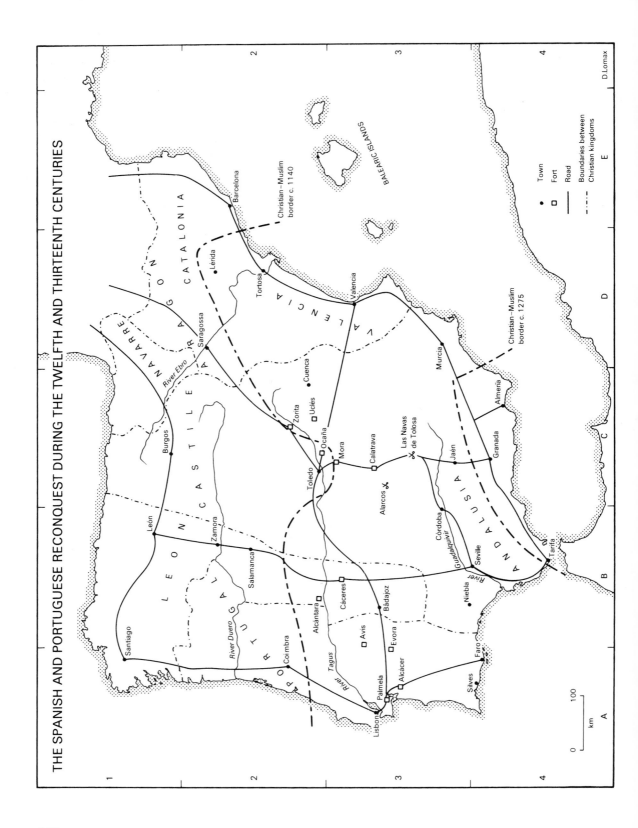

THE SPANISH AND PORTUGUESE RECONQUEST DURING THE TWELFTH AND THIRTEENTH CENTURIES

D.Lomax

Town
Fort
Road
Boundaries between
Christian kingdoms

untouched by Christian immigration, though reducing them to near-serfdom under a new landowning aristocracy from Aragon and Catalonia. Thus he strengthened the nobility throughout his realms; he inhibited Catalan migration, except to Murcia and the overseas islands which his descendants were to conquer; and he ensured that, whereas the peasantry enjoyed ever more favourable conditions in Castile, the reverse would be true in Catalonia.

D. Lomax

RELIGION

Latin Episcopal Sees at the End of the Thirteenth Century

By the end of the thirteenth century Latin Christianity had for the most part reached its furthest limits territorially until the beginning of European expansion overseas two centuries later. The extensive ecclesiastical provinces of central Europe bounded to the east and south upon territories that followed the Orthodox rite and to the north-east upon pagan Lithuania, which did not finally convert to Christianity until the late fourteenth century. The provinces of Gniezno, which corresponded to the Polish kingdom, and Esztergom and Kalocsa, which two were contained within the kingdom of Hungary, had all been established in the early years of the eleventh century, between 1000 and 1009, but the creation of new dioceses within them was not far advanced in the years since then. Kalocsa had recently acquired jurisdiction over Bosnia, following its absorption by Hungary in the course of a crusade against the heretics of the region. The great diocese of Prague, which together with Olmütz corresponded to the kingdom of Bohemia, was still dependent upon Mainz and was not to be erected into a separate province until 1344. In the north-east a number of episcopal sees had been set up in the first half of the thirteenth century to promote and accommodate missionary activity among the Baltic peoples, and these were consolidated into the province of Riga in 1253, with the exception of Reval, which was attached to the Scandinavian province of Lund. Within Scandinavia itself the process of conversion begun in the tenth century with the Danes had been carried forward and culminated in the erection of the three provinces of Lund in 1104, Trondhjem in 1152 and Uppsala in 1164, which three were coterminous with the boundaries of the kingdoms of Denmark, Norway and Sweden, respectively.

Across the North Sea in the British Isles a number of significant changes had been made since the eleventh century. In England the Norman conquerors respected the provincial boundaries but moved several sees from their Anglo-Saxon locations to different sites, centres of greater political and economic importance. Edward I's conquest of Wales in the late thirteenth century ended any lingering hopes that the Welsh bishops may have entertained of jurisdictional independence and effectively bound their sees to the province of Canterbury. In Scotland the diocesan confusion of the early Middle Ages was followed in the twelfth century by the foundation or re-foundation of firmly established sees, which thereafter enjoyed an uninterrupted succession of bishops until the abolition of the episcopate in the Reformation period. The efforts of successive twelfth-century archbishops of York to bring the Scottish church under their metropolitan jurisdiction failed everywhere but Whithorn. With the exception of Sodor and Man (the Isles) and Orkney, which formed a part of the province of Trondhjem, the remainder of the northern sees were made immediately subject to the jurisdiction of Rome and given the status of *filia specialis* to the apostolic see by Pope Celestine III in 1192, thus confirming what was in fact a political reality. Eventually, the sees of St Andrews and Glasgow were promoted to metropolitan dignity with their own suffragans in 1472 and 1492, respectively, and the sees of Whithorn, the Isles and Orkney were incorporated into the Scottish Church. Irish diocesan organization along the lines that obtained in the remainder of Latin Christendom was begun in the early twelfth century. The four provinces of Armagh, Cashel, Tuam and Dublin were established at the synod of Kells in 1152. This in fact took place a number of years before the English subjugation of Ireland, but Henry II was nevertheless able to play upon Roman suspicions of ecclesiastical irregularities there in order to obtain Pope Alexander III's approval for the conquest of the island.

Whereas provinces or dioceses in central Europe, Scandinavia and the British Isles either came to or had been specifically designed to correspond to political units, the ecclesiastical structure that had early evolved in the Frankish kingdoms and the Carolingian empire did not so readily reflect political boundaries. Thus, the eastern dioceses of the provinces of Reims and Lyon, both of which lay substantially within the kingdom of France, took in tracts of land across the border in the empire. Moreover, with a few exceptions such as the duchy of Normandy, which was coterminous with the province of Rouen, the boundaries of the various provinces and dioceses did not follow those of the greater fiefs. This could prove troublesome for both lay and ecclesiastical authorities. In particular, the long-standing aspirations of the Breton clergy to form a separate province under the metropolitan jurisdiction of Dol were not finally crushed until 1199, when Innocent III made decisive judgement in favour of the traditional claims of Tours. As in France, the pattern of provinces and dioceses in the kingdom of Germany was well established by the eleventh century. It was only in the eastern and south-eastern marches of the empire, in the provinces of Bremen-Hamburg, Magdeburg, and Salzburg, that new sees were erected in the eleventh, twelfth and thirteenth centuries. Thus, to the province of Salzburg, which at its establishment in 798 had only the three suffragans of Freising, Passau and Regensburg, and soon afterwards Brixen, were added the sees of Gurk in 1072, Chiemsee in 1215, Seckau in 1218 and Lavant in 1228. Few major changes took place in France, the empire or the central European kingdoms in the following centuries. A few new sees were raised in the eastern provinces. As a measure to combat heresy the diocese of Pamiers was erected in 1295, and in 1317 it and six other new sees were removed from the southern French province of Narbonne and assigned to the new metropolinate of Toulouse, while a few other sees were at the same time established in the provinces of Bourges, Bordeaux and Narbonne itself. In 1475, another new, small province, that of Avignon, was carved out of Arles.

It was in the Mediterranean that the most significant institutional developments since the early eleventh century took place. The gradual expulsion of the Saracens there opened up extensive territories in which to establish provinces and dioceses. In the Iberian peninsula, the aim was largely one of the re-foundation of episcopal sees at their ancient sites, and the reconquest that enabled this was nearly complete by the end of the thirteenth century, with only the Moorish kingdom of Granada remaining in the extreme south. The latter was eventually conquered and created into a province in 1492, at which time Valencia was also promoted to metropolitan status. In 1318 the province of Saragossa was established with jurisdiction over sees that formerly belonged to Tarragona. The Great Schism brought about the contraction of the province of Braga and the establishment of that of Lisbon, both within the confines of the kingdom of Portugal, which supported the Urbanist line of popes in opposition to neighbouring Castile. Likewise, the Saracen-dominated Sardinia and Corsica were conquered by the Genoese and Pisans and Sicily by the Normans in the eleventh century, which afforded the opportunity in each island for a new ecclesiastical ordering. Rival Pisa and Genoa themselves had each been promoted to metropolitans in 1092 and 1133, respectively. Further subdivision in northern Italy took place with the erection of the provinces of Florence in 1420 and Siena in 1459. The provincial fragmentation of southern Italy continued with the creation in the eleventh century of Rossano, Siponto, later translated to Manfredonia, Acerenza, Cosenza, Trani and Conza. Few changes took place in Italy in the later Middle Ages beyond the suppression or union of a number of smaller, poorer sees.

R.K. Rose

111

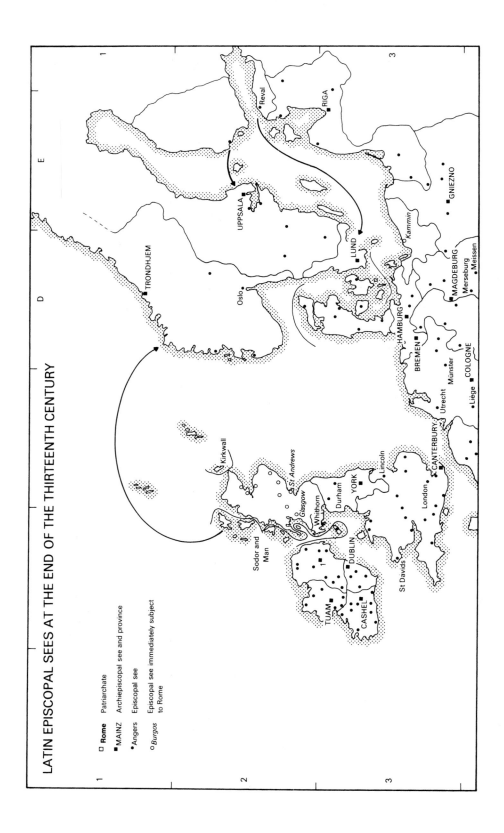

LATIN EPISCOPAL SEES AT THE END OF THE THIRTEENTH CENTURY

□ **Rome**   Patriarchate

■ **MAINZ**   Archiepiscopal see and province

● Angers   Episcopal see

○ *Burgos*   Episcopal see immediately subject
            to Rome

TRONDHJEM

Oslo

UPPSALA

Reval

RIGA

LUND

Kammin

GNIEZNO

MAGDEBURG
Merseburg
● Meissen

HAMBURG

BREMEN

Munster

Utrecht

COLOGNE

Liège

Kirkwall

Sodor and
Man

Glasgow

Whithorn

St Andrews

Durham

YORK

Lincoln

London

CANTERBURY

St Davids

DUBLIN

TUAM

CASHEL

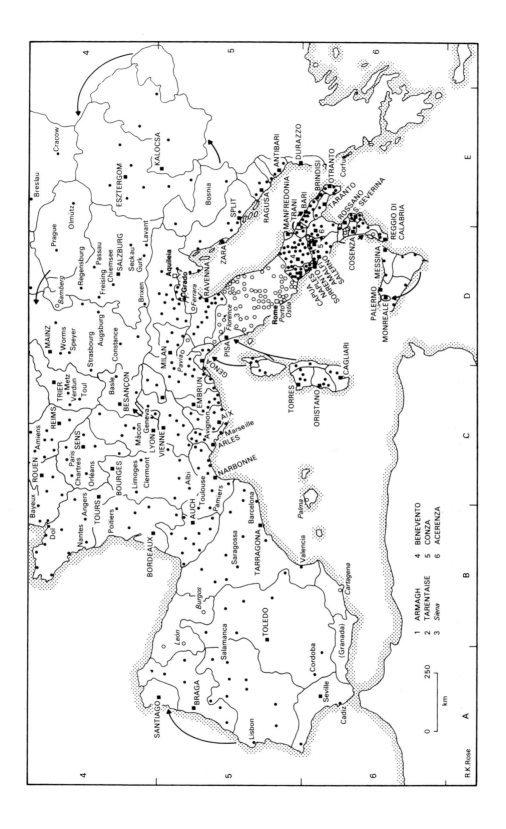

Cistercians, Premonstratensians and Others

The monastery of Cîteaux was founded in Burgundy in 1098 by Robert of Molesme and twenty-one companions. Robert had been abbot of more than one house and was the founder of Molesme, itself the head of a prosperous congregation; but he and his companions now wished to attempt to keep the *Rule* of St Benedict even better than they had previously done. Subsequent Cistercian writings attempted to show that Cîteaux was founded in reaction to the decadence of conventional Benedictinism, typified by Cluny; but although it is popularly supposed that the Cistercians attempted to follow the Benedictine *Rule* without the additional customs which had been developed in the tenth and eleventh centuries, it is now clear that they soon developed customs of their own which were partly based upon those of Cluny. By 1119, the Cistercian way of life had attracted new recruits, several new houses had been founded, and Pope Calixtus II approved legislation for an order as a whole. The Cistercians' originality lay in their rejection of tithes as a fitting source of monastic income; in their insistence on supporting themselves by agriculture and the labour of their own hands, and on only accepting donations of remote and unwanted lands to do this; and in their development of the use of lay brothers – already used to some extent in other new congregations – to help them.

The order was governed on federal lines, by visitation and annual assemblies of abbots in a General Chapter, set out in several versions of a document known as the *Charter of Charity*. The Cistercian habit was undyed (in contrast to the black robes of the earlier Benedictines) and their churches plain and unadorned with, eventually, their own architectural style – in the time of St Bernard of Clairvaux (d. 1153), the famous Cistercian leader, mystic and theologian, they generally had a square and plain east end in contrast to the semicircular ambulatory with radiating chapels found in many other churches. The design of Cistercian monastic buildings became standardized and is remarkable both for the use of diverted streams for sanitation and mills, and also for the strict separation of the quarters of the monks and the lay brothers. The Cistercian use of lay brothers to till marginal land put them in the forefront of the process of land clearing and reclamation, particularly on the eastwards-expanding German frontier and in northern England. By the end of 1151, there were over 330 Cistercian houses; the next century saw a steady but less remarkable expansion. The map shows some of the most important houses, or the earliest in their region, or those which had many 'daughter' houses founded from them.

The Premonstratensians, founded in 1120 by the famous preacher Norbert of Xanten (d. 1134), were an order of regular canons who followed not only the *Rule* of St Augustine, which became the most popular rule for canons in the twelfth century, but also customs based partly on those of Cluny and an organization which derived from the Cistercian *Charter of Charity*. They too adopted undyed habits and used lay brothers to help cultivate marginal lands, and they expanded into the border lands of Germany, although the conversion of the chapter of Magdeburg also meant a succession of Premonstratensian bishops there and elsewhere in Germany. Their numbers and expansion were never as dramatic as those of the Cistercians, but they were known throughout Europe. Other important twelfth-century groupings included that of Savigny which joined Cîteaux in 1147; the Order of Sempringham, a small English order founded in the 1130s by Gilbert for women and canons; and the famous house of Fontevrault, founded early in the century by Robert of Arbrissel, also for women. The Order of Grandmont, which grew up after the death in 1125 of its 'founder', Stephen of Muret, expanded considerably, but almost exclusively in France, in the twelfth century. It evolved its own *Rule* which stressed the need for communal poverty.

M. Dunn

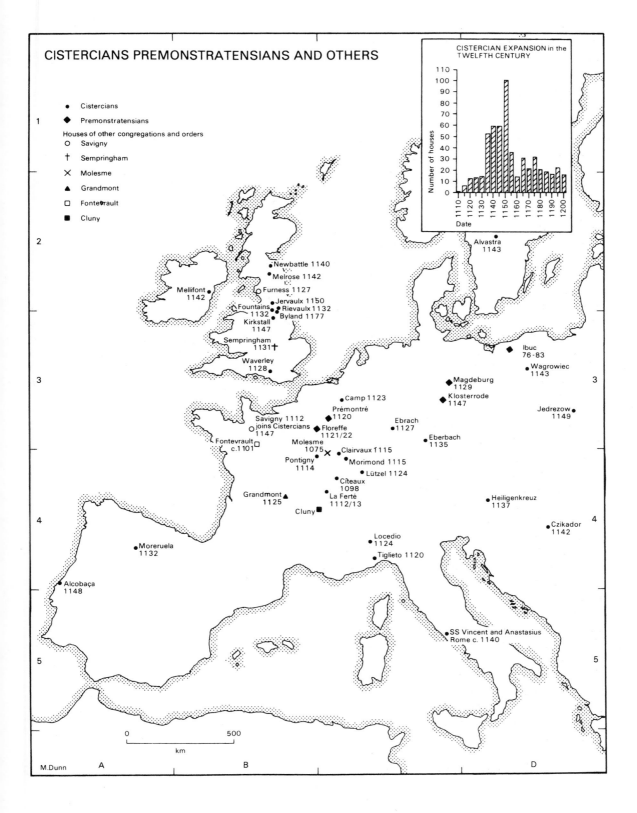

CISTERCIANS PREMONSTRATENSIANS AND OTHERS

Cistercians
Premonstratensians
Houses of other congregations and orders
Savigny
Sempringham
Molesme
Grandmont
Fontevrault
Cluny

CISTERCIAN EXPANSION in the TWELFTH CENTURY

Number of houses

Date

Alvastra 1143

Newbattle 1140
Melrose 1142
Furness 1127
Jervaulx 1150
Mellifont 1142
Fountains 1132
Rievaulx 1132
Byland 1177
Kirkstall 1147
Sempringham 1131
Waverley 1128

Ibuc 76-83
Wagrowiec 1143
Magdeburg 1129
Klosterrode 1147
Jedrezow 1149

Camp 1123
Prémontré 1120
Savigny 1112 joins Cistercians 1147
Floreffe 1121/22
Ebrach 1127
Eberbach 1135
Fontevrault c.1101
Molesme 1075
Clairvaux 1115
Pontigny 1114
Morimond 1115
Lützel 1124
Cîteaux 1098
Grandmont 1125
La Ferté 1112/13
Cluny
Heiligenkreuz 1137
Czikador 1142

Moreruela 1132

Locedio 1124
Tiglieto 1120

Alcobaça 1148

SS Vincent and Anastasius Rome c. 1140

0   500
km

M.Dunn   A   B   D

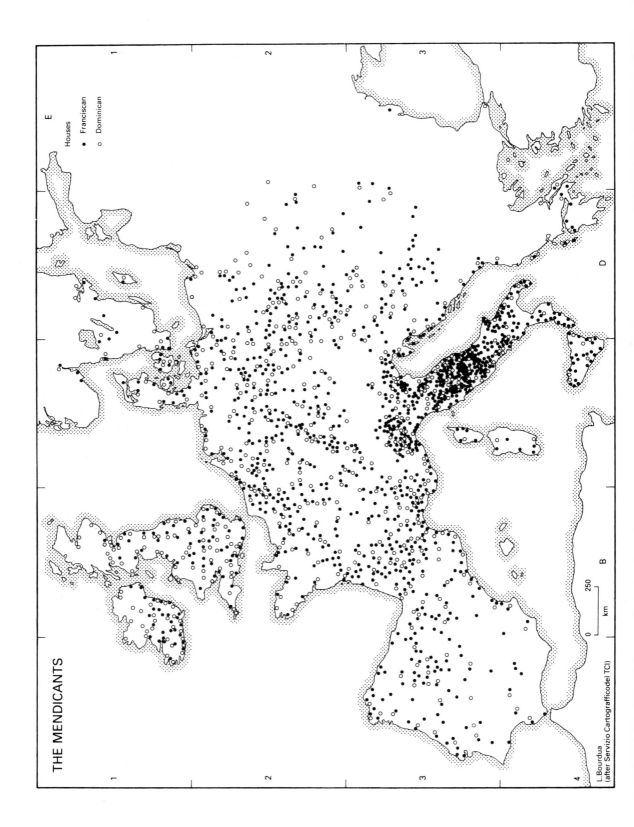

THE MENDICANTS

Houses
● Franciscan
○ Dominican

L. Bourdua
(after Servizio Cartografico del TCI)

0   250
km

Mendicants

The name mendicant (from *mendicare*, to beg) is applied to religious men and women who have taken vows of common renunciation of goods, chastity and obedience. The earliest orders were the Franciscans (founded by Francis of Assisi (*c.* 1172–1226) and approved in 1209), and the Dominicans (founded by Dominic of Caleruega (1170–1221) and approved in 1216). By the mid-century they also included the Carmelites who had originated from groups of hermits (Order of Our Lady of Mount Carmel) living in Palestine on the slopes of Mount Carmel, who migrated to Sicily, Italy, France and England in the 1230s. In 1247 their General, Simon Stock, approached Innocent IV for a modification in the *Rule* which allowed them to settle anywhere (including the towns), to lead a cenobitical style of life and adopt an active pastoral role in the towns. Similarly, groups of hermits in Lombardy, Tuscany and Romagna were united in 1256 with the Bonites, a congregation of penitents, who lived a life of preaching and mendicancy in north Italy. They also ministered to the townspeople of Europe (primarily in Italy but with priories in Spain, Germany, France, England and Scotland) and were renamed the Order of Friars Hermits of St Augustine.

The mendicant orders aimed to reintroduce the apostolic life of the gospels (or imitation of Jesus and the first apostles) into the growing towns of thirteenth-century Europe. Poverty, voluntarily embraced, was one intention, as was the idea of preaching to the unconverted or those who had strayed. The movement first emerged in Italy but quickly spread throughout Christendom. The mendicants were generally welcomed with enthusiasm but at times faced opposition from secular clergy because of the threat of competition, particularly after 1267 when Clement IV renewed their privilege of preaching, hearing confession and accepting burials without having to obtain diocesan consent. However, the papacy, usually supportive, sought to resolve such conflicts with bulls such as *Super cathedram* issued in 1300, which ordered that licenses must first be obtained before undertaking such activities.

The friars settled initially outside the walls of a city and moved into the centre from the 1230s onwards, into pre-existing sites, often derelict, which had been lent by a sympathetic local bishop, an individual or a city corporation. The first purposely built mendicant churches were tiny and simple and were quickly outgrown, thus necessitating the rebuilding which was executed in a new architectural style which recalled Cistercian models. This plan was ideally suited to preaching, with a spacious nave (single or aisled), optional transept and terminating in an apse or apsidal chapels at the east end.

Apart from their contribution to preaching, sermon-making and education, their artistic contribution was immense – each mendicant order attracted extensive patronage from families and confraternities which commissioned works of art in return for masses and/or burial. The Dominicans and Franciscans, in particular, had a considerable impact upon all subsequent forms of religious life including the Tertiaries. These, the Third Order, were groups of lay people who led a life of piety and charity and continued to live in their homes, married or not, and attached themselves to the mendicants for liturgical services.

L. Bourdua

Béguines and Beghards

Pious women known as Béguines first appeared in the Low Countries and the Rhineland in the early thirteenth century as part of a Europe-wide movement of popular religious revival. They grew rapidly in numbers and spread to northern France, Switzerland and central Europe. Their

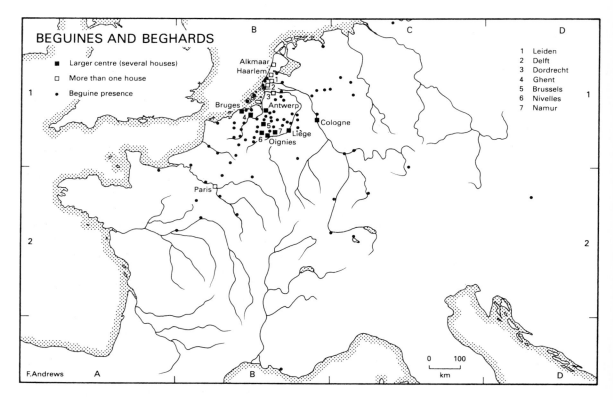

BEGUINES AND BEGHARDS

■ Larger centre (several houses)
□ More than one house
• Beguine presence

1 Leiden
2 Delft
3 Dordrecht
4 Ghent
5 Brussels
6 Nivelles
7 Namur

Alkmaar
Haarlem
Bruges
Antwerp
Cologne
Liège
Oignies
Paris

F. Andrews

0   100
km

male counterparts, the Beghards, were much fewer in number and followed rather than led the women. The origin of the names is unknown but was possibly associated with the Albigensian heresy. They were certainly intended to discredit women and men who lived a life of pious devotion, but followed no approved rule and took no irrevocable vows. Recruits included both members of the newly affluent bourgeoisie and poorer women who sometimes lived in Béguine hospitals. They are often elusive in the written records and the style of their communities was subject to regional variation, including some living alone or in small groups in a house or convent, while others inhabited a large Béguinage within an enclosure, or occasionally in Béguine parishes. Béguines and Beghards adopted voluntary poverty, renounced worldly goods, undertook to observe celibacy while in their communities and lived by the labour of their hands, often working in hospitals or cloth manufacture and occasionally resorting to begging. Their spirituality was frequently mystical, individ-

ualistic and marked by visionary experiences, and several were accomplished writers in the vernacular. Initially they were admired and supported by prominent clerics such as Jacques de Vitry (d. 1240) and Robert Grosseteste (d. 1253), and attracted lay patronage, for example from Louis IX of France, who established a Béguinage in Paris in 1264. As lay women living without a religious order, the Béguines also attracted hostility from some clerics who suspected them of heresy. Thus in 1310 Marguerite Porète was condemned and burnt with her mystical work, *The Mirror of Simple Souls*. The Council of Vienne in 1311–12 issued a broad condemnation of Béguines who 'lose themselves in foolish speculations ... promise obedience to nobody ... nor profess any approved rule'. 'Faithful' women who wished to live 'as the lord shall inspire them' were not condemned, but the decree forced numerous Béguines into more formal communities: many attached themselves to the houses of friars.

F. Andrews

The Papacy and the Conciliar Fathers of 1215

In his letter convoking the Fourth Lateran Council of 1215, *Vineam Domini Sabaoth* (19 April 1213), Pope Innocent III sought the widest possible attendance of Church dignitaries, including, for the first time, representatives from the cathedral chapters. Abbots of the monastic orders and lay envoys of the secular powers were also urged to attend. Thus the primacy of Rome as the centre of papal Christendom was to be symbolized by an ecclesiastical parliament on an unprecedented scale.

Besides the crucial issues of Church reform, the struggle against heresy, and the forthcoming crusade, the conciliar agenda also included such matters of ecclesiastical politics as the outcome of the German imperial election, the disputed primacy of the Spanish Church and the suspension of the Archbishop of Canterbury. A further vexed question involved the rights of the Count of Toulouse in the territories won by the Albigensian Crusade. All of these items of Church business influenced the geographical composition of the Fourth Lateran Council.

The gathering at Rome in November 1215 dwarfed previous Western ecumenical councils. Over 1,200 churchmen are known to have been present. Scots and Irishmen mingled with Hungarians, Poles and Sicilians. But the supposed ecumenicism and cosmopolitanism of the Fourth Lateran requires some qualification. The oriental Christians absented themselves, and the prelates from the Christian East were overwhelmingly transplanted Latins. The large delegations from Spain, Provence and England were in part motivated by specific regional concerns. Above all, the geographical distribution of the conciliar fathers reveals a Mediterranean and especially Italian numerical predominance at the Council, although Italian loyalties were fragmented and localized. The Scandinavian countries largely ignored the Council, and the politically divided German episcopate was certainly under-represented. Not all of the bishoprics immediately subject to Rome were actually located in Italy, but the concentration of Italian churchmen at the Fourth Lateran Council perhaps helps to explain the significance of the papacy's Italian policy, both in the papal states and in southern Italy, in the course of the thirteenth century.

G. Dickson

Shrines and Revivals: Popular Christianity, *c.* 1200–*c.* 1300

Pilgrimage to the holy shrines of Latin Christendom was a striking feature of popular religious experience from the early Middle Ages to the eve of the Reformation. Pilgrimages were undertaken to seek a miraculous cure at the tomb of a saint; to perform the penitential rite of the ascetic journey; and to receive the spiritual reward of an indulgence, such as the crusader's plenary indulgence for the Jerusalem pilgrimage. During the first of the medieval Jubilees – the remarkable Holy Year of 1300, the year in which Dante's celebrated *Divine Comedy* is set – Pope Boniface VIII granted a plenary indulgence to pilgrims who visited designated Roman stational churches. In addition to religious motives for pilgrimage, more secular cravings for travel, adventure or escape also played an important part in directing the footsteps of medieval proto-tourists.

Punitive pilgrimages were imposed by some secular powers (the Flemish towns, for instance), but they were especially utilized by the inquisitorial courts of Carcassonne, Albi and Toulouse as penances for the former heretics of Languedoc.

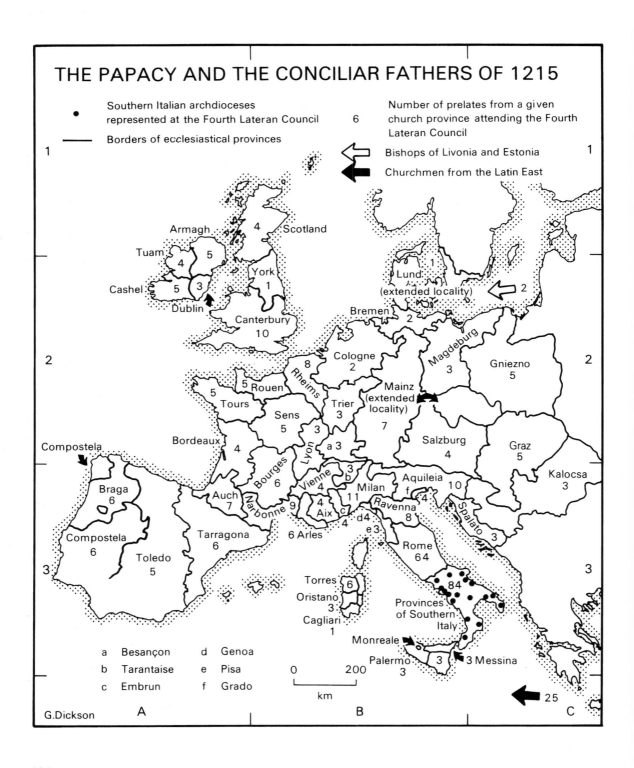

THE PAPACY AND THE CONCILIAR FATHERS OF 1215

•   Southern Italian archdioceses represented at the Fourth Lateran Council

—   Borders of ecclesiastical provinces

6   Number of prelates from a given church province attending the Fourth Lateran Council

⇦   Bishops of Livonia and Estonia

⬅   Churchmen from the Latin East

Armagh

Scotland 4

Tuam 5

4

Cashel 5   3

Dublin

York 1

Canterbury 10

Lund (extended locality) 1

Bremen 2

Magdeburg 3

Gniezno 5

Cologne 2

Rouen 5   5

Rheims 8

Tours 5

Sens 5

Trier 3

Mainz (extended locality) 7

Salzburg 4

Graz 5

Bordeaux

Bourges 6

Lyon 3

a 3

Vienne 4

b 3

Milan 11

Aquileia f 4 10

Kalocsa 3

Compostela

Braga 6

Auch 7

Narbonne 9

Aix c 4

d 4

Ravenna 8

Spalato 3

Compostela 6

Toledo 5

Tarragona 6

6 Arles

e 3

Rome 64

Torres 6

Oristano 3

Cagliari 1

Provinces of Southern Italy 84

Monreale

Palermo 3

3   3 Messina

a	Besançon	d	Genoa
b	Tarantaise	e	Pisa
c	Embrun	f	Grado

0   200

km

⬅ 25

G.Dickson

A   B   C

1   2   3

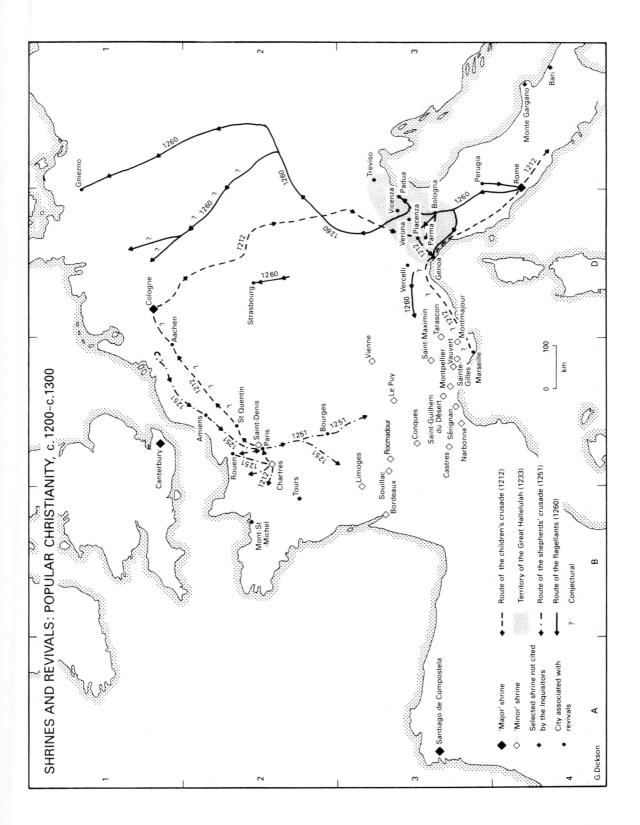

SHRINES AND REVIVALS: POPULAR CHRISTIANITY, c. 1200–c.1300

Route of the children's crusade (1212)

Territory of the Great Hallelulah (1233)

Route of the shepherds' crusade (1251)

Route of the flagellants (1260)

Conjectural

'Major' shrine

'Minor' shrine

Selected shrine not cited by the Inquisitors

City associated with revivals

G. Dickson

These Inquisitors drew upon an old distinction between 'major' and 'minor' pilgrimage sites. Here the shrines where the 'major' saints were venerated – St James of Compostela, Sts Peter and Paul of Rome, the Three-Kings of Cologne, and St Thomas Becket of Canterbury – provide us with the four outstanding 'high places' of thirteenth-century Christendom. On the other hand, the choice of 'minor' pilgrimage sites is not representative of the great number of regional and local shrines dotted throughout Europe, but instead reflects the southern French perspective of the Inquisitors and the locality of the penitent ex-heretics. A few of the most important shrines not mentioned by the Inquisitors have been marked on the map. A complete map of Christian holy places, however, listing all the miraculous images, translated Eastern saints' relics, pieces of the True Cross, venerated hosts and so on – could it be drawn – would be so detailed as to be virtually unreadable. Indeed, by the late Middle Ages, most localities in Christendom could lay claim to some saint or sacred object worthy of a pilgrim's devotion.

Like pilgrimage, many thirteenth-century revivals had an itinerant (or at least an ambulatory, processional) character. Like pilgrimage, too, revivals were instances of public, collective and popular religious behaviour. They began with a religious crowd, developed into a movement, and sometimes, as with the flagellants of 1260, created durable religious institutions. The flagellant movement of 1260 began in Perugia and completed its transalpine trek in 1261 in northern Poland. It was fundamentally penitential, prophetic and Christocentric in nature, although strongly influenced by its crusading context. In contrast, the children's crusade of 1212 and the shepherds' crusade of 1251 were both popular, i.e. unofficial, crusades: the papacy did not authorize them. The children's crusade of 1212 began with processions, which probably were held at Chartres, to obtain divine support for the threatened Spanish Church. Ultimately, the majority of its adherents settled in Mediterranean cities. The enthusiasts of the shepherds' crusade of 1251 proclaimed their intent to assist King Louis IX of France against the Saracens of Egypt. This movement, however, turned violent, anti-semitic and anti-clerical, and was put down by force. All three of these popular enthusiasms gained recruits along the line of march. These recruits were usually peasants, but also included townspeople, who joined when the enthusiasts passed through cities. The Lombard 'Great Hallelujah' of 1233 was itinerant only in respect to the huge crowds who gathered to hear the sermons of miracle-working friars. It was a revival promoted by Franciscan and Dominican friars, who emphasized preaching. It was a notable medieval peace movement.

Just as with both pilgrimages and crusades, such medieval revivals show how religious enthusiasm could mobilize large groups of ordinary believers and influence their behaviour in many ways.

G. Dickson

Heresy, the Albigensian Crusade and the Inquisition, *c.* 1200–*c.* 1240

Individuals of questionable orthodoxy as well as heretical sects could be found scattered throughout much of early thirteenth-century Europe. Paris in 1210 saw the burning of the pantheistic Amalricians, while Strasbourg a year or two later witnessed a greater conflagration, perhaps of the obscure Ortliebians. When the Stedinger peasants of northern Germany refused to pay their tithes to the archbishop of Bremen, they were declared heretical; Pope Gregory IX, who believed they were Luciferians, authorized the crusade which crushed them in 1234. Such pockets of heresy, however, did not constitute a major threat to the Church.

What worried a pope like Innocent III (1198–1216) was the danger of large concentrations

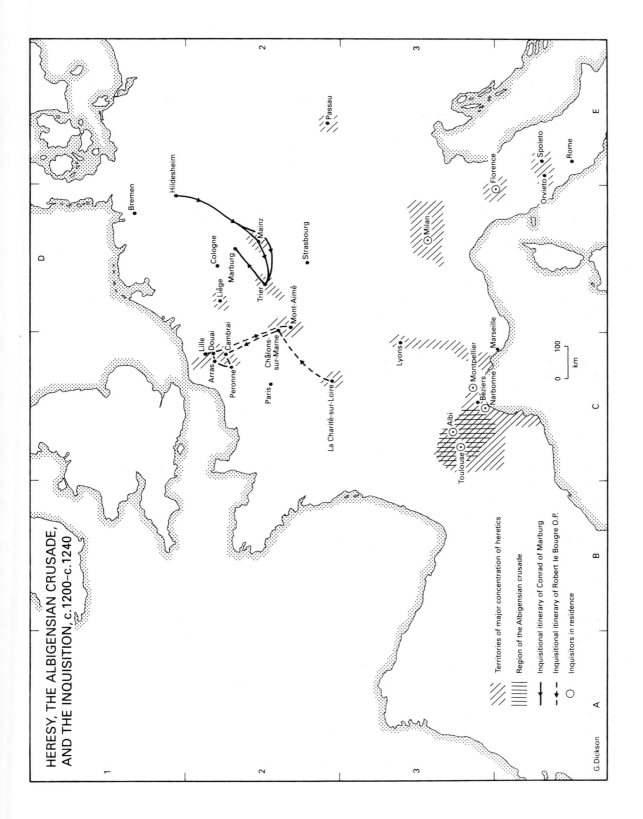

HERESY, THE ALBIGENSIAN CRUSADE,
AND THE INQUISITION, c.1200–c.1240

Territories of major concentration of heretics

Region of the Albigensian crusade

Inquisitional itinerary of Conrad of Marburg

Inquisitional itinerary of Robert le Bougre O.P.

Inquisitors in residence

G.Dickson

Bremen

Hildesheim

Cologne
Liège
Marburg
Trier
Mainz
Strasbourg
Mont-Aimé

Lille
Douai
Arras
Cambrai
Peronne
Châlons-sur-Marne
Paris

La Charité-sur-Loire

Lyons
Montpellier
Narbonne
Marseille
Béziers
Albi
Toulouse

Milan

Florence
Orvieto
Spoleto
Rome

Passau

0   100
km

of religious deviants existing in the midst of Catholic communities, while remaining relatively free to evangelize. The Cathars or Albigensians were dualists who had their own Church. Their holy men and women – known as the perfect – were actively proselytizing from the Pyrenees to the Papal State, almost to the outskirts of Rome. Also, the Poor Men of Lyon or Waldensians, laymen whose main heresy was to insist upon preaching the Gospel despite ecclesiastical prohibition, were gaining adherents in southern France and in the Lombard cities. The Waldensians and Cathars were opposed to one another, but they intermingled in southern Europe and, to an extent, in northern Europe as well. There were other heresies; but these were the most formidable. The last Cathar perfect was burnt as late as 1321. The Waldensians of the Piedmont survived until the Reformation.

The stronghold of the Cathars or Albigensians was in the lands of the count of Toulouse in south-west France. Here, because the heretics were so deeply entrenched in Languedocian society, the Church could not persuade or compel the secular nobility to suppress them on its behalf. Nor was the king of France, Philip II Augustus, willing to act. After the murder of his legate Peter of Castelnau in 1208, Pope Innocent III launched a crusade against the heretics and their supporters – a holy war for peace (against the mercenary *routiers*) and for the faith (against the heretical Albigensians). It was led by papal legates like the Cistercian abbot Arnold Aimery and the northern French baron Simon de Montfort. Towns were sacked, Cathar *perfecti* were massacred and lands were confiscated by the northerners. The crusade continued intermittently through the first half of the thirteenth century, although Catharism was by no means eradicated. In 1271, Languedoc passed to the French Crown. The Capetians were the crusade's ultimate beneficiaries.

While the Albigensian crusade was still in progress in 1212, Innocent III threatened the Milanese with a crusading army if they failed to repress the heretics in their city. Yet the crusade was a blunt instrument. The Inquisition was potentially more selective. Traditionally, it was the bishop's job to detect heretics within his diocese. Now specialists were needed. The Franciscan and especially the Dominican friars brought theological expertise and religious zeal to their task. The career of the Dominican Inquisitor, Robert le Bougre, active between *c.* 1232 and 1239, culminated in that year with the mass *auto da fé* of Cathars at Mont-Aimé in Champagne. The secular priest Conrad of Marburg was similarly relentless in his pursuit of Waldensians, Cathars and (alleged) Luciferians in the mid-Rhineland from *c.* 1227 until his assassination in 1233. The pope who had commissioned them both, Gregory IX (1227–41), established the Inquisition in Languedoc in 1233. Inquisitors were then based at Toulouse, Montpellier and Albi; at Narbonne there was already a Dominican Inquisitor, an appointee of the archbishop. Fixed inquisitorial tribunals in Italy also date from Gregory IX's pontificate; they become more plentiful thereafter. Particularly effective was the Inquisition of the dead. For a deceased testator to be found guilty of heresy meant that his heirs forfeited their estate. Property proved a powerful stimulus for orthodoxy.

G. Dickson

GOVERNMENT, SOCIETY AND ECONOMY

Provisioning War in the Twelfth Century

In the twelfth and thirteenth centuries some western European monarchies began to produce documents which recorded their activities in a more sustained and detailed way than before. From this period it is thus possible to reconstruct the practical workings of government. One of the best-documented of medieval governments was that of England, and the map shows the kind of detailed information that can be drawn from twelfth-century English records. In this case the information is drawn from the Pipe Rolls. These were accounts of the sums rendered by the sheriffs and other royal officials to the exchequer, the central financial institution. When the king took goods from the localities directly, these were credited to the sheriff's account. Plotted on the map is the amount of foodstuffs and materials provided for Henry II's expedition to Ireland in 1171–2.

This expedition, which brought an English king to Ireland for the first time, had been made necessary by developments in Ireland over the previous two years. In 1169 Norman-Welsh adventurers had landed in Leinster, initially serving as auxiliaries in the never-ending warfare of the Irish kings. In 1171, however, their leader, Richard fitz Gilbert ('Strongbow') had taken over Leinster itself. Henry II had no desire to see a new, independent principality so close to his own territories, especially one ruled by a politically suspect member of his own aristocracy. His expedition of 1171–2 secured both Strongbow's submission and the recognition of his overlordship by the Irish kings. It was the beginning of a political connection which survives, in part, to this day.

The king maintained an army of about 10,000 men in Ireland for six months. This included a prolonged stay during the winter months in Dublin, where a timber palace was constructed.

An army of this size, especially if sedentary for any length of time, could not live off the land and hence a great quantity of provisions had to be collected in England and transported to Ireland. The map shows how a successful twelfth-century monarchy could mobilize large-scale resources for warfare. Thousands of quarters of grain and hundreds of hogs were sent from virtually every part of the kingdom. Beans and cheese (not plotted) were collected. Ships' gear, such as canvas, was procured and seamen were levied from a dozen counties. Axes, shovels and nails were also dispatched – 60,000 nails and a thousand shovels came from the Forest of Dean, England's most important iron-working centre.

Bristol and Chester were the most important shipping points, but oats and other products of the northern counties were sent directly from Cumbrian ports. Naturally more food and material was raised in the counties nearer to Ireland, but the existence of water routes meant that even the eastern counties could contribute: grain was sent by river from Cambridge to Lynn, for example. The initial contact between Normans and Irish had been a matter of ambitious frontiersmen on a freelance expedition. From 1171 the English state was involved and hence the resources of a much larger area could be applied to support military or political involvement in Ireland. The food chain was extended; the acorns of Norfolk were being excreted in Dublin.

Other monarchs of this period also launched large-scale military expeditions. The kings of Germany, for example, repeatedly took armies of thousands southwards across the Alps. They left, however, no complex bureaucratic record of the provisioning of these troops. England is unique in the scope of its records rather than the scale of its undertakings. The existence of these

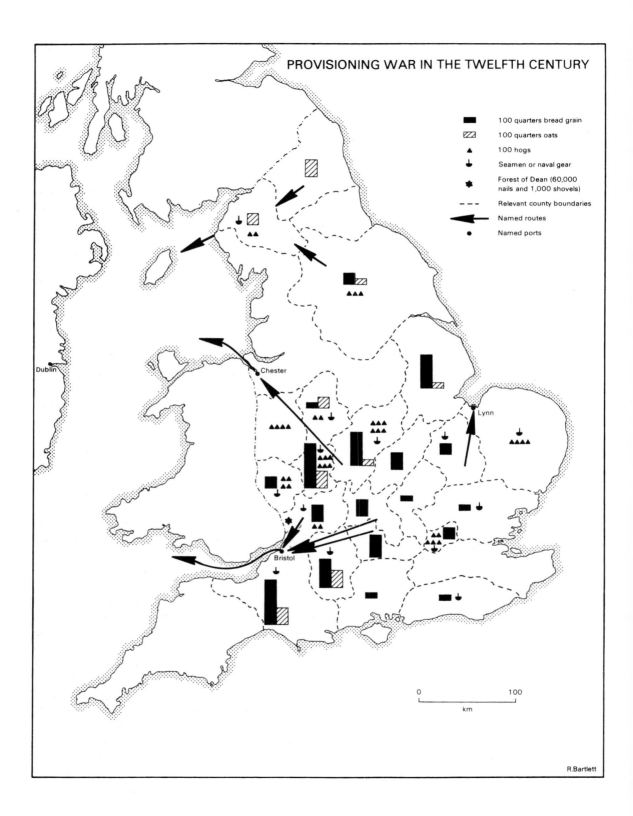

PROVISIONING WAR IN THE TWELFTH CENTURY

■ 100 quarters bread grain
▨ 100 quarters oats
▲ 100 hogs
⚓ Seamen or naval gear
✿ Forest of Dean (60,000 nails and 1,000 shovels)
- - - Relevant county boundaries
◀━ Named routes
● Named ports

Dublin

Chester

Lynn

Bristol

0   100
      km

R.Bartlett

records, however, enables us to anatomize some of these undertakings and produce a map illustrating a sophisticated twelfth-century state at work in one of its most characteristic activities.

R. Bartlett

The Rise of Representative Assemblies

Theories of 'representation' and 'consultation' appear in European writings from about 1000 together with the belief that consultation in government was natural and desirable. Early consultative assemblies were essentially enlarged royal councils, where matters touching the kingdom in general could be discussed. These were ill-defined bodies where membership was non-elective and 'representative' only in so far as the magnates who attended them were deemed to act on behalf of the wider populace. There was no suggestion that 'representation' derived from election, nor that it stemmed from any association with particular areas or social groups. In the late twelfth and thirteenth centuries the shifting burden of government, particularly of taxation, produced significant change in the range of consultation. Growing royal requirement for revenue to meet the costs of increasingly sophisticated government stimulated demands for wider consultation before the granting of taxation. Behind such developments lay recognition of the wealth and rising economic power of classes such as the townsmen and the royal desire to tap that wealth as a source of revenue.

First evidence for a widening of representation in royal councils to include non-aristocratic or clerical members comes from Spain. There the process arose from Alfonso IX of Leon's search for broad popular support to strengthen his hold on his throne. To an extraordinary meeting of his curia at León in 1188 he summoned town representatives as well as the bishops and magnates, initiating the type of wide-based assemblies referred to as '*cortes*'. This innovation recognized the power which the wealth of the towns commanded and which the king sought to harness to his own needs, fiscal and political. In subsequent *cortes*, as at Benavente in 1202 or León in 1208, townsmen were summoned specifically to assent to a tax. Similar developments in Sicily under Frederick II were also tied to the levying of taxes, such as that granted in 1231 by a wide-based council, and the need to secure broad-based support to facilitate collection. Summonses to townsmen were again issued in 1232 and the practice had become so deep-rooted that in 1267 Pope Clement IV instructed Charles of Anjou to consult his subjects before raising a tax. The military and financial demands of the struggle with Frederick II on the papal lands led there to increased consultation over the issue of taxation, with negotiations in assemblies coming to be dominated by the townsmen. Within the empire proper, royal power was considerably more circumscribed after the upheavals of the reign of Frederick II, but in the later thirteenth century under Rudolf I, regnal assemblies composed of men from all areas and social ranks were used as a means of re-establishing royal power through collective endorsement of legislation on a national level.

Moves towards increased representation in England arose largely from conflict between crown and baronage in the early thirteenth century. At the root of the conflict were basic economic issues, taxation and lack of consultation, and in 1215 clauses of Magna Carta were devoted to resolving such matters. In England, however, although the principle of no taxation without the 'common counsel' of the realm was established, the scope of consultation was restricted at first to the nobility, and only from the late 1260s were the boroughs represented in parliament on a regular basis. Increased representation in France arose from a different response to the same issue of taxation. There the king was for long able to levy taxes with the assent of his usual restricted circle of advisers,

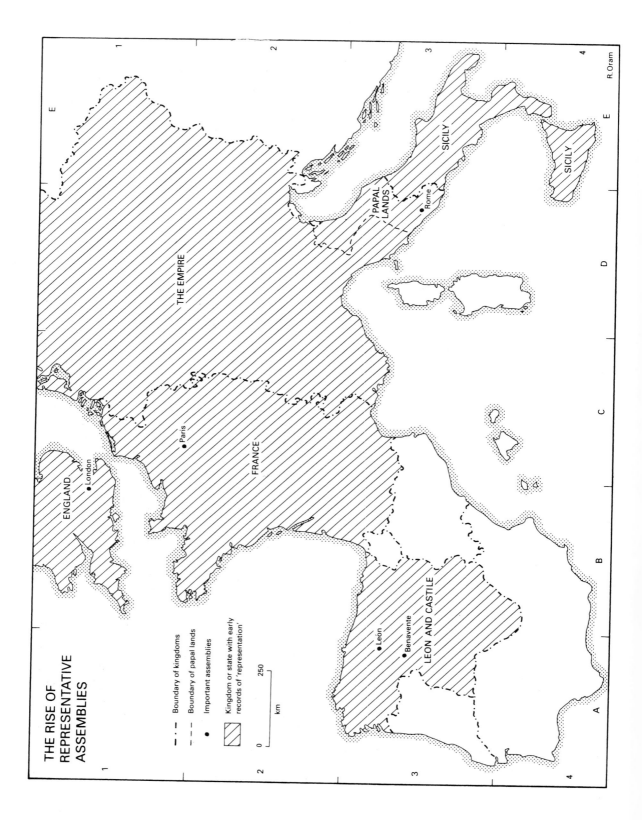

THE RISE OF
REPRESENTATIVE
ASSEMBLIES

Boundary of kingdoms
Boundary of papal lands
Important assemblies
Kingdom or state with early
records of 'representation'

km
0   250

ENGLAND
London

FRANCE
Paris

THE EMPIRE

PAPAL
LANDS
Rome

SICILY
SICILY

LEON AND CASTILE
León
Benavente

R. Oram

128

without any attempt to widen membership or make it more representative. Instead, there were moves towards negotiations between separate social groups and royal officials. In the thirteenth century towns negotiating payment of taxation sent representatives to regional meetings, while the nobility and the Church treated separately.

Despite the widening of the range of representation in royal assemblies throughout the thirteenth century there appears to have been no corresponding development of a theory of estates. Although society was seen as being composed of 'orders' there was no assumption that the orders needed separate representation. Moves towards divisions such as the three 'estates' of France, or the two 'houses' of parliament in England, although stemming from earlier circumstances, were largely developments of the fourteenth century.

R. Oram

European Fairs and Trade Routes

The central Middle Ages was, in general, an era of economic vitality. Population grew, more land was brought under cultivation and both the number and size of towns increased. Commercial activity also expanded as individuals sought to sell surplus produce and to purchase commodities which were not available locally. This trade was focused on the markets and fairs of the Middle Ages. Many of these had developed during the early medieval period, in an *ad hoc* style now difficult to trace, at locations such as castles and monasteries. At specific times of the year large numbers of people congregated in these places for judicial, religious and other purposes and merchants realized that such groups were potential consumers. Here, too, in an age without the resources or requirement for permanent trading centres, merchants could meet and deal with other merchants. In the central Middle Ages landlords came to recognize that, through the imposition of tolls and other levies, profit could be made from the commercial activity at such gatherings. Licence from a landlord to hold a market or fair could also help to stimulate the economic fortunes of a new town. Consequently markets and fairs became the subject of seigneurial protection and regulation and they came to acquire a legal status. Markets were normally weekly events and mainly of local importance. Fairs, by contrast, were less frequent occasions and in many places were held only on an annual basis. Most were of between several days and several weeks duration and attracted merchants from further afield than the local market. Although some, such as Bozen's wine fair, Medina del Campo's wool fair and Skania's herring fair, specialized in particular commodities, most provided a venue for the exchange of a diverse range of local and more distant wares. While the overwhelming majority of fairs were of a mainly regional significance, a few, facilitated by good communications and developments in transport, rose to international prominence. In some areas cycles of sequential, neighbouring fairs emerged, providing merchants with virtually year-long trading opportunities. One of the earliest cycles had developed in Flanders by the twelfth century, based on the fairs of Ypres, Lille, Mesen, Torhout and Bruges, which were held between February and November. The most famous cycle, however, was located in Champagne. From the Lagny fair in January/February merchants could progress to Bar-sur-Aube, Provins and Troyes, returning to Provins and then the second Troyes fair in November/December. The six Champagne fairs attracted merchants and merchandise from all over western Europe and were especially important as a point where Flemish cloth was exchanged for the commodities brought along the Rhône–Saône route by Italian merchants. In the wake of this commercial activity the Champagne fairs acquired equal significance as a financial centre where money was changed, credit arranged and

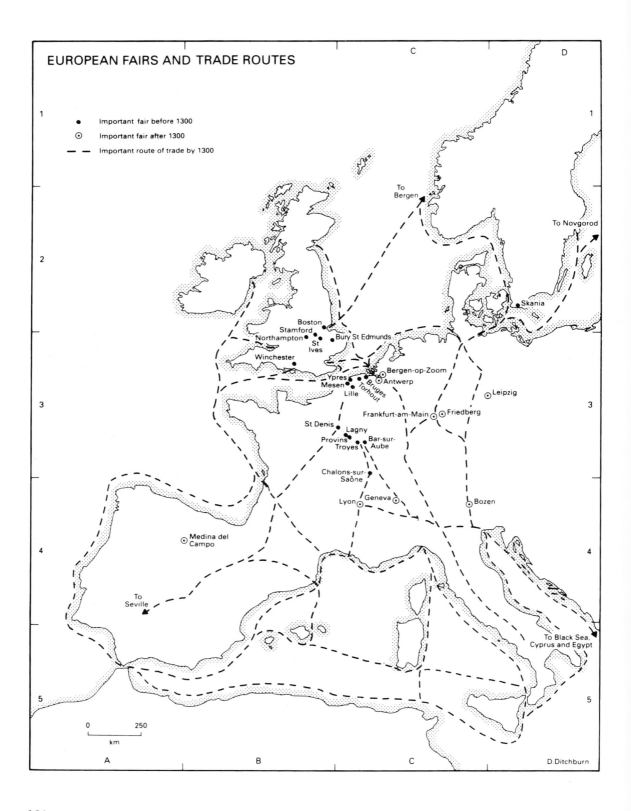

EUROPEAN FAIRS AND TRADE ROUTES

- ● Important fair before 1300
- ⊙ Important fair after 1300
- - - Important route of trade by 1300

To Bergen

To Novgorod

Skania

Boston
Stamford
Northampton
St Ives
Bury St Edmunds
Winchester

Bergen-op-Zoom
Antwerp
Ypres
Bruges
Mesen
Torhout
Lille

Leipzig

Frankfurt-am-Main
Friedberg

St Denis
Lagny
Provins
Troyes
Bar-sur-Aube

Chalons-sur-Saône

Lyon
Geneva
Bozen

Medina del Campo

To Seville

To Black Sea,
Cyprus and Egypt

0   250
km

A   B   C

D.Ditchburn

accounts settled. In the later Middle Ages other fairs, such as the Antwerp/Bergen-op-Zoom cycle and several in the developing regions of central and eastern Europe, rose to international stature. By contrast, however, the fairs of Flanders, Champagne and several others of international significance in the central Middle Ages were in decline by the early fourteenth century. In some instances local political instability contributed to this demise but economic factors were probably more important. The Champagne fairs were undermined by the development of the central Alpine passes and direct sea communications between Italy and northern Europe in the later thirteenth century. These new routes by-passed Champagne. The growing sophistication of business and financial techniques made direct personal contact between northern and southern European merchants in Champagne less necessary. More generally, commerce had become a year-long activity in the larger towns of western Europe. While markets remained central to commercial activity throughout the Middle Ages and after, it was no longer necessary to stimulate trading activity by means of a periodic fair.

D. Ditchburn

The Alpine Passes

The Alps were a major obstacle to the medieval traveller. By the later Middle Ages there were a few guides, hospices and some road improvements. Nevertheless, winter journeys were difficult or impossible and goods could only be transported by pack animals. The lack of maps, dangers from avalanches and wild animals, and sudden weather changes exacerbated the usual problems

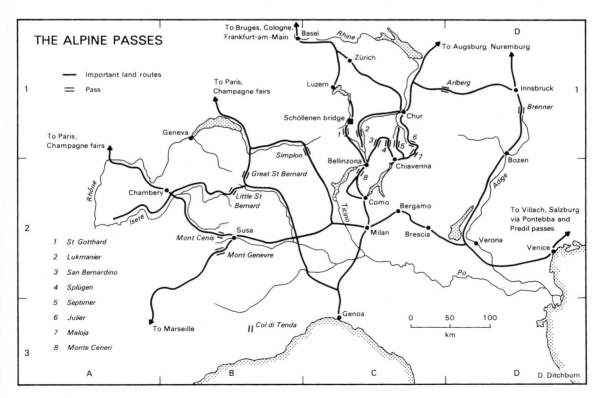

THE ALPINE PASSES

— Important land routes
= Pass

1 St Gotthard
2 Lukmanier
3 San Bernardino
4 Splügen
5 Septimer
6 Julier
7 Maloja
8 Monte Ceneri

D. Ditchburn

of travel. From Carolingian times the Great St Bernard and Mont Cenis passes were used most frequently. They provided direct routes from Italy to the Champagne fairs of the twelfth and thirteenth centuries, while emperors campaigning in Italy favoured them since their approach roads passed through usually unaligned territories. From the 1230s, when a bridge was constructed at Schöllenen, the western passes lost traffic to the Gotthard. It was easily reached from the north-west and the increasingly important south German fairs, such as Frankfurt-am-Main. Latterly English wool was also transported across the Gotthard, avoiding passage through hostile France. To the south, Monte Ceneri had a bad reputation for brigandage in the fifteenth century. Other central passes focused on Chur. The Septimer was the most popular of these, although it suffered from heavy snowfalls and a steep southern ascent. As military routes the central passes were less attractive as they converged on Como and Milan, traditionally hostile to emperors. After Austria's incorporation into the empire, armies increasingly used the Brenner. Its approach roads were direct and if necessary Verona could be easily by-passed. Low in height, it was also less susceptible to heavy snowfalls. With its proximity to Venice and the development of the central European economy in the later Middle Ages, the Brenner was also of growing commercial importance. It was one of the few passes across which wine could be transported and an important wine fair developed at Bozen. Further east, the Pontebba and, from the fourteenth century, the Predil, were used by merchants trading between the Veneto and Carinthia.

D. Ditchburn

The Larger Towns of Europe

Towns and townspeople provide a contrast to the predominantly rural landscape and agrarian society of the Middle Ages. In many countries walls physically separated towns from the surrounding countryside and, to some extent, townspeople were subject to different laws from others. Economically, however, town and country were more closely integrated: the produce of the countryside was bought and sold in towns and rural areas provided raw materials for the urban craft industries. A significant number of townspeople, especially in the smaller towns, were even engaged in agrarian pursuits. Most medieval towns were, by modern standards, small. Even although the number and size of towns grew to accommodate part of the rising population of the central Middle Ages, their population was usually numbered in hundreds rather than thousands. Of the largest urban communities, a disproportionate number were located in northern Italy. In this region about forty towns probably had a population of over 10,000, including four of Europe's largest urban centres, the ports of Genoa and Venice and the manufacturing centres of Milan and Florence.

Urban density was probably at least as great in both Flanders and Sicily where towns were generally smaller but more numerous. Calculating the exact population of medieval towns remains, however, difficult. Contemporary chroniclers routinely overestimated their size while little statistical data of the sort used by modern demographers survives for the medieval period. Instead historians have based their population estimates on a variety of other sources, including the physical size of towns, lists of townspeople compiled for taxation or military purposes and even figures of aggregate wine purchase. Such figures then require to be multiplied (selecting the appropriate multiplier is itself a controversial matter) to produce a population quotient. Different approaches can lead to gross discrepancies: Lucca's population has been estimated as 15,000 or 23,000; Paris's as 80,000 or 200,000; and London's traditionally as about 40,000 or more recently as at least 80,000. The accompanying map should, therefore, be regarded with caution.

D. Ditchburn

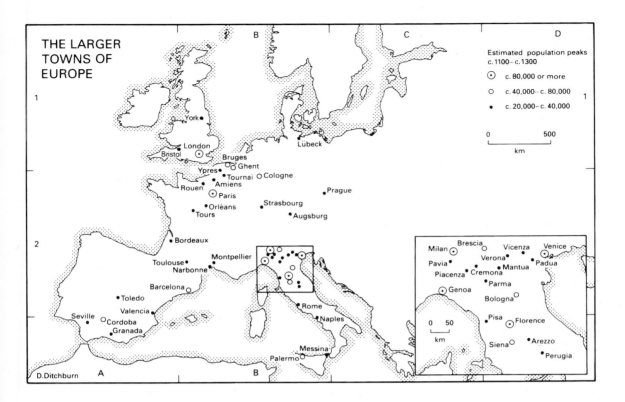

THE LARGER TOWNS OF EUROPE

Estimated population peaks
c.1100–c.1300

⊙ c. 80,000 or more

○ c. 40,000–c. 80,000

• c. 20,000–c. 40,000

0   500
km

York

London
Bristol
Bruges
Ghent
Ypres
Tournai
Cologne
Amiens
Rouen
Paris
Orléans
Tours
Strasbourg
Augsburg
Prague
Lübeck

Bordeaux

Toulouse
Narbonne
Montpellier

Barcelona

Toledo
Valencia
Seville
Cordoba
Granada

Rome
Naples

Messina
Palermo

Milan
Brescia
Vicenza
Venice
Pavia
Verona
Padua
Piacenza
Cremona
Mantua
Parma
Genoa
Bologna
Pisa
Florence
Siena
Arezzo
Perugia

0   50
km

D.Ditchburn

Families of Town Law

During the twelfth and thirteenth centuries many new towns were founded and old settlements raised to urban status. One common way of doing this was through the grant of the rights and privileges of an existing town. The result was the creation of 'families' of town law, groups of urban settlements whose legal arrangements were, at least initially, modelled on a 'mother town'. The mother town might be a major economic and political centre, like Lübeck, but some relatively unimportant places, like Breteuil in Normandy, also became the model for many towns spread over wide areas.

The degree of dependence between mother and daughter towns varied. Sometimes the new town was simply granted the customs of an existing town and there was no further connection. In other cases the affiliated town might turn to the mother town for a ruling when some point in the customs needed clarification. An even closer bond existed in town families such as that of Lübeck, whose mother town heard judicial appeals from the courts of daughter towns.

The three families of town law shown here have been chosen to illustrate the variety of the phenomenon. The first, the family of towns with the law of Breteuil, was modelled on the small Norman town of Breteuil, which was enfranchised by its lord, William fitz Osbern, around 1060. After the Norman Conquest of England fitz Osbern became earl of Hereford and introduced the law of Breteuil into his Marcher lordship, whence it spread into surrounding areas of England and Wales. The Anglo-Normans who invaded Ireland in the decades after 1169 included many men, like the de Lacys, from this part of the country, and when they founded boroughs, like the de Lacy foundation of Drogheda, they too granted the laws of Breteuil. In this way, by a series of feudal conquests,

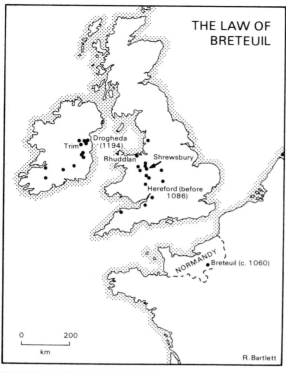

THE LAW OF BRETEUIL

Trim
Drogheda (1194)
Rhuddlan
Shrewsbury
Hereford (before 1086)
NORMANDY
Breteuil (c. 1060)

0   200
km

R. Bartlett

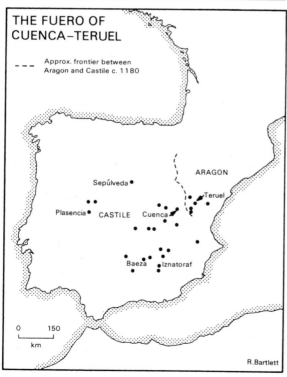

THE FUERO OF CUENCA-TERUEL

- - -   Approx. frontier between Aragon and Castile c. 1180

Sepúlveda
ARAGON
Teruel
Plasencia   CASTILE   Cuenca
Baeza   Iznatoraf

0   150
km

R. Bartlett

the laws of a small Norman town came to be adopted by dozens of settlements in England, Wales and Ireland.

The law of Breteuil did not consist of a large or well-defined body of customs, indeed, its essence seems to have been the limitation of judicial fines to the low sum of 12 d. The law or *fuero* of Cuenca was a very much more elaborate affair. It contained almost a thousand clauses, regulating matters as varied as inheritance rights, criminal law, military obligations, Christian–Jewish relations, irrigation and pasturage, the public baths and the penalties for taking roses and lilies from another's vineyard. This comprehensive code was granted by Alfonso VIII of Castile soon after he had conquered the town from the Muslims in 1177. At about the same time a very similar code was granted to Teruel, across the border in Aragon, by Alfonso II of Aragon. Thus the family of Cuenca–Teruel law spread across political boundaries. As the reconquest pushed south, more towns were granted the *fuero*, some, such as Baeza and Iznatoraf in Andalusia, becoming the mother towns for yet further settlements.

Lübeck law, originating in the twelfth century and codified in the thirteenth, was the basis for the most important of the three families of law shown here. It was a complex set of provisions governing commercial activity as well as criminal law and town government, and it provided the model for over a hundred towns founded along the Baltic shore in the thirteenth century. It served as the basic urban constitution for virtually all the towns of Mecklenburg and Pomerania. Because of its stress on urban independence some rulers found it suspect. The Teutonic Knights, for example, discouraged Lübeck law in their domains, preferring their own, less autonomous code, that of Kulm. Danzig and Memel, which originally had Lübeck law, were forced to abandon it under pressure from the Knights. Despite this resistance, however, Lübeck law was, in various forms, the dominant code of the Baltic, from the mother city itself to the frontiers of Russia.

R. Bartlett

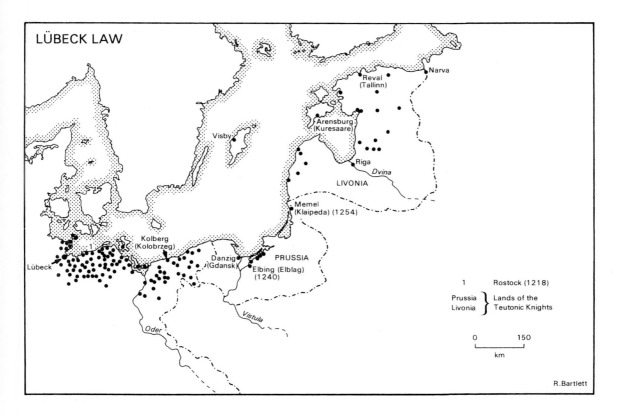

LÜBECK LAW

Narva
Reval
(Tallinn)
Arensburg
(Kuresaare)
Visby
Riga
Dvina
LIVONIA
Memel
(Klaipeda) (1254)
Kolberg
(Kolobrzeg)
Lübeck
Danzig
(Gdansk)
Elbing (Elblag)
(1240)
PRUSSIA
Vistula
Oder

1   Rostock (1218)

Prussia } Lands of the
Livonia } Teutonic Knights

0   150
         km

R.Bartlett

The Contado of Lucca in the Twelfth Century

The commune of Lucca is first recorded with consuls in 1119, though it may have been autonomous since the 1080s. Like other Italian cities, it aspired to control the whole of its diocese; like them, it had to fight rural lords and rival cities in order to do so.

The core of the diocese was the rich plain around the city, the Sei Miglia or 6-mile territory, fully ceded to city jurisdiction by Henry IV in 1081; in this area, rival powers were weak, except along the frontier with Pisa, and all were destroyed relatively early (though Ripafratta, taken in 1105, ended up under Pisan control). The major problem the city faced was access to the sea, normally through the territory of its enemy. The Lucchesi and Pisans fought many wars over the issue, particularly when the Lucchesi tried to establish a port in their own

diocese on the river Motrone, rather than go through Pisa. These wars reached their height in the 1170s, but they are a feature of the whole period. Elsewhere, Lucchese control was helped by the network of episcopal castles, for the bishop was generally a reliable associate of the commune, and by an early tendency for rural lords to live in the city. The military expansion of Lucca was largely along the major road routes east and south-east, and up the Serchio valley into the mountains. East and north, the Lucchesi found domination relatively easy, and they were only held back by the occasional hostile intervention of German emperors.

However, the Arno and Era valleys – in a geographical sense Pisa's hinterland – were absorbed into the latter's *contado* in the end, despite the episcopal castles in the area; the

135

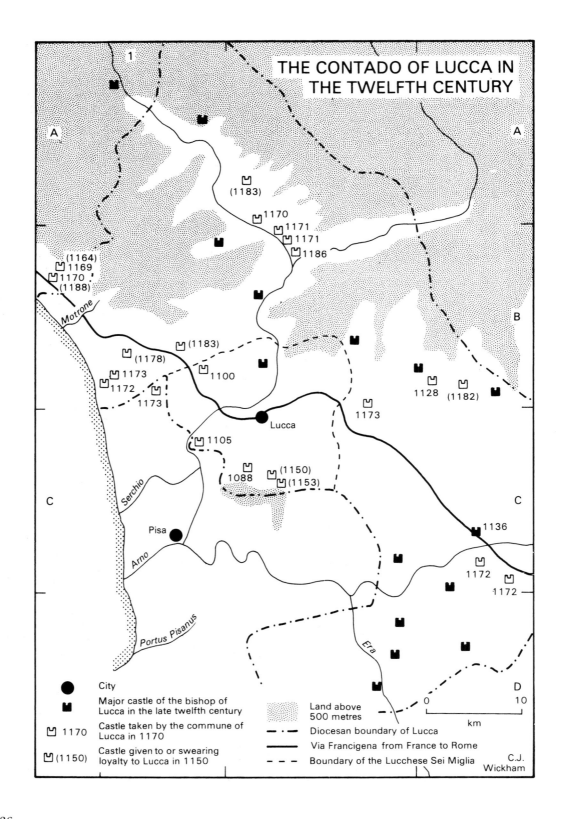

THE CONTADO OF LUCCA IN
THE TWELFTH CENTURY

(1183)

1170
1171
1171
1186

(1164)
1169
1170
(1188)

Motrone

(1183)

(1178)

1173
1172
1173

1100

1128   (1182)

1173

Lucca

1105

1088

(1150)
(1153)

Serchio

Pisa

1136

Arno

1172

1172

Era

Portus Pisanus

D

0   10

km

● City

Major castle of the bishop of
Lucca in the late twelfth century

1170   Castle taken by the commune of
Lucca in 1170

(1150)   Castle given to or swearing
loyalty to Lucca in 1150

Land above
500 metres

Diocesan boundary of Lucca

Via Francigena from France to Rome

Boundary of the Lucchese Sei Miglia

C.J.
Wickham

Lucchesi made no effective impact here. Hegemony over the rural lordships of the diocese was otherwise pretty complete well before the end of the century; only a rival city prevented it from being fully realized in the south, not any rural aristocrat.

C. Wickham

Communal Movements

Risings of townsmen against their ecclesiastical or lay lords not only demonstrated the growing importance of such groups in society but also frequently took on the form of communal movements, as in northern France, northern Spain, northern Italy, Flanders and some of the Rhine towns. A classic account of such a communal struggle in the northern French town of Laon in 1112 is given by the Benedictine Abbot Guibert of Nogent although it tends to be lost among his many stories and observations about miracles and even anecdotes of a folk-loric nature. Not that the religious dimension was irrelevant to communal movements. On the contrary, they were frequently influenced by the Christian value of love, also to be found in the 'Peace of God' movements which coincided with the emergence of the early communes and like them aimed to eliminate conflict and vendettas. Indeed the word 'commune' could be associated with the communion (*communio*) of Christians in the Eucharist, and it was not uncommon for the urban authorities of some towns of the later medieval and early modern period to attempt to disperse dangerous urban uprisings by confronting the rioters with consecrated hosts carried in

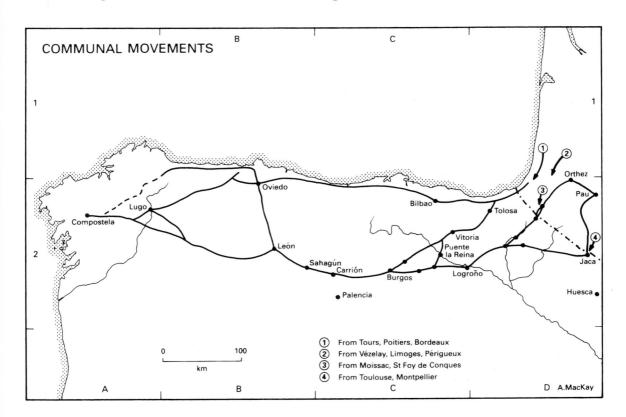

COMMUNAL MOVEMENTS

Oviedo
Bilbao
Lugo
Compostela
Tolosa
León
Vitoria
Puente la Reina
Sahagún
Carrión
Burgos
Logroño
Palencia
Orthez
Pau
Jaca
Huesca

0   100
km

① From Tours, Poitiers, Bordeaux
② From Vézelay, Limoges, Périgueux
③ From Moissac, St Foy de Conques
④ From Toulouse, Montpellier

A. MacKay

procession by members of the clergy.

The religious dimension was evident in other ways. The emergence of towns is frequently associated with economic causes such as the growth of trade and the appearance of markets, but these too were influenced by religious factors. The towns which grew up along the famous pilgrim route to Santiago de Compostela are a case in point. The townsmen who settled in Sahagún, for example, included pilgrims and others from the various regions of France and Italy, and even Germans and English. But although many of those who settled in Compostela, Sahagún, Carrión, Burgos and Palencia grew relatively prosperous as merchants and artisans, they found that their wealth and status was not accompanied by any participation in the local power structure, and chroniclers' accounts of some of the ensuing troubles are remarkably similar to that of Guibert of Nogent.

According to the anonymous chronicler of Sahagún, the town had been founded by Alfonso VI of León and Castile (1065–1109). However the king had taken care to protect the rights and jurisdiction of the monastery that already existed there. Thus if any townsmen held lands within the lordship of the monastery they could only do so on the terms and conditions laid down by the abbot; all those with houses in the town were to pay a yearly sum of money to the monastery as a rent and recognition of the monastic lordship, and all bread had to be baked in the monastery's oven. Friction over this latter requirement was resolved by commuting the obligation into yet another cash payment, the townsmen now having to pay one sum at Christmas for the oven and another at All Saints as rent and recognition of lordship.

The townsmen, however, not only resisted the lordship of the monastery but sought to replace its authority by their own. In a typical incident, for example, they forced their way into the monastic chapter, produced a document of new laws and customs which they themselves had drawn up, and forced the monks to sign in agreement.

Although the objective of such rebellions was to establish communal power, this was envisaged in practical terms and not as an abstract ideal. Frequently, too, the disturbances were linked to more widespread tensions, such as conflicts between the monarchy and nobility, or the townsmen recruited help from other discontented sectors of society, as they did in Compostela where they exercised *de facto* communal power for a whole year, during which the political and jurisdictional powers of the ecclesiastical lordship virtually ceased to exist.

A. MacKay

Settlement Patterns in Medieval Italy: (1) Nucleation (Monte Amiata in Southern Tuscany); (2) Dispersal (the Casentino in Northern Tuscany)

From the tenth century Italy, like other places in Europe, saw the development of a network of castles, fixing in place the slowly emerging structures of private political power that succeeded the public world of the Carolingians. In northern Europe, castles were usually aristocratic fortifications dominating pre-existing, often tightly structured, systems of village settlement and field division. In Italy villages were less stable and agriculture often less collectively controlled (no common fields or strip farming). Aristocratic fortifications here could have much more impact on settlement, notably in the relatively underpopulated central peninsula; the development of castles (*incastellamento*) could produce a network of fortified *villages*, which absorbed all other rural settlement, between *c.* 950 and *c.* 1200. Around and inland from Rome, for example, unfortified villages and dispersed farmsteads, which had been common earlier,

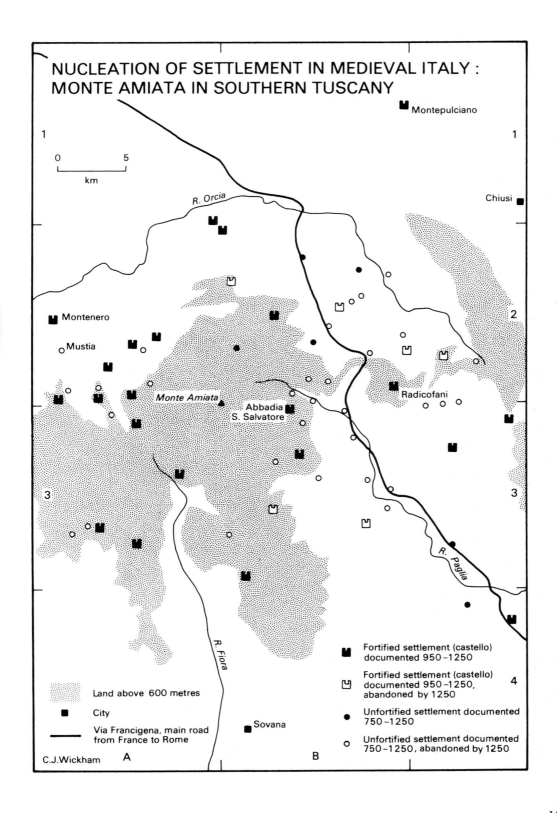

NUCLEATION OF SETTLEMENT IN MEDIEVAL ITALY : MONTE AMIATA IN SOUTHERN TUSCANY

Montepulciano

1

0   5
km

R. Orcia

Chiusi

Montenero

Mustia

Monte Amiata

Abbadia
S. Salvatore

Radicofani

3

2

3

R. Paglia

Fortified settlement (castello)
documented 950–1250

Fortified settlement (castello)
documented 950–1250,
abandoned by 1250

Unfortified settlement documented
750–1250

Unfortified settlement documented
750–1250, abandoned by 1250

4

Land above 600 metres

City

Via Francigena, main road
from France to Rome

R. Fiora

Sovana

C.J.Wickham   A   B

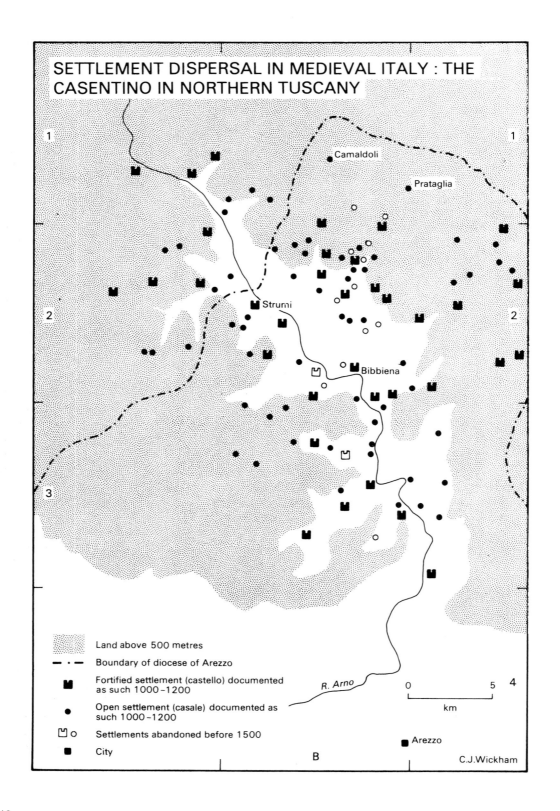

SETTLEMENT DISPERSAL IN MEDIEVAL ITALY : THE CASENTINO IN NORTHERN TUSCANY

Camaldoli

Prataglia

Strumi

Bibbiena

Land above 500 metres

Boundary of diocese of Arezzo

Fortified settlement (castello) documented as such 1000–1200

Open settlement (casale) documented as such 1000–1200

Settlements abandoned before 1500

City

R. Arno

0   5

km

Arezzo

B

C.J.Wickham

disappeared; aristocrats moved whole villages and groups of villages inside their fortifications, and independent peasants began to set up and live in their own castles if they wanted to stay independent.

The map on p. 139 shows this process at Monte Amiata in the south of Tuscany. In Tuscany, political breakdown was relatively slow and castles rare before 1000; but subsequently the major powers on the Amiata began to develop them, and settlement nucleation is very evident. West of the mountain, there is a fairly clear pattern of castles replacing open settlements in a one-to-one relationship: Mustia, for example, was a village directly replaced by Montenero. Whether settlements changed in type is unclear: Mustia may have been a nucleated village even before Montenero was built. But by *c.* 1200, after *incastellamento*, nucleated settlements predominated: documents show almost no isolated houses on the thirteenth-century Amiata. East of the mountain, settlement patterns certainly did change: a scatter of small sites overlooking the river valleys were in the eleventh century drawn into a smaller number of castles; and then, around 1150, this group focused on a smaller number still. The twenty-odd settlements, some very small, of *c.* 900 were reduced to two by *c.* 1200, Abbadia S. Salvatore (the castle of the monastery of S. Salvatore) and Radicofani. S. Salvatore could do this because it owned much of the land of the region, which was undersettled and in need of economic reorganization, which the monastery undertook. This sort of settlement change is in general an indicator of economic organization and of political control – though the monastery found its two big castles extremely difficult subjects, and eventually ceded them extensive rights.

Still in Tuscany, the Casentino (facing page) shows similar localization of private power, across the same period, but in a very different environment. It is much closer to a major city, Arezzo (the cities near the Amiata were weak): landowning by lay aristocrats and churches was much more fragmented here in the central Middle Ages, and peasant owners very numerous. Local lords built many *castelli*, more indeed than on the Amiata; but far fewer of them were population centres, and many must have been little more than fortified residences of petty aristocrats. A tight network of small open settlements survived almost without any break, and some of these were highly fragmented, with houses stretching from end to end of their territories. One of the few castles to establish itself as a real population centre was Bibbiena, a major base of Arezzo's powerful bishops. But Camaldoli, Prataglia and Strumi, the local monasteries whose archives survive, built no castles at all (though they received several from lay families): a military rhetoric for their power was evidently less necessary than on the Amiata. The importance of Bibbiena underlines the failure of most other local castles to expand: it looks as if aristocrats here never had the hegemony over the population that their peers had in the south. This pattern, of numerous small castles and surviving dispersed settlement, is common in the urbanized areas of the Po plain and northern Tuscany, and seems to indicate relatively fragmented political power and, sometimes, weak seigneurial rights.

C. Wickham

The Huerta of Valencia

Although the Cid had taken Valencia in 1094, it was reconquered by the Muslims in 1102 and did not fall definitively to the Christians until James I of Aragon succeeded in taking it in 1238. However, although the dramatic events created the illusion of a triumphant Christian victory, in reality the conquerors were prepared to come to terms with the defeated Muslims who remained, and above all to make use of their agrarian institutions and manpower. Thus the kingdom of Valencia after its reconquest contained several predominantly Christian cities, particularly Valencia itself, many towns in which Muslims and Christians lived together, and a countryside

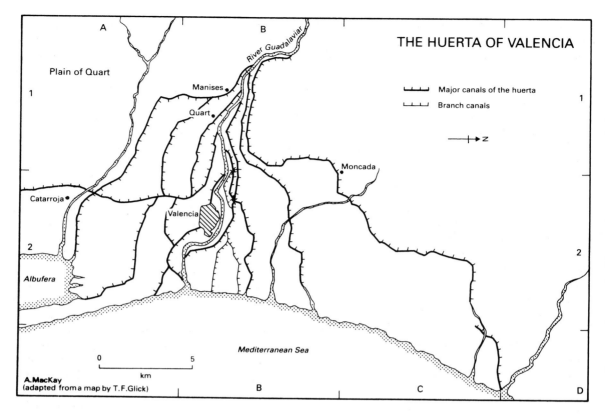

THE HUERTA OF VALENCIA

Major canals of the huerta

Branch canals

A.MacKay
(adapted from a map by T.F.Glick)

which, although under the political control of Christian lords, was mainly tenanted by Mudejars (Muslims living under Christian rule).

Along the Levantine coast of Spain some regions, notably those in and around the city of Valencia, were characterized by a rural economy with sophisticated irrigation systems in which thousands of small channels and ditches diverted water from the larger canals, distributing the precious liquid over large areas of territory. Rivers of course played an important role, particularly the Guadalaviar and the Júcar, but so too did small dams, divisors of currents, branches of

canals, *norias* (devices for lifting water, probably of Persian origin), and horizontal wells dispersing water by gravity flow (*qanats*).

The practical effects of irrigation imposed themselves on rural society, demanding co-operation of those who depended on water distribution and favouring small farms rather than large estates. Before conquering Játiva James I of Aragon himself described the patchwork landscape, the huertas of the area, the villages or *alquerías*, and the water-courses or *acequías* on which the inhabitants depended.

A. MacKay

The Thirteenth-Century Repopulation of Andalusia

The reconquest of Andalusia was largely due to Ferdinand III and his son Alfonso X, both of them kings of Castile. The former skilfully

exploited the internal weaknesses and divisions of the Almohad Empire, which had been plunged into crisis almost on the morrow of the great defeat it sustained at the battle of Las Navas de Tolosa (1212). Combining military aggression with surrender agreements, the Christians took the leading cities of the region: Andújar (1224), Baeza (1227), Ubeda (1232), Córdoba (1236), Jaén (1246) and Seville (1248). Alfonso X (1252–84) followed up on these successes, taking Cádiz (c. 1260), Niebla (1262) and Jerez and its territory (1264). The last significant conquest of the thirteenth century was Tarifa (1292), and already by this time the long-term military objective was to deprive the Moors of the control of the straits of Gibraltar.

In each case reconquest was followed up both by repopulation – that is, the introduction of new colonists from the north amongst whom massive amounts of lands were shared out – and by the civil and ecclesiastical reorganization of the conquered territories.

As in Valencia and Murcia, the repopulation of Andalusia was carried out according to the model of *repartimiento*. Briefly, this consisted of a royally ordered distribution of houses, lands, and rural properties between those who had participated in the campaigns of conquest and the new Christian colonists. The former – nobles, members of the royal family, leading churchmen, the military orders, soldiers and royal officials – were the main beneficiaries of these distributions and they received the best lands. But most of the lands were given to those who really were colonists or *repobladores*. They were given properties according to their socio-military status as knights (noble or urban) or plain foot-soldiers. The view, widely propagated by even eminent historians, that the Andalusian *latifundios* were created as a result of the conquest and the *repartimientos* is completely erroneous because every colonist was by definition a proprietor. For example the share of agricultural land assigned to a foot-soldier in Carmona or Vejer de la Frontera consisted of some 74 acres.

The Muslim population was systematically expelled from the towns and any areas of strategic value. Nevertheless, in the early stages a considerable number of Muslims remained in the villages and smaller urban nuclei by virtue of surrender agreements which guaranteed them their freedom of religion, their own laws and their properties. This situation lasted until the uprising of the subjected Muslims (*mudéjares*) in 1264. The outcome of this uprising was the defeat of the rebels, the conquest of some areas of territory (Jerez), and the expulsion and exile of most of the *mudéjares* who still remained in Andalusia. From this point on the Muslims were reduced to a small minority with hardly any demographic significance.

Andalusia was mainly repopulated by people of Castilian and Leonese origins, although there were colonists who came from the other Iberian kingdoms, like Catalans, Portuguese and Navarrese. In those places which were well connected with maritime trade – Seville, Jerez, Cádiz, Puerto de Santa María – foreigners appeared: English, French, Bretons, and above all Italians, especially the Genoese. The diagram shows the origins of the first colonists of Jerez de la Frontera. Yet despite the demographic efforts which the repopulation of Andalusia imposed on Castile, the region remained underpopulated during the thirteenth and fourteenth centuries. This was especially evident in the countryside, and this explains the foundation or repopulation of numerous rural nuclei throughout the later medieval period.

Administratively Andalusia was organized around the three 'kingdoms' of Jaén, Córdoba and Seville. In them royal jurisdiction was initially predominant and was exercised through a series of large municipalities or town councils endowed with extensive lands and municipal law codes or *fueros*. Nevertheless some lordships also came into being, almost all of them along the frontier with the kingdom of Granada and belonging to the military orders of Calatrava, Santiago and Alcántara.

An ecclesiastical organization was also set up or restored. Initially the region was divided into three diocesan areas: the bishoprics of Jaén and Córdoba, dependent on the archbishopric of Toledo, and the archbishopric of Seville. In 1263 the bishopric of Cádiz, dependent on Seville, was created.

M. González Jiménez

143

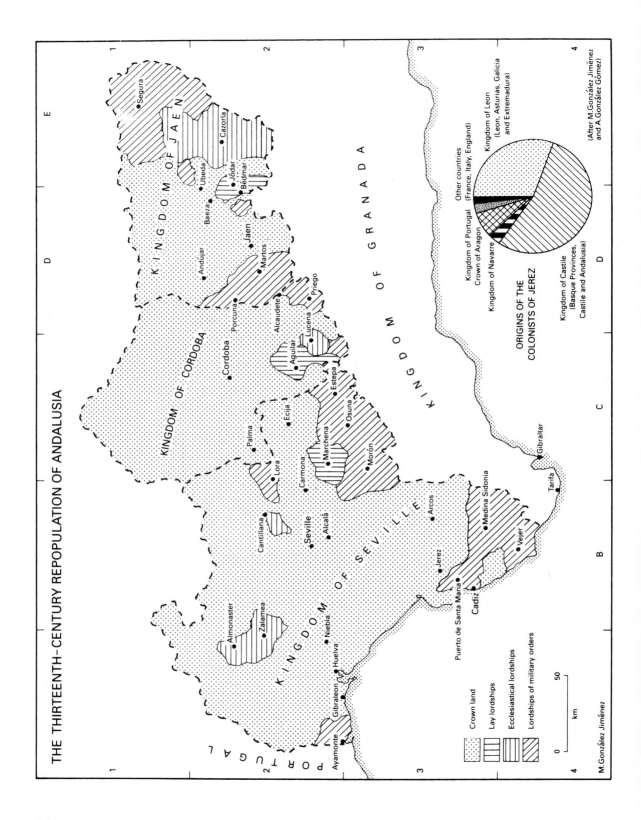

THE THIRTEENTH–CENTURY REPOPULATION OF ANDALUSIA

PORTUGAL

KINGDOM OF JAEN

Segura

Cazorla

Ubeda
Jódar
Bedmar

Baeza

Jaen
Andujar
Martos

KINGDOM OF CORDOBA

Priego
Alcaudete
Porcuna
Lucena
Aguilar
Cordoba

Estepa
Palma
Ecija
Osuna
Lora
Marchena
Carmona
Morón

KINGDOM OF GRANADA

KINGDOM OF SEVILLE

Almonaster
Zalamea

Niebla
Huelva
Gibraleon

Ayamonte

Cantillana

Seville
Alcalá

Arcos

Jerez
Puerto de Santa Maria
Cadiz

Medina Sidonia

Vejer

Gibraltar

Tarifa

Crown land
Lay lordships
Ecclesiastical lordships
Lordships of military orders

0   50
km

M. González Jiménez

ORIGINS OF THE
COLONISTS OF JEREZ

Other countries
(France, Italy, England)

Kingdom of Leon
(Leon, Asturias, Galicia
and Extremadura)

Kingdom of Portugal

Crown of Aragon

Kingdom of Navarre

Kingdom of Castile
(Basque Provinces,
Castile and Andalusia)

(After M. González Jiménez
and A. González Gómez)

144

Anti-Semitism, 1096–1306

The Middle Ages began with a fair degree of harmony existing between Jews and Christians. This *modus vivendi*, however, was shattered by the first crusade (1096). According to a Jewish chronicler, many who took the cross reasoned as follows: 'We are going ... to exact vengeance on the Ishmaelites yet here are the Jews ... whose forefathers slew him [Jesus]. First let us take vengeance on them.' By the summer of 1096 much of Rhineland Jewry had either been killed or forcibly converted. Such anti-Jewish violence was frowned on by the Church. According to Innocent III's *Constitutio pro Judaeis* of 1199 Jews were to be tolerated 'in accordance with the clemency that Christian piety imposes'. The Church was concerned, however, to distinguish Jews from Christians physically (by, for example, the 'Jewish badge'), socially (by discouraging all manner of social intercourse) and politically (by prohibiting Jews from exercising authority over Christians). Such regulations also found their way into secular law, though they did not affect the legal status of Jewry; Jews had to be humbled but they were not legally defined as being of servile status. To be sure, the term *servi regi* was applied to the Jews of Aragon (first to Teruel, 1176), and the term *servi camarae* was applied to the Jews of the Holy Roman Empire (first in Sicily by Frederick II, 1236). These terms, however, were not descriptive of a servile Jewish status; rather they were used to press certain jurisdictional rights over Jews in the face of a competing jurisdiction.

While official ecclesiastical and lay policies for the most part sought to protect Jews, the religious consciousness of people tended to emphasize the demonic nature of the Jew. This was most apparent in the blood libel and in the charge of host desecration, both of which often led to anti-Jewish violence. According to the blood libel, from the time Jesus had been crucified the Jews thirsted, particularly at Easter time, for the pure and innocent blood of Christian children. The libel of host desecration appeared only after the Lateran Council of 1215 had formulated the doctrine of transubstantiation. Jews were thought to bribe Christians into supplying them with a host (the body of Jesus) which they then tortured. Such a charge in Roettingen in 1298 led to a wave of massacres throughout Bavaria and adjoining regions.

The demonic nature of Jewry was further emphasized by the artistic depiction of Jews as *incubi* and the like. In contrast to the sweet-smelling 'odour of sanctity', the foul *foetor judaicus* was ascribed to Jews. That innocent Christians were exploited by Jewish usurers was another charge that found adherents in Church, state and populace. Jews, indeed, were often engaged in money-lending and tax collection; this fact, which was the cause of much antagonism, was itself the result of attempting to leave the practice of money-lending to the Jews, who were not 'brothers' in the mystical body of Christ. Jews could, of course, join this body by converting, and the Mendicant Orders, particularly the Dominicans, mounted a campaign of conversion in the thirteenth century which manifested itself in conversionist sermons, directed at Jews, and in the staging of public debates, such as that held before the court of James I (Barcelona, 1263). The failure of this 'dream of conversion' led to the more strident view that Jews were unassimilable to the Christian social body and ought therefore to be either forcibly segregated or expelled. The latter course was adopted in England in the first general expulsion of the Jews in 1290, and later in France in 1306.

P. Hersch

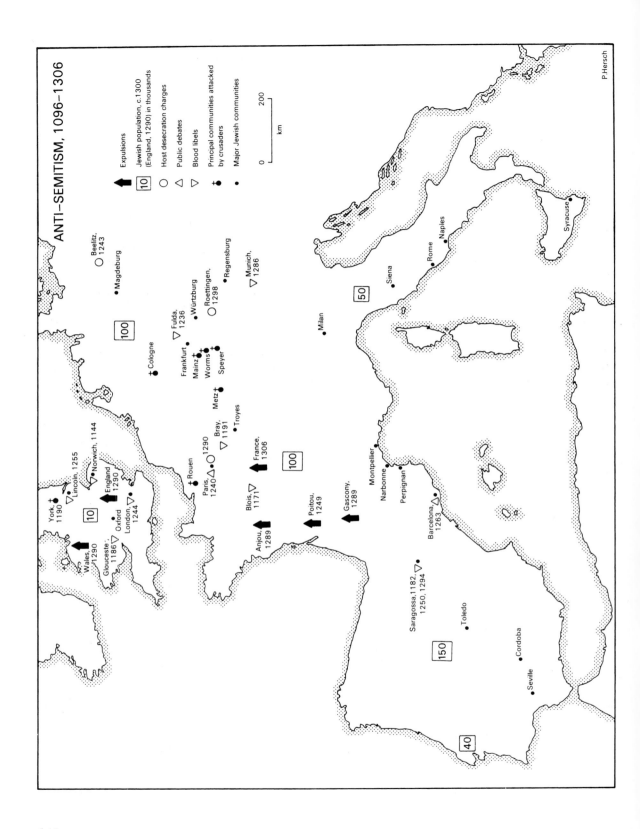

ANTI-SEMITISM, 1096–1306

Expulsions

Jewish population, c.1300
(England, 1290) in thousands

Host desecration charges

Public debates

Blood libels

Principal communities attacked
by crusaders

Major Jewish communities

P.Hersch

km

0   200

Beelitz,
1243

Magdeburg

Fulda,
1236

Würtzburg

Roettingen,
1298

Regensburg

Munich,
1286

Cologne

Frankfurt

Mainz

Worms

Speyer

Metz

Troyes

Milan

Siena

Rome

Naples

Syracuse

Bray,
1191

France,
1306

Lincoln, 1255

Norwich, 1144

Rouen

Paris,
1240

England
1290

Blois, 1171

Anjou,
1289

Poitou,
1249

Gascony,
1289

York,
1190

Oxford

London,
1244

Gloucester,
1186

Wales,
1290

Montpellier

Narbonne

Perpignan

Barcelona,
1263

Saragossa,1182,
1250, 1294

Toledo

Cordoba

Seville

146

CULTURE

The Twelfth-Century Renaissance: Translation and Transmission

The 'Twelfth-Century Renaissance' is a convenient historiographical label and, despite re-evaluations, Haskins' vision of this cultural achievement, published in 1927, remains the starting-point for its study. He portrayed a reinvigorated interest in Latin and its ancient classics, the revival of Roman Law, greater sophistication in historical writing and the rise of universities. Above all, because of the repercussions for the philosophical and scientific thought-worlds, he emphasized the translations of texts unavailable to the West for generations.

The pre-eminent centres of translation were in Sicily (including southern Italy) and Spain. In Sicily, various writings were translated directly from the Greek, including Ptolemy's Almagest and works by Euclid and Proclus. With a medical school at Salerno, a demand for medical texts, especially Galen, became prominent. This was met by men like Burgundio of Pisa, a jurist who visited Constantinople several times. Burgundio and other Italians also translated theological works by the Greek Fathers. However, the main impetus was directed at translating ancient

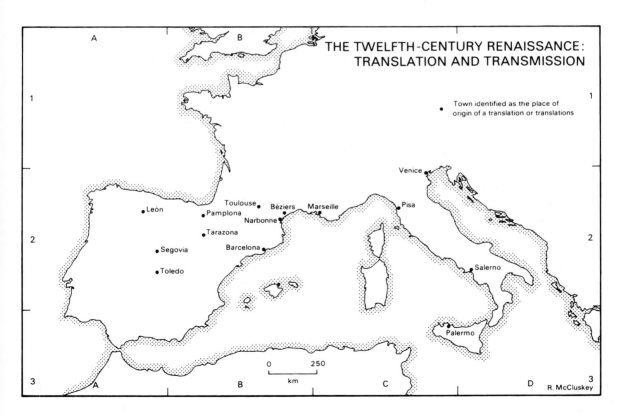

THE TWELFTH-CENTURY RENAISSANCE: TRANSLATION AND TRANSMISSION

• Town identified as the place of origin of a translation or translations philosophy, oftentimes with Arabic commentary, and mathematics and astronomy. Translations from Arabic in Spain were principally devoted to these subjects and, most significantly, to recovering Aristotle's works. The place of Toledo as the leading Spanish centre needs qualification – the idea of a 'school' under Archbishop Raymond (1125–52) appears premature – but, from the second half of the century, Toledo undoubtedly attracted scholars of quality, including the enormously productive Gerard of Cremona. Other centres are identifiable: Hugh of Santalla in Tarazona, Plato of Tivoli in Barcelona, Robert of

Chester in Segovia. Herman of Carinthia was in León in 1142 and in Toulouse and Béziers in 1143, translating as he went.

It is not fully understood how manuscripts of Aristotle and others were transmitted to the West's intellectual centres. Probably, the wandering scholars themselves played a major part in the dissemination. It fell to men like St Thomas Aquinas (1225–74) to systematize the 'new' knowledge and harmonize it to the fundamentals of Christian theology.

R. McCluskey

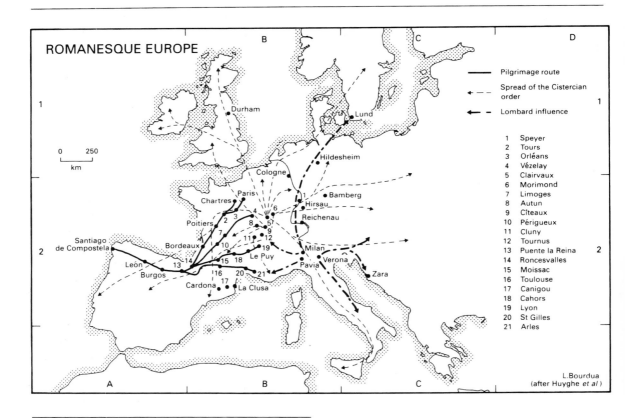

Romanesque Europe

'Romanesque' was a term first used by Charles de Gerville, a Norman archaeologist, to describe western architecture from the fifth to the thirteenth centuries. It is now applied to a more restricted type of architecture and decorative

arts which evolved in western Europe in the eleventh and twelfth centuries. Technically speaking, Romanesque architecture amounts to a complete building system executed by highly skilled workers. Developments included the replacement of timber roofing with stone groin and barrel vaults, for timber churches made them vulnerable to fire. At first only small spaces were vaulted, but eventually this would include the vaulting of elongated naves, made possible only by strengthening the structure of the building. What is known as 'the first international romanesque style' began in Lombardy where one bay of a church between the apse and the nave was vaulted (e.g. San Ambrogio, Milan). The next step took place in Catalonia where entire churches were vaulted with barrel vaulting, such as San Vicente de Castillo at Cardona and St-Martin-du-Canigou. The culminating point in the development of Romanesque architecture is, however, in England at Durham cathedral, with its ribbed vaulting throughout supported by cylindrical and compound piers.

Travelling ateliers of masons from Lombardy were called on by abbots and bishops to rebuild churches which had either suffered damage following the upheavals and invasions of the tenth century, or were newly built by reformed religious orders. These naturally spread up the Rhine as far north as Sweden. Once assembled, the ateliers gave training to locals and eventually these areas became centres from which craftsmen could be sent elsewhere. Hence the diffusion of regional trends throughout much of Europe. The Cluniac and Cistercian Orders played an important role in the patronage during this period. The pilgrimage roads to Rome, Jerusalem and particularly Santiago de Compostela were also an important factor in the dissemination of style. Amongst notable examples of pilgrimage churches are Ste Foy at Conques; St Martial at Limoges; St Sernin at Toulouse and Santiago de Compostela.

L. Bourdua

Gothic Europe

The term 'Gothic' was coined in Italy as a later expression of contempt to describe medieval architecture as a whole. However, Gothic architecture evolved over the course of four centuries (twelfth to sixteenth), and required more sophisticated building methods than its Romanesque predecessor. Developments included greater use of cross-ribbed vaulting to roof larger areas than previously, a system of supports including exterior flying buttresses, the substitution of walls by large windows of multi-coloured glass, and more complex façades with portals and programmes of sculpture. The greatest technical developments occurred in the Ile-de-France, where builders refused to use rib vaulting with heavy Norman walls and consequently developed more adventurous vaulting techniques. The solutions were to reinforce piers by creating more projections on the wall, either by grouping clusters of engaged columns inside, or using bigger buttresses outside. Vault cells assumed a pointed shape, as did the arch, and the vault was also made lighter through the use of well-cut stones of thin ashlar, instead of the rubble previously employed. New exterior flying buttresses reduced the thrust of the vaults and despite their structural purpose became things of beauty. The rebuilding of the abbey church of St Denis, situated north of Paris, marked a turning point in the development of the style. The wide gothic *chevet* (a double ambulatory) was created, an open structure with no walls between chapels, articulated by two rows of slender columns; stained glass was also used on an unprecedented scale. A parallel development was the rebuilding of Sens cathedral, where from the very start it was intended to cover the nave and choir with a cross-ribbed vault.

Most French cathedrals were designed on such an ambitious scale that few were ever finished as intended. (The desire for verticality was so great that Beauvais cathedral remained unfinished.) English Gothic churches were lower than French ones, with more complex rib-

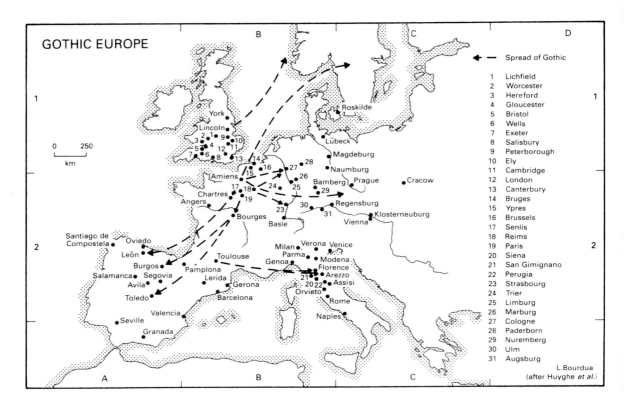

GOTHIC EUROPE

Spread of Gothic

1 Lichfield
2 Worcester
3 Hereford
4 Gloucester
5 Bristol
6 Wells
7 Exeter
8 Salisbury
9 Peterborough
10 Ely
11 Cambridge
12 London
13 Canterbury
14 Bruges
15 Ypres
16 Brussels
17 Senlis
18 Reims
19 Paris
20 Siena
21 San Gimignano
22 Perugia
23 Strasbourg
24 Trier
25 Limburg
26 Marburg
27 Cologne
28 Paderborn
29 Nuremberg
30 Ulm
31 Augsburg

vaulting designs (e.g. St Hugh's choir at Lincoln cathedral) and differing façades. In Germany, the influence set in during the thirteenth century (e.g. Cologne cathedral), as in Spain (e.g. the cathedrals of Burgos and Toledo). In Italy, apart from Cistercian abbeys (such as Fossanova), the style retained more Romanesque features.

L. Bourdua

The Travels of Villard de Honnecourt

The architectural style now known as the Gothic had its origins in northern France in the second quarter of the twelfth century. The twelfth and thirteenth centuries saw a vast amount of building in western Europe and French architecture was the increasingly fashionable model. This can be observed in the geographical spread of the Gothic style and can occasionally be documented, as in the hiring of William of Sens to rebuild Canterbury cathedral in 1174 or in the presence of a mason from Paris in Wimpfen, who, it was noted in the late thirteenth century, built in the French style.

In the years around 1230 a French traveller, keenly interested in architecture, made a series of drawings, which are now in the *Bibliothèque Nationale* in Paris (ms. fr. 19,093). At some stage he wrote (or perhaps dictated) a series of captions in the French of Picardy. (Two hands added further texts later in the century.) The name he gives is usually modernized as Villard de Honnecourt. The varied contents include architectural details, plans, carpentry, mechanical devices, figure subjects (several after sculpture, both contemporary and antique) and animals (some copied from bestiaries and some perhaps from

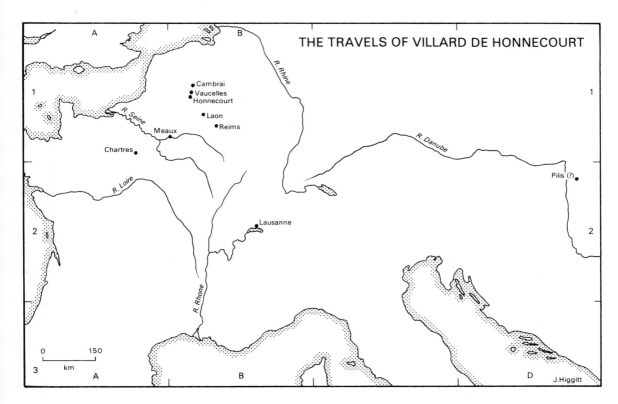

THE TRAVELS OF VILLARD DE HONNECOURT

J.Higgitt

life). There are also diagrammatic representations of ideas deriving from the practice of masons and carpenters and figurative drawings based on geometric schemata. In both the latter and in his 'preface' he lays self-conscious emphasis on geometry.

Villard has generally been thought of as a master mason who prepared a set of annotated drawings for the edification of his workshop. Recently his architectural competence has been questioned. Other suggestions are that he was a sculptor, or a metalworker, or a clerk with architectural, artistic and mechanical interests.

Whatever his trade, he tells us that he travelled to many lands, including Hungary. His sketches show that he visited modern buildings and building sites at Cambrai (near Honnecourt), Laon, Lausanne, Meaux, Reims and Vaucelles. Recent excavations at the site of the Cistercian abbey of Pilis in Hungary revealed tiles similar to those he sketched in Hungary. Whether artisan or clerk or some combination of the two, Villard was alert and well-travelled, and his book shows one way in which (mainly French) visual and technical ideas were collected and, perhaps, diffused.

J. Higgitt

The Spread of the Old French Epic
(The Roland Legend)

The skirmish at Roncesvaux produced a legend of great vitality. Roland's name is first associated with the battle in the ninth-century *Vita Caroli*, written in court circles at Aachen by Eginhard. A note in an eleventh-century chronicle from San Millán de la Cogolla (Castile) adds a mythic dimension to Charlemagne and his twelve 'nephews', increases the role of the Moors ('Saracens') and associates many French epic heroes with the battle. *C.* 1100 the archetype of the extant poems was produced in Normandy, possibly by a literate poet exploiting oral traditions. This version gave rise to the oldest manuscript of the *Chanson de Roland*, copied in England *c.*1150. Material gathered in England was transmitted to Norway and thence to Denmark to form the two versions of the Old Norse *Karlamagnús Saga* (thirteenth century). In the course of the twelfth

century semi-independent versions arose in central and eastern France, emphasizing romance features centred on Roland's fiancée, Aude. Over the next two centuries the *Roland* was translated into English, Welsh, Middle High German, Provençal, Aragonese and the Franco-Italian koïné of the Veneto. Two versions of Roland's youthful deeds (*Enfances*) were produced: *Aspremont*, in the Norman kingdom of Sicily, *c.* 1190, and *Girart de Vienne*, by Bertrand de Bar-sur-Aube, *c.* 1175, linking the legend of Roland to that of the Narbonnais clan. Roland's incestuous birth is closely linked to legends of Charlemagne's early years, recorded, amongst other places, in the now lost Castilian *Mocedades de Mainete* and the German *Karl der Grosse* by Der Stricker. As pseudo-history the legend served crusading purposes in the *Historia Caroli Magni*

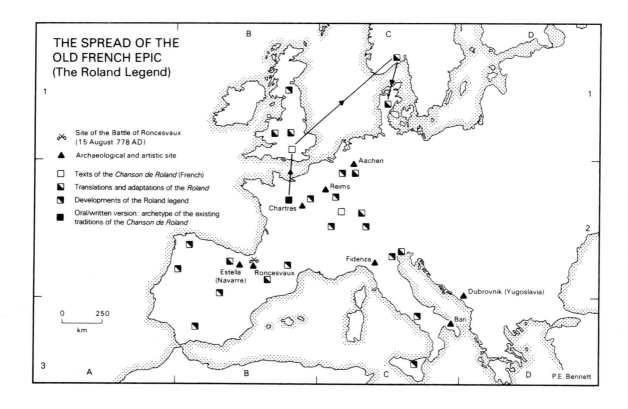

THE SPREAD OF THE
OLD FRENCH EPIC
(The Roland Legend)

✂ Site of the Battle of Roncesvaux
(15 August 778 AD)

▲ Archaeological and artistic site

☐ Texts of the *Chanson de Roland* (French)

◪ Translations and adaptations of the *Roland*

◪ Developments of the Roland legend

■ Oral/written version: archetype of the existing
traditions of the *Chanson de Roland*

Aachen

Reims

Chartres

Estella
(Navarre)   Roncesvaux

Fidenza

Dubrovnik (Yugoslavia)

Bari

0   250
km

P.E. Bennett

152

('Pseudo Turpin Chronicle') an early version of which is preserved in the *Codex Calixtinus* in Compostela. It also provided material for official chronicles of France (fourteenth century) and to bolster the prestige of the house of Burgundy in the fifteenth. The lasting appeal of the legend is seen in the fourteenth-century *Entrée d'Espagne* and *Prise de Pampelune*, both written in the region of Padua and inspiring Ariosto and Boiardo, in the folk tales of Liège and Naples, generating puppet theatres still extant, and in similar tales circulating in Andalusia and Portugal whence they were carried to the New World and to Goa, where they are still productive. Artistic representations of the legend abound, ranging from the Romanesque capitals at Estella and Fidenza to the thirteenth-century 'Charlemagne Window' at Chartres, Gothic statues at Reims, the reliquary of Charlemagne in Aachen (1200–15) and the fifteenth-century statue of Roland in Dubrovnik. Now lost is a twelfth-century mosaic floor dealing with the Battle of Roncesvaux in the cathedral in Bari.

P.E. Bennett

Troubadours: Centres of Creativity and Travels of the Poets

Some 400 troubadours are known, authors of over 4,000 poems, coming from all strata of society. The earliest whose songs survive is Guillaume IX, duke of Aquitaine, writing at his courts in Poitiers and Bordeaux, and doubtless elsewhere on travels that took him to the Holy

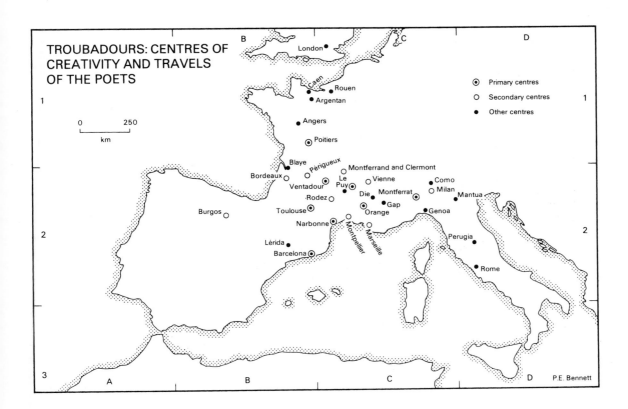

TROUBADOURS: CENTRES OF CREATIVITY AND TRAVELS OF THE POETS

0 250 km

⊙ Primary centres
○ Secondary centres
● Other centres

London
Caen
Rouen
Argentan
Angers
Poitiers
Blaye
Périgueux
Montferrand and Clermont
Bordeaux
Le Puy
Vienne
Como
Ventadour
Die
Montferrat
Milan
Mantua
Rodez
Gap
Toulouse
Orange
Genoa
Burgos
Narbonne
Perugia
Marseille
Montpellier
Lérida
Barcelona
Rome

P.E. Bennett

Land and to Spain. He was also in contact with the courts of Anjou and Ventadour. He lived from 1071 to 1127. Bernart de Ventadour (*fl.* 1150–1200) was of poor birth, working for Ebles II ('The Singer') of Ventadour, as well as in Narbonne and Toulouse. He also wrote for Eleanor of Aquitaine with whom he travelled to Normandy and England, writing at least one extant poem north of the Channel. Marcabru, a Gascon of humble origins, was in contact with Jaufré Rudel, prince of Blaye, who died on crusade in 1148 or 1149, giving rise to a romantic legend. Marcabru also worked for the courts of Aragon and Castile. Most troubadours seem to have been peripatetic, the great Guillaume IX, Richard I of England, Alfonso II of Aragon, for reasons of state, others to follow their lords. Peire Vidal worked not only for the count of Toulouse and king of Aragon but also for the marquis of Montferrat, like many late twelfth- and early thirteenth-century troubadours, with whom he visited Cyprus and perhaps Constantinople. The routes taking Gausbut de Poicebot from the Limousin to Spain are less well charted; like the earlier Gascon poet *Cercamon* ('Search

the World') he may have been the archetypal 'wandering troubadour'. Other poets, however, remained at home: Maria de Ventadour, Raimbaut d'Orange, the countess of Die, Peire d'Alvernhe in Clermont. Major centres like Vienne, seat of the Dauphin, Le Puy, which lent its name to northern French poetic societies, and Toulouse, home of the 'Floral Games' of the fourteenth-century troubadour revival, proved magnets to many poets. Not all troubadours were Provençal. Lanfranc Cigala and Fouquet de Marseille, bishop of Toulouse, were from Genoa; the former wrote there. Sordel was from Mantua; Guillem de Cabestaing and Guillem de Bergedan were Catalan; all three travelled in France and Spain. Much of this movement, and the concomitant cultural diffusion, stemmed from the vast and interconnected politico-geographical influence of the houses of Anjou, Aragon-Toulouse and Provence, which, together with transalpine houses like Montferrat, provided a continuing tradition of poetic patronage, as well as producing poets among their own members.

P.E. Bennett

Languages, *c.* 1200

The map outlines the linguistic situation *c.* 1200. A map covering the end of the first millennium would have looked very different, since, apart from Latin – the almost universal language of literacy – other languages mainly existed as more or less distinct (and largely unwritten) dialects from which, in ensuing centuries, there would emerge the first signs of maturing written (and hence standardizing) forms. It was in the twelfth and thirteenth centuries (very occasionally earlier, sometimes later) that vernacular languages began to be prominently recorded; then we can detect converging developments which became the bases of later standard and national forms. Spoken and regional forms – always perhaps the primary language of troubadours, preachers and ordinary people – developed into national writ-

ten forms with the impetus of social, cultural and political evolution.

Virtually all the languages of Europe are descended from a postulated common prehistoric origin – Indo-European. The exceptions are Basque, whose origins seem more primitive still, and perhaps Albanian; and interloping languages of the Finno-Ugric family – Hungarian, and Estonian and Finnish.

Under the Roman Empire, Latin was the learned *lingua franca* throughout Europe. In the very early Middle Ages, Slavic and Magyar incursions westward surrounded the Latin-speaking province of Dacia: hence the separate development of Rumanian. It is from Slavic that Russian, Polish, Czech, Slovak, Slovenian, Serbo-Croatian, Macedonian and Bulgarian ultimately

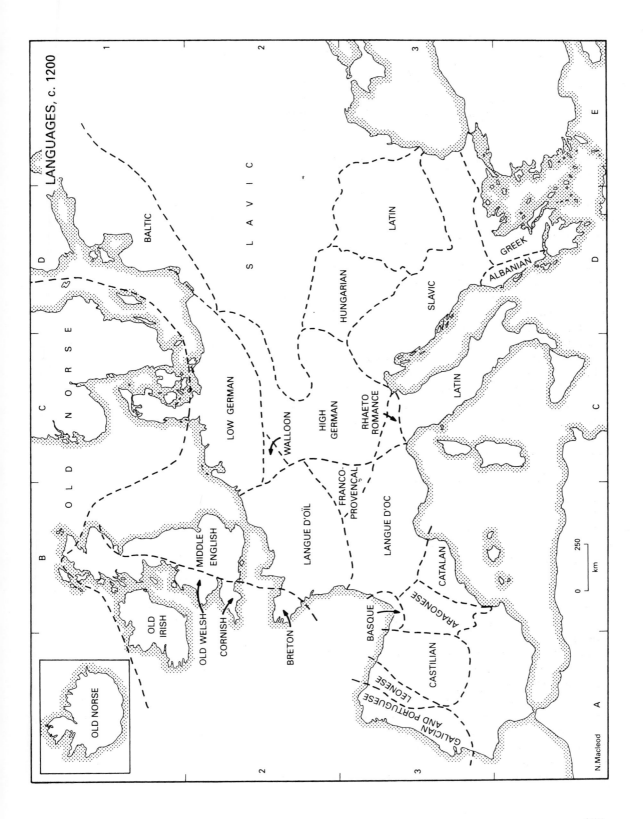

LANGUAGES, c. 1200

OLD NORSE

BALTIC

S L A V I C

LATIN

HUNGARIAN

GREEK

ALBANIAN

SLAVIC

LOW GERMAN

WALLOON

HIGH GERMAN

RHAETO ROMANCE

LATIN

MIDDLE ENGLISH

OLD IRISH

OLD WELSH

CORNISH

BRETON

LANGUE D'OÏL

FRANCO-PROVENÇAL

LANGUE D'OC

CATALAN

ARAGONESE

BASQUE

CASTILIAN

LEONESE

GALICIAN AND PORTUGUESE

OLD NORSE

250

km

0

N. Macleod

155

develop. Related, at least by contact if not by descent, are the Baltic languages of Lithuania and Latvia.

In northern Europe, the languages of Sweden, Denmark, Norway, Iceland and the Faroes began to develop separately out of Old Norse between 1150 and 1250.

Before the turn of the thirteenth century various phonological developments served to distinguish Low German (the precursor of Dutch, Flemish and Frisian) from (southern) High German, from which modern standard German evolved.

In medieval France a similar dialectal division holds between northern and central dialects (grouped as *langue d'oïl*) and the dialects of the south (*langue d'oc*). It was from one of the north-central forms, *francien*, the dialect of the Ile-de-France, that modern standard French developed.

Among various languages of the Iberian peninsula, one in particular occupied more and more territory with comparative rapidity: Castilian.

In thirteenth-century Italy much literary and non-literary material was still written in Latin. It was in the early part of the fourteenth century that Tuscan, specifically the Tuscan of Florence, emerged as the literary language of Italy.

In the British Isles medieval English, which had been very much to the fore in developing a written vernacular standard in Anglo-Saxon times, again emerged and would soon be ascendant, despite linguistic incursions from Scandinavia and France. In the east, north and south of the Forth Scots began to emerge as a separate standard language before 1400. Other regions of northern and western Britain became the locations of various (and, once, more prominent) Celtic languages – the descendants of Brythonic in Wales and Cornwall, and of Goidelic in Ireland and Scotland.

N. Macleod

THE LATE MIDDLE AGES
(*c.* 1300–*c.* 1500)

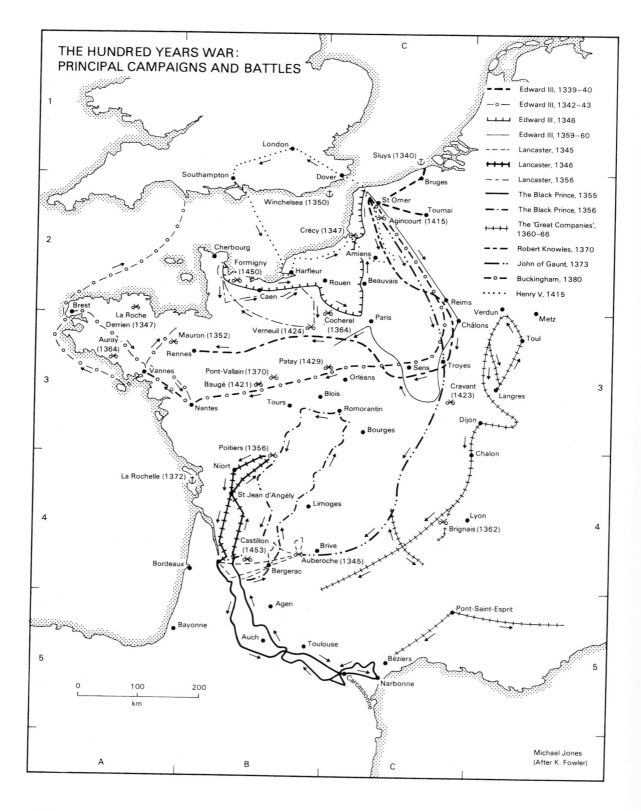

THE HUNDRED YEARS WAR:
PRINCIPAL CAMPAIGNS AND BATTLES

▬ ▬ ▬	Edward III, 1339–40
—o—	Edward III, 1342–43
⊢⊣⊢⊣	Edward III, 1346
——	Edward III, 1359–60
– – –	Lancaster, 1345
✚✚✚	Lancaster, 1346
— — —	Lancaster, 1356
▬▬▬	The Black Prince, 1355
▬·▬·▬	The Black Prince, 1356
┼┼┼┼	The 'Great Companies', 1360–66
▬ ▬ ▬	Robert Knowles, 1370
▬··▬··▬	John of Gaunt, 1373
—o—o—	Buckingham, 1380
··········	Henry V, 1415

London
Southampton
Dover
Sluys (1340)
Bruges
Winchelsea (1350)
St Omer
Tournai
Crécy (1347)
Agincourt (1415)
Cherbourg
Amiens
Formigny (1450)
Harfleur
Caen
Rouen
Beauvais
Brest
Reims
Verdun
Metz
La Roche
Derrien (1347)
Cocherel (1364)
Paris
Châlons
Toul
Auray (1364)
Mauron (1352)
Verneuil (1424)
Rennes
Vannes
Patay (1429)
Sens
Troyes
Pont-Vallain (1370)
Cravant (1423)
Baugé (1421)
Orléans
Langres
Nantes
Tours
Blois
Romorantin
Dijon
Bourges
Chalon
Poitiers (1356)
Niort
Limoges
Lyon
La Rochelle (1372)
Brignais (1362)
St Jean d'Angély
Castillon (1453)
Brive
Bordeaux
Auberoche (1345)
Bergerac
Agen
Pont-Saint-Esprit
Bayonne
Auch
Toulouse
Béziers
Narbonne
Carcassonne

0   100   200
km

Michael Jones
(After K. Fowler)

POLITICS

The Hundred Years War

The long-term causes of 'the Hundred Years War' (a description for the conflicts traditionally covering the years 1337–1453) lay in the claims of the king of France, following the treaty of Paris (1259), to sovereignty over the duchy of Guyenne (or Aquitaine), then held by his liege vassal, the king of England. Difficulties in implementing this complex treaty and subsidiary agreements (Amiens, 1279; Paris, 1303), allied to a more precise definition of sovereign rights, provoked conflict. In 1294 Philip IV declared Guyenne forfeit and invaded the duchy. Although peace was soon restored and diplomats tried to resolve the long-standing problems, these efforts failed as both sides became entrenched in their positions. In 1324 Guyenne was again confiscated and, although peace was agreed in 1327, the French handed back a diminished duchy (holding on to the Agenais) and demanded reparations. Nor was tension subsequently eased by the Process of Agen (1332). By now other causes intensified ill-feeling. The French alliance with Scotland, first formed in 1295, was renewed and resulted in French intervention in support of David Bruce and a series of English invasions of Scotland between 1332 and 1337. There was rivalry for allies in the Netherlands, where economic factors were important because of the staple Anglo-Flemish wool trade. At sea piracy and naval activities connected with French crusading plans further exacerbated bad relations.

The extinction of the Capetian dynasty in the direct line (1328) was a turning point because it allowed Edward III to claim the Crown of France. At the time Philip of Valois, the nearest adult male claimant, was preferred as king. Edward, under the tutelage of Isabella and Mortimer, performed homage for his French lands. But after further efforts to resolve arguments over Guyenne, Edward undermined the basis on which Anglo-French relations had been predicated by claiming the Crown of France. This he did tentatively and momentarily in 1337, then more permanently from January 1340. This may have been pure expediency, but it has been pointed out that Edward's strategy up to 1360 suggests that he increasingly believed in his claim, even that the Crown was almost within his grasp following spectacular victories (Crécy, 1346; Poitiers, 1356). In any event, once adopted, the title 'king of France' was incorporated into the royal style until George III renounced it in 1801, apart from 1360–9 when an attempt was made to implement the treaty of Brétigny (1360) which ended the first major phase of the war.

If completed, this treaty would have given the English an enlarged and sovereign Guyenne, including Poitou, Saintonge, Périgord, Quercy and the Rouergue, vindicating Edward's resort to force. For, after a false start that brought little advantage by campaigning in the Low Countries and indeed led to bankruptcy, with the opening of the Breton succession war (1341–64) and campaigns in Normandy and Guyenne, the fame of English arms and chivalry spread throughout Europe. In 1359 Edward even prepared for his coronation at Reims but the failure of this campaign led to renewed negotiations with John II, captured at Poitiers, and to the partition of France in the treaty of Brétigny.

Failure to implement this treaty led to a renewal of war in 1369. Charles V quickly won most of the lands his father lost, leaving English Guyenne reduced to a rump around Bordeaux and Bayonne. However, the effort to drive the English out completely proved to be beyond the means of a war-torn country. With bases at Calais, Cherbourg and Brest, and the alliance, uncertain though it often was, of French princes like

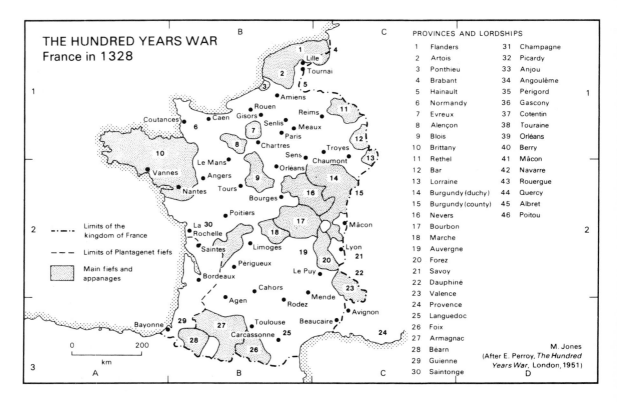

THE HUNDRED YEARS WAR
France in 1328

PROVINCES AND LORDSHIPS

1	Flanders	31	Champagne
2	Artois	32	Picardy
3	Ponthieu	33	Anjou
4	Brabant	34	Angoulême
5	Hainault	35	Périgord
6	Normandy	36	Gascony
7	Evreux	37	Cotentin
8	Alençon	38	Touraine
9	Blois	39	Orléans
10	Brittany	40	Berry
11	Rethel	41	Mâcon
12	Bar	42	Navarre
13	Lorraine	43	Rouergue
14	Burgundy (duchy)	44	Quercy
15	Burgundy (county)	45	Albret
16	Nevers	46	Poitou
17	Bourbon		
18	Marche		
19	Auvergne		
20	Forez		
21	Savoy		
22	Dauphiné		
23	Valence		
24	Provence		
25	Languedoc		
26	Foix		
27	Armagnac		
28	Béarn		
29	Guienne		
30	Saintonge		

Limits of the
kingdom of France

Limits of Plantagenet fiefs

Main fiefs and
appanages

0   200
km

M. Jones
(After E. Perroy, *The Hundred
Years War*, London, 1951)

the count of Flanders, duke of Brittany or king of Navarre, who held extensive lands in northern France, the English continued to maintain a presence. Moreover from the start both sides had involved their neighbours and war flared up elsewhere, notably after 1365 in the Iberian peninsula.

The war developed a momentum of its own. Many participated for profit or excitement. From the 1340s both kings found it hard to control troops who recognized their distant authority. Parts of northern, central and south-western France especially, although no area was entirely spared, suffered from a lawless soldiery. For a period in the 1350s and 1360s bands of English, Breton, Gascon, Navarrese, German and other mercenaries or *routiers* pursued private gain and formed the Great Companies which even tyrannized the pope at Avignon and defeated the duke of Bourbon at Brignais (1362). Civil wars in Flanders and Brittany or conflicts between powerful nobles added to the violence. Independent captains set up garrisons

in districts between zones of English or French allegiance and cruelly exploited the population. Uprisings like the Jacquerie (1358) or the Tuchinat from the 1360s were fuelled by the distress caused by the *routiers*. The same phenomenon affected widespread regions from the 1420s when the freebooters earned the name of 'flayers' (*écorcheurs*). It was in this form that many people experienced the reality of war; others were victims of the great *chevauchées* launched by the English; others suffered in the long sieges of which those of Calais (1346–7), Rennes (1356–7), St-Sauveur (1374–5), Rouen (1418–19) and Orléans (1428–9) are the best-known.

The pattern of short campaigns or longer sieges interspersed with truces and negotiations, established from the first years of the war, most obviously shaped events from 1369 to 1415. If Richard II did not pursue with conviction the conflict he inherited but looked for peace (a twenty-eight-year truce came into force in 1398) and Henry IV was largely prevented from

160

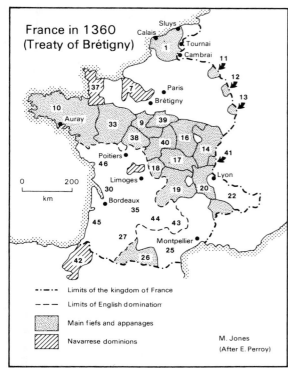

France in 1360
(Treaty of Brétigny)

Sluys
Calais
Tournai
Cambrai
1
11
12
37
7
Paris
Brétigny
13
10
Auray
33
9
39
38
40
16
14
41
Poitiers
46
17
18
Lyon
Limoges
30
19
20
22
Bordeaux
35
44
43
45
27
Montpellier
25
42
26

0   200
km

- · - · - Limits of the kingdom of France
- - - Limits of English domination
▨ Main fiefs and appanages
▧ Navarrese dominions

M. Jones
(After E. Perroy)

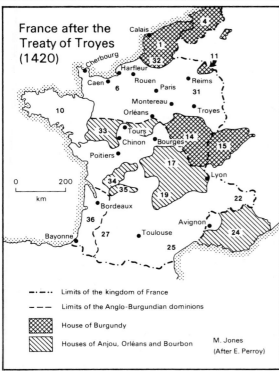

France after the
Treaty of Troyes
(1420)

Calais
4
1
32
11
Cherbourg
Harfleur
Caen
6
Rouen
Paris
Reims
31
10
Montereau
Orléans
Troyes
33
Tours
Chinon
Bourges
14
Poitiers
15
17
Lyon
34
35
19
22
Bordeaux
36
Avignon
Bayonne
27
Toulouse
24
25

0   200
km

- · - · - Limits of the kingdom of France
- - - Limits of the Anglo-Burgundian dominions
▨ House of Burgundy
▧ Houses of Anjou, Orléans and Bourbon

M. Jones
(After E. Perroy)

re-opening the war by revolts and illness, Henry V had few qualms about the justice of his cause. After his request that the terms of Brétigny be fulfilled was rejected, he launched the *chevauchée* that culminated in victory at Agincourt (1415). Thereafter, taking advantage of French divisions, he determined on a systematic conquest beginning with Normandy (1417–19). In 1419 the murder of John the Fearless, duke of Burgundy, drove his successor, Philip the Good, into an English alliance, delivered Paris to Henry and enabled him to attempt a novel solution to the war.

If it can be argued that up to 1419 Henry worked within the Brétigny tradition of trying to obtain extensive territories in full sovereignty (for which the claim to the French Crown might be seen as a cloak), in 1420 he adopted a new approach. In the treaty of Troyes he came to terms with Queen Isabella and the Burgundians to disinherit the dauphin – the future Charles VII – and marry Catherine, daughter of Charles VI, thus settling the Crown on them and their issue and forming the double monarchy of England and France. The premature death of Henry, two months before that of Charles VI (1422), leaving the infant Henry VI, ruined the chances of this audacious plan, though Henry VI was later crowned king at Paris (1431). For the revival of the fortunes of Charles VII, 'the king of Bourges', slowly wore down English resistance. Too much significance should not be attached to the exploits of Joan of Arc, like the relief of Orléans (May 1429), but the renewed confidence of the French monarchy, seen in the coronation which followed, was buoyed up by the defection of the Burgundians from their English allegiance in the treaty of Arras (1435). In 1436 Paris was recaptured by Constable Richemont, whilst from 1439 financial reforms also prepared the way for the restoration of royal authority. In England support for the war was at a low ebb. In 1444 a new truce was agreed at Tours. Henry VI undertook to marry Charles VII's niece, and to return Maine. By 1449 Charles was ready to launch his reformed army. A brilliant campaign saw the reconquest of Normandy (1449–50). In 1451 Guyenne capitulated and although it reverted to the English in 1452, resources dispatched for its defence proved inadequate. In 1453 the veteran commander John Talbot, earl of Shrewsbury, who with a handful of other outstanding captains had propped up the occupation of Normandy since 1422, was defeated and killed at Castillon in the last major battle of the war. Bordeaux yielded in October; no peace was sealed but the war was over. Beginning as a quarrel between lord and vassal, it had long since become a conflict between 'autonomous and self-contained kingdoms . . . and Frenchmen and Englishmen began to hate one another as Englishmen and Frenchmen' (Le Patourel).

M. Jones

The Growth of the Burgundian State

The rise and fall of this state under its Valois dukes – Philip the Bold (1363–1404), John the Fearless (1404–19), Philip the Good (1419–67) and Charles the Bold (1467–77) – was a spectacular development. When the last Capetian duke of Burgundy died (1361), his lands escheated to the French Crown and John II conferred the duchy on his youngest son Philip (1363). His fortunes were further enhanced when he married the late duke's widow (1369) because she was heiress to the counties of Flanders, Artois, Rethel, Nevers and Burgundy. After almost fifty years of scheming and indirect influence in the duchy of Brabant, this duchy together with that of Limbourg fell into Philip the Good's hands (1430). In 1421 he had purchased the county of Namur. Between 1428 and 1433 the counties of Hainault, Holland and Zeeland were inherited by him, and in 1443 he made good claims to the duchy of Luxembourg. In the south, in addition to the duchy and county of Burgundy, the county of Charolais was bought (1390) and John the Fearless acquired those of Tonnerre and Mâcon. Burgundian influence was also felt in many of the enclaves and prince-bishoprics along the border between France and the empire, especially when ducal bastards were appointed as bishops. Thus, partly by dynastic accident and partly through deliberate policy, the dukes controlled a large complex of territories. These extended some 500 miles from north to south and between 150 and 250 miles from east to west at their maximum, though the two main blocs centring on Flanders and the Low Countries and on the two Burgundies were usually separated by a gap of *c.* 150 miles. Charles the Bold in particular tried to bridge this by acquiring intervening lands – bringing him into conflict with his neighbours, especially in Bar, Lorraine and Alsace.

Held together largely by personal ties between the duke (or his family) and the separate territories, including the highly urbanized Low Countries and the rich agricultural and human resources of Burgundy, the state remained primarily a dynastic creation though it developed certain institutions enabling the duke to exercise rule more effectively throughout his lands. A common currency was created (1433). Estates General were held. Representatives from every quarter could be found at court or in the duke's council and administration. The chivalric order of the Golden Fleece (1430) focused the loyalty of the high nobility of blood and service from all over the duke's dominions. For contemporaries Philip the Good or Charles the Bold was 'the great duke of the west' (*le grand duc du Ponant*). With more than 3 million subjects, the dukes had enormous resources of wealth and manpower. Their prestige equalled that of ancient kingdoms and aspirations for a crown first clearly emerged with Philip the Good in the 1440s. Under Charles it seemed that a new Middle Kingdom would appear. In 1473 Charles even had his coronation robes made in preparation for an interview at Trier with Emperor Frederick III, who was expected to decree his elevation. Sadly deceived when Frederick secretly left without a formal declaration, Charles redoubled his efforts to capture the

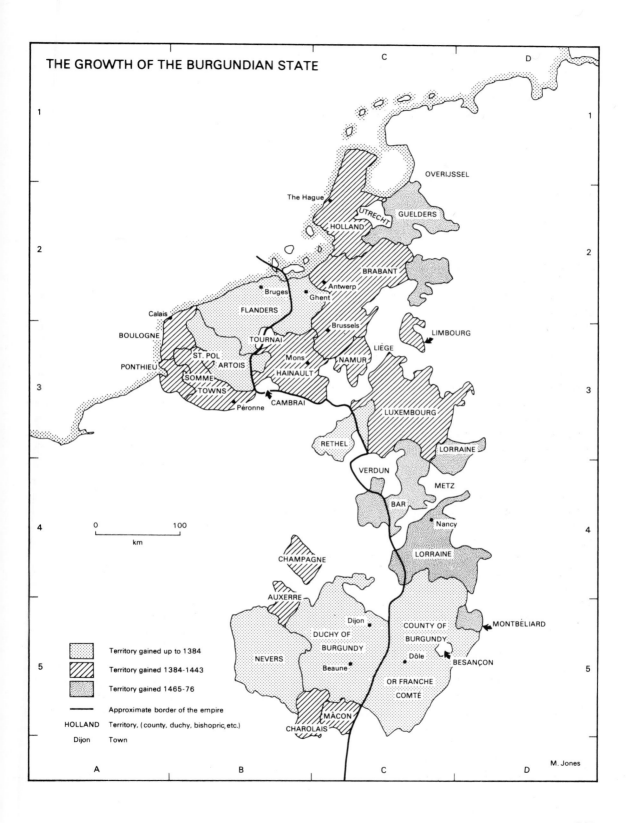

THE GROWTH OF THE BURGUNDIAN STATE

OVERIJSSEL

The Hague
UTRECHT
GUELDERS
HOLLAND

BRABANT

Bruges
FLANDERS
Antwerp
Ghent

Calais

BOULOGNE
Brussels
LIMBOURG

PONTHIEU
TOURNAI
ST. POL
ARTOIS
Mons
NAMUR
LIÈGE
SOMME
TOWNS
HAINAULT
Péronne
CAMBRAI
LUXEMBOURG

RETHEL
LORRAINE

VERDUN
METZ

BAR

Nancy

CHAMPAGNE
LORRAINE

AUXERRE

Dijon
COUNTY OF
BURGUNDY
MONTBÉLIARD

DUCHY OF
BURGUNDY

NEVERS
Dôle
BESANÇON
Beaune
OR FRANCHE
COMTÉ

MÂCON
CHAROLAIS

0   100
km

	Territory gained up to 1384
	Territory gained 1384-1443
	Territory gained 1465-76
——	Approximate border of the empire
HOLLAND	Territory, (county, duchy, bishopric, etc.)
Dijon	Town

M. Jones

duchy of Lorraine. But defeated by the Swiss (Morat and Granson, 1476) and the Lorrainers (Nancy, 1477), urged on by Louis XI of France and assisted by Charles' many enemies in the Rhineland and elsewhere, Charles' death before Nancy (5 January 1477) signalled the end of the Valois duchy. The main beneficiaries were the French king, who repossessed all the French fiefs of the duke except Flanders, and the house of Habsburg. For the duke's only heiress, Mary, desperate for protection against French aggres-sion, married Maximilian, son of Frederick III (August 1477). Despite internal disputes in the Low Countries and Mary's premature death (1482), Maximilian managed to preserve the imperial fiefs of Burgundy, together with Flanders. Ephemeral and personal, the Valois duchy of Burgundy yet left an important heritage to successor states. Belgian and Dutch historians, in particular, have seen the period of Valois rule as decisive in the development of their nations.

M. Jones

The Scottish Wars of Independence

Edward I of England's efforts to take over Scotland in the 1290s sparked off a long sequence of cross-border invasions and raids punctuated by some devastating battles; but neither side could force the other to give in. The main war zone stretched across middle Britain, roughly from the Tyne north to the Forth. But the regions beyond that zone were perhaps more significant: Scottish raids could never get far enough south to put unbearable pressure on the English Crown (nor, though it was tried in 1315, could that be done via Ireland); conversely, it was beyond English power permanently to dominate Scotland north of the Forth, yet without that Scotland could never be conquered. This was understood by Edward I, whose northern campaigns of 1296 and 1303 (map A) produced massive (but temporary) Scottish submissions; and by Robert I (Robert Bruce), whose great achievements in the south – including victory at Bannockburn (1314), and English recognition of Scottish independence (1328) – were only possible after he had won northern Scotland from his English and Scottish enemies (1307–13) (map A). And when the war reopened in 1332 after Robert I's death, Edward III soon accepted the impossibility of conquering the north; instead, he overran and annexed about half of southern Scotland (map B). By the later fourteenth century, the main issue in Anglo-Scottish warfare (border raiding apart) was the Scottish recapture of this English-held territory. It was mostly achieved by 1384, and thereafter the warfare gradually petered out. But some places stayed in English hands until well into the fifteenth century; the last to be regained by the Scots was Berwick, in 1461 – which was lost again, permanently, in 1482 (map B).

A. Grant

Wales: The Principality and the Marches

During most of the thirteenth century the balance of territorial advantage between the Welsh rulers, the Marcher lords and the Crown had constantly shifted. But two broad tendencies were apparent: the growing assertiveness of royal government, and the emergence of the princes of Gwynedd as effective overlords of native Wales. These developments helped to make the Welsh war of 1282–3 far more radical in its effects than its many predecessors. Edward I evicted Llywelyn ap Gruffydd from north Wales, and seized his principality for the Crown; the take-over was aided by the firmer structure that Gwynedd had recently developed, and by the

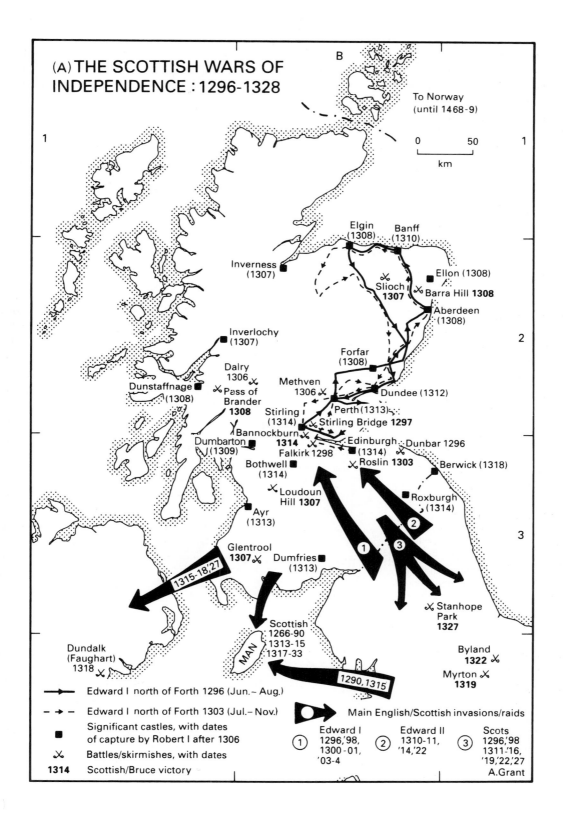

(A) THE SCOTTISH WARS OF INDEPENDENCE : 1296-1328

B

To Norway (until 1468-9)

0   50

km

Elgin (1308)
Banff (1310)
Inverness (1307)
Ellon (1308)
Slioch 1307
Barra Hill 1308
Aberdeen (1308)
Inverlochy (1307)
Forfar (1308)
Dalry 1306
Methven 1306
Dundee (1312)
Dunstaffnage (1308)
Pass of Brander 1308
Perth (1313)
Stirling (1314)
Stirling Bridge 1297
Bannockburn 1314
Dumbarton (1309)
Edinburgh (1314)
Dunbar 1296
Falkirk 1298
Bothwell (1314)
Roslin 1303
Berwick (1318)
Loudoun Hill 1307
Roxburgh (1314)
Ayr (1313)
Glentrool 1307
Dumfries (1313)
1315-18,'27
Stanhope Park 1327
Scottish 1266-90 1313-15 1317-33
MAN
Byland 1322
Dundalk (Faughart) 1318
Myrton 1319
1290,1315

Edward I north of Forth 1296 (Jun.– Aug.)

Edward I north of Forth 1303 (Jul.– Nov.)

Significant castles, with dates of capture by Robert I after 1306

Battles/skirmishes, with dates

1314 Scottish/Bruce victory

Main English/Scottish invasions/raids

① Edward I 1296,'98, 1300-01, '03-4

② Edward II 1310-11, '14,'22

③ Scots 1296,'98 1311-'16, '19,'22,'27

A.Grant

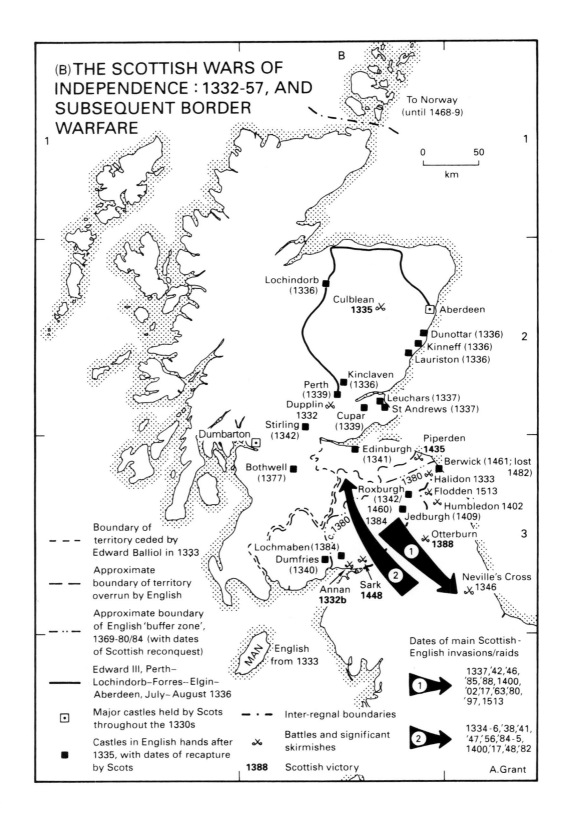

(B) THE SCOTTISH WARS OF INDEPENDENCE : 1332-57, AND SUBSEQUENT BORDER WARFARE

To Norway (until 1468-9)

0   50
km

Lochindorb (1336)
Culblean 1335
Aberdeen
Dunottar (1336)
Kinneff (1336)
Lauriston (1336)
Kinclaven (1336)
Perth (1339)
Dupplin 1332
Leuchars (1337)
St Andrews (1337)
Cupar (1339)
Stirling (1342)
Dumbarton
Edinburgh (1341)
Piperden 1435
Berwick (1461; lost 1482)
Bothwell (1377)
Halidon 1333
Roxburgh (1342/1460)
Flodden 1513
Humbledon 1402
Jedburgh (1409)
1384
Otterburn 1388
Lochmaben (1384)
Dumfries (1340)
Neville's Cross 1346
Annan 1332b
Sark 1448

MAN
English from 1333

Boundary of territory ceded by Edward Balliol in 1333

Approximate boundary of territory overrun by English

Approximate boundary of English 'buffer zone', 1369-80/84 (with dates of Scottish reconquest)

Edward III, Perth– Lochindorb–Forres–Elgin– Aberdeen, July–August 1336

Major castles held by Scots throughout the 1330s

Castles in English hands after 1335, with dates of recapture by Scots

Inter-regnal boundaries

Battles and significant skirmishes

1388   Scottish victory

Dates of main Scottish- English invasions/raids

1337,'42,'46, '85,'88,1400, '02,'17,'63,'80, '97,1513

1334-6,'38,'41, '47,'56,'84-5, 1400,'17,'48,'82

A.Grant

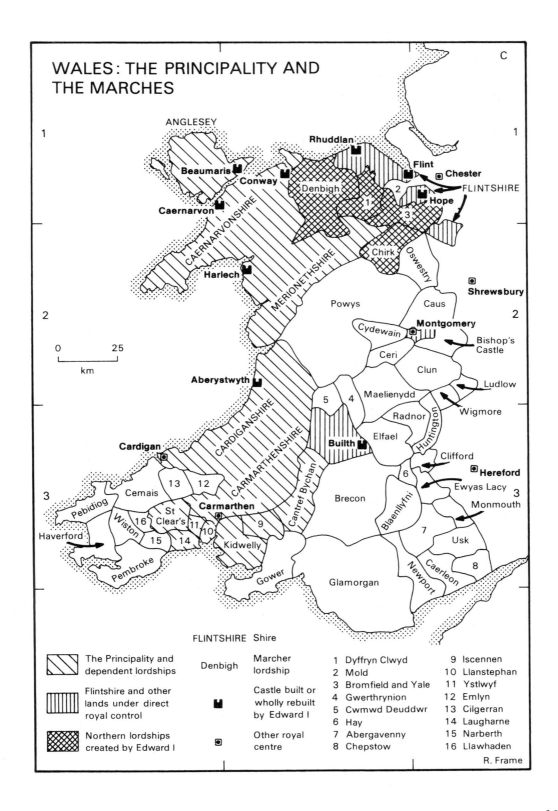

WALES: THE PRINCIPALITY AND THE MARCHES

C

ANGLESEY

1

Rhuddlan

Flint

Chester

Beaumaris

Conway

Denbigh

1

FLINTSHIRE

Caernarvon

2

Hope

CAERNARVONSHIRE

3

Harlech

MERIONETHSHIRE

Chirk

Oswestry

Powys

Caus

Shrewsbury

2

Cydewain

Montgomery

2

Bishop's
Castle

Ceri

0   25

Clun

km

Aberystwyth

Maelienydd

Ludlow

5   4

Wigmore

CARDIGANSHIRE

Radnor

Elfael

Huntington

Builth

Clifford

Cardigan

Hereford

Cemais

13   12

6

Ewyas Lacy

3

Pebidiog

CARMARTHENSHIRE

Monmouth

3

Brecon

Haverford

Wiston

16

St
Clear's

11

Carmarthen

Blaenllyfni

7

Usk

15   14

10

Kidwelly

9

Caerleon

8

Pembroke

Cantref Bychan

Newport

Gower

Glamorgan

FLINTSHIRE Shire

The Principality and dependent lordships	Denbigh	Marcher lordship
Flintshire and other lands under direct royal control		Castle built or wholly rebuilt by Edward I
Northern lordships created by Edward I		Other royal centre

1 Dyffryn Clwyd	9 Iscennen
2 Mold	10 Llanstephan
3 Bromfield and Yale	11 Ystlwyf
4 Gwerthrynion	12 Emlyn
5 Cwmwd Deuddwr	13 Cilgerran
6 Hay	14 Laugharne
7 Abergavenny	15 Narberth
8 Chepstow	16 Llawhaden

R. Frame

167

defection of members of its ministerial class.

Edward's victory saw the former heartland of Llywelyn's power organized into the shires of Anglesey, Caernarvon and Merioneth, now controlled from Caernarvon by an English justiciar and chamberlain. Royal castles, often accompanied by boroughs where English settlement was promoted, were built at strategic points. This new area of Crown authority, with Edward's conquests in west Wales and the old royal lordships of Cardigan and Carmarthen, formed the Principality which from 1301 was usually bestowed upon the king's eldest son. In the north-east, apart from the county of Flint which was ruled from Chester, most of the gains were distributed to English aristocrats, who also built castles, established boroughs, and displaced native populations. This added to the mosaic of jurisdictionally privileged Marcher lordships which already occupied most of south Wales and the borders. In the later Middle Ages there were some Welsh risings, but only that of Owain Glyn Dŵr in the reign of Henry IV was other than localized and transient. In the more stable political conditions the Principality and the Marches were available for economic exploitation by the English Crown and nobility, with whom the Welsh squirearchy – displaying an intriguing mixture of careerism and resentment – took service.

R. Frame

Ireland: English and Gaelic Lordship, *c.* 1350

Whereas in the later Middle Ages the Welsh political map tended towards greater neatness and stability, that of Ireland remained fluid. In the mid-thirteenth century Ireland had probably seemed more firmly within English control than Wales: English lords dominated about three-quarters of the country, and there was no single centre of native rule to match Gwynedd. In the age of Edward I, when royal administration was growing at the expense of baronial jurisdictions, and the Dublin government was raising men, money and provisions for the Welsh and Scottish wars, the situation might still have been regarded with some satisfaction from Westminster.

The fourteenth century saw English Ireland weakened by famine, plague, emigration, the division of lordships among absentee heiresses, Scottish invasion, and the growth of Gaelic military capacity close to Dublin. The retreat was slow and patchy. Even at the height of English power not just the unshired north and the western fringes but also enclaves of upland and bog in southern and eastern Ireland had remained Irish in culture and subject only to superficial influence. In the later Middle Ages the areas of Gaelic custom and lordship expanded. But it should not be imagined that English rule was restricted to the hinterland of Dublin and a few coastal towns; even in the late fifteenth century – the era of the 'Pale' – the contraction was never so drastic. Royal authority penetrated, however unevenly and indirectly, into a sizeable world where gentry communities, urban elites, Anglo-Irish magnates, and Gaelic lords coexisted in complex local balances, and where English and Irish custom interacted. Across the official administrative divisions lay other boundaries and zones of command whose informal and shifting character makes them impossible to depict precisely. The map provides a – necessarily impressionistic – view of the gulf between the theoretical extent of royal administration and the regions actually subject to English law and government.

R. Frame

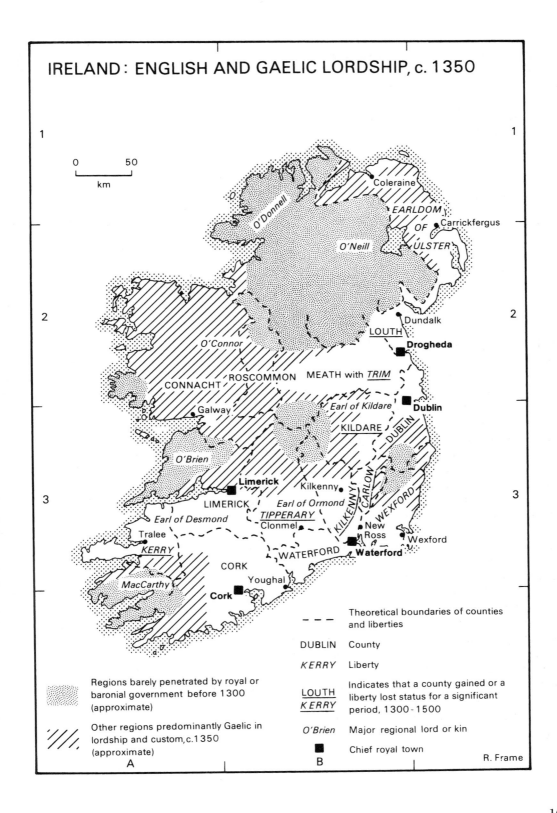

IRELAND: ENGLISH AND GAELIC LORDSHIP, c. 1350

0   50
km

Coleraine

EARLDOM

Carrickfergus

O'Neill

OF

ULSTER

O'Donnell

Dundalk

LOUTH

Drogheda

O'Connor

MEATH with *TRIM*

CONNACHT   ROSCOMMON

Galway

Earl of Kildare

Dublin

KILDARE

DUBLIN

O'Brien

CARLOW

WEXFORD

Limerick

Kilkenny

LIMERICK   *Earl of Ormond*

KILKENNY

Earl of Desmond   *TIPPERARY*

New
Ross

Clonmel

Tralee

Wexford

KERRY

WATERFORD

Waterford

CORK

Youghal

MacCarthy

Cork

Theoretical boundaries of counties
and liberties

DUBLIN   County

KERRY   Liberty

<u>LOUTH</u>   Indicates that a county gained or a
<u>*KERRY*</u>   liberty lost status for a significant
period, 1300 - 1500

Regions barely penetrated by royal or
baronial government before 1300
(approximate)

O'Brien   Major regional lord or kin

Other regions predominantly Gaelic in
lordship and custom, c.1350
(approximate)

■   Chief royal town

R. Frame

A   B

169

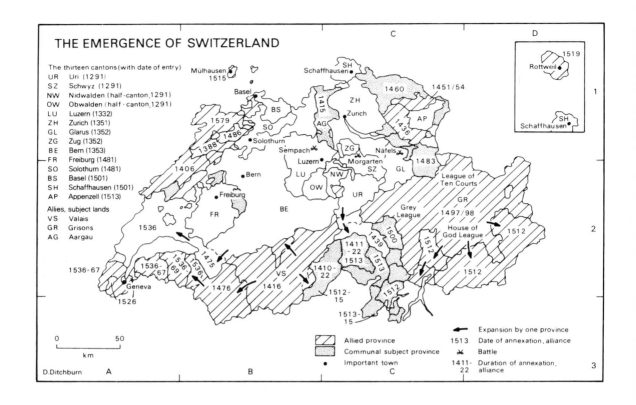

THE EMERGENCE OF SWITZERLAND

The thirteen cantons (with date of entry)

UR   Uri (1291)
SZ   Schwyz (1291)
NW   Nidwalden (half-canton,1291)
OW   Obwalden (half-canton,1291)
LU   Luzern (1332)
ZH   Zurich (1351)
GL   Glarus (1352)
ZG   Zug (1352)
BE   Bern (1353)
FR   Freiburg (1481)
SO   Solothurn (1481)
BS   Basel (1501)
SH   Schaffhausen (1501)
AP   Appenzell (1513)

Allies, subject lands

VS   Valais
GR   Grisons
AG   Aargau

Allied province
Communal subject province
•   Important town

Expansion by one province
1513   Date of annexation, alliance
Battle
1411-   Duration of annexation,
22   alliance

D.Ditchburn

0   50
km

The Emergence of Switzerland

The 1291 pact between Uri, Schwyz and Nidwalden, later joined by Obwalden, traditionally marks the birth of Switzerland. Motivated by the desire to constrain Habsburg overlordship, this was probably the revival of an older alliance. After 1291 the cantons successfully played the Habsburgs off against other imperial families and in 1315 they defeated the Habsburgs at Morgarten. To further secure their quasi-autonomous status, allies were sought and Luzern, a town closely connected economically and ecclesiastically, joined in 1332. Temporary alliances with Zurich, Zug and Glarus, all wary of Habsburg intentions, were made permanent shortly afterwards. Bern, a less obvious ally, joined in 1352. For the next century and a half the eight cantons (sometimes together, sometimes on their own) were embroiled in wars, some defensive, some expansionist. Habsburg power was further limited by victories at Sem-

pach (1386) and Näfels (1388), and the joint cantonal occupation of Aargau in 1415. Victory in the Swabian War of 1499 confirmed Switzerland's de facto independence from the empire. Bern's chief preoccupation was in the west, where she clashed with Burgundy. Not until Duke Charles the Bold's defeat and death at Nancy, in 1477, was this threat removed. Uri spearheaded southern expansion. Swiss participation in the Holy League secured the acquisition of the Ticinese provinces from Milan in 1512/13. Swiss influence also grew through a series of alliances with neighbouring provinces. There was reluctance, however, to admit new cantons. Appenzell was only admitted in 1513. Freiburg and Solothurn entered in 1486, following their support in the Burgundian wars, while Basel and Schaffhausen, allies in the Swabian War, joined in 1501.

Unity was, however, originally based only on

the desire to maintain cantonal independence. Initially there were no central institutions and cantonal interests frequently clashed. Yet, due to military success, the fragile unity of the unusual alliance between towns and rural communities was preserved.

D. Ditchburn

Late Medieval Scandinavia: Unity and Disunity

In 1360–1 the Danish king Valdemar Atterdag conquered Scania from Sweden and then Öland and Gotland. This provoked a war with the Hanse, which perceived a threat to its commercial interests. Although Valdemar was supported by his son-in-law Hakon VI of Norway, the Hanse triumphed. Its domination of Scandinavia was confirmed by the Peace of Stralsund in 1370. The Peace of Vordingborg in 1435, following further conflict with Denmark over the imposition of shipping tolls at the Sound, reaffirmed

Hanseatic commercial privileges. Thereafter, faced with growing Dutch competition and renewed Danish hostility, the Hanse maintained its commercial domination of Scandinavia with difficulty. In 1387 Valdemar's formidable daughter Margaret had become regent of Denmark and Norway. At the invitation of discontented magnates, she invaded Sweden, defeating the Swedish king Albrecht at Aasle in 1389. Stockholm submitted in 1395 and the Scandinavian kingdoms were formally united by the Union of

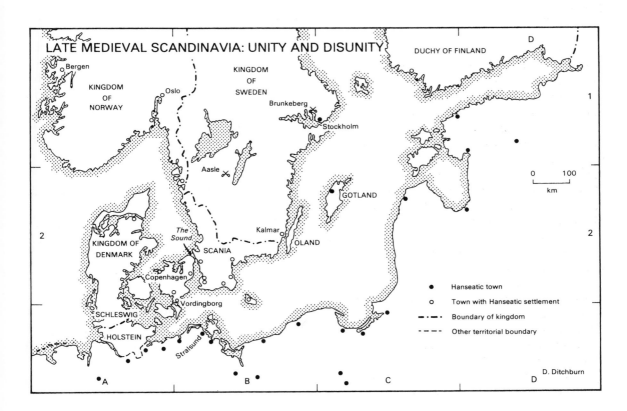

LATE MEDIEVAL SCANDINAVIA: UNITY AND DISUNITY

DUCHY OF FINLAND

KINGDOM OF NORWAY — Bergen, Oslo

KINGDOM OF SWEDEN — Brunkeberg, Stockholm, Aasle

GOTLAND

Kalmar, The Sound, SCANIA, ÖLAND

KINGDOM OF DENMARK — Copenhagen, Vordingborg

SCHLESWIG, HOLSTEIN, Stralsund

0 100 km

● Hanseatic town
○ Town with Hanseatic settlement
–·–·– Boundary of kingdom
– – – Other territorial boundary

D. Ditchburn

Kalmar in 1397. Gotland was conquered in 1409, while in 1460 King Christian I was also elected duke of Schleswig and Holstein. Nevertheless the growth of royal power had its limitations. Orkney and Shetland were ceded to Scotland in 1468–9. In Denmark and Sweden the monarchy remained elective. Powerful magnates in particular resented the imposition of heavier taxation and the appointment of foreign and non-noble officials. Discontent was greatest in Sweden. Revolts were led by Engelbrecht Engelbrechtson and Karl Knutson, who was elected King Charles VIII of Sweden in 1448. The revolts were suppressed in 1457 but resumed in 1464. After the Swedish regent Sten Sture defeated the Danes at Brunkeberg in 1471, the Danish kings Christian I and John struggled to maintain their authority in Sweden. They received support from their kinsman James IV of Scotland and took advantage of divisions among the Swedish nobility. The Swedish resistance was generally backed by the Hanse. It was not until 1523, however, that the Union of Kalmar was finally dissolved.

D. Ditchburn

Emperors and Princes: Germany in the Later Middle Ages

German settlement respected few natural or political frontiers in the Middle Ages. In the Tirol it had spread south of the Alps and in the east beyond the frontiers of the German kingdom. By contrast the Valois rulers of the Low Countries were Frenchmen who sought ultimately to establish their own kingdom while Bohemia was the heartland of both the Luxembourg dynasty of German kings and the Czech national movement led by Jan Hus and his followers. Limited geographical and ethnic unity was matched by monarchical weakness. The German kingdom was part of the Holy Roman Empire and, following coronation by the pope, German kings were styled emperor. Yet little of the empire, and even less of the emperors' pretensions to political leadership of the entire West, remained intact following the Hohenstauffen dynasty's clash with the papacy and the ensuing interregnum between 1250 and 1273. Thereafter imperial authority was in practice confined largely to Germany and the increasingly Germanic nature of the imperial monarchy was confirmed by the formal exclusion of the papacy from imperial elections in 1338. The rules for imperial elections were further clarified in the Golden Bull of 1356 with the designation of seven (German) electors. Even within Germany, however, the elective nature of kingship constrained monarchical power. Despite an almost unbroken succession of emperors from the Luxembourg family between 1346 and 1437, and then from the Habsburg family after 1438, no king could be certain that his heir would inherit the title. Moreover, the resources of German kings were scant. Most of the imperial lands had been usurped during the conflicts of the thirteenth century. Little other than the imperial towns remained and these were frequently mortgaged. Royal rights over the fragmentary morass of ecclesiastical and secular principalities had also diminished, partly through immunities granted in return for political support and partly through neglect. In the Golden Bull Charles IV (1347–78) recognized the impossibility of retrieving the situation by formally granting the electors extensive rights and freedoms from royal interference. These were privileges to which other princes also aspired. With limited resources and rights kings lacked the need and ability to develop strong institutions of central government. Beset by such difficulties the monarchy failed to emerge as a focus for political unity and, instead, German kings invested their energies in the augmentation of family lands (*Hausgut*) rather than imperial possessions (*Reichsgut*). In this the Habsburgs were strikingly successful. By 1300

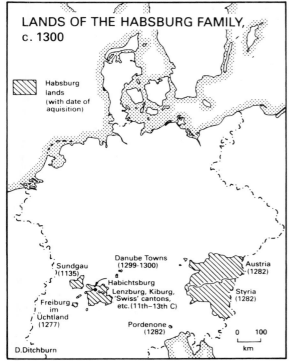

LANDS OF THE HABSBURG FAMILY, c. 1300

Habsburg lands (with date of aquisition)

Sundgau (1135)

Danube Towns (1299-1300)

Austria (1282)

Habichtsburg
Lenzburg, Kiburg, 'Swiss' cantons, etc.(11th–13th C)

Styria (1282)

Freiburg im Üchtland (1277)

Pordenone (1282)

0   100
km

D.Ditchburn

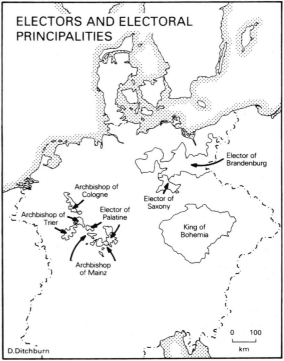

ELECTORS AND ELECTORAL PRINCIPALITIES

Elector of Brandenburg

Archbishop of Cologne

Elector of Saxony

Archbishop of Trier

Elector of Palatine

King of Bohemia

Archbishop of Mainz

0   100
km

D.Ditchburn

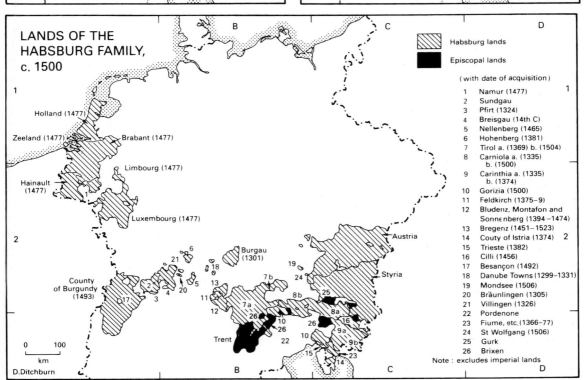

LANDS OF THE HABSBURG FAMILY, c. 1500

Habsburg lands

Episcopal lands

(with date of acquisition)

1   Namur (1477)
2   Sundgau
3   Pfirt (1324)
4   Breisgau (14th C)
5   Nellenberg (1465)
6   Hohenberg (1381)
7   Tirol a. (1369) b. (1504)
8   Carniola a. (1335)
         b. (1500)
9   Carinthia a. (1335)
         b. (1374)
10   Gorizia (1500)
11   Feldkirch (1375–9)
12   Bludenz, Montafon and
         Sonnenberg (1394–1474)
13   Bregenz (1451–1523)
14   Couty of Istria (1374)
15   Trieste (1382)
16   Cilli (1456)
17   Besançon (1492)
18   Danube Towns (1299–1331)
19   Mondsee (1506)
20   Bräunlingen (1305)
21   Villingen (1326)
22   Pordenone
23   Fiume, etc.(1366–77)
24   St Wolfgang (1506)
25   Gurk
26   Brixen
Note : excludes imperial lands

Holland (1477)

Zeeland (1477)

Brabant (1477)

Limbourg (1477)

Hainault (1477)

Luxembourg (1477)

County of Burgundy (1493)

Burgau (1301)

Austria

Styria

Trent

County of Burgundy (1493)

0   100
km

D.Ditchburn

they possessed Austria, Styria and various lands and jurisdictions around their ancestral castle of Habichtsburg. Other lands were acquired before 1500 by imperial grant, marriage, inheritance, purchase and conquest while Habsburg influence was exerted on ecclesiastical principalities such as Trent, Brixen and Gurk. The territorial ambitions and achievements of the Habsburgs were unusual in extent rather than in essence though the growth of princely power, even that of the Habsburgs, was neither swift, unchallenged nor without setbacks. Penury forced many princes to mortgage or sell their lands while the custom of partible inheritance led to the division of many principalities between heirs. There were often aggressive neighbours to contend with: the Habsburgs lost the Swiss cantons and the Hungarians occupied part of their eastern territories in the 1480s. Within many principalities the estates (gatherings of lesser nobles, clergymen, townsmen and occasionally, as in Tirol, of peasants) exploited princely weakness and often acquired considerable influence in return for settling magnate disputes or granting taxation. Only as the Middle Ages came to a close did princes overcome such problems. Lordship gradually became more territorial: the Electors Palatine, for example, exchanged other princes' serfs in the Palatinate for their own serfs elsewhere. The gradual introduction of regular taxation, primogeniture (which ended the fragmentation of lands) and notions of Roman law (which exalted the prince's position) further bolstered princely authority. Viewed from the perspective of an accretion of princely power, German developments slowly but more closely parallel growing royal power elsewhere in Europe.

D. Ditchburn

Northern Italy from the Rise of the *Signori* to the Peace of Lodi

From the later thirteenth century control of many north Italian city-states passed from oligarchic communal governments to dynastic *signorie*. This was particularly the case in the Trevisan March, Lombardy, Emilia and the Marches where many *signori* came to control more than one town. The nineteenth-century characterization of these rulers as 'despots' reflects their contemporary designation as 'tyrants', but underestimates the elements of continuity between the communal and signorial regimes: both were very violent, neither was democratic. Indeed, the change of regime did not generally lead to radical transformations in the conduct of government. The *signori* gained the ascendant gradually, often holding office in the commune and using their wealth and political skills to extend their control over the communal bureaucracy and to suppress opposition. Smaller towns in their control were generally allowed a considerable degree of self-government and the administrative structures of the communes frequently survived. Once in power the *signori* sought to legitimize their position and establish a hereditary right to govern, cultivating prestige through marriage alliances, artistic patronage, honours and titles, such as papal vicar or imperial duke, the latter a title acquired from the Emperor by Giangaleazzo Visconti of Milan in 1395. In the search for political ascendancy, violence was ever-present. Factionalism within towns frequently led to plots and assassinations such as that of Bartolomeo della Scala in 1381 at the instigation of his brother Antonio, who sought to ensure his own control of the *signorie* of Verona and Vicenza. At the same time the struggle for supremacy between city-states led to almost constant warfare. The growing use of mercenary companies (often composed from foreign troops) led by *condottieri* (often lords of smaller centres such as the Malatesta in Rimini) increased the general political instability. The

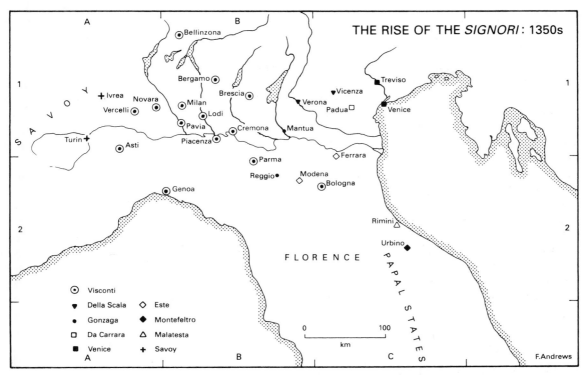

THE RISE OF THE *SIGNORI*: 1350s

Bellinzona

Bergamo

Treviso

Vicenza

Ivrea Novara Milan Brescia Verona Padua Venice

Vercelli Lodi

Pavia Cremona Mantua

Turin Piacenza

Asti

Parma Ferrara

Reggio Modena

Bologna

Genoa

S A V O Y

F L O R E N C E

Rimini

Urbino

P A P A L   S T A T E S

	Visconti		Este
	Della Scala		Montefeltro
	Gonzaga		Malatesta
	Da Carrara		Savoy
	Venice		

0   100
km

F. Andrews

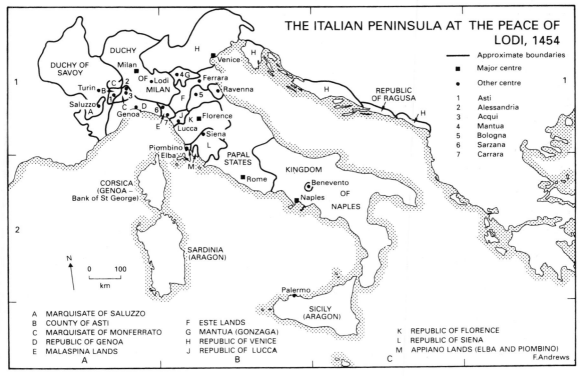

THE ITALIAN PENINSULA AT THE PEACE OF LODI, 1454

DUCHY OF SAVOY

DUCHY

Milan

Venice

OF Lodi

MILAN

Ferrara

Ravenna

Turin

Saluzzo

Genoa

Florence

Lucca

Siena

Piombino

Elba

CORSICA
(GENOA –
Bank of St George)

PAPAL
STATES

Rome

REPUBLIC
OF RAGUSA

KINGDOM

Benevento

Naples

OF

NAPLES

SARDINIA
(ARAGON)

Palermo

SICILY
(ARAGON)

—— Approximate boundaries

■ Major centre

● Other centre

1 Asti
2 Alessandria
3 Acqui
4 Mantua
5 Bologna
6 Sarzana
7 Carrara

N

0   100
km

A	MARQUISATE OF SALUZZO	F	ESTE LANDS	K	REPUBLIC OF FLORENCE
B	COUNTY OF ASTI	G	MANTUA (GONZAGA)	L	REPUBLIC OF SIENA
C	MARQUISATE OF MONFERRATO	H	REPUBLIC OF VENICE	M	APPIANO LANDS (ELBA AND PIOMBINO)
D	REPUBLIC OF GENOA	J	REPUBLIC OF LUCCA		
E	MALASPINA LANDS				

F. Andrews

first map shows the situation in the 1350s when the lands of the Visconti of Milan had extended to absorb several neighbouring cities. The situation was, however, fluid and smaller centres frequently changed hands: in 1336 the della Scala had controlled Brescia, Padua, Treviso, Feltre, Belluno, Parma and even Lucca but their defeat in 1339 at the hands of Florence and Venice (the only two major cities to remain ostensibly republican in form though the differences were often little more than a matter of diplomatic rhetoric) restricted the della Scala to Verona and Vicenza. The second map shows the situation at the peace of Lodi in 1454. In the intervening years the Milan-based *signorie* of the Visconti had expanded under Giangaleazzo and then partly fragmented following his sudden death in 1402. It was substantially restored once his son, Filippo Maria, came of age but in the 1420s war broke out between the long-standing enemies, Milan and Florence. Over the following decades most of the Italian peninsula became involved. Venice, increasingly concerned about the security of its hinterland and now intent upon a policy of expansion on the mainland

(*terraferma*), joined an intermittent alliance with Florence against Milan. Later both Alfonso of Naples and papal forces were drawn into the conflict. Filippo Maria's death without legitimate male heirs in 1447 transformed the situation. The Visconti regime in Milan was replaced by the short-lived 'Ambrosian Republic' (1447–50). After the failure of the republic, named after the patron saint of the city, Milan fell under the control of Francesco Sforza, a *condottiere* who had fought for both Milan and Florence and who in 1441 had married Filippo Maria's daughter, Bianca. On 9 April 1454 Milan and Venice agreed to the peace of Lodi. The other major powers, Florence, the papacy and Naples, eventually also adhered to the peace. Together these five principal powers of Italy founded the Italian (or Italic) League. This sought, with limited success, to promote political stability in the peninsula by recognizing the territorial status quo, regulating military resources and establishing ground rules for the pursuit of war. Remarkably, it was to last for forty years.

F. Andrews

The Expansion of the Crown of Aragon

James I (1213–76) conquered Majorca (1229), Menorca (1232), Ibiza (1235) and Valencia (1238). Subsequently Corsica and Sardinia were added to the Mediterranean possessions of the Crown of Aragon, an uprising against the Angevins in Sicily in 1282 led to its acquisition, and Alfonso V (1416–58) devoted his reign to southern Italy, which he conquered, despite papal and Angevin opposition, after the death of Joanna II of Naples (1435).

The importance attached to Mediterranean possessions by Aragonese kings entailed serious repercussions for their realms in Spain. Peter III (1276–85) might have curbed the Aragonese nobility but for his preoccupation with Sicily, and succeeding kings had to accept constitutional limitations.

Institutional innovations were linked to the

problem of 'absentee monarchy'. Kings had to delegate powers to *procuradores*, and from the late fourteenth century there appeared lieutenants-general or viceroys in Sardinia, Sicily and Majorca, a pattern repeated in Aragon, Catalonia and Valencia as a result of Alfonso V's absence in Italy.

The powers of monarchs and their officials were severely curtailed by the various *cortes* of the federation. Consent was necessary for all laws and grievances redressed before financial aid was granted. Between meetings of the *cortes* royal officials were controlled by standing committees. The origins of the Catalan *Diputació* or *Generalitat* date from the late thirteenth century when delegates were appointed to deal with problems once the representatives had dispersed, their main task being to control the raising and spending of money. By 1359 the *Generalitat* was a permanent body, and similar institutions were set up in Aragon and Valencia in 1412 and 1419. Controlling royal authority, the *cortes* were not democratic; they represented the privileged, defending the interests of the oligarchs who dominated the towns and the countryside.

A. MacKay

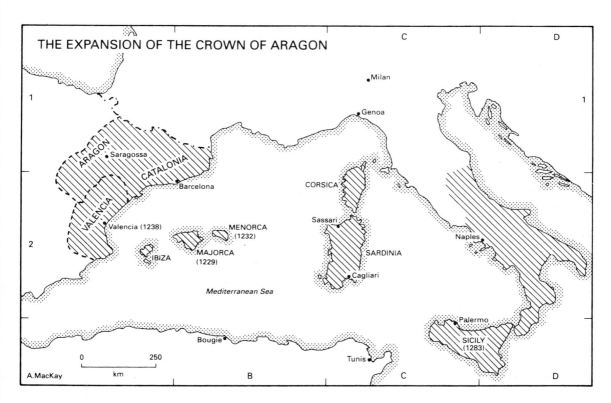

THE EXPANSION OF THE CROWN OF ARAGON

ARAGON · Saragossa
CATALONIA
· Barcelona
VALENCIA
Valencia (1238)
· IBIZA
MENORCA (1232)
MAJORCA (1229)
Milan
Genoa
CORSICA
Sassari
SARDINIA
Cagliari
Naples
Palermo
SICILY (1283)
Bougie
Tunis
Mediterranean Sea
0   250   km
A.MacKay

The Wars of the Roses

This name, symbolizing the dynastic conflict of the Houses of Lancaster and York, was apparently coined by Sir Walter Scott to describe the civil wars fought mainly in England and Wales between 1455 and 1485. They started with risings by Richard, duke of York, aimed at ousting the favourites of Henry VI (1452, 1455, 1459). But in 1460, after victory in another rising, York claimed the throne, a claim implemented by his son, who was proclaimed Edward IV in 1461. His rule was challenged in 1469–70 by some of his own supporters, who restored Henry VI: in 1471 the exiled Edward invaded England and regained the Crown. In 1483 Edward's brother Richard, duke of Gloucester, seized it from his young son Edward V. Richard III defeated a revolt that autumn, but in 1485 he was killed fighting Henry Tudor, representing the Lancastrian interest, at Bosworth. Plots and attempted risings on behalf of Yorkist pretenders recurred over the next twelve years, but were speedily crushed by Henry VII.

The Wars of the Roses were mostly highly mobile campaigns, with few prolonged sieges: protagonists aimed to catch opponents unprepared and to secure cities and boroughs, above all London and York, with minimal disruption, so as not to alienate support. The sometimes

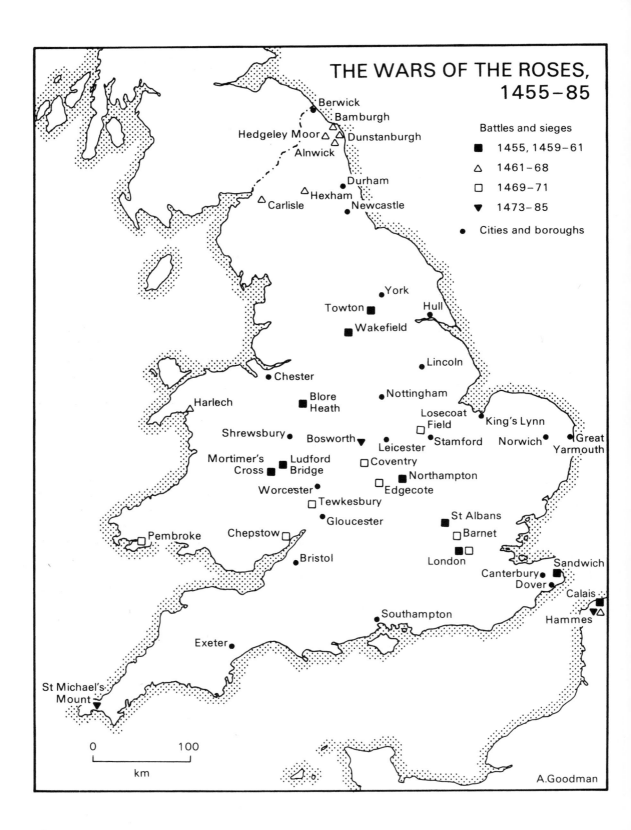

THE WARS OF THE ROSES, 1455–85

Battles and sieges
- ■ 1455, 1459–61
- △ 1461–68
- □ 1469–71
- ▼ 1473–85
- • Cities and boroughs

Berwick
Bamburgh
Hedgeley Moor
Dunstanburgh
Alnwick
Durham
Hexham
Carlisle
Newcastle
York
Towton
Hull
Wakefield
Lincoln
Chester
Nottingham
Blore Heath
Losecoat Field
King's Lynn
Harlech
Shrewsbury
Bosworth
Stamford
Norwich
Great Yarmouth
Leicester
Mortimer's Cross
Ludford Bridge
Coventry
Worcester
Northampton
Edgecote
Tewkesbury
St Albans
Gloucester
Chepstow
Barnet
Pembroke
London
Bristol
Sandwich
Canterbury
Dover
Calais
Southampton
Hammes
Exeter
St Michael's Mount

0   100
km

A. Goodman

lengthy struggles to control geographically marginal castles in Northumberland (1461–4) and Wales (1461–8) formed an exceptional phase. Urban and rural communities in most parts of England and Wales were involved at different times in arraying for campaigns, manning local defences and victualling armies. But such involvement tended to be patchily regional, reflecting the rivalries and ambitions of particular magnates and their local clientage networks:

a lot of campaigns, lasting only a few weeks, were too short for widespread damage. Only in the crisis years of 1459–61 and 1469–71 did the conflicts acquire fuller dimensions. Occasionally foreign princes and foreign mercenaries were drawn into the Wars: exiles launched invasions from Calais, Ireland (possessions of the English Crown), Scotland, Zeeland, Brittany and Normandy.

A. Goodman

Late Medieval Scotland: Crown and Magnates, *c.* 1400 and *c.* 1460

At the end of the fourteenth century (map A), Scotland's old territorial pattern of 'provincial' earldoms and lordships was essentially intact, but two new 'scattered' earldoms, Douglas and Crawford, had been created. The Douglases – major recipients of royal rewards after the Wars of Independence – had gained vast estates throughout the country, especially in the borders and south-west. Meanwhile many of the other earldoms – and indeed the Crown – had come to the Stewarts. Collectively they were the greatest kindred of all, but in *c.* 1400 they were riven by quarrels between Robert III, his son and his brothers, and the Crown's effective power-base had contracted into the south-west. By *c.* 1460, however, Scotland's territorial structure had been transformed (map B). Most 'provincial' earldoms and lordships were in Crown hands – chiefly as a result of forfeitures following confrontations between James I (1406–37) and his

Stewart kinsmen, and between James II (1437–60) and the eighth earl of Douglas. Now – outside the Highlands – sheriffdoms, not earldoms and lordships, provided the geopolitical framework, while the Crown's main power-base had been relocated centrally, in Lothian (around Edinburgh) and in Fife, Stirlingshire and Perthshire. And now the magnates had scattered estates and local spheres of influence rather than provinces. That applied to the new earldoms created by James II for his supporters, except for the new 'provincial' earldoms of Argyll (Campbells) and Huntly (Gordons). These were bulwarks on the frontiers of the Highlands against the MacDonald Lordship of the Isles – the vast Gaelic power-block built up by the heads of Clan Donald (earls of Ross, 1437–75), which dominated most of the Highlands from the 1410s to the 1490s.

A. Grant

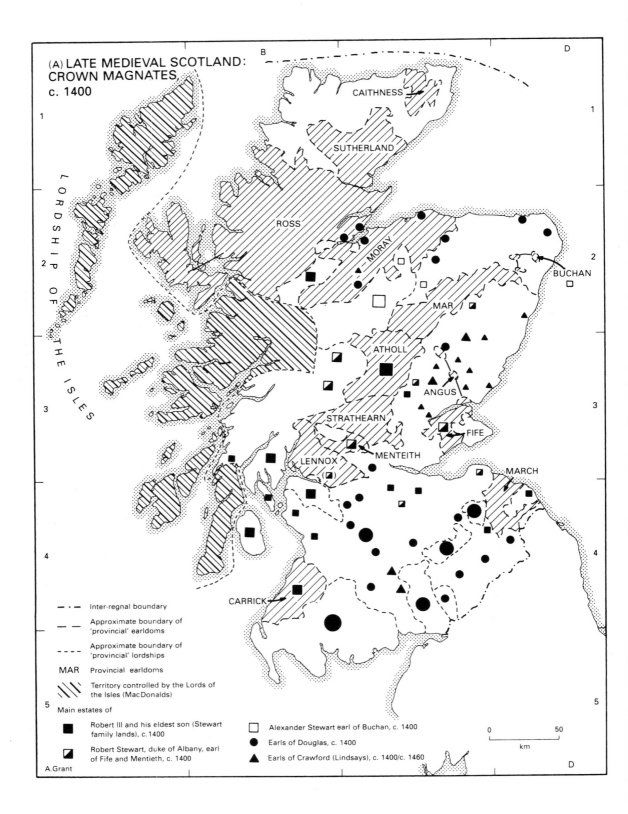

(A) LATE MEDIEVAL SCOTLAND: CROWN MAGNATES, c. 1400

CAITHNESS

SUTHERLAND

ROSS

MORAY

BUCHAN

MAR

ATHOLL

ANGUS

STRATHEARN

FIFE

LENNOX

MENTEITH

MARCH

CARRICK

LORDSHIP OF THE ISLES

Inter-regnal boundary

Approximate boundary of 'provincial' earldoms

Approximate boundary of 'provincial' lordships

MAR   Provincial earldoms

Territory controlled by the Lords of the Isles (MacDonalds)

Main estates of

■ Robert III and his eldest son (Stewart family lands), c. 1400

◪ Robert Stewart, duke of Albany, earl of Fife and Mentieth, c. 1400

□ Alexander Stewart earl of Buchan, c. 1400

● Earls of Douglas, c. 1400

▲ Earls of Crawford (Lindsays), c. 1400/c. 1460

0   50
km

A. Grant

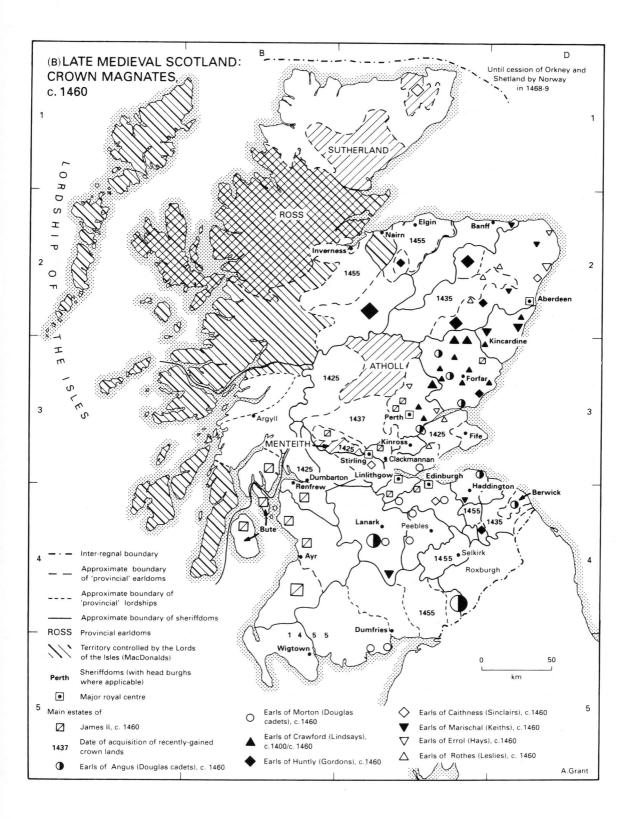

(B) LATE MEDIEVAL SCOTLAND:
CROWN MAGNATES
c. 1460

Until cession of Orkney and
Shetland by Norway
in 1468-9

SUTHERLAND

ROSS

Elgin
Banff
Nairn
Inverness
1455
1455
Aberdeen
1435
Kincardine
ATHOLL
Forfar
1425
Perth
1437
1425
Fife
Kinross
1425
Clackmannan
Argyll
MENTEITH
1425
Stirling
1425
Linlithgow
Edinburgh
Dumbarton
Haddington
Renfrew
Berwick
1455
1435
Lanark
Peebles
Selkirk
1455
Roxburgh
Ayr
1455
Dumfries
Wigtown
1 4 5 5

0   50
km

Inter-regnal boundary

Approximate boundary
of 'provincial' earldoms

Approximate boundary of
'provincial' lordships

Approximate boundary of sheriffdoms

ROSS   Provincial earldoms

⬔   Territory controlled by the Lords
of the Isles (MacDonalds)

Perth   Sheriffdoms (with head burghs
where applicable)

⊙   Major royal centre

Main estates of

▱   James II, c. 1460

1437   Date of acquisition of recently-gained
crown lands

◐   Earls of Angus (Douglas cadets), c. 1460

○   Earls of Morton (Douglas
cadets), c. 1460

▲   Earls of Crawford (Lindsays),
c. 1400/c. 1460

◆   Earls of Huntly (Gordons), c.1460

◇   Earls of Caithness (Sinclairs), c. 1460

▼   Earls of Marischal (Keiths), c. 1460

▽   Earls of Errol (Hays), c. 1460

△   Earls of Rothes (Leslies), c. 1460

A. Grant

181

Late Medieval Iberia

From 1350 to 1389 a long struggle was waged for control of the kingdom of Castile. It began primarily as a civil war between Peter I (1350–69) and a coalition of nobles led by his illegitimate half-brother, Henry of Trastámara, but both sides sought foreign support, particularly from France and England (already opposed in the Hundred Years War).

In 1365 the exiled Henry of Trastámara invaded Castile, aided by French and English mercenaries, and proclaimed himself king as Henry II (1366). Peter fled to Bayonne and, helped by the English, mounted a counter-invasion, defeating the Trastámarans at Nájera (1367). His triumph was brief. Charles V of France gave full backing to yet another invasion by Henry, and Peter was finally defeated and murdered by his half-brother at Montiel (1369).

But the threat to the Trastámaran dynasty continued. In 1371 John of Gaunt, duke of Lancaster, married Peter's eldest daughter and claimed the Castilian throne. Portugal also became involved. The heiress to its throne married John I of Castile in 1383 and when the latter invaded their kingdom the Portuguese, assisted by English archers, inflicted a crushing defeat on the Castilians at Aljubarrota (1385). Lancaster landed in La Coruña in 1386, but his invasion was a failure, the Castilians subsequently buying off his claims to the throne with the promise of large payments of cash, and both sides agreeing to a marriage between Gaunt's daughter, Catherine of Lancaster, and John I's heir, the future Henry III of Castile (1390–1406).

On the death of Henry III his younger brother Ferdinand, co-regent during the minority of John II (1406–54), dominated the political scene. Winning fame by taking Antequera from the Moors (1410), Ferdinand successfully put forward his claims to the Crown of Aragon after the death of the childless Martin I (1395–1410) being 'elected' king at the Compromise of Caspe (1412). But his short reign in Aragon (1412–16) was marked by his continued interest in Castilian politics and the promotion of his family's interests.

His sons were to dominate the political scene: Alfonso V of Aragon (1416–58) devoted himself mainly to Italian affairs; John, who inherited the family's vast landed possessions in Castile remained absorbed in that kingdom's political affairs despite becoming king of Navarre in 1425 and succeeding his brother in the Crown of Aragon (1458–79); Henry became Master of the Order of Santiago and involved himself in constant political intrigues until his death in 1445.

Opposed to them in Castile was the powerful royal favourite Alvaro de Luna who advocated exalted claims of royal absolutism on behalf of the king and defeated the Aragonese party at a crucial battle at Olmedo in 1445, only to fall himself victim to court intrigue and be executed in 1453. After an auspicious start the next reign, that of Henry IV (1454–74), degenerated into anarchy, the most serious crisis arising from an attempted deposition-in-effigy of the king at Avila in 1465 and the 'election' of his half-brother Alfonso as a rival king. After Alfonso's death in 1468, the political factions prepared for a crisis in the succession. Although it was alleged that he was both impotent and a homosexual, Henry IV claimed to have fathered a daughter, Juana 'la Beltraneja' (a name deriving from her putative father, the king's favourite Beltrán de la Cueva); against her were ranged those who supported the claims of Isabella (the king's half-sister) and Ferdinand of Aragon (the son of John II of Aragon, and Isabella's husband since 1469). Isabella and Ferdinand won the civil war, and on the death of John II of Aragon in 1479 Castile and Aragon were 'unified' under the Catholic Kings (as Ferdinand and Isabella are usually known). Their respective realms, however, continued to retain widely differing institutions. Muslim Granada was conquered in 1492, Columbus 'discovered' America in the same year, and the kingdom of Navarre was incorporated to Castile in 1512.

A. MacKay

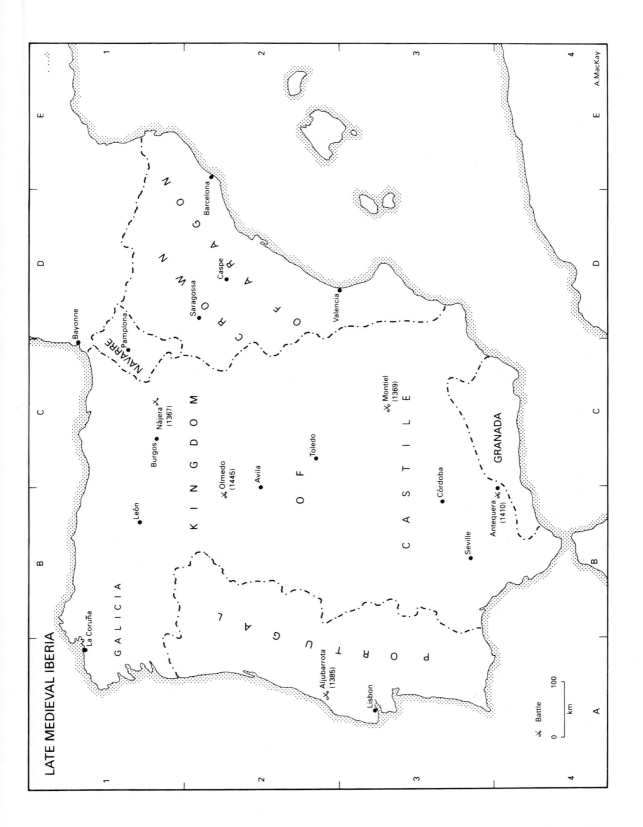

LATE MEDIEVAL IBERIA

A. MacKay

Bayonne

NAVARRE
Pamplona

Barcelona

Caspe

Saragossa

A R A G O N

Valencia

Burgos
Nájera (1367)

K I N G D O M

Olmedo (1445)

Avila

Toledo

Montiel (1369)

C A S T I L E

O F

León

GALICIA

La Coruña

P O R T U G A L

Córdoba

Antequera (1410)

GRANADA

Seville

Aljubarrota (1385)

Lisbon

⚔ Battle

0   100
        km

The Advance of the Turks and the Crusade in the Later Middle Ages

In the early fourteenth century the Byzantines lost western Anatolia to the Turks, of whom the most successful were the Ottomans who established themselves opposite Constantinople. This blocked further expansion until 1354, when involvement in the Byzantine civil wars allowed the Ottomans to establish a bridgehead at Gallipoli. This became their base for the conquest and settlement of Thrace, completed with their victory in 1371 over the Serbs at the battle of the Maritsa. Turkish expansion has been attributed to the *ghazi*-ethos, i.e. the Turks were warriors for the faith bent on extending the frontiers of Islam. They were also pastoralists seeking new lands for their flocks. They fed on the weakness of their opponents. In 1387 Thessalonica, the second city of the Byzantine Empire, voluntarily submitted to the Ottomans. In 1389 the Serbs were defeated at Kossovo and became their tributaries. In 1393 the Ottomans entered Trnovo and annexed Bulgaria. They were also taking over the Turkish emirates in Anatolia, including in 1397 Karaman. Constantinople only survived because of Tamburlane who invaded Anatolia and in 1402 defeated the Ottomans at Ankara. They needed nearly twenty years to recover from this defeat, but under Murad II (1421–51) almost all the losses in the Balkans and in Anatolia, Karaman excepted, were made good. Murad also put Ottoman power on a sounder basis by regulating recruitment into the janissaries, the slave troops who formed the core of the Ottoman army. It was left to his son Mehmed the Conqueror (1451–81) to take Constantinople in 1453, thus endowing the Ottomans with a worthy capital, capable of holding their territories together and of enhancing the authority of the sultan. Mehmed rounded off his territories by annexing the remnants of the Byzantine Empire in the Peloponnese (1460), Trebizond (1461) and Karaman (1468). Already a major power, the Ottomans were poised for the mastery of the Mediterranean.

The threat from the Turks gave a new lease of life to the crusade which had lost its purpose after the fall of Acre in 1291. The Knights Hospitallers led the way. In 1308 they seized Rhodes from the Byzantines and used it as a base against Turkish piracy in the Aegean. Their success encouraged crusading activity which suited Venetian commercial interest and pandered to nostalgia for the glories of the crusade. There was a fashion for the creation of chivalric orders dedicated to the promotion of the crusade. The main success came with the crusade of 1344, which conquered Smyrna, handing it over to the Knights Hospitallers. The initiative thus wrested from the Turks in the Aegean, the focus of the crusade now became Cyprus, where Peter I was preparing a crusade against the Mamluks of Egypt. Alexandria was stormed in 1365, but any further progress was dampened by the Venetians who feared for their trade with Egypt.

The Ottoman advance into the Balkans shifted crusading interest to Byzantium. In 1366 Amadaeus of Savoy went to the rescue of his cousin, the Emperor John V Palaiologos. The survival of Constantinople was a matter of urgency for the Hungarian King Sigismund, if only to divert the Ottomans from his frontiers. He was able to tap the crusading idealism of the French courts, already exploited in 1390 by the Genoese with Louis of Bourbon's crusade against Tunis. The new crusade was led by John the Fearless, the son and heir of the duke of Burgundy. The French met the Ottomans at Nicopolis in 1396 and were hopelessly defeated. This disaster effectively ended French participation in the crusade, though the Burgundian court continued to pay enthusiastic lip-service to the ideal. The crusade against the Ottomans became very much a Hungarian preserve. It came to grief in 1444 at Varna where a Hungarian crusade marching to the relief of Constantinople was defeated in a desperate two-day battle. Thereafter the crusade was relegated to the realms of wishful thinking. The Ottomans had proved too strong.

M. Angold

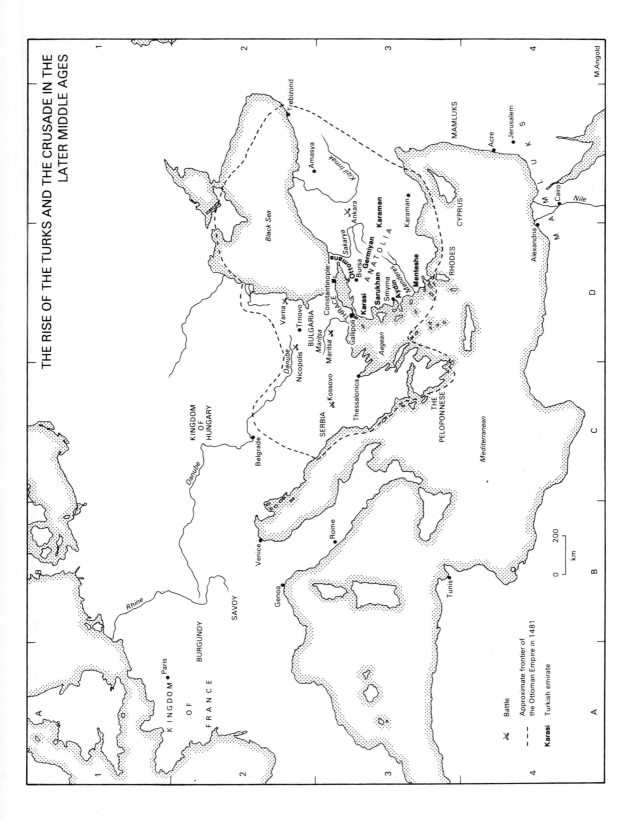

THE RISE OF THE TURKS AND THE CRUSADE IN THE LATER MIDDLE AGES

M. Angold

Battle

Approximate frontier of
the Ottoman Empire in 1481

Karasi Turkish emirate

185

The Rise of Muscovy and the Union of Lithuania and Poland

Kiev fell to the Mongols in 1240. The principality of Kiev along with the other south Russian principalities was swept away. In the north a number of principalities survived as tributaries of the khan of the Golden Horde. Leaving aside the city-state of Novgorod the most important was the principality of Vladimir-Suzdal, the ruler of which was recognized as Grand Prince by the khan. From the turn of the thirteenth century it lost its ascendancy to the principalities of Tver' and Moscow. Both were situated close to the headwaters of the major Russian rivers, which ensured that they had good communications and avenues of expansion. Moscow was perhaps less exposed, being protected by marshes to the west and thick forest to the east, but the decisive

factor in its favour was the combination of the approval of the Mongols and the backing of the Orthodox Church. The princes of Moscow preferred to co-operate with the Mongols rather than oppose their rule. From the reign of Prince Ivan Kalita (1328–41) the khans consistently bestowed the title of Grand Prince on the princes of Moscow and with it seniority over the other Russian princes. Ivan also ensured that Moscow would become the permanent residence of the metropolitan of Kiev and all Russia, the head of the Russian Church, who was appointed from Constantinople. The metropolitan acted as arbiter between the Russian princes and normally used his influence to further Moscow's political interests. By 1380 the strength of Moscow was

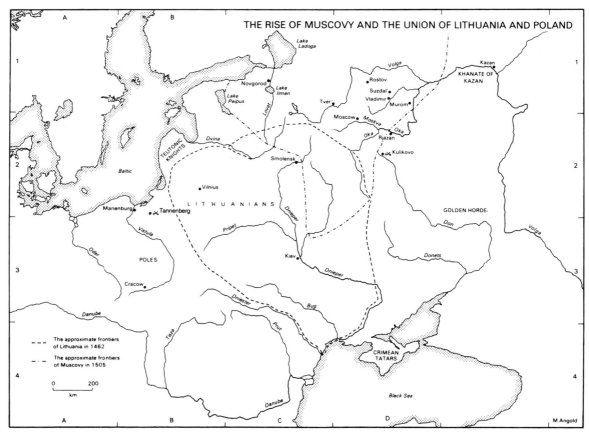

such that its prince Dimitri Donskoj was able to challenge the Mongols and win a great victory over them at Kulikovo. Though obliged two years later to submit once again to Mongol overlordship, he preserved the title of Grand Prince and his pre-eminence among the Russian princes. A succession struggle later slowed down the momentum of Muscovite expansion. It was left to Ivan III (1462–1505) to complete the 'Gathering in of the Russian Lands' around Moscow. The culmination was the annexation of Novgorod in 1478 and of Tver' in 1485. Ivan had already thrown off the Mongol yoke once and for all in 1480.

The rise of Moscow was aided by the willingness of local boyars and princely families to take service with the Muscovite ruler. Along his western frontier this was often a response to the threat posed by the Lithuanians. From the early thirteenth century the pagan Lithuanians had become a formidable military power, as they strove to escape subjugation by the Teutonic Knights, who had conquered neighbouring Prussia. The Lithuanians soon began to extend their sway south-eastwards into the southern Russian lands, where the retreat of the Mongols had left a political vacuum. By the mid-fourteenth century there was a strong possibility that the ruling dynasty would accept the Orthodox Christianity of their Russian subjects. In 1352 their ruler Olgerd tried to get his candidate recognized at Constantinople as metropolitan of Kiev and all Russia, which was a direct challenge to the prince of Moscow. To show his sincerity Olgerd adopted Orthodoxy along with members of his family shortly before his death in 1377, but the civil war which ensued produced a new alignment. His son Jagello turned to the Poles for support. Under Casimir the Great the Poles were rivals of the Lithuanians in southern Russia, but Casimir died in 1370, leaving only daughters. The Crown of Poland went with the hand of his daughter Jadwiga, who in 1386 married Jagello. This created a union of the Crowns of Lithuania and Poland. The price was the conversion of the still largely pagan Lithuanians to Catholicism. This was to inject a religious edge into the continuing rivalry of Lithuania and Moscow.

The Union of Lithuania and Poland worked well, largely because Jagello concentrated on Polish affairs and left Lithuania to his cousin Vitovt. They co-operated against the Teutonic Knights. Their victory in 1410 at Tannenberg hastened the decline of the Knights as a political force. The administration of Lithuania and Poland was reunited under Casimir IV (1447–92), but he lost the initiative against Moscow. His alliance in 1480 with the Mongol khan exposed his territories to the raids of Moscow's allies, the Crimean Tatars. The effort to stem Moscow's westward advance ended in the treaty of 1503. Lithuania retained the towns of Kiev and Smolensk, but otherwise recognized Moscow's hold on the disputed borderlands.

M. Angold

RELIGION

The Avignon Papacy and Papal Fiscality

From 1305 to 1378 the papacy was removed from Rome and for nearly all of this period resident at Avignon, a city situated on the river Rhône in Provence, then part of the empire. Petrarch (d. 1374) likened life at the papal court in Avignon to the legendary vice, corruption and greed of Babylon, a literary device used to criticize worldly tendencies in the Church by Joachim of Fiore in the twelfth century and more latterly by the Spiritual Franciscans. 'Babylonian Captivity' has since then gained currency as a term to describe this period of papal history, but the

Avignon popes were rather more exiles than captives. The rivalries of great Roman families had played a significant part in the ignominious end of Boniface VIII, and dissensions between Guelphs and Ghibellines in northern Italy led to the endemic wars that kept the popes across the Alps, even though they themselves took an active part in these conflicts. The plans of Clement V (1305–14) and John XXII (1316–34) to return to Italy gave way to their successors' complacency over being absent from Rome. Nevertheless there was a general, although unjustifiable, opinion

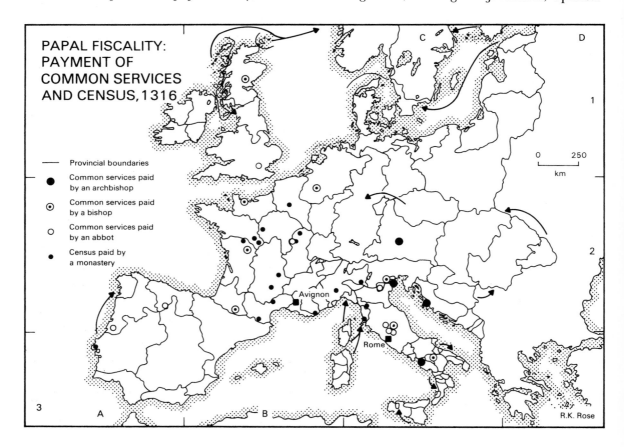

PAPAL FISCALITY:
PAYMENT OF
COMMON SERVICES
AND CENSUS, 1316

—— Provincial boundaries

● Common services paid by an archbishop

◉ Common services paid by a bishop

○ Common services paid by an abbot

● Census paid by a monastery

Avignon

Rome

0   250
km

R.K. Rose

that the papacy was in the French king's pocket and a feeling that the ills of the Church would be rectified by the pope's return to Rome. After Urban V (1362–70) made what amounted to a visit in 1369–70, Gregory XI's (1370–8) resettlement in Rome in 1377 proved permanent, but after his death the Church was beset by the Great Schism with the establishment of a rival line of popes at Avignon.

Beyond all else contemporaries condemned the grasping nature of the Avignon popes, who found themselves requiring additional funds to support a burgeoning bureaucracy and to finance the Italian wars. This need was exacerbated by falling revenues from the papacy's territorial possessions in Italy, due to the political upheaval there. Like any bishop, the pope derived his income from both temporal and spiritual sources, the latter of which were to become increasingly important. These originally consisted of nominal payments in recognition of papal authority, such as the census paid by a number of monasteries and Peter's pence paid by certain countries. In the thirteenth and early fourteenth centuries popes levied occasional tenths of the assessed value of benefices to finance crusades, but most of the money collected went to lay rulers and was not used for its intended purpose. More lucrative were the exactions made in connection with the increasing practice of papal provision, or the pope's direct appointment to dignities and benefices: common services paid by archbishops, bishops and abbots and annates paid by other provisors. The former amounted notionally to one-third and the latter to the whole of the assessed annual income, which was lower than the true value. In theory, the pope's right to provide to any church was well worked out by now, but under John XXII the fiscal benefits of the practice were better realized. His constitution *Execrabilis* (1317) was enacted to end the abuse of pluralism, but he also reserved to himself the disposal of benefices thus left vacant, enabling him to collect annates, then still a novelty in most of Europe. During his pontificate the provision of bishops and abbots began to become commonplace. The map opposite, derived from records of payment to the apostolic camera, shows how common services came to be exploited as a source of income, by comparing the first and the last full years of John XXII's pontificate. In both years the total census collected was near 100 florins. In contrast, common services were becoming the Holy See's principal source of income. In 1316–17 twenty-one prelates paid 9,343 florins, but in 1332–3 nearly one hundred churchmen paid about 38,370 florins, or more than a four-fold increase.

R.K. Rose

The Great Schism and the Councils

Following the death in March 1378 of Gregory XI, who the previous year had returned the papacy to Rome, sixteen cardinals met in conclave. On 8 April they elected Bartolomeo Prignano, archbishop of Bari, as Urban VI, amidst raucous demands from the populace for a Roman pope. Although the regularity of his election might be doubted because of the disturbances, in its aftermath it is clear that the cardinals did in fact recognize and treat Urban as the legitimate pope. Only after four months did thirteen of the electors, weary of their master's violent outbursts, desert him and declare his election invalid. In a second conclave at Fondi, in the kingdom of Naples, they elected the French king's cousin Robert of Geneva as Clement VII. Unable to dislodge Urban from Rome, Clement quite naturally chose to establish his court at Avignon, where five of Gregory XI's cardinals had obstinately remained in residence.

Allegiance to the rival popes largely reflected the national political alignments of Europe. Charles V of France had from the start encouraged the cardinals in their rebellion and prompted Joanna of Naples to follow his lead. It was natural therefore that England should remain loyal to Urban, while Scotland, France's ally, accepted the French pope. Within France itself,

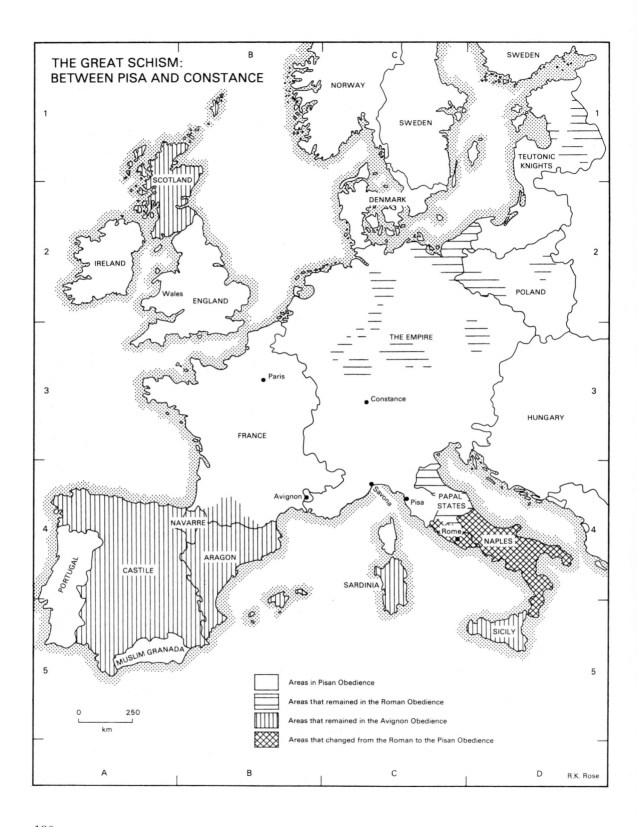

THE GREAT SCHISM:
BETWEEN PISA AND CONSTANCE

Areas in Pisan Obedience

Areas that remained in the Roman Obedience

Areas that remained in the Avignon Obedience

Areas that changed from the Roman to the Pisan Obedience

R.K. Rose

the clergy of Flanders and the English enclaves of Calais and Gascony rejected Clement. The emperor, Charles IV, along with other rulers of central Europe and Scandinavia, recognized Urban VI, but parts of the German kingdom, especially those bordering France, followed the opposite course. Urban engineered the downfall of Joanna of Naples, but his own creature also turned against him. Naples did not become officially Urbanist until 1400, though the Roman pope had until then enjoyed support in the kingdom. Portugal wavered between Rome and Avignon until 1385, when it finally embraced the former. The kings of Castile, Aragon and Navarre deferred their decisions until 1381, 1386 and 1390, respectively, when each in turn recognized Clement.

While military action proved to be futile, the delicate question of how to heal the schism was debated in the universities. Jurists and theologians were in universal agreement that a pope could only be deposed for heresy, but neither pontiff was alleged to be a heretic. As early as 1379, Henry of Langenstein and Conrad of Gelnhausen, both of the University of Paris, advocated the calling of a general council, as superior to the pope, to examine the criminal misconduct of Urban VI and the illegal election of Clement VII. But it was generally accepted that only a pope could summon a general council. The scandal of the schism deepened when the Roman cardinals elected Boniface IX after Urban's death in 1389. Despite exhortations from the French crown not to proceed with an election after Clement died in 1394, his cardinals proclaimed Benedict XIII pope. Afterwards, the resignation of both popes, greatly promoted by Parisian scholars Pierre d'Ailly and Jean Gerson, was the most widely favoured means of ending the schism. In 1407 a meeting at Savona was arranged between Benedict and Gregory XII, Roman pontiff since the previous year, but Gregory could not bring himself to make the final leg of the journey. Frustrated by inaction, cardinals from both camps joined together and summoned a general council to meet at Pisa in March 1409. Without universal support and of doubtful legitimacy, it was a sham, and the end result was not one pope but three. It was still generally acknowledged that only a council could solve the problem. The deadlock was broken by the emperor-elect, Sigismund, who summoned the council of Constance, which met between 1414 and 1417. The Pisan pope, John XXIII, and Gregory XII resigned, but Benedict XIII kept up the pretence until his death in 1423. The council was careful not to elect the one, new pope, Martin V, until all 'nations' were represented, in November 1417.

R.K. Rose

The Papal States

The papal states were the basis for the papacy's temporal power. Founded in 754 (when Pepin, king of the Franks, granted Pope Stephen II the exarchate of Ravenna and the Pentapolis) they were directly governed by the pope as secular ruler and acquired political autonomy from neighbouring powers in the thirteenth century. Despite an extensive network of roads, largely based on ancient Roman routes, the diverse terrain of the states presented formidable administrative problems. The key cities of Rome, surrounded by an infertile coastal plain, and Bologna, in the productive region of Romagna, were separated by the Apennine passes and the wealthy march of Ancona, a hilly region of varied economic activity and numerous small *signori*. The whole area was ruled by papal governors or rectors based in Perugia, Orvieto, the Patrimony of St Peter in Tuscia, Romagna and elsewhere. During the papal absence in Avignon (1309–77) de facto authority was usurped by numerous communes and latterly by signorial dynasties such as the Malatesta of Rimini and the Montefeltro of Urbino. The Roman hinterland was likewise dominated by families such as the Orsini, Caetani, Colonna, da Vico and Anguillara,

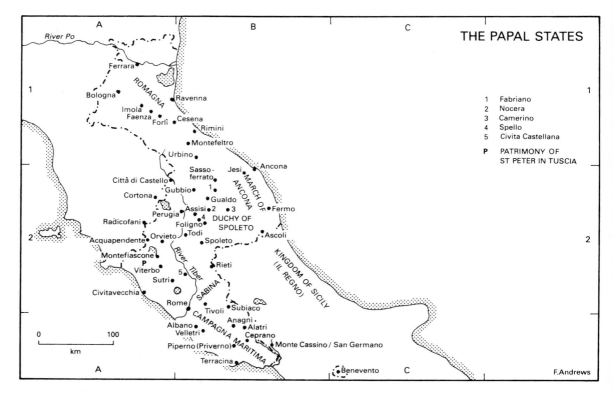

THE PAPAL STATES

1 Fabriano
2 Nocera
3 Camerino
4 Spello
5 Civita Castellana
P PATRIMONY OF
   ST PETER IN TUSCIA

F. Andrews

while Rome itself remained faction-ridden despite Cola di Rienzo's attempt to reorganize city government in 1347. Bologna, meanwhile, had rebelled in 1334. For decades the region was beset by warfare. In 1353–67 Cardinal Egidio (Gil) de Albornoz was charged by Innocent VI to restore papal fortunes. Through military and diplomatic means some recognition of papal authority was achieved and the legitimacy of some *signori* was recognized by their appointment as papal vicars. After the return of the popes to Rome the papal states shared in the crisis of papal power provoked by the Great Schism and the Conciliar Movement: Ladislao of Naples, for example, seized Rome in 1408 and 1413. Papal authority was precariously re-established by Eugenius IV (1431–47). Thereafter, income from the papal states did much to bolster financially a now spiritually weakened papacy.

F. Andrews

Byzantine Cultural and Monastic Centres

The loss of Egypt and Syria to the Arabs in the seventh century deprived the Byzantine Empire of many of its major cultural centres. These included Alexandria, along with Athens, the major university, and Beirut, the main centre of legal studies. Constantinople was left with a virtual monopoly of higher education, scholarship and letters. Even here the university established in 425 disappeared. Education was a matter of private tutors and private schools. State supervision was limited to the provision of funds to selected masters and schools. There was no

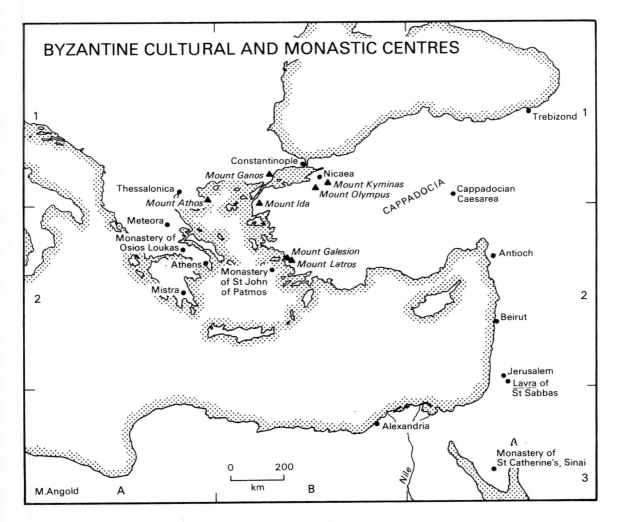

BYZANTINE CULTURAL AND MONASTIC CENTRES

Trebizond

Constantinople

Mount Ganos ▲

Nicaea

▲ Mount Kyminas

Mount Olympus

Thessalonica

CAPPADOCIA

Cappadocian
Caesarea

Mount Athos ▲

▲ Mount Ida

Meteora

Monastery of
Osios Loukas

Antioch

Mount Galesion

Mount Latros

Athens

Monastery
of St John
of Patmos

Mistra

Beirut

Jerusalem
Lavra of
St Sabbas

Alexandria

Nile

0   200
km

Monastery of
St Catherine's, Sinai

M.Angold   A   B

institution of higher education approaching the model of the western university. Byzantium inherited the Hellenistic educational curriculum with its emphasis on rhetoric. Speculative thought, whether philosophical or theological, remained a private concern. This remained true in the twelfth century when the supervision of education came under the patriarchs of Constantinople. The disintegration of the Byzantine Empire after the Latin conquest of 1204 meant that Constantinople lost its cultural monopoly. Byzantine scholars found refuge at Nicaea and at Trebizond. After the recovery of Constantinople in 1261 the Emperor Michael VIII Palaiologos took steps to revive education and scholarship,

but Constantinople never regained its cultural monopoly, being challenged by Thessalonica in the fourteenth century. In the final phase Mistra became the most prestigious centre of Byzantine scholarship thanks to the activities of the Platonist George Gemistos Plethon and his circle.

While education and scholarship were the preserve of a tiny elite, monasticism involved the whole of Byzantine society. Constantinople was always the major centre of Byzantine monasticism. From its foundation in the mid-fifth century the monastery of St John Stoudios at Constantinople was always among the most prestigious. Its rule served as a model for many other monastic foundations, though Byzantium had no monastic orders as such. Instead, there were Holy Mountains. The most famous and enduring example is Mount Athos, which is a confederation of monasteries under the presidency of a *protos*. Other examples were Olympus, Latros, Ida, Kyminas, Galesion and Ganos. The Meteora in Thessaly became an important monastic centre from the mid-fourteenth century. The rock-monasteries of Cappadocia indicate the hold that monasticism enjoyed in the provinces. Contact was maintained with distant orthodox monastic centres, such as St Catherine's on Mount Sinai, while the *lavra* of St Sabbas outside Jerusalem exerted a deep influence on Byzantine monasticism with its combination of the coenobitic and eremitical life.

M. Angold

The Bohemian Lands and the Hussite Wars, 1415–37

In the fourteenth century the Bohemian Lands (Bohemia and Moravia) became the administrative centre of the Holy Roman Empire. Charles IV, emperor and king of Bohemia, was responsible for transforming Prague into a splendid imperial capital in the late Gothic style. Among the emperor's most important achievements was the foundation of the oldest university in central Europe at Prague in 1347.

The university rapidly became a hotbed of heresy, producing a number of important preachers and reformers such as Jan Hus and his principal follower Jakoubek of Stříbro. This climate of dissent was aggravated by Wenceslas IV's weak government and a lack of direction from the Catholic Church after the Schism of 1378. The deposition of Wenceslas from the imperial throne (1400) and the Decree of Kutná Hora (1409), whereby the Czechs gained a controlling majority in the administration of the university, meant that the international significance of Bohemia and the Prague university diminished. Bohemia became isolated and shunned abroad as the home of heresy.

Following the burning of Hus in 1415 and their condemnation by the Council of Constance, the Hussites enshrined certain demands for reform in the Four Articles of Prague (1420): the free preaching of the Word of God, communion in both kinds, the confiscation of the secular property of the clergy and the punishment of public sin. But the new movement soon splintered into several factions: on the right were the Utraquists who demanded no more than the right to receive communion in both kinds (*sub utraque specie*); in the centre was the moderate party led by Jakoubek of Stříbro; on the left were the Taborites, adherents of chiliasm or Millenarianism; on the extreme left were the Adamites, a sect which went naked and denied the doctrine of the Real Presence.

The areas of greatest Hussite activity were Prague, where Hus and his followers preached at the Bethlehem Chapel, north-west, west and south Bohemia; Moravia and Slovakia remained Catholic throughout the Hussite Wars. The Taborites, consisting mainly of peasants and gentry, founded the town of Tábor (1420) and established a municipal form of government which abolished the feudal system. The movement soon spread to the so-called Five Towns – Plzeň, Slaný, Žatec, Louny and Klatovy – which were regarded by the radical preachers as the final refuge of the elect against the Anti-Christ.

In 1420 an anti-Hussite crusade under Wenceslas's brother, Sigismund, king of Hungary and Holy Roman emperor, marched into Bohemia and captured Prague where Sigismund was crowned. The Taborites, led by the dynamic Jan Žižka, came to the rescue and drove the crusaders out of Prague. A second Catholic assault later the same year also met with disaster. Following a third victory over the crusaders the next year (1421), the Bohemian diet met at Čáslav where it accepted the Four Articles of Prague as law and rejected Sigismund's claim to the throne.

The Hussites undertook their own religious

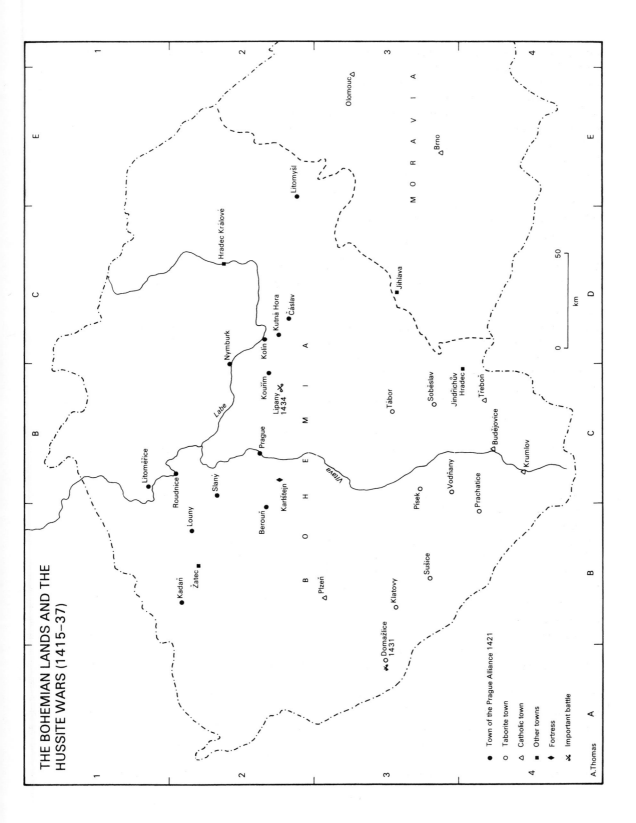

THE BOHEMIAN LANDS AND THE
HUSSITE WARS (1415–37)

MORAVIA

Olomouc △

△ Brno

Litomyšl ●

Hradec Králové ■

Jihlava ■

Kutná Hora ●
Čáslav ●

Nymburk ●

Kolín ●

Kouřim ●
Lipany ✗
1434

B O H E M I A

Tábor ○

Soběslav ○

Jindřichův
Hradec ■

Třeboň △

Prague ●

Litoměřice ●

Roudnice ◆

Slaný ●

Louny ●

Karlštejn ◆

Berouň ●

Vltava

Písek ○

Vodňany ○

Prachatice ○

Budějovice ○

Krumlov △

Labe

Kadaň ●

Žatec ■

△ Plzeň

Klatovy ○

Sušice ○

Domažlice ○
1431 ✗

●		Town of the Prague Alliance 1421
○		Taborite town
△		Catholic town
■		Other towns
◆		Fortress
✗		Important battle

A. Thomas

50
km
0

195

crusades abroad into Poland and Germany led by Žižka's successor Prokop Holý. Internecine strife among the heretics enabled further Catholic invasions in 1427 and 1431 when Sigismund's forces were decisively defeated at the Battle of Domažlice. By the 1430s, however, the moderate wing of the Hussites were seeking a peaceful solution to the Bohemian question. Their initiative resulted in an agreement between the Utraquist nobility and the Catholics (the Compactata of Basel). The two forces allied to crush the extremists at the Battle of Lipany in May 1434. The destruction of the Taborite cause cleared the way for further negotiations. The Utraquists abandoned their insistence on the obligatory use of the chalice throughout Bohemia, but demanded that the new archbishop should be of the Utraquist persuasion. In 1436 the Compactata of Basel was ratified at Jihlava and Sigismund returned to Prague as king in August 1436. This event marked the beginning of a new *modus vivendi* between Hussites and Catholics which was to last until the loss of Czech independence in 1620.

A. Thomas

GOVERNMENT, SOCIETY AND ECONOMY

The Growth of Royal Fiscality and Administration in France

Between the early Middle Ages and the thirteenth century the king of France derived his income not from taxes on his subjects at large but almost exclusively from his own estates (*domaine*) like any other great landholder. But under Philip IV (1285–1314) this ordinary income, even when augmented by careful exploitation of sovereign rights and boosted by windfalls when the Crown attacked privileged groups like the Lombards, Jews and Templars, failed to cover royal needs and further revenue raised by taxation, usually termed 'extraordinary' taxation, was required. A crusading tithe levied on the clergy in 1147 and 1188 provided a model. In the thirteenth century the king raised similar tenths (*décimes*) from ecclesiastics at frequent intervals, with or without papal approval, and this remained a valuable source of income. But Philip IV, justifying his demands by pleas of evident necessity and defence of the realm in an emergency, now sought war subsidies directly from his lay subjects, though he normally also had to summon the feudal host (*arrière-ban*) beforehand. He also experimented with indirect taxes (*impôts*) on the sale of basic foodstuffs, drink and manufactured goods, together with customs dues like the *maltôte* (1295). At the same time the rudimentary financial administration was transformed, though it was the mid-fourteenth century before a proper system for collecting revenue derived from sources other than the royal *domaine* was devised. The Templars, who had acted as royal bankers since the mid-twelfth century, were relieved of their duties in the 1290s and a royal *trésor* was set up. Accounting took place before an enlarged *curia de compotis* (1289) or *chambre des comptes*, which functioned fully as a court by the 1320s, even if it was 1381 before its first *président* appeared, and

control of *impôts*, now termed *aides*, passed after 1390 to the *Cour des aides* and a *Cour du trésor* took over supervision of domainal revenues.

However, the idea that extraordinary revenues should constitute a regular and permanent source of income in peacetime for the Crown was long resisted. Some great duchies and counties like Brittany, Burgundy, Flanders and Gascony managed to preserve their fiscal autonomy. There was a failure to devise standard national means either for authorizing taxation or for levying and collecting it and much was left to local endeavours, with the Crown simply grateful to receive a proportion of what it demanded. Philip IV called an assembly or Estates General and his successors found it expedient to summon them occasionally, or meetings of regional Estates for northern and southern France (Languedoil and Languedoc) to consider the imposition of a particular tax – but it was to obtain their counsel rather than their consent. After 1439, however, the next meeting of the Estates General did not take place until 1484. In contrast, between 1330 and 1430 other more local provincial Estates were formed. Some, like those of Normandy, claimed the right to consent to taxes and were indeed consulted according to circumstance or tradition. Some modification of the form or burden of taxation could thus be negotiated. But from an early point the Crown, frustrated by the delays such consultation inevitably entailed (for decisions taken by Estates General had to be ratified by local Estates and taxes granted in the larger bodies were seldom collected), began to decide in advance the sum required and simply ordered provincial assemblies to authorize its levying. This they normally did by sharing out their quota amongst those liable to taxation in their area, the division

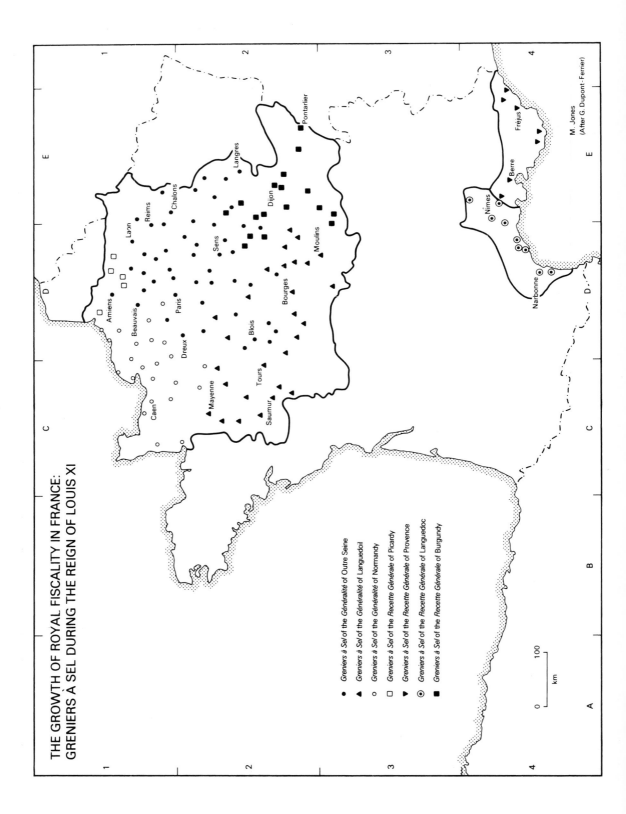

THE GROWTH OF ROYAL FISCALITY IN FRANCE:
GRENIERS À SEL DURING THE REIGN OF LOUIS XI

M. Jones
(After G. Dupont-Ferrier)

Greniers à Sel of the Généralité of Outre Seine
Greniers à Sel of the Généralité of Languedoïl
Greniers à Sel of the Généralité of Normandy
Greniers à Sel of the Recette Générale of Picardy
Greniers à Sel of the Recette Générale of Provence
Greniers à Sel of the Recette Générale of Languedoc
Greniers à Sel of the Recette Générale of Burgundy

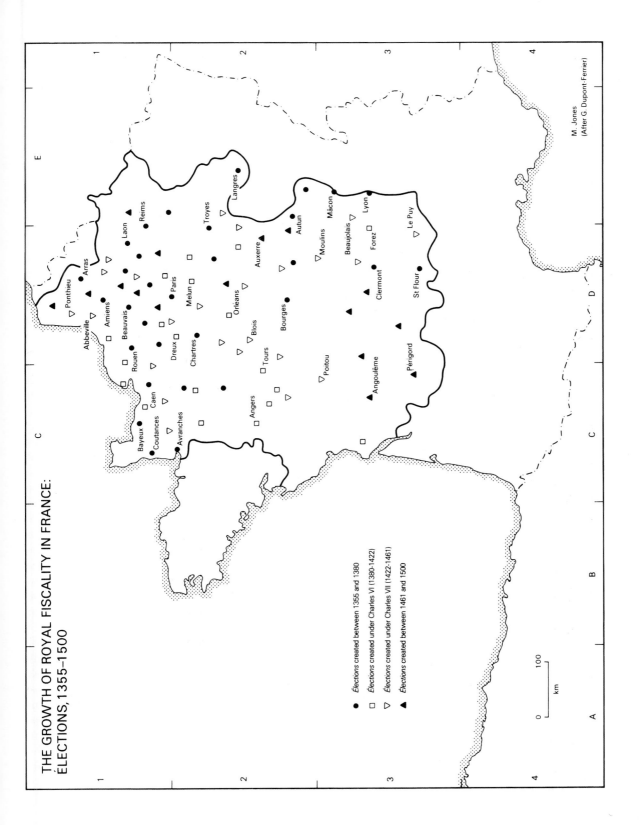

THE GROWTH OF ROYAL FISCALITY IN FRANCE:
ÉLECTIONS, 1355–1500

Élections created between 1355 and 1380
Élections created under Charles VI (1380-1422)
Élections created under Charles VII (1422-1461)
Élections created between 1461 and 1500

M. Jones
(After G. Dupont-Ferrier)

199

(*répartition*) being based on information derived from great inquiries, like that of 1328, into the number of hearths or households (*feux*) in the regions under royal control. Hence the hearth tax (*fouage*) was the main form of direct taxation. Established during Philip IV's reign in the Midi, after 1355 it was applied in Languedoil also, where from the 1380s it was normally termed the *taille*. With demographic changes, especially consequent upon the Black Death, revision of the number of *feux* was necessary, and the concept of the fiscal household made up of a varying number of real households emerged. From the start exemption from the *fouage* and *taille* was claimed by the nobility, clergy and certain other privileged groups (royal officials, for example) – though they did not always enjoy it, especially in the almost permanent state of war which afflicted France after 1337.

It was this war with England that revealed how inadequate the Crown's income from war subsidies still was. After recourse to traditional means of raising extra income, especially currency manipulation, a series of taxes, already tried in limited form, were generalized. In 1341 a sales tax on salt, the *gabelle*, was imposed. Though it was dropped in 1346, it was revived between 1356 and 1380 and from 1383 became a permanent item in royal revenue. In the fifteenth century it was raised from about one-third of the kingdom at royal warehouses (*greniers*) where the salt was deposited before sale. But the really critical period for the establishment of both direct and indirect taxes was 1355–70. An already serious political crisis in 1355 deepened in 1356 when John II was captured at Poitiers. To meet the enormous ransom of 3 million *écus* (£500,000) forced loans were levied and the traditional feudal aid was granted – but this was levied as a *fouage* while, at the same time, the sales tax (*aides*) was also extended, accustoming subjects to paying taxes now on an annual basis, not only because of evident necessity but also for the common benefit. To collect this money royal France was divided into new administrative districts. The Estates of 1355–6 nominated collectors known as *élus* (hence *élections* for their circumscriptions). The *élections*

were usually based on existing dioceses and were eventually grouped into regional *recettes générales* supervised by general councillors. From 1436 there were four main *recettes* under four *trésoriers* and four *généraux*. The addition of new territories to the royal *domaine* in the later fifteenth century meant that by Louis XII's reign (1498–1514) there were ten or eleven *recettes*, and some eighty-five *élections*. From 1360 the Crown had taken over the nomination and payment of the *élus* and their subordinates.

By this means a large proportion of John II's ransom was paid and the Crown came to depend on the regular levying of taxes. But on his deathbed Charles V (1364–80), conscious of the tradition that such taxation was still considered exceptional, abolished the *fouage*. Military and political crises allowed his successor to re-establish both the *fouage* and the *aides*, which had been cancelled after Charles died, and these taxes were collected regularly until the Crown's position was once again weakened after 1412. Charles VII (1422–61) was forced to consult extensively with various representative assemblies early in his reign. The *taille* was not levied between 1412–23 nor *aides* from 1418–28. But after 1428 the king began to take taxes without consent, and the Estates at Orléans in 1439 were the last to give general approval to raising the *taille*. In 1443 Languedoc and Dauphiné bought off the *aides* by conceding an annual lump sum, the *équivalent*. By this time the distinction between the *pays d'états*, regions with representative institutions, and those lacking them, *pays d'élections*, had clearly emerged, though it apparently made little difference to their relative burden of taxation. Normandy, a *pays d'états*, for example, produced between a sixth and third of royal revenue after its reconquest (1450). By then Charles VII raised annually about 1.2 million *livres* from the *taille*. Under Louis XI (1461–83) the annual income of the Crown rose dramatically to about 4.7 million *livres*. Of this only about 100,000 came from the *domaine*, 650,000 from *aides* and no less than 3.9 million from the *taille*. By far the largest cost to the Crown was its expenditure on the army established on a permanent basis in the 1440s and enormously expanded by Louis XI. During the minority of Charles VIII (1483–90) there was an inevitable reaction against royal fiscality. The Estates General of 1484 reduced both the level of taxation and the size of the army, but the beginning of French intervention in Italy soon raised the burden of taxation in the 1490s to 4 million *livres*.

M. Jones

Burgundian Administration

Recognizing local privileges, ducal government had a federal quality. But gradually certain central institutions emerged. A chancellor headed an omnicompetent ducal council. Finances were under a treasurer while a receiver-general, though not controlling all local receipts, handled revenues from all the duke's lands. Regional receivers were accountable before *chambres des comptes* at Lille (founded by the count of Flanders, 1382) and Dijon (reorganized, 1386). Subsequently *chambres* also emerged at Brussels and The Hague. From *c.* 1430–68 the duke disposed of important funds through establishing a *trésor de l'épargne*. Charles also appointed a treasurer of wars. In both these cases French or Breton practice was imitated. From the 1440s *commis sur le fait des finances*, chief financial officers, supervised their administration and advised the council. Locally, efforts were made to rationalize institutions in neighbouring territories. The two Burgundies and some adjacent territories – Flanders and Artois, Brabant and Limbourg, Holland and Zeeland – were often administratively combined. Northern predominance (in Charles' reign the Netherlands pro-duced five times more revenue than the two Burgundies) was marked early in Philip the Good's reign by the removal of responsibility for auditing the accounts of the ducal household, together with those of the receiver-general, from Dijon to Lille. From 1473 Charles attempted to establish alongside the newly created sovereign *parlement* for his Netherlandish territories at Malines a new *chambre des comptes* to replace those of Lille and Brussels. Other sovereign courts existed in Hainault (Mons) and the Franche Comté (Dôle), though the *parlement* at Beaune remained subject to the Paris *parlement*, which also heard appeals from Artois and Flanders. Most territories had representative institutions, like the Estates of Artois or Four Members of Flanders, and dukes consulted them, especially for taxes (*aides*). From 1425 Estates in adjacent territories tended to hold joint meetings; one such in 1464 is usually regarded as the first Estates General of the Low Countries which had an important future role, especially after Charles' death (1477).

M. Jones

Castilian *Corregidores*

Although officials known as *corregidores* were already in existence during the early fourteenth century, the Castilian monarchy only began to make extensive use of them from the reign of Henry III (1390–1406) onwards. Initially, they were the ideal agents to represent the Crown in dealing with problems in royal towns, and they disposed of important powers over the political and economic life of the towns to which they were sent. Theoretically they were dispatched at the invitation of the towns, but in practice the king often appointed them without consultation. The salaries of these *corregidores*, who were not usually natives of the areas in which they operated, were paid by the towns where they resided, and this fact, coupled with their powers of

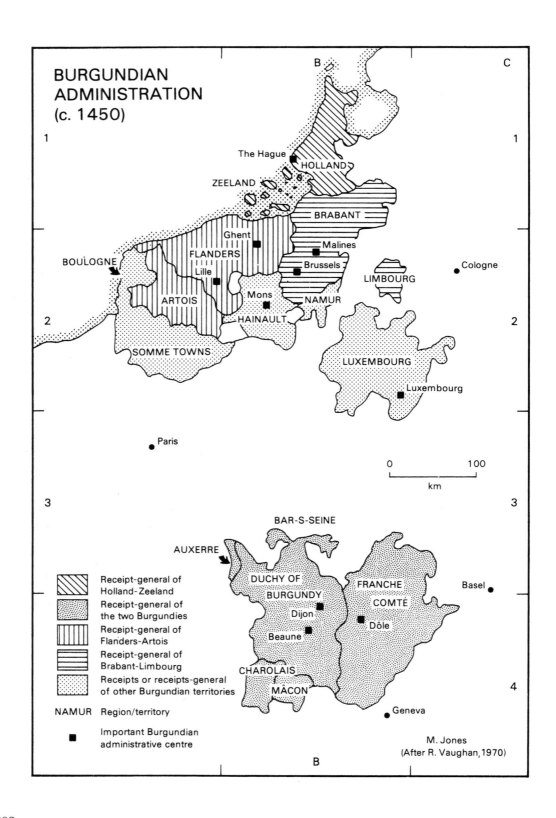

BURGUNDIAN
ADMINISTRATION
(c. 1450)

B · C

1 · 1

The Hague
HOLLAND

ZEELAND

BRABANT

Ghent
FLANDERS · Malines
Lille · Brussels
LIMBOURG · Cologne
BOULOGNE

ARTOIS · Mons · NAMUR

HAINAULT

2 · SOMME TOWNS · LUXEMBOURG · 2

Luxembourg

Paris

0 · 100
km

3 · BAR-S-SEINE · 3

AUXERRE

DUCHY OF · FRANCHE
BURGUNDY · COMTÉ · Basel

Receipt-general of
Holland-Zeeland

Receipt-general of · Dijon
the two Burgundies · Dôle

Receipt-general of · Beaune
Flanders-Artois

Receipt-general of · CHAROLAIS
Brabant-Limbourg

Receipts or receipts-general · MÂCON · 4
of other Burgundian territories

NAMUR   Region/territory · Geneva

■   Important Burgundian
administrative centre · M. Jones
(After R. Vaughan, 1970)

B

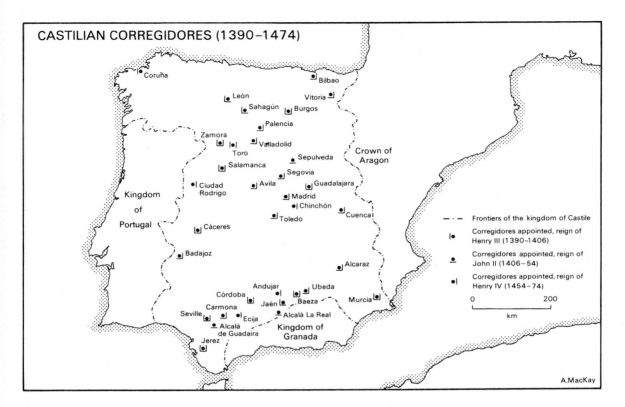

CASTILIAN CORREGIDORES (1390–1474)

Coruña
Bilbao
León
Vitoria
Sahagún
Burgos
Palencia
Zamora
Valladolid
Toro
Sepulveda
Crown of
Aragon
Salamanca
Segovia
Ciudad
Rodrigo
Avila
Guadalajara
Madrid
Chinchón
Cuenca
Toledo
Cáceres
Badajoz
Alcaraz
Kingdom
of
Portugal
Andujar
Córdoba
Ubeda
Carmona
Jaén
Baeza
Murcia
Seville
Ecija
Alcalá La Real
Alcalá
de Guadaira
Kingdom of
Granada
Jerez

— · — Frontiers of the kingdom of Castile

Corregidores appointed, reign of
Henry III (1390–1406)

Corregidores appointed, reign of
John II (1406–54)

Corregidores appointed, reign of
Henry IV (1454–74)

0   200
km

A.MacKay

intervention, aroused the hostility of urban oligarchies.

Most *corregidores* were either minor nobles or men with legal training (*letrados*). The main problems that they had to contend with were internal urban disorders arising from clan-like feuds amongst regional elites, abuses in the administration of justice, corrupt levying and auditing of municipal finances, and the usurpation of royal and municipal rights by the Church and the nobility.

The Catholic Monarchs, inheriting this system from their predecessors, extended appointments so considerably that by 1494 there were fifty-four *corregidores* in existence. However, although the increasing use of these officials generally enhanced royal power considerably, abuses by individual *corregidores* were frequent. Moreover during the reign of Henry IV the appointment of some *corregidores* fell into the hands of great nobles, and from the reign of John II onwards the Crown on the whole failed to support the attempts by *corregidores* to prevent the great aristocracy from usurping urban territories. When many Castilian towns rebelled in 1520 in the Revolt of the *Comuneros*, informed contemporaries agreed that abuses in the royal control of the system of *corregidores* had constituted a major cause of urban unrest.

A. MacKay

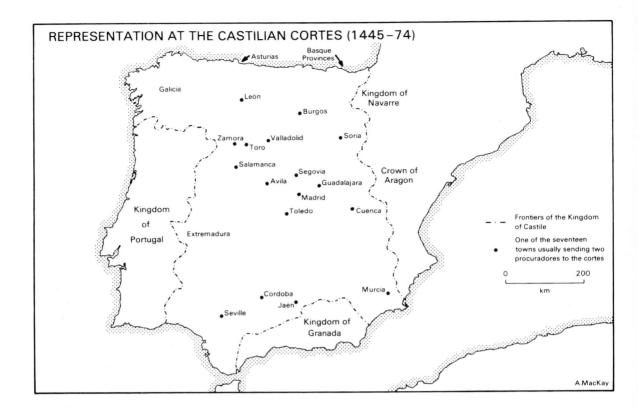

REPRESENTATION AT THE CASTILIAN CORTES (1445–74)

Asturias — Basque Provinces

Galicia

León

Burgos

Kingdom of Navarre

Zamora — Valladolid — Soria
Toro

Salamanca

Segovia — Crown of Aragon

Avila — Guadalajara

Madrid

Kingdom of Portugal — Toledo — Cuenca

Extremadura

Cordoba — Murcia
Jaén

Seville — Kingdom of Granada

— · — Frontiers of the Kingdom of Castile

• One of the seventeen towns usually sending two procuradores to the cortes

0 — 200
km

A.MacKay

Representation at the Castilian *Cortes*, 1445–74

During the fifteenth century the influence of the Castilian *cortes* declined sharply, and this was paralleled by its increasingly unrepresentative nature. The attendance of the first and second estates was irregular since the king only summoned those individuals whom he wanted to attend and the clergy and nobility took little interest in *cortes* proceedings. Thus, meeting irregularly and only when summoned by the king, the *cortes* was frequently nothing much more than an assembly of representatives of the third estate (*procuradores*) and royal officials, its main functions being to vote taxation and to present petitions, often evasively answered, to the king.

Forty-nine towns were represented in the *cortes* of 1391, but by the mid-fifteenth century this number had decreased to a maximum of only seventeen towns. These were all royal towns, the inhabitants of noble and ecclesiastical lordships being theoretically represented by the first and second estates. In practice, therefore, complete regions, such as Galicia, the Basque provinces, Asturias and Extremadura were not represented.

The selection of *procuradores* was controlled by the urban oligarchies, although the king himself occasionally intervened to nominate individuals. The *cortes* of Zamora of 1432 formally reaffirmed what had for long been practice – namely, that no non-noble could be a *procurador*. By this time, too, the *procuradores'* expenses were being paid by the Crown. In general, therefore, these *procuradores* were not necessarily more representative of the interests of townspeople than bishops were of the inhabitants living in their lordships.

They could readily agree to taxes which they themselves did not have to pay, and the oligarchies they represented, proud of their participation in the *cortes*, could even expect to derive some benefit from agreeing to royal requests to spend other people's money.

A. MacKay

Parliamentary Representation in Later Medieval England

Representatives of shires, cities and boroughs were summoned to some parliaments in the reign of Edward I (1272–1307) and were customarily summoned from the reign of his son Edward II (d. 1327) onwards. Writs were sent from chancery to sheriffs ordering them to cause elections of two shire knights each to be held in thirty-seven shires. Cheshire and County Durham, where respectively the earls of Chester and bishops of Durham exercised regal authority, were unrepresented. Only occasionally were those elected actually knights; more commonly they were gentlefolk, often lawyers and stewards of estates busy in local administration. Under the Lancastrian kings in the fifteenth century there was legislation to ensure that the elections in the shire court reflected truly the will of better-off, resident freeholders.

The number of boroughs which were ordered to elect two burgesses (London was unique in electing four citizens) and which sent them fluctuated in the period. According to Professor McKisack, an average of seventy cities and boroughs were represented in Edward II's parliaments and of eighty-three in the parliaments of Richard II (reigned 1377–99). The map shows cities and boroughs which returned in the early decades of the fifteenth century. Northern England was poorly represented compared with England south of the river Trent, with two unenfranchised shires and few cities and boroughs. Many enfranchised boroughs were dwindling into insignificance in terms of population and wealth by the fifteenth century, when there was a tendency for such boroughs to return members of aristocratic rather than bourgeois status, often non-resident. Gentlefolk had come to consider it prestigious and useful to sit in the Commons House, even as burgesses: the outnumbered shire knights apparently controlled the business of the House. By the time the 'Good Parliament' met in 1376, shire knights and burgesses were in the habit of sitting and debating together: then, under the leadership of the first known Commons Speaker, they demonstrated a remarkable ability to press reform of government on the Crown.

A. Goodman

The Government of Later Medieval Germany

The limited powers of the German monarchy were reflected in the rudimentary nature of Germany's institutions of central government. The chancery was responsible for issuing royal charters and letters though it was small compared to that in other countries. Germany's representative assembly, the *Reichstag*, had developed by the later Middle Ages from an advisory into a legislative body. Its membership, still somewhat fluid in the fifteenth century, comprised the electors, prelates, princes, some lesser lords and representatives of the imperial towns.

PARLIAMENTARY
REPRESENTATION
IN LATER
MEDIEVAL ENGLAND

— · — National boundaries
— — Shire boundaries

Shires without
parliamentary
representation

• Cities and boroughs
which elected
representatives in the
early fifteenth century

1 Northampton
2 Cambridge
3 Huntingdon
4 Bedford
5 Southampton
6 Winchester
7 Worcester
8 Newcastle under Lyme
9 Salisbury
10 Reading

A
Newcastle
Bishopric
of Durham
Carlisle
Cumberland
Appleby
Northumberland
Scarborough
Yorkshire
York
Hull
Lancashire
Grimsby
Lincolnshire
Lincoln
Derbyshire
Earldom
of Chester
Derby
Nottingham
R. Trent
Boston
Bishop's
Lynn
Great
Yarmouth
Norwich
Norfolk
Shrewsbury
Stafford
Leicester
Shropshire
Coventry
Warwick
Leominster
Herefordshire
Hereford
Gloucester
Gloucestershire
Suffolk
Ipswich
Essex
Colchester
Maldon
Oxford
London
Wallingford
Berkshire
Rochester
Bristol
Bath
Wiltshire
Wells
Surrey
Guildford
Canterbury
Kent
Sandwich
Somerset
Bridgewater
Taunton
Hampshire
Sussex
Rye
Dover
Devon
Dorset
Chichester
Portsmouth
Exeter
Cornwall

0   100
km

A.Goodman

I Westmorland   VI Leicestershire   XI Bedfordshire
II Staffordshire   VII Rutland   XII Hertfordshire
III Worcestershire   VIII Northamptonshire   XIII Middlesex
IV Warwickshire   IX Huntingdonshire   XIV Buckinghamshire
V Nottinghamshire   X Cambridgeshire   XV Oxfordshire

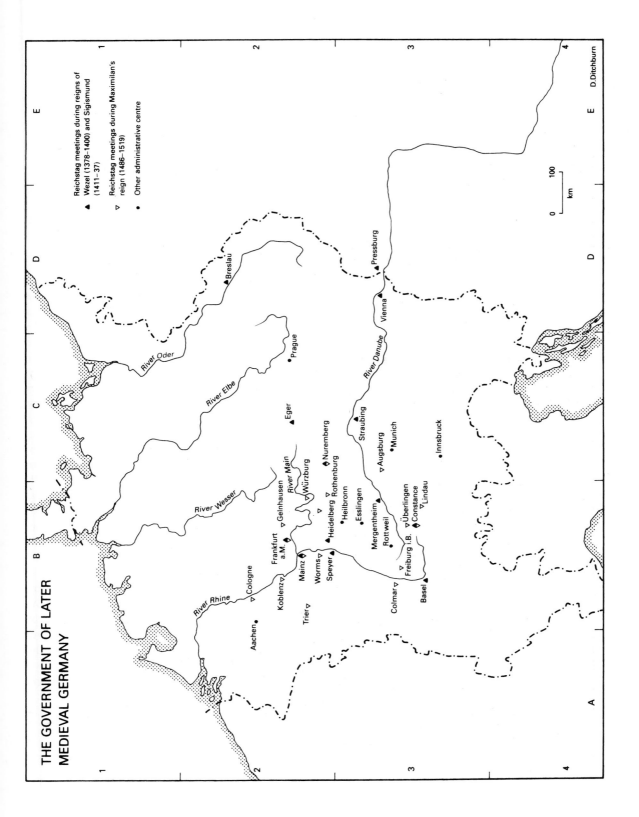

THE GOVERNMENT OF LATER
MEDIEVAL GERMANY

Reichstag meetings during reigns of
Wezel (1378–1400) and Sigismund
(1411–37)

Reichstag meetings during Maximilian's
reign (1486–1519)

Other administrative centre

0   100
km

D.Ditchburn

River Oder

Breslau

River Elbe

Prague

Eger

River Wesser

River Main

Nuremberg

Würzburg

Gelnhausen

Frankfurt
a.M.

Rothenburg

Heidelberg

Heilbronn

Esslingen

Mergentheim

Cologne

Koblenz

Mainz

Worms

Speyer

Rottweil

Überlingen

Freiburg i.B.

Constance

Lindau

Colmar

Basel

Trier

Aachen

River Rhine

Straubing

River Danube

Augsburg

Munich

Innsbruck

Vienna

Pressburg

The electors, constituted as the *Kurverein*, and urban envoys, constituted from the 1470s as the Urban diet, sometimes met independently of the *Reichstag* in order to articulate their respective interests. The *Reichstag* itself met frequently in the later Middle Ages though absenteeism, especially among northern members, was rife and the acceptance and implementation of its decisions only partial. Neither the *Reichstag* nor the emperor provided an effective remedy for Germany's pressing need for public peace and justice. Repeated attempts to outlaw feuding were ineffective and the provision of royal courts inadequate. The emergence of a chamber court (*Kammergericht*) – but with limited competence and resources – was paralleled by the demise of the royal court of justice (*Reichshofgericht*) in the mid-fifteenth century following widespread grants of immunity from its jurisdiction. Royal taxation, meanwhile, remained largely *ad hoc* and meagre compared to that elsewhere. Several plans for reinvigorating imperial government were advanced in the fifteenth century though it was only after the deliberations of the emperor-elect Maximilian and the *Reichstag* held at Worms in 1495 that reforms were actually implemented. Following the declaration of a perpetual public peace and the prohibition of feuding, the *Kammergericht* was transformed into the *Reichskammergericht*, a supreme appellate court with a staff of salaried professional judges. The costs of this court and an imperial army were to be met from a new imperial property tax, the 'common penny' (*Gemeiner Pfennig*). Inability to enforce payment of the tax undermined the other reforms and the *Gemeiner Pfennig* was soon abandoned. Instead the government resorted for finance to *Kammerzieler*, a small biennial tax to support the *Reichskammergericht*, and other traditional but irregular levies including 'Roman money' (*Römermonate*), an aid originally intended to finance imperial coronations in Rome which evolved into a levy for military

purposes. Maximilian was less enthusiastic about other reforms discussed at Worms, including the proposal associated with Berthold von Henneberg, archbishop of Mainz, to establish a permanent executive council. This body (the *Reichsregiment*) was, however, appointed in 1500. Presided over by the king or his deputy, its twenty members included representatives of the electors, other *Reichstag* estates and six newly established constituencies or 'circles' (*Kreise*), who together were entrusted with extensive powers over royal justice, finance and foreign policy. Ill-resourced, without means of asserting its authority and regarded with suspicion by Maximilian, the *Reichsregiment* floundered within two years though it was revived later in the sixteenth century. In consequence of political particularism and the limited success of the attempted governmental reforms, Germany lacked an equivalent to London, Paris or Edinburgh which were emerging as national administrative centres. The *Reichstag* assembled in a variety of locations though usually, and increasingly under Maximilian, in central or southern Germany. The Urban diet convened at Frankfurt, Speyer, Heilbronn and Esslingen and the *Kurverein* in yet other towns. The *Kammergericht* frequently sat at Rottweil. The *Reichskammergericht* was assigned to Frankfurt, where imperial elections were usually held, though royal coronations took place at Aachen. The royal insignia was lodged at Munich, then Karlstein near Prague and from 1424 at Nuremberg, where the *Reichsregiment* too was based. But in other respects, just as Prague may be regarded as the centre of Charles IV's (1347–78) empire, so Innsbruck was the centre of Maximilian's kingdom. It was in the administrative centre of his Tirolean lands that Maximilian first based his imperial chancery and court and here too that he established the imperial archive.

D. Ditchburn

208

The Spread of the Black Death

The appearance and rapid spread of the Black Death or plague in Europe was facilitated by the *pax mongolica* and by those widespread trade-routes which medieval merchants had established between Europe and Central Asia. The Black Death spread across Central Asia from China during the 1340s and, infecting Genoese merchants at the Crimean port of Caffa in 1347, it almost immediately reached Constantinople and was then rapidly disseminated along the trade routes to the Mediterranean and western Europe. By the end of 1348 it had affected most of southern and western Europe, appearing in England at Melcombe Regis during the summer, and in the course of the next two years it spread over the rest of the British Isles, Germany and Scandinavia.

The bubonic plague was a disease of black rats which affected humans when the bacillus was spread by the *Xenopsylla Cheopis* 'carrier' flea, especially during periods of warm weather. The pneumonic plague was a deadlier and more contagious variation of the same disease. It seems to have been a secondary stage or extension of the bubonic plague and was spread not by the *X. Cheopis* carrier but by breathing in the bacilli of infected people.

Given the absence of adequate statistical data and variation in the incidence of the phenomenon, it is impossible to be precise about the number of people who were wiped out by this pandemic disaster. Shaken by the calamity, contemporaries might understandably have exaggerated the results. The chronicler Froissart, for example, claimed that 'at least a third of all the people in the world died then'. Yet perhaps Froissart was not too wide of the mark and it may be suggested, with all due caution, that between one-quarter and one-third of the population of western Europe died as a result of the plague. However, this estimate must also be considered within the context of the significant variations in the incidence of mortality. Some towns, and especially ports, suffered huge losses. Albi, Castres and Florence, for example, probably lost over half their populations, Genoa and Hamburg two-thirds, and Bremen up to three-quarters. On the other hand Bohemia, Poland, Hungary, and perhaps the central plateaus of Castile seem to have been less affected by the plague.

Horrendous though the Black Death was, it was not an isolated phenomenon, and it is important to bear in mind the periods both before and after the pandemic. The Black Death had been preceded by years of famine, particularly the great famine of 1315–17 in north-western Europe, and it is probable that population growth in general had already been checked before the pandemic. Consequently, Malthusian analysis would suggest that the expansion of the twelfth and thirteenth centuries created a situation where population growth outstripped food resources, with the result that crises of subsistence became more serious and facilitated the 'collapse' of the four-teenth century. By the same token the distinctive land:population ratios of central and eastern Europe and some areas of the Iberian peninsula meant that these regions were relatively better endowed with land than they were with colonists and settlers, and this in turn may help to explain why they were less affected by the Black Death.

After the Black Death the plague became endemic for the remainder of the Middle Ages (and beyond), with sporadic outbreaks of the disease occurring at different times and in different places. These outbreaks, which were more pronouncedly urban in character, not only helped to check the recovery of the population but also seem to have hit hardest at those who lacked immunity – hence, for example, the 'Pestilences of the Children' in England in 1361 and in Catalonia in 1362–3 ('*mortaldad de los infants*').

A. MacKay

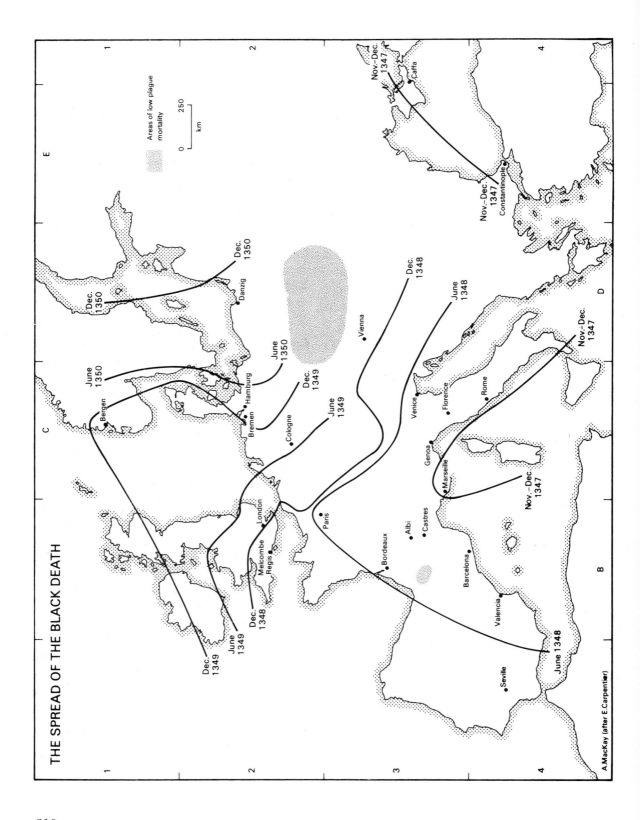

THE SPREAD OF THE BLACK DEATH

Areas of low plague mortality

0 250 km

Dec. 1350
Danzig
Dec. 1350
June 1350
Bergen
Hamburg
Bremen
Cologne
Dec. 1349
June 1349
Vienna
Dec. 1348
June 1348
Venice
Florence
Rome
Genoa
Marseille
Nov.–Dec. 1347
London
Melcombe Regis
Dec. 1348
June 1349
Dec. 1349
Paris
Bordeaux
Albi
Castres
Barcelona
Valencia
June 1348
Seville
Nov.–Dec. 1347
Caffa
Nov.–Dec. 1347
Constantinople

A.MacKay (after E.Carpentier)

The German Hanse

The term 'Hanse', usually referring to a group of merchants or towns, was widely known in medieval Europe. The most important Hanse was the German Hanse or Hanseatic League, formed by the merchants and towns of northern and central Germany, though there were also two non-urban members, the peasant community of Ditmarschen in Holstein and the grand master of the Teutonic Order. The lifeblood of the German Hanse was trade. Its members, active in northern Europe from the twelfth century until the League's demise in the seventeenth century, dominated Baltic trade during the thirteenth and fourteenth centuries.

The origins of the German control of Baltic trade lay in the German colonization of Slav lands east of the Elbe. Lübeck, the League's unofficial capital, was founded in 1143 and other new towns, frequently based on existing Slav settlements, followed. Germans, then, dominated the towns of northern Europe, and German merchants from the twelfth century visited the traditional entrepots of northern Europe, such as Visby. Nonetheless the Baltic was ill-equipped to meet all their demands. Germans were therefore forced to travel further afield: to Russia, Norway, Britain, the Low Countries, France and, by the fifteenth century, the Mediterranean.

They sold all the products of their home regions, but their grain, above all, was vital to both the urbanized Low Countries and those areas unable to produce sufficient corn themselves. Indeed, the control of grain supplies allowed Germans to win privileges for themselves, especially in Norway, where other foreign merchants were virtually excluded. This, coupled with their development of ships, such as the 'cog' and 'hulk', suited to the transportation of bulk produce, and also the adoption of Flemish and Italian trading techniques, precipitated the German domination of Baltic trade.

Yet it was among the communities of German merchants abroad that the Hanse emerged. Frequently grouped together in self-contained settlements, merchants co-operated to defend and extend their privileges. Such a community emerged at Visby by c. 1160. Others followed, notably at the four Hanseatic staple towns ('Kontors') of Novgorod, Bergen, London and Bruges. Co-operation gradually developed between the German towns too. The catalyst to this was the desirability of co-ordinating a response to common enemies, in the absence of protective imperial authority. Initially this was on a regional basis against pirates and local princes. By the late thirteenth century threats to merchants in Novgorod, Flanders and Norway prompted more widespread urban co-operation, in the shape of trade embargoes and blockades. The zenith of urban co-operation was reached in 1367–70. In the face of Danish and Norwegian threats of political hegemony the towns pursued a successful military response. Yet even at this highpoint, the Hanse was more concerned to protect its commercial interests than pursue territorial aggrandisement.

In the fifteenth century the Hanse faced growing challenges to its commercial domination. English, Dutch, Scottish, Italian and south German merchants all attempted to intervene in the Baltic's lucrative trade, while within the towns the ruling mercantile elites faced increasing discontent from middling merchants and craftsmen. The response to these threats was mixed and the Dutch, in particular, developed their share of Baltic trade dramatically. Such setbacks were due largely to the Hanse's inability to maintain a united response. There was little institutional unity to ensure that all the towns agreed to, or implemented Hanseatic policy. Different regions, which had always had different commercial interests, were able to follow conflicting policies. Such differences became even starker in the sixteenth and seventeenth centuries. Faced with the resurgence of the Scandinavian and Slav kingdoms, with their territorial ambitions, the Hanse became increasingly impotent. Though individual Hanseatic towns continued to prosper, the last Hanseatic Diet met in 1669, hoping for better times. They were not to come.

D. Ditchburn

211

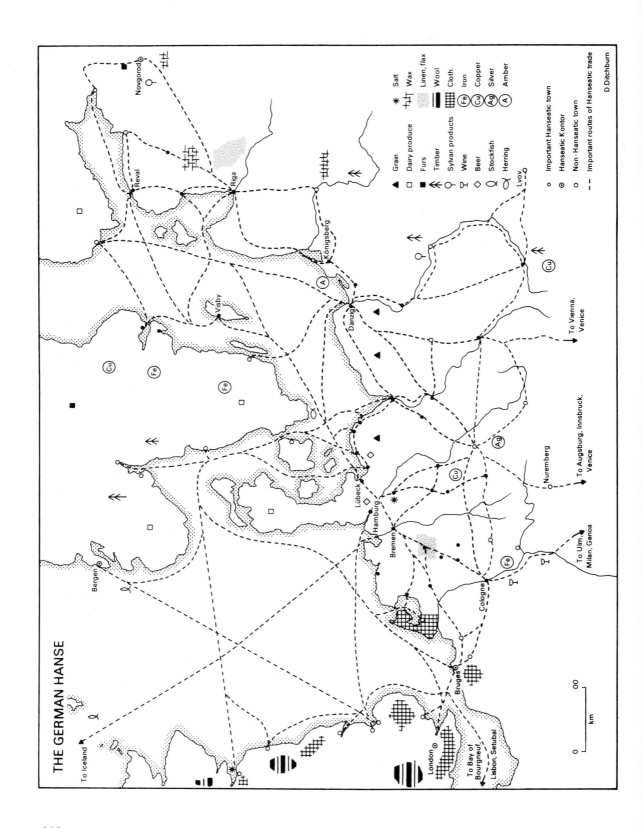

THE GERMAN HANSE

To Iceland

Bergen

Reval

Novgorod

Riga

Visby

Königsberg

Danzig

Lübeck

Hamburg

Bremen

Lvov

Nuremberg

Cologne

Bruges

London

To Vienna, Venice

To Augsburg, Innsbruck, Venice

To Ulm, Milan, Genoa

To Bay of Bourgneuf, Lisbon, Setubal

D.Ditchburn

Salt
Wax
Linen, flax
Wool
Cloth
Iron   Fe
Copper Cu
Silver Ag
Amber   A

Grain
Dairy produce
Furs
Timber
Sylvan products
Wine
Beer
Stockfish
Herring

○ Important Hanseatic town
◉ Hanseatic Kontor
○ Non-Hanseatic town
-- Important routes of Hanseatic trade

km
0   00

Financial Centres in Western Europe

The religious, political and economic life of late medieval Europe was highly monetized. The revenues remitted to the curia at Avignon during the pontificate of John XXII (1316–34), for example, almost averaged 230,000 Florentine gold florins per year, similar amounts were paid to the cardinals, litigation was expensive, and when the papacy was based in Rome pilgrims brought considerable sums of money. Crusading activities likewise involved enormous expenditure, as did the Hundred Years War whether on ransoms, protection money (*appatissements*) or wages paid to mercenaries, of whom the most famous fought in the Great Companies operating in France and Spain during the fourteenth century. A memorable description of the profits made by freebooters in the Great Companies was given by the Bascot de Mauléon to the chronicler Jean Froissart in an interview in 1388.

If a map of the main financial centres cannot do justice to such religious and military aspects, the traditional focus of attention on outstanding families of financiers, such as the Frescobaldi, Bardi, Peruzzi, Medici and Fugger, or even individuals like William de la Pole or Jacques Coeur, also obscures others whose total contributions were of greater value. In aggregate the lesser markets and fairs, as well as rural monetary transactions of all kinds were of enormous significance to economic life, the sale of cereals, livestock, cloth, and wine or malt being essential features of small market-towns and villages. For every urban market in Leicestershire and Nottinghamshire, for example, there were six village markets.

As for the prominent financiers, their activities usually combined different functions. The Medici, for example, acted as papal bankers, and others burned their fingers by over-investing in the ventures of princes, from the Florentine companies of the Bardi, Peruzzi and Acciauoli, involved in loans to fourteenth-century rulers in Naples and England, to the sixteenth-century Fuggers who financed Charles V of Spain.

The most prominent entrepreneurs in the financial markets of western Europe were the Italians, particularly the Florentines and Genoese. They were usually both merchants and bankers, and their success owed much to advanced commercial techniques. These allowed them to organize their affairs from a home base and use 'partnerships' or 'correspondents' abroad. Insurance and accounting became specialized activities. Double-entry book-keeping was increasingly used as were different kinds of account books, for example to keep track of an individual's investments (including everything from trade to marriage contracts and dowries), or to maintain balances between a home company and branches abroad. Permanent banking centres were scattered throughout western Europe, but international banking was also catered for at the great international fairs, those of Champagne in the thirteenth century, and of Geneva, Medina del Campo and Lyon later on. Payments were normally made by bills of exchange, using the services of Italian or south German bankers. They involved the advance of funds at one financial or banking centre and the paying out of the amount involved at another centre, almost invariably in another currency. Exchange rates fluctuated. In theory, therefore, it was possible for a bill to be dishonoured at its destination and then to be rechanged back to its place of origin at a different exchange rate and at a profit. This gave rise to the practice of dry exchange, that is using bills of exchange as a pretext or cover for usury.

Frequently great financial and banking dynasties eventually reneged on their entrepreneurial background. This may have been partly due to a guilt complex about an incompatibility between their activities and religious values. The Peruzzi even opened up an account in their books on behalf of '*Messer Dommeneddio*' ('Mr God'), the profits being given to the poor, and the account being the only one to show a credit balance when their company failed. More generally it was a drive for political power and respectability. The Medici ruled Florence, became popes (Leo X and Clement VII), and even married royalty (Catherine de Medici, queen of France).

A. MacKay

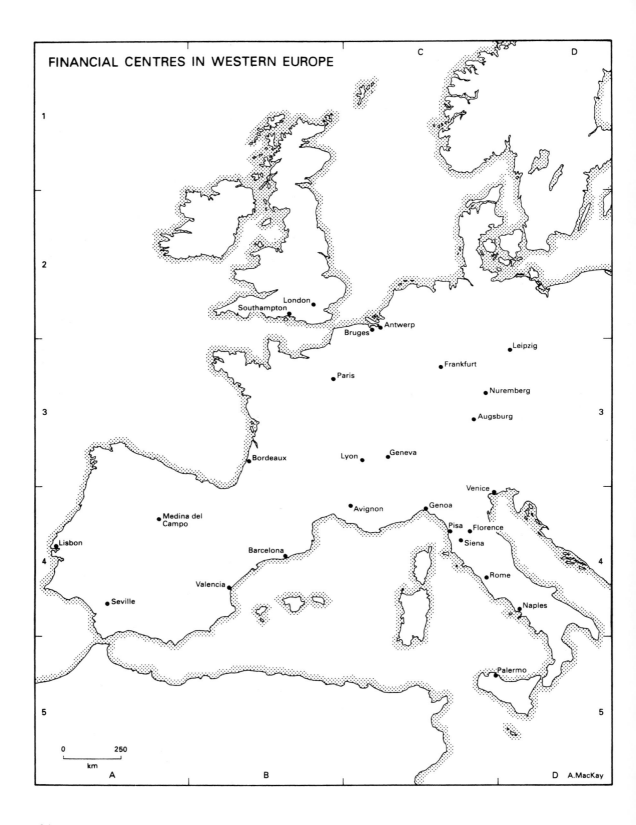

FINANCIAL CENTRES IN WESTERN EUROPE

London
Southampton
Bruges · Antwerp
Leipzig
Frankfurt
Paris
Nuremberg
Augsburg
Bordeaux
Lyon · Geneva
Venice
Avignon · Genoa
Medina del Campo
Pisa · Florence
Siena
Lisbon
Barcelona
Rome
Valencia
Naples
Seville
Palermo

0   250
km

A   B

D A.MacKay

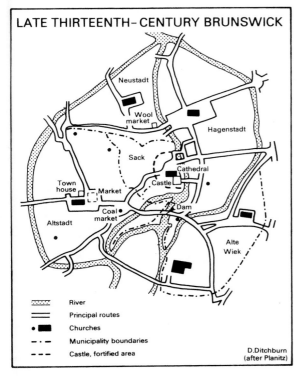

LATE THIRTEENTH-CENTURY BRUNSWICK

Legend:
- River
- Principal routes
- Churches
- Municipality boundaries
- Castle, fortified area

D. Ditchburn
(after Planitz)

Late Thirteenth-Century Brunswick

Brunswick, the largest city in medieval Lower Saxony, is one of the earliest examples of a 'multi-town'. Most German 'multi-towns' had two or three constituent towns. Brunswick was unusual in that it had five. The earliest, dating from the tenth century, were at Sack (around the fortified castle and cathedral) and Alte Wiek, a market-based settlement. In the eleventh century a mercantile quarter grew at Altstadt, while Duke Henry the Lion of Saxony founded Hagenstadt and Neustadt in the twelfth century. The three new towns had their own councils by the thirteenth century (before the two old ones). In 1269 they established a general council to overlook matters of common concern. Although the existence of councils in the component towns, increasingly styled municipalities, was confirmed in 1299, the general council began to dominate internal and external matters.

D. Ditchburn

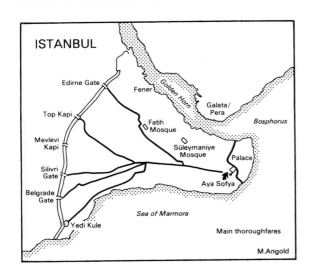

ISTANBUL

M. Angold

Istanbul

The city which the Ottoman Turks conquered from the Byzantines in 1453 was nigh derelict. Its restoration was among the most urgent tasks facing Mehmed the Conqueror. He drafted in settlers from all parts of his empire. His success is revealed by a census of the city made in 1477. There were at least 16,324 households, representing a total population of perhaps 100,000. Muslims formed about three-fifths of the population; Greeks just under a quarter, already concentrated in Fener, where the patriarchate found a resting place. The next largest community were the Jews – about a tenth of the population. Though always cosmopolitan, Istanbul was a thoroughly Muslim city. St Sophia was turned into the chief mosque. Mehmed had the Fatih mosque constructed on the site of the Church of the Holy Apostles. Attached to these were reli-

215

gious, charitable and educational institutions and, by way of endowment, markets, shops and workshops. The foundation of such complexes – or *imârets* – was typical of the growth of the city. The Conqueror's example was followed by his viziers and his successors. Among the most impressive is the Süleymaniye built by Süleyman the Magnificent (1520–66). By his reign the population of Istanbul was approaching the half million mark.

M. Angold

Novgorod in the Later Middle Ages

Novgorod, in existence by the ninth century, was the seat of a bishopric, and from 1165 an archbishopric. It was also by the later Middle Ages the centre of a large city-state with far-flung trading interests. The town was divided by the River Volkov, but linked by a bridge. The St Sophia side was dominated by the cathedral and its surrounding fortress, the Kremlin. The market place, close to the wharfs on the commercial side, was surrounded by mercantile churches, such as St John's Church of the Russian merchants, and the Good Friday Church of the Russian long-distance merchants, and trading depots, such as the Gotenhof of the Gotland merchants and the Hanse's St Petershof. Politically, until its conquest by Ivan III of Russia in 1478, Novgorod was dominated by its archbishop and a group of urban dwelling nobility. For administrative purposes the city was divided into fifths and these in turn into smaller units, the smallest of which was the street.

D. Ditchburn

The Swabian Town League

Later medieval German urban leagues were temporary alliances between neighbouring towns. They were usually directed against knights and princes who threatened urban trading monopolies and jurisdictions. Despite their prohibition in the Golden Bull (1356), leagues

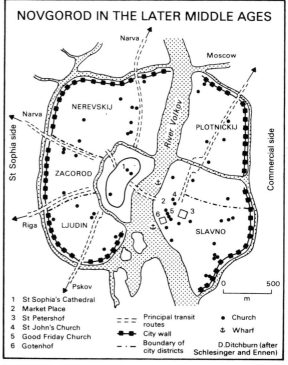

NOVGOROD IN THE LATER MIDDLE AGES

1 St Sophia's Cathedral
2 Market Place
3 St Petershof
4 St John's Church
5 Good Friday Church
6 Gotenhof

= = = Principal transit routes
●—■—● City wall
— · — Boundary of city districts

● Church
⚓ Wharf

D.Ditchburn (after Schlesinger and Ennen)

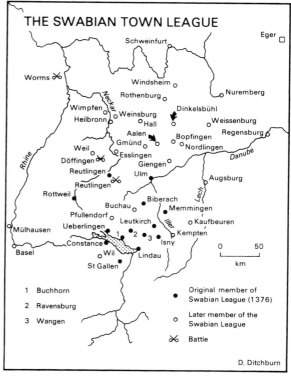

THE SWABIAN TOWN LEAGUE

1 Buchhorn
2 Ravensburg
3 Wangen

● Original member of Swabian League (1376)
○ Later member of the Swabian League
⚔ Battle

D. Ditchburn

flourished because weak kings failed to defend urban interests. When Charles IV and Wenzel imposed high taxation on some towns, and mortgaged others to their princely enemies in order to fund their dynastic ambitions, fourteen towns under Ulm's leadership formed the Swabian Town League in 1376. The League defeated its main local enemy, the count of Wurtemberg, at Reutlingen (1377), encouraging other towns, notably Regensburg (1381) and Nuremberg (1384) to join. Alliances were made with the Rhenish League (1381) and Swiss Confederation (1385), and the League received implicit imperial recognition in 1384. Nevertheless in 1388 the princes defeated the Swabian League at Döffingen and its Rhenish allies at Worms. The leagues gradually fell apart thereafter and were again proscribed by the Pacification of Eger (1389).

D. Ditchburn

Late Medieval Seville

Within its walls the great trading city of Seville covered an area of 682 acres, and to this must be added the extra-mural districts such as Triana. The original nucleus, characterized by small blocks of buildings and irregular streets, was in the south-east. Towards the north the blocks of buildings were larger and the streets rectilinear, above all in the north-west part which came into existence later. The large blocks of areas taken up by the monasteries and convents were prominent (there were nineteen by 1500), above all those established in the thirteenth century and situated along the western front.

Administratively the city was divided into twenty-eight parishes and five districts, and its population rose from approximately 5,000 *vecinos* (heads of households) in the 1430s to 7,000 *vecinos* in the 1480s, excluding temporary resi-

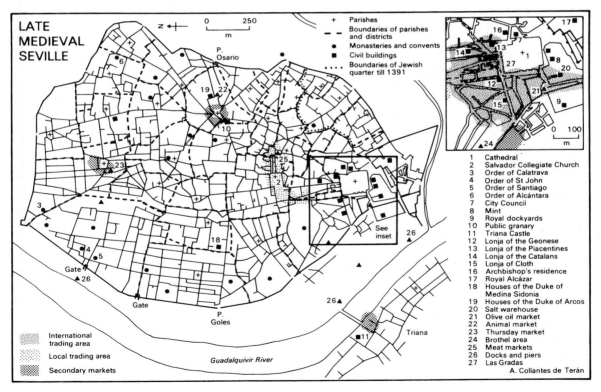

LATE MEDIEVAL SEVILLE

z

0 250 m

+ Parishes
– – Boundaries of parishes and districts
● Monasteries and convents
■ Civil buildings
···· Boundaries of Jewish quarter till 1391

P. Osario

See inset

0 100 m

Gate

Gate

P. Goles

Triana

Guadalquivir River

International trading area
Local trading area
Secondary markets

1 Cathedral
2 Salvador Collegiate Church
3 Order of Calatrava
4 Order of St John
5 Order of Santiago
6 Order of Alcántara
7 City Council
8 Mint
9 Royal dockyards
10 Public granary
11 Triana Castle
12 Lonja of the Geonese
13 Lonja of the Piacentines
14 Lonja of the Catalans
15 Lonja of Cloth
16 Archbishop's residence
17 Royal Alcázar
18 Houses of the Duke of Medina Sidonia
19 Houses of the Duke of Arcos
20 Salt warehouse
21 Olive oil market
22 Animal market
23 Thursday market
24 Brothel area
25 Meat markets
26 Docks and piers
27 Las Gradas

A. Collantes de Terán

dents and the exiguous minorities of Jews and Muslims. This population was unevenly distributed, with the highest densities being in the southern part of the city. Here were to be found the centres of civil power, such as the *alcázar* or royal palace, the city council, the admiralty and the customs headquarters; the cathedral; the most important markets; the *alcaicería* or silk exchange; the area where international trade was transacted; the *lonjas* or commercial centres of merchants from different nations; and all those associated with these activities, such as money-changers, bankers and notaries. The urban configuration here had for the most part been inherited from the Muslims.

To the north of the city gates of Osario and Goles there was a lesser density of population, a predominance of occupations relating to agriculture, fishing and seamanship, and a large number of labourers. Moreover this was an area almost totally lacking in a co-ordinating infrastructure, apart from a market to supply the locality with provisions and another weekly market, for probably the same purpose, held every Thursday.

The houses of great nobles and patrician oligarchs were not in one particular district but dispersed throughout the city.

A. Collantes de Terán

Deserted English Villages: Regional and Temporal Incidence, *c.* 1100–*c.* 1500

'There was probably never a decade in the Middle Ages which did not see the death of one or more villages' (M. Beresford, 1954/1983).

Beresford's outline of the spatial and temporal incidence of village desertions has been modified little by subsequent research except perhaps to indicate a higher casualty rate in the period before the Black Death. The absence of tax assessments before 1297 and the imperfections of later sources and archaeological dating methods inhibit accurate dating of many known desertions. Most disappearances can, however, be located within broad time periods. With the notable exception of the central Midlands, John Hales' observation in 1549 that 'the chief destruction of villages was before the reign of King Henry the Seventh' (i.e. 1485) holds true.

The incidence and causes of desertions varied regionally and over time. A universal feature, however, especially marked before the late fourteenth century, was the greater vulnerability of smaller villages. Factors such as soil type and proximity to neighbours may have restricted growth and predisposed smaller villages to loss of economic viability when the agricultural terms of trade shifted unfavourably and certain demographic conditions prevailed.

Twelfth-century desertions were largely due to the sheep farming activities of Cistercian Houses and local factors such as coastal erosion and border raids. Desertions between the late thirteenth and mid-fourteenth centuries can be attributed to the retreat from marginal land colonized during the population expansion of the late Middle Ages, due to a combination perhaps of soil exhaustion and the demographic contraction under way before the Black Death. Recurrent plague epidemics thereafter rarely caused the demise of villages directly. Rather, the casualties of the next 150 years seem associated with the continued abandonment of marginal arable land and the emergent comparative advantage of pastoral production occurring in the context of demographic stagnation and demand shifts. Particularly at risk were places, many in the Midland counties, where the relative advantage of pastoral or arable production was not strong.

Enclosures, so villainized by contemporary commentators, were clearly, then, a symptom rather than a cause of village desertion prior to 1500.

E.M. Turner

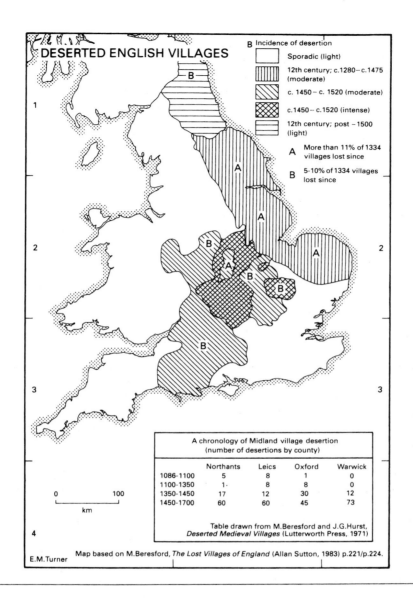

DESERTED ENGLISH VILLAGES

B Incidence of desertion

	Sporadic (light)
	12th century; c.1280–c.1475 (moderate)
	c. 1450 – c. 1520 (moderate)
	c.1450 – c.1520 (intense)
	12th century; post – 1500 (light)
A	More than 11% of 1334 villages lost since
B	5-10% of 1334 villages lost since

A chronology of Midland village desertion
(number of desertions by county)

	Northants	Leics	Oxford	Warwick
1086-1100	5	8	1	0
1100-1350	1·	8	8	0
1350-1450	17	12	30	12
1450-1700	60	60	45	73

Table drawn from M.Beresford and J.G.Hurst,
Deserted Medieval Villages (Lutterworth Press, 1971)

0 ——— 100
km

E.M.Turner
Map based on M.Beresford, *The Lost Villages of England* (Allan Sutton, 1983) p.221/p.224.

Late Medieval Transhumance in Western Europe

Transhumance is the seasonal movement of livestock (notably sheep) in April/May and September/October between winter and summer pastures allowing the avoidance of variations in climate, the displacement in Europe being one of altitude. It differs from nomadism in that in transhumance there is a permanent dwelling for part of the year. In 'normal' transhumance the permanent (winter) home is in the lowlands, while in 'inverse' transhumance the permanent (summer) home is in the mountains. Since large numbers of sheep were moved over long distances, late medieval transhumance involved considerable organization, as the fixed

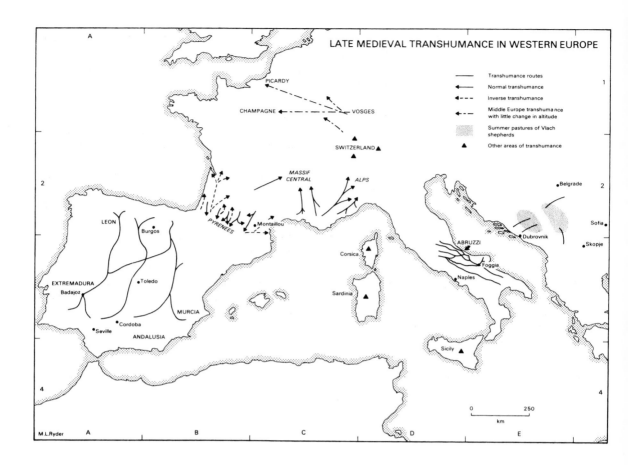

Transhumance routes

Normal transhumance

Inverse transhumance

Middle Europe transhumance with little change in altitude

Summer pastures of Vlach shepherds

Other areas of transhumance

PICARDY

CHAMPAGNE

VOSGES

SWITZERLAND

MASSIF CENTRAL

ALPS

Belgrade

Sofia

LEON

Burgos

PYRENEES

Montaillou

Corsica

Dubrovnik

Skopje

ABRUZZI

Foggia

EXTREMADURA

Badajoz

Toledo

MURCIA

Sardinia

Naples

Cordoba

Seville

ANDALUSIA

Sicily

M.L.Ryder

0   250

km

routes on the map help to illustrate. These tracks varied from subsidiary ones only 10 metres wide to main routes at least 20 metres wide. Each had a strip of pasture on one or both sides which increased the width by a further 100 metres on average.

Transhumance was carried out in Yugoslavia by Vlach shepherds, the summer settlement being the *katun*. It was particularly important to the economy of Dubrovnik. Inverse transhumance occurred in some places, as well as 'oscillating' transhumance in which the permanent home lies on the migration route and accommodates the flocks in spring and autumn. In Italy transhumance between the Abruzzi mountains and the Apulian Tavoliere was based on routes known as *tratturi delle pecore*. In the fifteenth century, as a result of intervention by Alfonso I of Aragon, sales of wool and sheep were

centred on Foggia and transhumance was regulated by an institution known as the *Dogana*. The *tratturi*, therefore, linked the *Dogana* of Foggia with the highland areas of the Abruzzi. In the kingdom of Castile transhumance was catered for by numerous tributary tracks (*cañadas*) which fed three main north–south routes (*cañadas reales*). All were marked by stone pillars 1.5 metres high at 100-metre intervals. In the thirteenth century royal recognition of the *Mesta*, an association of stockmen, strengthened existing rights of way, and the Crown derived income from the *servicio* and *montazgo* taxes levied on the movement of sheep. Southern France was characterized by both normal and inverse transhumance. *Carraïrés*, dating from the thirteenth century and formalized by *Statuts de la Transhumance* in the sixteenth century, were routes which were fed by narrower *drailles*. In Alpine transhumance, typified by Switzerland, pastures at different altitudes were emphasized more than the tracks. The pastures all fell within the mountain area and were grazed successively as the season advanced: *hofweiden* at 1,000 metres, *vorweiden* up to 1,500 metres, and *alpweiden* up to over 2,000 metres.

Although it is difficult to reconstruct routes for northern Europe, not included on this map, northern areas also had transhumance. In Iceland there was oscillating transhumance with sheep being wintered away and only going to higher ground during July and August. In Norway the movements were eastwards from the west coast and valleys, into the mountains, while in Sweden the movements were westwards, the summer settlement being the *seter*. The evidence for transhumance in the British Isles also lies more in summer settlements than in migration routes, which probably became green drove roads and even ordinary roads, just as the sum-mer settlements became permanent hill farms. In Wales the summer settlement was the *hafod* (in contrast to the lowland *hendre*). In the Pennines and Cumbria inverse transhumance persists, with the wintering on low ground of sheep in their first year. Pennine place names ending in 'sett' derive from *seter*, indicating transhumance and Scandinavian influence. In Cumbria the Norse ending for *seter* is 'erg', an Irish loan word for summer settlement, which itself indicates that transhumance took place in Ireland. There was transhumance in all the mountainous areas of Scotland, the summer settlement being the shieling.

Fascinating insights into the lives of shepherds of the Pyrenean village of Montaillou have been afforded by the early fourteenth-century Inquisition Register of Jacques Fournier, bishop of Pamiers.

M.L. Ryder

European Expansion at the End of the Middle Ages

During the fourteenth century the trade of Genoese, Castilians and Portuguese expanded in the region of North Africa. Factories were established on the Moroccan coast, traders accompanied caravans across the Sahara to the Niger towns and maritime expeditions visited the Atlantic Islands, raiding the Canaries for slaves which fetched a good price in Mediterranean Europe. The Genoese also invested extensively in sugar production in the southern parts of the Iberian peninsula.

Early in the fifteenth century permanent settlements were made by French and Castilians in the Canary Islands and this prompted the Portuguese for their part to occupy the Azores and Madeira where the Genoese soon introduced the growing of sugar cane. The Portuguese nobility also turned their attention to warfare in Morocco once the Hundred Years War in the Iberian peninsula finally came to an end in 1411. The main object of the party led by the Infante Dom Henrique (Henry the Navigator) was to seize Moroccan territory and major assaults were launched on Ceuta, Tangier, Alcacer and Arzila which all fell into Portuguese hands by 1471. The Portuguese nobility also raided for slaves along the African coast and in the Canary Islands. During the regency of the Infante Dom Pedro (1440–9) the Portuguese, encouraged by the high price of slaves, sailed south of the Sahara to trade with the well-organized kingdoms of the Senegambia region, discovering that gold and ivory could also be obtained in exchange for salt, horses, wheat and cloth which came from the Mediterranean countries or the islands.

Trading was of less interest to the Portuguese nobility than obtaining territory or holding military commands. While willing to acquire seigneurial rights in the various islands that were

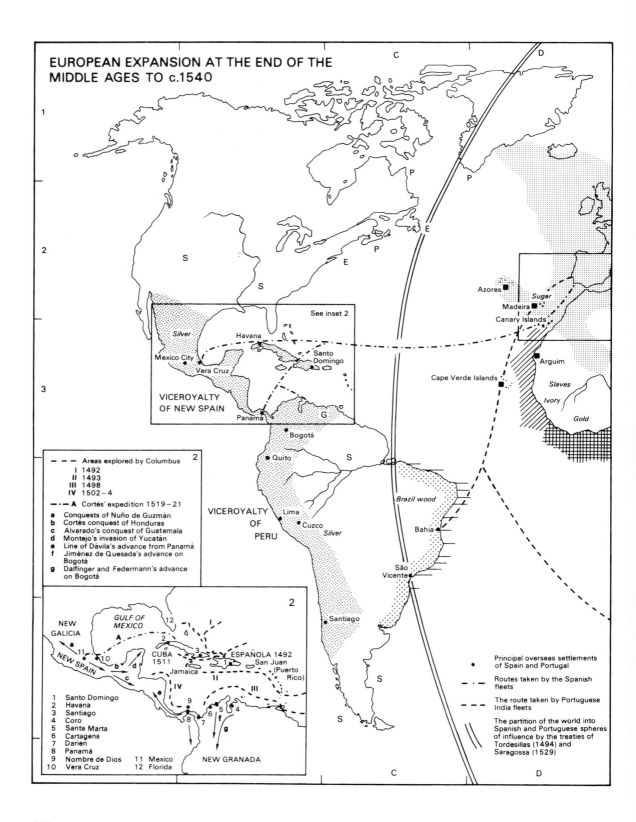

EUROPEAN EXPANSION AT THE END OF THE MIDDLE AGES TO c.1540

Azores
Sugar
Madeira
Canary Islands

Arguim

Cape Verde Islands

Slaves

Ivory

Gold

See inset 2

Silver

Havana

Mexico City

Vera Cruz

Santo Domingo

VICEROYALTY
OF NEW SPAIN

Panamá

G

Bogotá

Quito

S

Brazil wood

Areas explored by Columbus
  I 1492
 II 1493
III 1498
IV 1502–4
A Cortés' expedition 1519–21
a Conquests of Nuño de Guzmán
b Cortés conquest of Honduras
c Alvarado's conquest of Guatemala
d Montejo's invasion of Yucatán
e Line of Dávila's advance from Panamá
f Jiménez de Quesada's advance on
    Bogotá
g Dalfinger and Federmann's advance
    on Bogotá

VICEROYALTY
OF
PERU

Lima

Cuzco

Silver

Bahia

São
Vicente

Santiago

S

Inset 2

NEW
GALICIA

GULF OF
MEXICO

NEW SPAIN

A

CUBA
1511

ESPAÑOLA 1492

San Juan
(Puerto
Rico)

Jamaica

Santiago

Coro

NEW GRANADA

1 Santo Domingo
2 Havana
3 Santiago
4 Coro
5 Santa Marta
6 Cartagena
7 Darien
8 Panamá
9 Nombre de Dios
10 Vera Cruz
11 Mexico
12 Florida

• Principal overseas settlements
   of Spain and Portugal

–·–·– Routes taken by the Spanish
   fleets

– – – The route taken by Portuguese
   India fleets

The partition of the world into
Spanish and Portuguese spheres
of influence by the treaties of
Tordesillas (1494) and
Saragossa (1529)

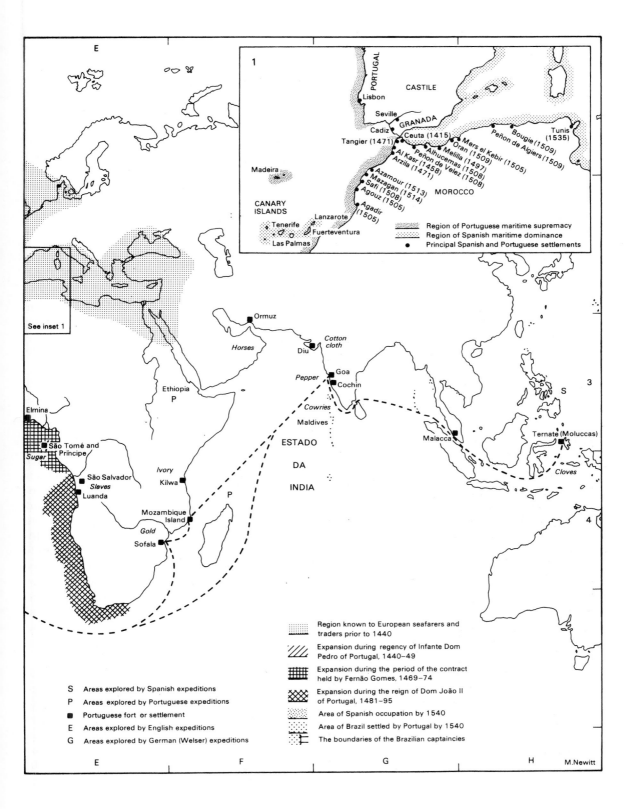

Inset 1

PORTUGAL

CASTILE

Lisbon

Seville

Cadiz

GRANADA

Tangier (1471)

Ceuta (1415)

Bougie (1509)

Tunis (1535)

Mers el Kebir (1509)

Peñon de Algiers (1509)

Melilla

Oran (1509)

Alhucemas (1497)

Al Kasr

Peñon de Velez (1508)

Arzila (1471)

Azamour (1513)

Mazagan (1514)

Safi (1508)

Agouz (1505)

Agadir (1505)

MOROCCO

Madeira

CANARY ISLANDS

Tenerife

Lanzarote

Fuerteventura

Las Palmas

Region of Portuguese maritime supremacy

Region of Spanish maritime dominance

● Principal Spanish and Portuguese settlements

See inset 1

Ormuz

Cotton cloth

Diu

Horses

Ethiopia

P

Pepper

Goa

Cochin

Elmina

Cowries

Maldives

São Tomé and Principe

Sugar

ESTADO

DA

INDIA

Malacca

Ternate (Moluccas)

São Salvador

Slaves

Luanda

Ivory

Kilwa

P

Cloves

Mozambique Island

Gold

Sofala

S   Areas explored by Spanish expeditions

P   Areas explored by Portuguese expeditions

■   Portuguese fort or settlement

E   Areas explored by English expeditions

G   Areas explored by German (Welser) expeditions

Region known to European seafarers and traders prior to 1440

Expansion during regency of Infante Dom Pedro of Portugal, 1440–49

Expansion during the period of the contract held by Fernão Gomes, 1469–74

Expansion during the reign of Dom João II of Portugal, 1481–95

Area of Spanish occupation by 1540

Area of Brazil settled by Portugal by 1540

The boundaries of the Brazilian captaincies

M.Newitt

discovered, the nobility were more interested in Moroccan and Spanish adventures and between 1469 and 1474, during the reign of Afonso V, the trade with Africa was leased to a Lisbon merchant, Fernão Gomes. Gomes' captains explored the Gulf of Guinea discovering the lucrative opportunities for trade in gold. Trade was interrupted by war with Castile between 1474 and 1479. Europe's first colonial war took place in the Canaries and along the coast of Guinea and the threat posed by Castile encouraged the Portuguese Crown to give direct control of the African trade to the Infante João. Before he came to the throne in 1481, the Treaty of Alcaçovas between Castile and Portugal had made the first partition of territory – Castile conceding the Atlantic Islands and the Guinea trade to Portugal in return for being confirmed in the sovereignty of the Canary Islands.

After the fall of Granada in 1492 the Castilians began to exploit their openings overseas. Expeditions were mounted against Morocco in imitation of the Portuguese, and the Canary Islands were parcelled out among would-be conquerors. It was the desire to exploit the opportunities presented by the treaty that led Isabella of Castile to grant a contract to the Genoese adventurer, Columbus, to undertake voyages and conquests to the west. The Portuguese meanwhile had continued to expand their trade under direct royal auspices. A castle was built at Elmina in 1482 to dominate the gold trade and an official royal factory was opened at the court of the king of the Congo to channel the slave trade of the region through royal hands. It was the Crown also which organized the exploratory voyages of Diogo Cão (1483–6) and Bartolomeu Dias (1487–9), and the overland journey of Pero de Covilhão who was dispatched to India, Africa and Arabia to spy out the opportunities of royal trade.

After Columbus' discoveries in 1492, not only the Caribbean islands but the whole of the New World threatened to pass out of the Castilian Crown's control since Columbus' contract had granted him the hereditary governorship of any lands he discovered. In its anxiety to establish royal authority, the Castilian Crown hastened to organize voyages of its own and set in motion the struggle for the control of the New World between rival *conquistadores* and between the *conquistadores* and the Crown. The scramble for conquest between the Spaniards based in Santo Domingo who set out to conquer Cuba and then Mexico and Honduras, and those based in Darien and Panama who pushed north into Nicaragua and then organized the conquest of the Inca empire, was mirrored in the competition between the Spaniards of Santa Marta and Cartagena and the Germans in Venezuela for the conquest of the Colombian plateau.

The individual rivalries of the *conquistadores* gave way to a struggle between the conquerors and the Crown, aided and abetted by the Church, for the control of the spoils. The struggle was not finally resolved until the 1550s when the Pizarro brothers were dead, the Welser control over Venezuela had ceased and the viceroyalties of Peru and Mexico were finally established.

The Portuguese, meanwhile, had established a maritime trading empire. In the Atlantic it was based initially on the gold trade of Elmina and the Brazilwood trade of the American coast. However, the expansion of the Genoese sugar production from one island group to another led to the emergence, first in São Tomé and then in Brazil, of the classic triangular Atlantic commerce which linked the slave trade of mainland Africa with the sugar-growing regions and the sugar market in Europe. In the east the Portuguese tried to impose a royal trading monopoly on the spice trade of Malabar and the Moluccas, and on the international trade in horses, ivory and gold. This monopoly was to be operated from a number of fortified ports which guarded the access to the western Indian Ocean and which acted as customs posts for the regulation of all eastern commerce.

Since 1479 the Iberians had managed to avoid conflict. At Tordesillas in 1494 they agreed to divide the Atlantic world between them and when Magellan, a Portuguese sailing in Castilian service, found an alternative route to the Far East in 1519, the Iberian monarchs again avoided conflict by extending the partition to the eastern hemisphere at the treaty of Saragossa in 1529. The peaceful settlement of the dispute was greatly assisted by the fact that the Spaniards had not found a way of sailing back across the Pacific. However, the separate development of the empires was to come to an end in 1545 when the Spaniards made the first of the great discoveries of silver mines in South America. The flow of silver to Europe was to provide the means to meet the huge deficit on trade which the Portuguese ran with the countries of the Indian Ocean and the Far East. Peruvian silver was to travel via Seville to India and China and for the first time weld the economies of the world together as one.

M. Newitt

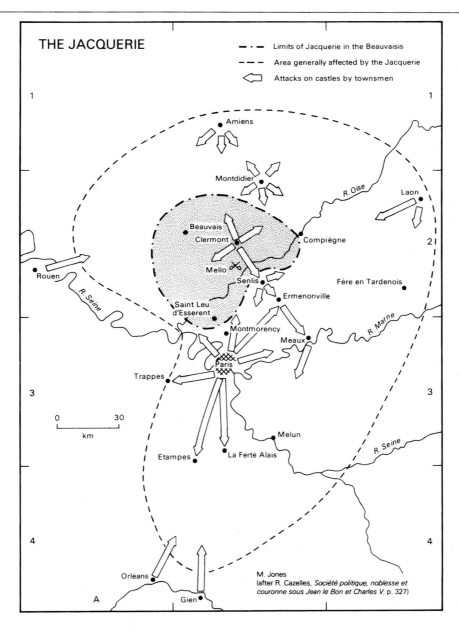

THE JACQUERIE

— · — Limits of Jacquerie in the Beauvaisis
– – – Area generally affected by the Jacquerie
◁ Attacks on castles by townsmen

Amiens
Montdidier
R. Oise
Laon
Beauvais
Clermont
Compiègne
Rouen
Mello
Fére en Tardenois
R. Seine
Senlis
R. Marne
Saint Leu d'Esserent
Ermenonville
Montmorency
Meaux
Paris
Trappes
Melun
0   30
km
Etampes
La Ferté Alais
R. Seine
Orléans
Gien
A

M. Jones
(after R. Cazelles, *Société politique, noblesse et couronne sous Jean le Bon et Charles V*, p. 327)

225

The Jacquerie

This brief and violent uprising against the nobility broke out on 28 May 1358. Centred on the Beauvaisis, disturbances affected areas from Picardy to Orléans, especially after Etienne Marcel, leader of the Parisian merchants in dispute with the government, joined the rebels and encouraged towns to attack seigneurial castles. Normally described as a peasants' revolt, most known rebels were rural artisans, such as coopers and stone-cutters, together with some minor clergy, petty royal officials and a few more well-to-do men. Led by Guillaume Cale and Jean Vaillant, rebel bands sustained an orgiastic destruction of noble property for a fortnight. By 8 June, however, urban interests, with Marcel the key figure, predominated.

Possible long-term causes included a painful re-adjustment following the Black Death, the difficulties of an unpopular government, led by the dauphin, in the war with the English, and criticism of a nobility failing in its role as protectors of the peasantry. The immediate causes lay in the struggle between the dauphin and Marcel. An order promulgated on 14 May, calling for the strengthening or destruction of seigneurial strongholds, probably sparked off the revolt. Intended to improve security when the Paris region was threatened by soldiers temporarily unemployed because of an Anglo-French truce, some interpreted the measure as a tightening of hated seigneurial authority, whilst Marcel saw it as the dauphin's attempt to exert further pressure on Paris. Marcel sent forces against his noble adversaries in alliance with the rebels. But in doing so he alienated an ally, Charles II, king of Navarre, who ambushed and executed Cale before dispersing his forces at Mello, whilst Gaston, count of Foix relieved Meaux. The nobles exacted a terrible revenge on a defenceless peasantry, whilst Marcel fell to a Parisian plot. By 10 August the dauphin, who had been on the point of fleeing, felt secure enough to issue letters of pardon to all involved and some semblance of peace was re-established. The Jacquerie left a legacy of class hatred and fear, symbolized by the way its name was subsequently attached to other rebellions.

M. Jones

The Peasants' Revolt of 1381

The Revolt broke out in late May and early June 1381, first in Essex villages on the Thames estuary, then on the opposite bank in Kent. Rebel armies formed in both shires and met up after being admitted to London. There the youthful Richard II had to concede the abolition of serfdom, a low level of land rents and voluntary terms of employment. The rebels executed 'traitors', including royal officials whom they blamed for a recently imposed poll tax. But on 15 June the rebel captain Wat Tyler, whilst making more radical demands, was mortally injured by the king's entourage: his demoralized supporters were rounded up and allowed to leave London.

The Essex and Kent risings were signals for widespread riots, attacks on property and coercion of landlords and officials. Big rebel bands formed in Hertfordshire, the East Midlands and East Anglia, some coercing a particular landowner or elite group, others roaming around to victimize and extort. But the Revolt in south-east England was generally stamped out in the second half of June and in July by Bishop Despenser of Norwich and by royal forces. The king revoked his pardons: a few hundred of the rebels died in battle or by execution.

The extent of participation in the Revolt is hard to determine. In the areas mainly affected many communities did not rise: evidence accu-

THE PEASANTS' REVOLT OF 1381

- – – – Shires mainly involved
- • Cities, boroughs and towns involved
- ✚ Religious institutions targeted

YORKSHIRE

Scarborough
York
Beverley

Chester Abbey

Lynn
Norwich
Great Yarmouth
NORFOLK

Peterborough Abbey
NORTHAMPTON
HUNT-INGDON
CAMBRIDGE
Ely
SUFFOLK
Northampton
Cambridge
Bury St Edmunds Abbey
Ipswich

Worcester Priory

Dunstable Priory
HERTFORD
ESSEX
St Albans Abbey
Ashridge College
Waltham Abbey
MIDDLESEX
London
Rochester
Canterbury
SURREY
Guildford
Maidstone
KENT

Hospital of St John, Bridgwater
Winchester

SUSSEX

0   50
km

A   B   A.Goodman

mulates of action by manorial tenants against their lords elsewhere in England. In Essex, Kent, Suffolk and Hertfordshire well-to-do peasants, holders of local office, were well-represented among the rebels. A few East Anglian gentlefolk joined in. Urban participation was widespread and crucial to many rebel successes. In Yorkshire risings were against unpopular urban regimes. At St Albans and Bury St Edmunds risings led or encouraged by urban elites were directed against the abbeys which controlled them: attacks on ecclesiastical landlords, especially abbots and monks, were conspicuous in the Revolt. Though enjoying only brief successes, the Revolt helped make the governing elites more cautious about the imposition of taxes on the commons and about resisting the trends to rent out demesne lands, commute servile works and grant higher wages.

A. Goodman

227

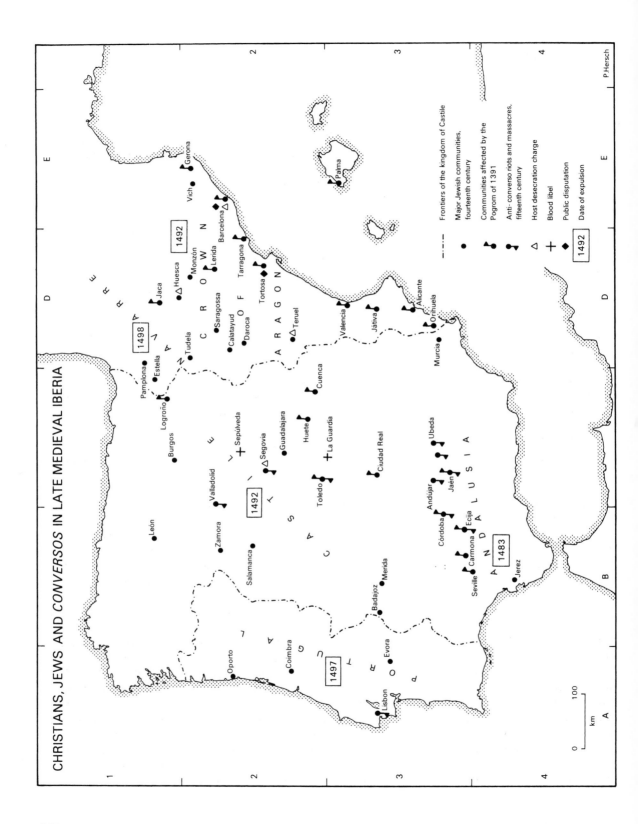

CHRISTIANS, JEWS AND *CONVERSOS* IN LATE MEDIEVAL IBERIA

Frontiers of the kingdom of Castile

Major Jewish communities, fourteenth century

Communities affected by the Pogrom of 1391

Anti-*converso* riots and massacres, fifteenth century

Host desecration charge

Blood libel

Public disputation

Date of expulsion

1492

P.Hersch

km

0   100

Christians, Jews and *Conversos* in Late Medieval Iberia

The tensions between Christians and Jews that were a feature of European life were also present in the Iberian peninsula. They were however tempered by a measure of *convivencia* in a land where Christian, Muslim and Jew dwelt side by side. Thus there were no anti-Jewish riots in Castile during the Black Death, although such riots did occur in the Crown of Aragon which was more open to the currents of mainstream European anti-semitism.

From the mid-fourteenth century, however, *convivencia* began to break down in the face of an increasing exclusivity. In the late 1370s Ferrant Martínez, the archdeacon of Ecija, began a campaign against the Jews which culminated in a wave of massacres throughout Castile and the Crown of Aragon during the summer of 1391. Many Jews were killed; many submitted to baptism to save their lives. Although forced conversion was in theory frowned upon by the Church, *conversos* were nevertheless considered to be technically Christians and were prohibited from returning to Judaism. Thus *converso* communities sprang up alongside decimated Jewish ones or, as in the case of Barcelona, supplanted the Jewish community altogether. Henceforth Jewish life would tend to shift from the large towns to smaller rural centres.

If forced conversion was meant to solve 'the Jewish problem', it only compounded it in Christian eyes. The sincerity of *converso* faith was inevitably questioned – and all the more fiercely by 'Old Christians' who saw former Jews successfully scaling the social, economic and political barriers which, as Jews, they had previously found insurmountable. Accordingly in the anti-*converso* uprising in Toledo in 1449 'statutes' were drafted by the Toledan Old Christians which prohibited *conversos* from holding all offices and benefices. Anti-*converso* violence, which surfaced again in Toledo in 1467, was particularly acute in the massacres which were perpetrated in many Andalusian towns in 1473.

The existence of the *converso* communities led to greater pressure on the Jews, for they were perceived as the cause of continuing crypto-Judaism amongst *conversos*. To combat this, segregatory laws were promulgated in 1412 designed 'to seek the best method ... so that Christian believers ... shall not be brought into any errors as a result of close contact with the infidels'. In 1415, after the Disputation at Tortosa, similar decrees were enacted in Aragon.

Christian zealots, however, were not satisfied with segregation and the limiting of Jewish rights. Two courses of action, it was argued, were required. First, crypto-Judaism could only be overcome by the introduction of an Inquisition; second, Jewish influence over the *conversos* could only be overcome by their expulsion. These ideas, adumbrated in works such as Alonso de Espina's *Fortalitium Fidei*, continued to gain ground, and on 27 September 1480 the Catholic Monarchs appointed Inquisitors in Castile who began their work in Seville shortly after (1481). *Conversos*, often subjected to torture, were discovered to be crypto-Jews and received varying punishments, ranging from pilgrimage to death by burning. During the first decade of the Inquisition's operations over 10,000 *conversos* were condemned. The expulsion of the Jews was authorized on 31 March 1492; in May those Jews who refused to convert left for Portugal, North Africa and Turkey. Those who fled to Portugal only found temporary refuge, for five years later they again faced the problem of forcible conversion. As in Spain, this led to the rise of crypto-Judaism, and on 23 May 1536 an Inquisition was set up on the Spanish model.

With the expulsion of the Jews anti-semitism took on a more racial tone. It is true that anti-Jewish libels had already reappeared in an anti-*converso* form, as in the famous blood libel trial of the case of 'the holy child of La Guardia' (1490–1). Similarly *conversos*, like Jews, kept hosts for evil purposes. But now purity of blood (*limpieza de sangre*) became an obsession and, although many *conversos* managed to hide their 'defect', those who were known not to possess 'pure' blood increasingly found themselves barred from entering many offices in Church and State.

P. Hersch

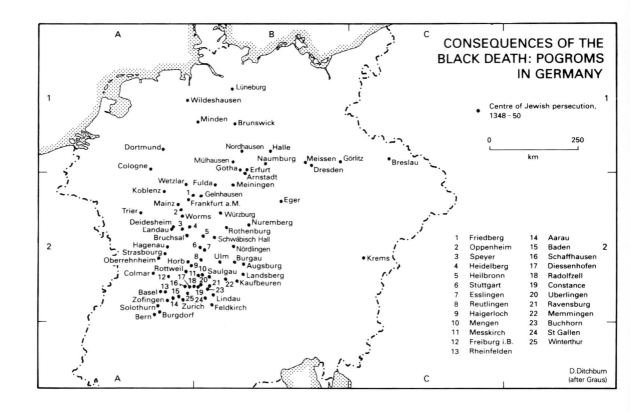

- Centre of Jewish persecution, 1348 - 50

0   250
km

1	Friedberg	14	Aarau
2	Oppenheim	15	Baden
3	Speyer	16	Schaffhausen
4	Heidelberg	17	Diessenhofen
5	Heilbronn	18	Radolfzell
6	Stuttgart	19	Constance
7	Esslingen	20	Uberlingen
8	Reutlingen	21	Ravensburg
9	Haigerloch	22	Memmingen
10	Mengen	23	Buchhorn
11	Messkirch	24	St Gallen
12	Freiburg i.B.	25	Winterthur
13	Rheinfelden		

D.Ditchburn
(after Graus)

Consequences of the Black Death: Pogroms in Germany

The Jewish communities of medieval Germany resided mainly in towns and often in particular districts of towns. On several occasions, notably in the wake of the first and second crusades, these religiously and physically distinctive communities had been subjected to persecution. The advent of the Black Death unleashed a further bout of persecution, some spontaneous, some planned, in over eighty towns between November 1348 and August 1350. Ignorance of the explanations for the dissemination of plague led to accusations across much of Europe that 'outsiders' had poisoned supplies of drinking water. In some areas foreign pilgrims were held responsible for this: in Germany, among other places, suspicion fell on the Jews. Yet fear of the onset of plague, rather than the search for scapegoats after its outbreak, accounts for the German

massacres which occurred *before* the arrival of plague. Likewise pogroms frequently occurred *before* the arrival in towns of Flagellants who have often been accused of whipping up anti-Jewish sentiment in a time of fear. Rather, such attitudes were perhaps encouraged consciously or unconsciously by local preachers with many of the pogroms occurring on Sundays or feast days. Traditionally the pogroms of the 1340s have also been seen as an expression of political tension between the unrepresented crafts (seen as hostile to Jews) and the governing patriciate (seen as protective of Jewish communities or prepared to acquiesce in their massacre in order to appease the craftsmen). Of late this interpretation has been dismissed although the cancellation of debts owed to murdered Jews benefited debtors of diverse social standing. The political background to the pogroms is, however, significant. As rival contenders asserted their claim to the Crown, none was in a position to exercise the traditionally protective role assumed by emperors towards Jewish communities. The cluster of pogroms in Meissen and Thuringia reflected the anti-Jewish sentiments of the local lord. By contrast only one pogrom, at Krems, occurred in lands firmly controlled by the more sympathetic Habsburgs.

D. Ditchburn

CULTURE

Knightly Journeys

During the later Middle Ages many European knights set off on extended travels, some of them for the express purpose of taking part in international jousting tournaments or chivalric passages-at-arms. Accounts of their deeds as knights-errants, either singly or as part of 'a team', to some extent recall the later Grand Tour but even more forcibly modern football tournaments (similar rules; the same emphasis on distinguishing strips and colours; the same cult of the player who distinguished/distinguishes himself above the rest; written accounts emphasizing the *visual* aspects of events). Other knights ventured into the relatively unknown parts of the world, rather like space-travellers.

At the end of the fourteenth century the conquests of the great Mongol leader Tamerlane (d. 1405) threatened the West and made travels in Central Asia more precarious. An early fifteenth-century visitor there was the Castilian noble Ruy Gonzales de Clavijo, who was sent on an embassy to Tamerlane's court by Henry III of Castile. Although the king had already exchanged ambassadors and presents with Tamerlane, no account of the embassies or travels survives.

Clavijo's account of his embassy is rather dry and factual, but this is a feature which enhances the information he supplied. Embarking at Puerto de Santa María (near Cadiz) on a vessel captained by a member of the Genoese family of the Centurione, Clavijo set off with his companions in May 1403. He began to write up his experiences from the day on which he embarked.

Clavijo's account is particularly interesting because of the light it throws on Tamerlane's enhancement of his capital at Samarkand, the fostering of links with Russia, India and Alexandria, and his observations on the trade connections from China to Ormuz (on the Persian Gulf), the activities of the Venetians and Genoese, and the importance of Christian-controlled ports such as Trebizond on the Black Sea and Caffa in the Crimea.

Clavijo returned to Castile in March 1406. Landing in San Lucar de Barrameda, he then went to the city of Seville and thereafter sought out the royal court (still itinerant) at Alcalá de Henares in order to report on his mission.

A. MacKay

Margery Kempe

Born *c.* 1373 in the prosperous port of King's Lynn, the daughter of John Brunham, a substantial oligarch who was several times mayor of the town and one of its Members of Parliament, Margery at the age of 20 married John Kempe. However she seems to have spent most of her subsequent life travelling, motivated by a religious wanderlust that usually took the form of frequent and incessant pilgrimages: to Jerusalem and the Holy Land, northern Italy, Santiago de Compostela, Norway, northern Germany, and places in England such as York, Walsingham and Leicester. On her travels she left her husband behind, although on occasion at least she was asked whether she had his written permission to journey alone in this way. Probably illiterate, yet with a sound knowledge of some of the scriptures, she began to dictate her experiences to a sympathetic priest round about 1436. What emerges from her *Book* or *Life* is hardly a traveller's

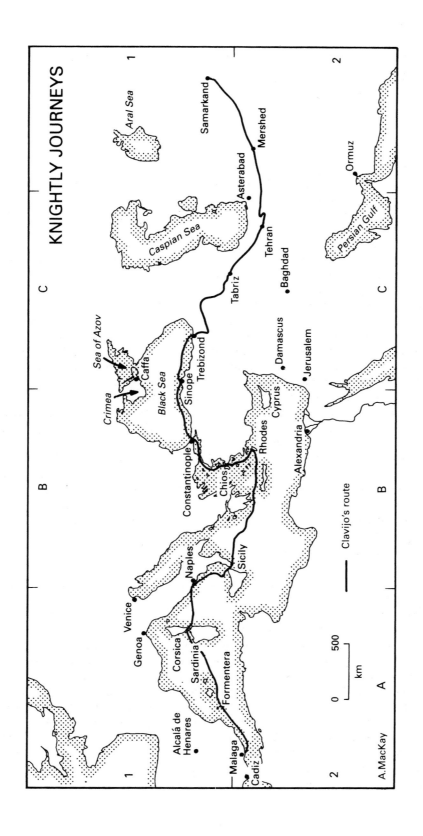

KNIGHTLY JOURNEYS

Aral Sea

Samarkand

Mershed

Asterabad

Caspian Sea

Tehran

Baghdad

Tabriz

Ormuz

Persian Gulf

Sea of Azov

Caffa

Crimea

Black Sea

Trebizond

Sinope

Damascus

Jerusalem

Cyprus

Rhodes

Constantinople

Chios

Alexandria

Venice

Naples

Sicily

Genoa

Corsica

Sardinia

Formentera

Alcalá de Henares

Malaga

Cadiz

Clavijo's route

0   500

km

A.MacKay

MARGERY KEMPE

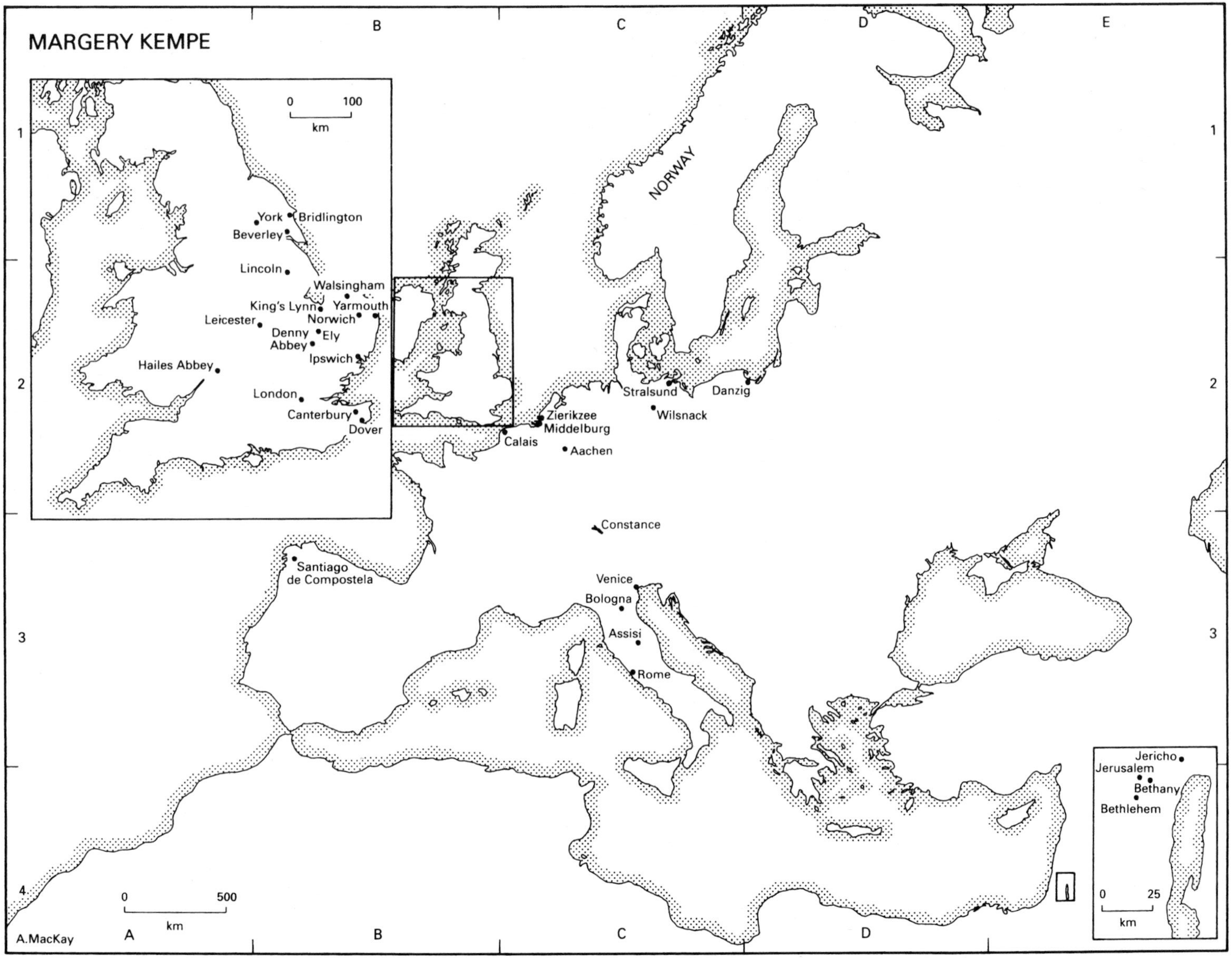

A B C D E
1 2 3 4
0 100 km
York
Bridlington
Beverley
Lincoln
Walsingham
King's Lynn
Yarmouth
Norwich
Leicester
Denny Abbey
Ely
Ipswich
Hailes Abbey
London
Canterbury
Dover
NORWAY
Stralsund
Danzig
Wilsnack
Zierikzee
Middelburg
Calais
Aachen
Constance
Santiago de Compostela
Venice
Bologna
Assisi
Rome
Jericho
Jerusalem
Bethany
Bethlehem
0 25 km
0 500 km
A.MacKay

account as one might imagine today; rather it is the description of a succession of emotionally charged religious experiences frequently associated with the places she visited.

When she visited Jerusalem, for example, she arrived there, like Christ, on a donkey. Then at Calvary she had a vision of Christ: not Christ as God but Christ as Man, a suffering human covered in blood, brutally nailed to the Cross. Such visions may well have been influenced by the Franciscan spirituality of the period, but in the view of most of her contemporaries Margery took matters to extremes, particularly since her ecstatic experiences usually took the form of noisy and prolonged bouts of crying, sobbing and roaring, frequently taking place in church and in public. When travelling, her fellow-pilgrims, determined to combine their religious duties with the enjoyment of pleasant company, food and good wine, clearly found her abstemious excesses and constant discoursing on spiritual matters intolerable.

Although Margery's *Book* does not obviously refer to her experiences in modern terms, the evidence does suggest that she may have suffered from some form of post-natal depression after the birth of her first child (by the time she was 40 she had given birth to fourteen children). Yet in some ways her actions were almost logical. For example, as an avid and frequent partaker of the Eucharist (literally the body and flesh of Christ) she compensated for this excess by becoming a vegetarian. She also had the ability to disturb members of the ecclesiastical hierarchy, powerful and humble alike. No stranger to sexual temptation herself, as she recounts vividly, she once turned the tables on a monk by telling him that he had sinned with women, only to be asked by her unfortunate and puzzled victim whether she knew if the women in question were married or single.

Eccentric to a degree and even suspected of being a Lollard, Margery was not perhaps entirely untypical. The number of documented female religious visionaries increased sharply during the later medieval and early modern period. Indeed Margery herself was aware of some of them. She visited the famous anchorite Julian of Norwich, went in Rome to the premises where St Bridget of Sweden had died, and may even have modelled herself to some extent on the Brabantine *béguine* Mary of Oignes (d. 1213) who also sobbed uncontrollably, persuaded her husband to live chastely, had the gift of visions and prophecies, and was devoted to the Eucharist and Christ's Passion.

A. MacKay

The Spread of Printing

Johann Gutenberg, already involved in printing experiments during the 1430s, is usually credited with producing the first printed book, using moveable type, at Mainz in 1454 or 1455. This was the 'Gutenberg' or 'Forty-two Line' Bible, consisting of 643 pages arranged in double columns of forty-two lines. Of some 200 copies, forty-eight have survived: the survival of printed texts is more likely than that of manuscripts.

Increased literacy and the slow production rate of manuscript copiers ensured that printing spread rapidly throughout Germany and (from 1464) Italy, and to Paris and Seville by 1470. Printing was introduced to the Low Countries from 1474, England from 1476 and most other European countries by 1500, though not until 1507 in Scotland.

Being commercial enterprises, presses initially concentrated on printing 'best sellers', especially Bibles, popular religious works (such as the mystical treatise, the *Imitation of Christ*, by Thomas à Kempis) and school books (such as Donatus' *Grammar*). The availability of paper, increasing use of spectacles and printing of books (albeit in limited quantity) further stimulated a growth in that literacy which had partly provoked the initial spread of printing. Indeed, the towns in which printing flourished (usually

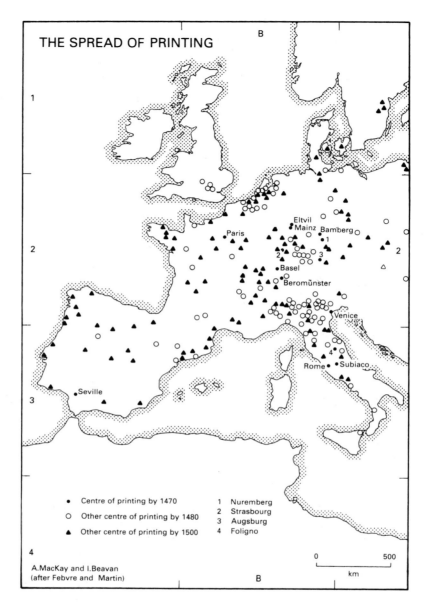

THE SPREAD OF PRINTING

Eltvil
Mainz Bamberg
1
2 3
Paris
Basel
Beromünster
Venice
4
Rome Subiaco
Seville

	Centre of printing by 1470	1	Nuremberg
	Other centre of printing by 1480	2	Strasbourg
	Other centre of printing by 1500	3	Augsburg
		4	Foligno

A.MacKay and I.Beavan
(after Febvre and Martin)

0   500
km

commercial rather than ecclesiastical centres) were often relatively well provided with schools.

Co-operation between humanists and printers stimulated the Bible-oriented concentration of reformers like Erasmus and Luther, an emphasis which was subsequently adopted by Catholic reformers too, the Complutensian Polyglot Bible published at Alcala under the patronage of Cardinal Cisneros being a celebrated example.

A professional copier of manuscripts working under pressure could produce some four hundred folios in six months. In comparison some 6 million books (representing thousands of different titles) had been printed by the start of the sixteenth century. Scholars could obtain a vast array of texts from one bookshop instead of tramping round many different manuscript shops or monastic libraries. Princes, too, succumbed to the attraction that influenced others: the Emperor Maximilian, for example, had himself portrayed in a printer's workshop.

A. MacKay and I. Beavan

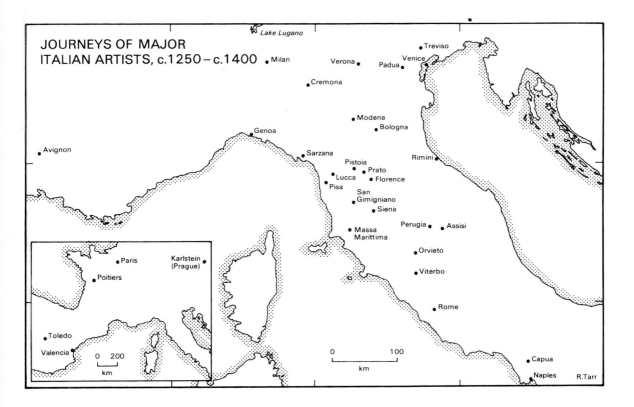

JOURNEYS OF MAJOR ITALIAN ARTISTS, c.1250 – c.1400

Journeys of Major Italian Artists Between *c.* 1250 and *c.* 1400

The establishment of the actual presence of artists in specific centres of artistic activity at various times is important for our understanding of the way aspects of art, such as style, technique, iconography and prestige, might be assessed in their historical context. Very often tantalizing similarities exist between the work of two artists in style or iconography, for example, and the temptation has always been to assume that there must have been some direct contact between them. However, with the development of more systematic art-historical scholarship this tendency has been modified so that such spontaneous assumptions have been called into question, unless firm documentation makes the connection quite clear. Emphasis has been placed on known chronological facts so that it might be seen at what period during an artist's

development he may have affected or been affected by the work of another. Consequently, whatever knowledge we have of journeys or visits made by artists to centres where others were working is of distinct value.

In terms of the effect of one artist's work on another, it is not always necessary to show their presence in particular places as panel paintings and also small sculptures may well have been transported from one place to another. However, with fresco painting and large-scale sculpture the presence of the artist in a particular place must be assumed and it is of great help to know the dates of such visits.

In the list as set out the purpose is to record these visits when they are securely known, and also, where a question mark is added, to record fairly well-substantiated visits.

As might be expected, there is a great deal of movement between centres in the various regions of Italy. This is important to establish, as Italy was at that time an accumulation of different states with quite widely divergent cultural backgrounds, so that the interchange of artistic ideas between them is in itself significant. However, the most striking journeys were made to other parts of Europe, for example that of the Florentine artist Starnina to Spain or that of the Sienese Simone Martini to Avignon. The natural barrier of the Alps may have restricted travel, but we have one reference to a Sienese architect, Ramo di Paganello, who returned from somewhere beyond the Alps to Siena in 1281, and the Sienese painter, Duccio, may well have been in Paris in 1296 and 1297. Indeed, we know that the Roman mosaicist Filippo Rusuti was working as a painter for the French king in Poitiers in 1308.

As the list shows, individual artists, perhaps for reasons of reputation, or possibly through lack of work, travelled more or less widely. Giotto, for example, travelled the length and breadth of Italy and may also have been as far afield as Provence. Others, however, seem to have stayed put, like his pupil, Taddeo Gaddi, who may never have moved out of Tuscany. It is also possible to speculate on the itinerary of journeys like, for example, one by Tomaso da Modena who painted frescoes in Treviso which would have demanded his presence there, and who, around 1360, was commissioned to make some panels for Charles IV's palace at Karlstein outside Prague. Although he could have sent these pictures, Treviso is on the way, as it were, from Modena to Prague, and so it is not impossible that he made what would have been at the time a quite adventurous journey.

Useful though the known evidence is, it must always be borne in mind that, like any historical evidence, it may not give the whole picture. No doubt there was much more interaction and contact than has come down to us and we must assume that artists made more journeys and travelled more often than the surviving records enable us to know for certain.

R. Tarr

ARTISTS (BIRTH) AND DATES OF THEIR SOJOURNS IN THE VARIOUS CENTRES

Sculptors and Architects

Nicola Pisano (c. 1210, Apulia?) Capua 1240s; Lucca 1258; Pisa 1260; Siena 1265–8; Pistoia 1273; Perugia 1277–84?

Giovanni Pisano (c. 1250, Pisa) Siena 1265–8; Perugia 1277–84?; Siena 1284–96; Massa Marittima? 1287; Pisa 1298; Pistoia 1300–1; Pisa 1302–10; Padua? *c.* 1305–6; Prato *c.* 1312; Genoa? 1313; Siena 1314.

Arnolfo Di Cambio (c. 1245, Florence) Siena 1265–8; Rome 1276?–7; Viterbo? 1276; Perugia 1281; Orvieto? 1282?; Rome 1285, 1293, 1300; Florence 1296, 1300–2.

Tino Da Camaino (c. 1280–5) Pisa *c.* 1306–15; Siena 1319–20; Florence 1321–3; Naples 1323/4–37.

Lorenzo Maitani (c. 1275, Siena) Orvieto 1310–30; Perugia 1317, 1319–21; Siena 1322.

Andrea Pisano (c. 1290, Pontedera, near Pisa) Florence 1330–40; Pisa? 1343–7?; Orvieto 1347–8.

Nino Pisano (c. 1315?) Pisa? 1342?; Orvieto 1349–53; Pisa 1357–8.

Andrea Orcagna (c. 1308, Florence) Florence 1343/4–57; Orvieto 1358–60; Florence 1364–8.

Giovanni Di Balduccio (c. 1300, Pisa?) Pisa 1317–18; Bologna 1320–5?; Sarzana? 1327–8; Milan *c.* 1334–60.

Bonino Da Campione (c. 1330, Campione, L. Lugano) Cremona 1357; Milan 1363; Verona 1374.

Painters

Coppa Di Marcovaldo (c. 1230, Florence) Florence? 1261; Pistoia 1265–9, 1274; Orvieto? 1265–8?

Cimabue (c. 1250, Florence?) Rome 1272; Assisi 1270s–1280s; Pisa 1301–2.

Filippo Rusuti (c. 1260, Rome) Poitiers 1308.

Cavallini (c. 1255, Rome) Naples 1308.

Duccio (c. 1255, Siena) Florence? 1285; Paris 1296–7.

Giotto (1265/75, Florence) Rome? 1300; Assisi 1309; Padua c. 1305–13?; Naples 1328–32 (possible journeys to Rimini, Avignon).

Simone Martini (c. 1290, Siena) Naples 1317; Assisi 1330s?; Avignon 1340–4.

Matteo Giovannetti (c. 1310, Viterbo) Avignon 1344–5.

Pietro Lorenzetti (c. 1295, Siena) Assisi 1316–19?

Ambrogio Lorenzetti (c. 1300, Siena) Florence 1321–7.

Barna Da Siena (c. 1320, Siena) San Gimigniano 1350s?

Taddeo Gaddi (c. 1310, Florence) Pisa 1342; Pistoia? 1353.

Giovanni Da Milano (c. 1330, Como?) Florence c. 1350–66; Prato 1354; Rome 1369.

Tomaso Da Modena (c. 1325, Modena) Treviso 1350s; Karlstein (Prague) 1360?

Giusto De' Menabuoi (c. 1350, Florence) Padua 1370.

Altichiero (c. 1350, Verona) Padua 1379–84.

Agnolo Gaddi (c. 1350, Florence) Rome 1369; Prato 1392–5.

Spinello Aretino (c. 1360, Arezzo) Florence 1387; Pisa 1391–2; Siena 1408.

Starnina (1354, Florence) Toledo and Valencia 1398–1401.

R. Tarr

The Rediscovery of Classical Texts

One factor that inaugurated the Renaissance was a more accurate knowledge of the ancient world. Petrarch (1304–74), pursuing the original texts of classical authors, was the first to feel the need for a precise picture of antiquity. When in Avignon, he profited from the riches of French libraries and from international contacts: in 1328 Landolfo Colonna brought from Chartres the rare Fourth Decade of Livy's *History of Rome*, enabling Petrarch to assemble the most complete and accurate text of Livy since antiquity; by 1354 other friends had obtained copies of Plato and Homer in Greek for him. In 1333 Petrarch himself discovered the lost *Pro Archia* of Cicero in a monastery in Liège. This was important, not least because the speech in defence of the poet Archias contained a famous encomium of the 'studia humanitatis'. The phrase became the slogan for disciplines which humanists championed: grammar, rhetoric, poetry, history and moral philosophy. In 1345 Petrarch made another discovery in the cathedral library of Verona – Cicero's *Letters to Atticus*. These personal letters allowed for a more accurate historical picture of Cicero and encouraged Petrarch and later humanists to publish their personal correspondence.

Boccaccio (1313–75), following Petrarch's example, inspected the library of the great abbey at Monte Cassino. There in 1355 he transcribed for Petrarch another speech of Cicero, Varro's *De Lingua Latina* and Apuleius' *The Golden Ass*, a text which not only influenced the author of the *Decameron* but also many other European novelists. The most important manuscript from Monte Cassino, containing Tacitus' *Annals* XI–XV and *Histories* I–V, also found its way to Florence, possibly by the agency of Boccaccio. Tacitus' condemnation of the Roman emperors shaped the republican 'Civic Humanism' of men like Leonardo Bruni (1370–1444). The century ended with Salutati discovering Cicero's *Ad*

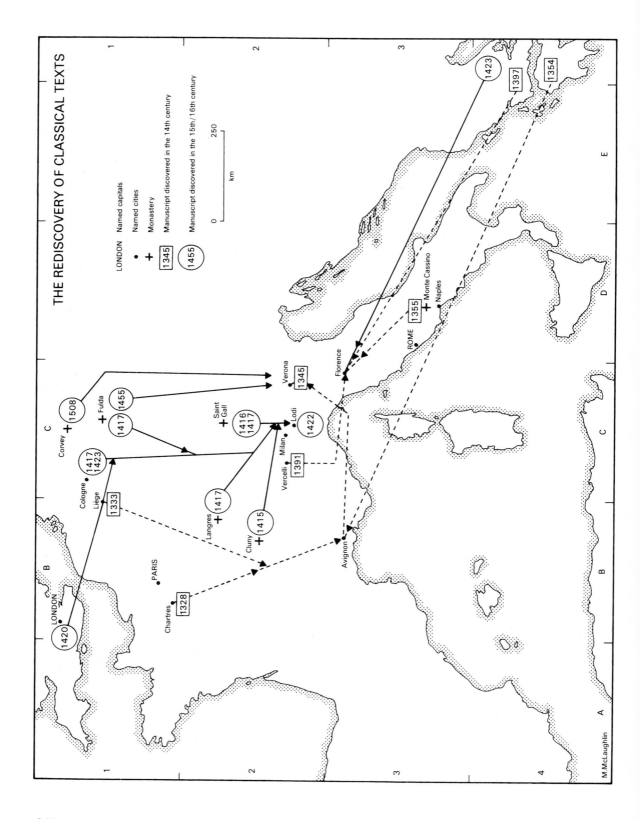

THE REDISCOVERY OF CLASSICAL TEXTS

LONDON Named capitals
• Named cities
+ Monastery
1345 Manuscript discovered in the 14th century
1455 Manuscript discovered in the 15th/16th century

km
0 250

M.McLaughlin

240

Familiares in a manuscript from Vercelli in 1391.

Enthusiasm for original texts expanded in the fifteenth century, leading to the recovery of most of the classical writings known today. Though only the most important can be mentioned, the map shows how the pace of discoveries increased and how, following Petrarch in the fourteenth century, the major figure of the new century was Poggio Bracciolini (1380–1459). When not on secretarial duty at the Council of Constance, Poggio combed the adjacent monasteries: he found two speeches of Cicero at Cluny (1415), the complete text of Quintilian's *Education of the Orator* in St Gall (1416), which stimulated the many Renaissance treatises on education, the poems of Lucretius, Manilius and Silius Italicus in other monasteries (1417), and in London (1420) and Cologne (1423) he came across what remains of Petronius' *Satyricon*. In Italy the complete texts of Cicero's *Orator* and *De Oratore* along with his unknown *Brutus* were discovered by Gherardo Landrianni at Lodi (1422). This manuscript provided the stimulus and terminology for Italian humanists to write the literary histories of their own time. In 1429 Nicholas Cusanus brought to Rome a manuscript containing twelve plays of Plautus, which with the comedies of Terence were influential in shaping Renaissance comedy in Europe. The two most significant texts after 1450 were Tacitus' *Minor Works*, brought from Fulda to Rome (1455), and Tacitus' *Annals* I–VI which reached Rome from Corvey (1508) and led to the printing of the first edition of Tacitus' *Complete Works* (1515).

Interest in Greek texts also began in the Trecento with Petrarch and Boccaccio reading Homer in Latin translation. But in 1397 Manuel Chrysoloras came to Florence and taught humanists like Bruni to read Greek and translate Plutarch and Plato into Latin. An idea of the enthusiasm for Greek can be gained from Giovanni Aurispa's return from Greece in 1423 with 238 manuscripts. In 1438 the Council of Ferrara-Florence encouraged a further influx of Greek scholars, as did the fall of Constantinople (1453). Amidst this popularity for Greek culture Marsilio Ficino (1433–99) translated the whole of Plato into Latin (1485) and while Aristotle's *Poetics* shaped literary criticism in the sixteenth century, the vogue for Plato was to engulf Europe and challenge the medieval domination of Aristotle in the field of philosophy.

M.L. McLaughlin

The Rise of Universities

The first universities emerged after a period of development which began in the late eleventh century. This process can only be understood in the context of economic growth and urban expansion since large numbers of economically unproductive scholars could only gather on a permanent basis when towns could offer adequate accommodation and regular markets at which basic necessities could be bought. From the early twelfth century there were more and more urban schools, centred on cathedrals or individual masters. They were very different from the monastic schools which had long dominated the world of learning. The atmosphere was highly competitive because masters needed to attract and retain the students who paid the fees which enabled the urban schools to survive. It was common for masters to set up school with the intention of poaching a rival's pupils. Institutionally, the situation was highly fluid with masters moving in and out of fashion very quickly. During the twelfth century the schools gradually became more permanent, each school embracing a number of masters. By 1200 the earliest universities had become established at Bologna and Paris. These *studia generalia*, as they were known, were essentially corporations or guilds. In Bologna the guilds were formed by students, and the students regulated the lives of the masters. Paris, however, was run by the masters;

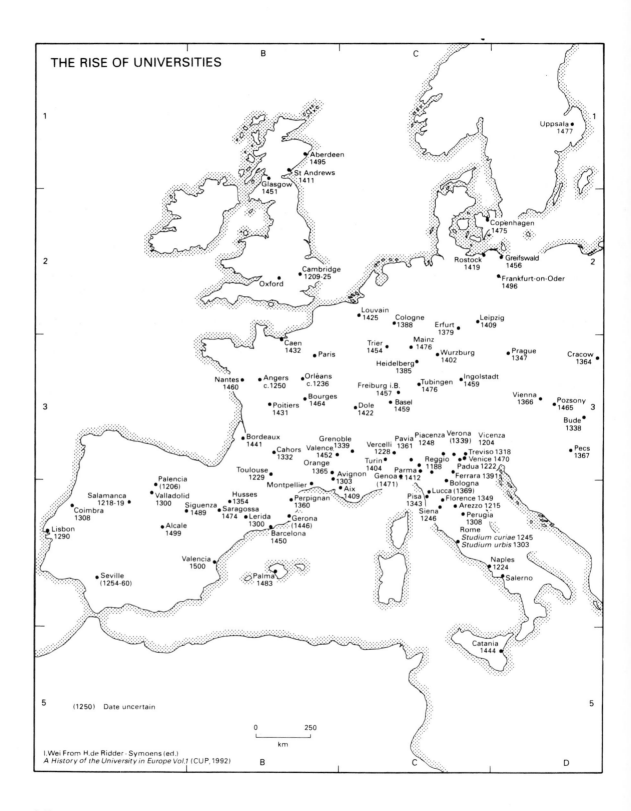

THE RISE OF UNIVERSITIES

Uppsala 1477

Aberdeen 1495
St Andrews 1411
Glasgow 1451

Copenhagen 1475

Rostock 1419
Greifswald 1456
Frankfurt-on-Oder 1496

Cambridge 1209-25
Oxford

Louvain 1425
Cologne 1388
Erfurt 1379
Leipzig 1409

Caen 1432
Paris
Trier 1454
Mainz 1476
Wurzburg 1402
Prague 1347
Cracow 1364

Heidelberg 1385

Nantes 1460
Angers c.1250
Orléans c.1236
Freiburg i.B. 1457
Tubingen 1476
Ingolstadt 1459
Vienna 1366
Pozsony 1465

Bourges 1464
Dole 1422
Basel 1459
Bude 1338

Poitiers 1431

Bordeaux 1441
Grenoble 1339
Valence 1452
Vercelli 1228
Pavia 1361
Piacenza 1248
Verona (1339)
Vicenza 1204
Pecs 1367

Cahors 1332
Turin 1404
Treviso 1318
Venice 1470

Toulouse 1229
Orange 1365
Avignon 1303
Genoa (1471)
Parma
Reggio 1188
Padua 1222
Ferrara 1391
Bologna

Palencia (1206)
Montpellier
Aix 1409
Lucca (1369)
Florence 1349

Salamanca 1218-19
Valladolid 1300
Husses 1354
Perpignan 1360
Pisa 1343
Siena 1246
Arezzo 1215
Perugia 1308

Coimbra 1308
Siguenza 1489
Saragossa 1474
Lerida 1300
Gerona (1446)
Rome
Studium curiae 1245
Studium urbis 1303

Lisbon 1290
Alcale 1499
Barcelona 1450
Naples 1224
Salerno

Valencia 1500

Seville (1254-60)
Palma 1483

Catania 1444

(1250)   Date uncertain

0   250
km

I. Wei From H. de Ridder - Symoens (ed.)
A History of the University in Europe Vol.1 (CUP, 1992)

242

they formed the corporations and students obtained their rights through association with their masters. Subsequent universities followed one or other of these models more or less closely. Crucial to the emergence of a university was the grant of privileges from pope, emperor, king or commune. These privileges usually included an element of juridical autonomy, the right to elect officers, powers to make statutes, and other keys to independence. While grants of privileges to the earliest universities simply recognized and reinforced developments which had already taken place, many later universities were deliberately 'founded'.

Universities very quickly developed a system of faculties. A *studium generale* would have a faculty of arts and at least one other faculty teaching theology, canon law, Roman law or medicine. Key textbooks emerged in what could now be called academic disciplines. Certain basic teaching techniques became established and were used in all disciplines. Lectures consisted of commentary on set texts while disputations involved debate in which the participants were required to take different sides. Scholars who worked in this context developed new ways of thinking in many fields of study.

The process by which universities were set up across Europe was far from smooth. Indeed universities were highly controversial: they had both passionate supporters and vitriolic critics. This is scarcely surprising in view of the roles which many scholars claimed to play in society. Masters of theology at the University of Paris, for example, considered it their responsibility to remove doubt and error, to elucidate the truth, to defend the faith against heretics, and to train others how to preach, teach and see to the cure of souls throughout Christendom. Certainly universities had a major impact on many aspects of medieval society. Scholars played an important role in shaping attitudes and opinions in many areas of life. University men also left the academic world to pursue careers in secular and ecclesiastical administration at every level. The culture of the medieval intellectual was thus an essential part of medieval society.

I. Wei

SUGGESTIONS FOR FURTHER READING

The suggestions which follow are intended for the school or undergraduate student, or the general reader, who wishes to seek more information on particular topics. Quite deliberately, therefore, most references are to modern publications in English. The bibliography is arranged in order of the appearance of the corresponding map. In addition to material cited under specific headings, the following introductory works are of relevance to a variety of topics:

M. Barber, *The Two Cities*, London, 1991.

R. Collins, *Early Medieval Europe, 300–1000*, London, 1991.

G. Holmes (ed.), *The Oxford History of Medieval Europe*, Oxford, 1992.

H.G. Koenigsberger, *Medieval Europe, 400–1500*, Harlow, 1987.

D. Nicholas, *The Evolution of the Medieval Europe: Society, Government and Thought in Europe, 312–1500*, Harlow, 1992.

S. Reynolds, *Kingdoms and Communities in Western Europe, 900–1300*, Oxford, 1984.

The Roman Empire in 395 AD

A. Cameron, *The Later Roman Empire*, London, 1993.

A. Cameron, *The Mediterranean World in Late Antiquity, AD 395–600*, London, 1993.

E. Gibbon, *The Decline and Fall of the Roman Empire*, revised by J.B. Bury, 3 vols, London, 1900.

A.H.M. Jones, *The Later Roman Empire, 284–602*, 2 vols, Oxford 1964.

D. Kagan (ed.), *The End of the Roman Empire: Decline or Transformation?*, 2nd edn, Lexington, MA, 1978.

The Barbarians

T.S. Burns, *A History of the Ostrogoths*, Bloomington, 1984.

F.M. Clover, *The Late Roman West and the Vandals*, Aldershot, 1993.

E. James, *The Franks*, Oxford, 1988.

J. Moorhead, *Theoderic in Italy*, Oxford, 1993.

H. Wolfram, *History of the Goths*, Berkeley and London, 1988.

The Empire of Justinian

J.B. Bury, *History of the Later Roman Empire from the Death of Theodosius to the Death of Justinian*, London, 1923, volume 2.

W.H.C. Frend, *The Rise of the Monophysite Movement*, Cambridge, 1972.

J. Moorhead, *Justinian*, Harlow, 1994.

The Expansion of Islam

F.N. Donner, *The Early Islamic Conquests*, Princeton, 1981.

W.E. Kaegi, *Byzantium and the Early Islamic Conquests*, Cambridge, 1992.

H. Kennedy, *The Prophet and the Age of the Caliphates: The Islamic Near East from the Sixth to the Eleventh Centuries*, London and New York, 1986.

M.A. Shaban, *Islamic History, A.D. 600–750: A New Interpretation*, Cambridge, 1971.

Italy in the Eighth Century

T.S. Brown, *Gentlemen and Officers: Imperial Administration and Aristocratic Power in Byzantine Italy 554–800 A.D.*, London, 1984.

P. Llewellyn, *Rome in the Dark Ages*, London, 1971.

T.F.X. Noble, *The Republic of Saint Peter*, Philadelphia, 1984.

G. Tabacco, *The Struggle for Power in Medieval Italy: Structures of Political Rule*, Cambridge, 1989.

C. Wickham, *Early Medieval Italy*, London, 1980.

The Carolingian Empire under Charlemagne
Division of the Carolingian Empire, 843

P. Godman and R. Collins (eds), *Charlemagne's Heir: New Perspectives on the Reign of Louis the Pious*, Oxford, 1990.

L. Halphen, *Charlemagne and the Carolingian Empire*, Amsterdam, 1977.

R. McKitterick, *The Frankish Kingdoms under the Carolingians*, London, 1983.

R. McKitterick (ed.), *Carolingian Culture: Emulation and Innovation*, Cambridge, 1994.

J. Nelson, *Charles the Bald*, London, 1992.

P. Riché, *The Carolingians: A Family Who Forged Europe*, Philadelphia, 1993.

T. Reuter, *Germany in the Early Middle Ages, 300–1056*, London, 1991.

The Byzantine Empire under the Macedonian Dynasty

H. Ahrweiler, *Byzance et la Mer*, Paris, 1966.

D. Obolensky, *The Byzantine Commonwealth*, London, 1971.

G. Ostrogorsky, *History of the Byzantine State*, 2nd edn, Oxford, 1968.

A. Toynbee, *Constantine Porphyrogenitus and His World*, Oxford, 1973.

Vikings

R.T. Farrell (ed.), *The Vikings*, Chichester, 1982.

J. Jesch, *Women in the Viking Age*, Woodbridge, 1991.

F.D. Logan, *The Vikings in History*, 2nd edn, London, 1991.

P. Sawyer, *Kings and Vikings*, London, 1982.

Magyars

C.A. Macartney, *Hungary: A Short History*, Edinburgh, 1962.

T. Reuter, *Germany in the Early Middle Ages, 300–1056*, London, 1991.

The East European States, *c.* 1000

F. Dvornik, *The Making of Central and Eastern Europe*, London, 1949.

F. Dvornik, *The Slavs: Their Early History and Civilisation*, Boston, 1956.

F. Dvornik, *The Slavs in European History and Civilisation*, Rutgers, 1962.

J.V.A. Fine, *The Early Medieval Balkans*, Ann Arbor, 1983.

D. Obolensky, *The Byzantine Commonwealth*, London, 1971.

A.P. Vlasto, *The Entry of the Slavs into Christendom*, Cambridge, 1970.

France and its Principalities, *c.* 1000

J. Dunbabin, *France in the Making, 843–1180*, Oxford, 1985.

E. Hallam, 'The king and the princes in eleventh-century France', *Bulletin of the Institute of Historical Research*, 53 (1980), pp. 143–56.

England before the Normans

J. Campbell (ed.), *The Anglo-Saxons*, Oxford, 1982.

D.N. Dumville, *Wessex and England from Alfred to Edgar*, Woodbridge, 1992.

D.P. Kirby, *The Earliest English Kings*, London, 1991.

H.R. Loyn, *The Governance of Anglo-Saxon England, 500–1087*, London, 1984.

B. Yorke, *Kings and Kingdoms of Early Anglo-Saxon England*, London, 1990.

Spanish and Portuguese Reconquest

D. Lomax, *The Reconquest of Spain*, London, 1978.

A. MacKay, *Spain in the Middle Ages: From Frontier to Empire, 1000–1500*, London, 1977.

B.F. Reilly, *The Contest of Christian and Muslim Spain, 1031–1157*, Cambridge, MA and Oxford, 1992.

B.F. Reilly, *The Two Spains*, Cambridge, 1993.

Ottonian/Saxon Empire, 962

K.J. Leyser, *Medieval Germany and Its Neighbours, 900–1250*, London, 1982.

K.J. Leyser, *Rule and Conflict in an Early Medieval Society: Ottonian Saxony*, London, 1979.

T. Reuter, *Germany in the Early Middle Ages, 300–1056*, London, 1991.

Christianity and Paganism

J.N. Hilgarth, *Christianity and Paganism, 350–750*, Philadelphia, 1986.

R.A. Markus, *Christianity in the Roman World*, London, 1974.

R.A. Markus, *The End of Ancient Christianity*, Cambridge, 1990.

Early Monasticism to 547

O. Chadwick, *John Cassian*, Cambridge, 1950.

D.J. Chitty, *The Desert a City*, Oxford, 1966.

T. Fry (ed.), *The Rule of St Benedict*, Collegeville, MN, 1980

C.H. Lawrence, *Medieval Monasticism*, 2nd edn, London, 1989.

Northern European Monasticism

H.B. Clarke and M. Brennan (eds), *Columbanus and Merovingian Monasticism*, British Archaeological Reports, International Series 13, Oxford, 1981.

F. Prinz, *Frühes Mönchtum in Frankenreich*, Munich, 1965.

T. Reuter (ed.), *The Greatest Englishman: Essays on St Boniface and the Church at Crediton*, Exeter, 1980.

J. Ryan, *Irish Monasticism, its Origins and Early Development*, Dublin, 1932.

Byzantine Missions among the Slavs

R. Browning, *Byzantium and Bulgaria*, London, 1975.

F. Dvornik, *Byzantine Missions among the Slavs*, New Brunswick, 1970.

D. Oblensky, *The Byzantine Commonwealth*, London, 1971.

A.P. Vlasto, *The Entry of the Slavs into Christendom*, Cambridge, 1970.

Tenth- and Eleventh-Century Centres of Reform

J.C. Dickinson, *The Origins of the Austin Canons and their Introduction into England*, London, 1950.

K. Hallinger, *Gorze-Kluny*, 2 vols, *Studia Anselmiana*, 22–5, 1950–1.

N. Hunt (ed.), *Cluniac Monasticism in the Central Middle Ages*, London, 1971.

C.H. Lawrence, *Medieval Monasticism*, 2nd edn, London, 1989.

Episcopal Sees in Europe at the End of the Tenth Century

R. Bartlett, *The Making of Europe: Conquest, Colonization and Cultural Change, 950–1350*, London, 1993.

G. Tellenbach, *The Church in Western Europe from the Tenth to the Early Twelfth Century*, Cambridge, 1993.

The Influx of Relics into Saxony

W. Lammers (ed.), *Die Eingliederung der Sachsen in das Frankenreich*, Darmstadt, 1970.

Royal Carolingian Residential Villas

R. Samson, 'Carolingian palaces and the poverty of ideology', in M. Locock (ed.), *Meaningful Architecture: Social Interpretations of Buildings*, Aldershot, 1994.

Anglo-Saxon Burhs and Mints

R.H.M. Dolley (ed.), *Anglo-Saxon Coins*, London, 1961.

H.R. Loyn, *The Governance of Anglo-Saxon England*, London, 1984.

H.R. Loyn, *Anglo-Saxon England and the Norman Conquest*, 2nd edn, London, 1991.

Royal Itineraries: Eleventh-Century France and Germany

C. Brühl, *Fodrum, Gistum, Servitium regis: Studien zu den wirtschaftlichen Grundlagen des Königtums im Frankenreich und in den Nachfolgestaaten*, 2 vols, Cologne, 1968.

England under William I

M. Chibnall, *Anglo-Norman England*, Oxford, 1986.

R. Fleming, *Kings and Lords in Conquest England*, Cambridge, 1991.

B. Golding, *Conquest and Colonisation: The Normans in Britain, 1066–1100*, Basingstoke, 1994.

H.R. Loyn, *The Norman Conquest*, London, 1965.

Early Medieval Towns

T.S. Brown, *Gentlemen and Officers: Imperial Administration and Aristocratic Power in Byzantine Italy, 554–800 A.D.*, London, 1984. [for Ravenna]

T.S. Brown, 'The interplay of Roman and Byzantine traditions in the Exarchate of Ravenna',

Settimana di Studio del Centro Italiano di Studi sull' Alto Medioevo, 33 (1988).

G. Dagron, *Naissance d'une capitale: Constantinople et ses institutions de 330 à 451*, Paris, 1974.

R. Hodges, *The Anglo-Saxon Achievement*, London, 1989. [for Hamwic]

R. Hodges and D. Whitehouse, *Mohammed, Charlemagne and the Origins of Europe*, London, 1983.

R. Krautheimer, *Rome: Profile of a City, 312–1308*, Princeton, 1980.

P. Llewellyn, *Rome in the Dark Ages*, London, 1971.

C. Mango, *Le developpement urbain de Constantinople (IV–VIIe siècles)*, Paris, 1985.

W. Muller-Winer, *Bildlexikon zur Topographie Istanbuls*, Tübingen, 1977.

T.F.X. Noble, *The Republic of St Peter: The Birth of the Papal State, 680–825*, Philadelphia, 1984.

P. Sherrard, *Constantinople: Iconography of a Sacred City*, London, 1965.

O. von Simson, *Sacred Fortress*, Chicago, 1948. [for Ravenna]

Trade Routes of the Carolingian Empire

R. Hodges and D. Whitehouse, *Mohammed, Charlemagne and the Origins of Europe*, London, 1983.

H. Jankuhn, *Haithabu*, 6th edn, Neumunster, 1976.

H. Pirenne, *Mohammed and Charlemagne*, London, 1939.

The Economy of San Vincenzo

R. Hodges, *A Dark-Age Pompeii: San Vincenzo al Volturno*, London, 1990.

R. Hodges (ed.) *San Vincenzo al Volturno: The 1980–1986 Excavations*, 2 vols, British School at Rome Archaeological Monographs, 1993–5.

C. Wickham, *La terra di San Vincenzo al Volturno e il problema dell' incastellamento di Italia centrale*, Florence, 1985.

Irish and Anglo-Saxon Centres on the Continent

J.J.G. Alexander, *Insular Manuscripts: 6th to the 9th Century*, London, 1978.

L. Bieler, *Ireland: Harbinger of the Middle Ages*, London, 1963.

W. Levison, *England and the Continent in the Eighth Century*, Oxford, 1946.

H. Lowe (ed.), *Dir Iren und Europa in früheren Mittelalter*, 2 vols, Stuttgart, 1982.

C.H. Talbot, *The Anglo-Saxon Missionaries in Germany*, New York, 1954.

Bede's World

P.H. Blair, *The World of Bede*, 2nd edn, Cambridge, 1990.

J. Campbell, *The Anglo-Saxons*, Oxford, 1982.

H. Mayr-Harting, *The Coming of Christianity to Anglo-Saxon England*, London, 1972.

P. Riché, *Education et culture dans l'Occident barbare VIe–VIIIe siècles*, Paris, 1962.

Angevins and Capetians in the Later Twelfth Century

J. Gillingham, *Richard the Lionheart*, 2nd edn, London, 1989.

J. Gillingham, *The Angevin Empire*, London, 1984.

E.M. Hallam, *Capetian France, 987–1328*, London, 1980.

R. Mortimer, *Angevin England, 1154–1258*, Oxford, 1994.

R.V. Turner, *King John*, Harlow, 1994.

W.L. Warren, *Henry II*, London, 1973.

Frederick Barbarossa, Germany and the Lombard League

B. Arnold, *Princes and Territories in Medieval Germany*, Cambridge, 1991.

H. Fuhrmann, *Germany in the High Middle Ages, c. 1050–1200*, Cambridge, 1986.

A. Haverkamp, *Medieval Germany 1056–1273*, 2nd edn, Oxford, 1992.

J.K. Hyde, *Society and Politics in Medieval Italy*, London, 1973.

K. Jordan, *Henry the Lion: A Biography*, Oxford, 1985.

P. Munz, *Frederick Barbarossa: A Study in Medieval Politics*, London, 1969.

G. Tabacco, *The Struggle for Power in Medieval Italy: Structures of Political Rule*, Cambridge, 1989.

D. Waley, *The Italian City Republics*, 3rd edn, London, 1988.

The Empire of the Comneni (1081–1185)

M.J. Angold, *The Byzantine Empire, 1025–1204: A Political History*, London, 1984.

A. Harvey, *Economic Expansion in the Byzantine Empire, 900–1200*, London, 1990.

A.P. Kazhdan and A.W. Epstein, *Change in Byzantine Culture in the Eleventh and Twelfth Centuries*, Berkeley, Los Angeles and London, 1985.

P. Magdalino, *The Empire of Manuel I Komnenoz, 1143–1180*, Cambridge, 1993.

Anglo-Norman Penetration of Wales and Ireland Scotland in the Central Middle Ages

G.W.S. Barrow, *The Anglo-Norman Era in Scottish History*, Oxford, 1980.

G.W.S. Barrow, *Kingship and Unity: Scotland, 1000–1306*, London, 1981.

R.R. Davies, *Domination and Conquest: The Experience of Ireland, Scotland and Wales 1100–1300*, Cambridge, 1990.

A.A.M. Duncan, *Scotland: The Making of the Kingdom*, Edinburgh, 1975.

M.T. Flanagan, *Irish Society, Anglo-Norman Settlement, Angevin Kingship*, Oxford, 1989.

R. Frame, *The Political Development of the British Isles, 1100–1400*, Oxford, 1990.

The Normans in Southern Italy and Sicily

C.N.L. Brookes, *The Normans in Sicily and Southern Italy*, Oxford, 1977.

H.E.J. Cowdrey, *The Age of Abbot Desiderius: Monte Cassino, the Papacy and the Normans in the Eleventh and Early Twelfth Centuries*, Oxford, 1983.

G.A. Loud, *Church and Society in the Norman Principality of Capua 1058–1197*, Oxford, 1985.

D. Matthew, *The Norman Kingdom of Sicily*, Cambridge, 1992.

D. Waley, *The Papal State in the Thirteenth Century*, London, 1961.

The Crusades and the Templars

M. Barber, *The New Knighthood: A History of the Order of the Temple*, Cambridge, 1993.

M. Benvenisti, *The Crusaders in the Holy Land*, Jerusalem, 1970.

M. Bull, *Knightly Piety and the Lay Response to the First Crusade*, Oxford, 1993.

A. Forey, *The Military Orders from the Twelfth to the Early Fourteenth Centuries*, Basingstoke, 1992.

W.C. Jordan, *Louis IX and the Challenge of the Crusade*, Princeton, 1979.

H.E. Mayer, *The Crusades*, 2nd edn, Oxford, 1988.

J. Riley-Smith, *The Crusades: A Short History*, New Haven, 1987.

J. Riley-Smith (ed.), *The Atlas to the Crusades*, London, 1990.

J. Riley-Smith, *What Were the Crusades?* 2nd edn, Basingstoke, 1992.

S. Runciman, *A History of the Crusades*, 3 vols, Cambridge, 1951–4.

K.M. Setton (ed.), *A History of the Crusades*, 6 vols, 2nd edn, Madison, 1969–90.

Frederick II, the Papacy and Italy
Italy in the Second Half of the Thirteenth Century

D. Abulafia, *Frederick II: A Medieval Emperor*, London, 1988.

J.K. Hyde, *Society and Politics in Medieval Italy*, Basingstoke, 1973.

J. Larner, *Italy in the Age of Dante and Petrarch*, Harlow, 1980.

D. Mack Smith, *A History of Sicily: Medieval Sicily, 800–1713*, London, 1968.

S. Runciman, *The Sicilian Vespers*, Cambridge, 1958.

G. Tabacco, *The Struggle for Power in Medieval Italy: Structures of Political Rule*, Cambridge, 1989.

D. Waley, *The Papal State in the Thirteenth Century*, London, 1961.

The *Ostsiedlung*
The Scandinavian Kingdoms, Germans and the Baltic

R. Bartlett, *The Making of Europe: Conquest, Colonization and Cultural Change, 950–1350*, London, 1993.

E. Christiansen, *The Northern Crusades: The Baltic and the Catholic Frontier, 1100–1525*, London, 1980.

B. Sawyer and P. Sawyer, *Medieval Scandinavia*, Minneapolis and London, 1993.

The Přemyslide–Habsburg Conflict

J. Bérenger, *A History of the Habsburg Empire, 1273–1700*, Harlow, 1994.

The Mongol–Tatar Invasions of the Thirteenth Century

J. Fennell, *The Crisis of Medieval Russia, 1200–1304*, London, 1983.

D. Morgan, *The Mongols*, Oxford, 1986.

P. Ratchnevsky, *Genghis Khan: His Life and Legacy*, ed. T.N. Haining, Oxford, 1991.

J.J. Saunders, *The History of the Mongol Conquests*, London, 1971.

France in the Reign of Philip the Fair

M. Barber, *The Angevin Legacy and the Hundred Years War, 1250–1340*, Oxford, 1990.

J. Favier, *Philippe le Bel*, Paris, 1978.

J.R. Strayer, *The Reign of Philip the Fair*, Princeton, 1980.

Spanish and Portuguese Reconquest in the Twelfth and Thirteenth Centuries

D. Lomax, *The Reconquest of Spain*, London, 1978.

A. MacKay, *Spain in the Middle Ages: From Frontier to Empire, 1000–1500*, London, 1977.

J.F. O'Callaghan, *A History of Medieval Spain*, Ithaca, 1975.

B.F. Reilly, *The Contest of Christian and Muslim Spain, 1031–1157*, Oxford, 1992.

Latin Episcopal Sees in the Thirteenth Century

R. Bartlett, *The Making of Europe: Conquest, Colonization and Cultural Change, 950–1350*, London, 1993.

C. Morris, *The Papal Monarchy: The Western Church from 1050–1250*, Oxford, 1989.

Monks, Mendicants, Béguines and Beghards

B.M. Bolton, *The Medieval Reformation*, London, 1983.

B.M. Bolton, 'Some Thirteenth-century Women in the Low Countries', *Niederlands Archief voor Kerkgeschiednis*, 61 (1981).

R.B. Brooke, *The Coming of the Friars*, London, 1975.

J.R. Burton, *The Monastic and Religious Orders in Britain, 1000–1300*, Cambridge, 1994.

W.A. Hinnebusch, *The History of the Dominican Order*, 2 vols, New York, 1973.

C.H. Lawrence, *The Friars*, London, 1994.

C.H. Lawrence, *Medieval Monasticism*, 2nd edn, London, 1989.

L.J. Lekai, *The White Monks*, Okauchee, 1953.

L.K. Little, *Religious Poverty and the Profit Economy*, London, 1978.

E.W. McDonnell, *The Béguines and Beghards in Medieval Culture*, New Brunswick, 1954.

L.J.R. Milis, *Angelic Monks and Earthly Men: Monasticism and its Meaning to Medieval Society*, Woodbridge, 1992.

J. Moorman, *A History of the Franciscan Order From its Origins to the Year 1517*, Oxford, 1968.

C. Neel, 'The Origins of the Béguines', *Signs*, 14 (1989).

R.W. Southern, *Western Society and the Church in the Middle Ages*, Harmondsworth, 1973.

The Papacy and the Conciliar Fathers of 1215

B.M. Bolton, 'A Show with a Meaning: Innocent III's Approach to the Fourth Lateran Council, 1215', *Medieval History*, 1 (1991).

H. Jedin, *et al.*, *History of the Church*, vol. 4, London, 1980.

J. Sayers, *Innocent III: Leader of Europe, 1198–1216*, London, 1993.

Shrines and Revivals, c. 1200–c. 1300

G. Dickson, 'The advent of the pastores (1251)', *Revue Belge de Philologie et d'Histoire*, 66 (1988).

G. Dickson, 'The flagellants of 1260 and the crusades', *Journal of Medieval History*, 15 (1989).

G. Dickson, 'Stephen of Cloyes, Philip Augustus and the Children's Crusade of 1212', in B.N. Sargent-Baur (ed.), *Journeys Towards God: Pilgrimage and Crusade*, Kalamazoo, 1992.

J. Sumption, *Pilgrimage: An Image of Mediaeval Religion*, London, 1975.

B. Ward, *Miracles and the Medieval Mind*, London, 1982.

Heresy, Albigensian Crusade and Inquisition

B. Hamilton, *The Medieval Inquisition*, London, 1981.

M. Lambert, *Medieval Heresy*, 2nd edn, Oxford, 1992.

W.L. Wakefield, *Heresy, Crusade and Inquisition in Southern France, 1100–1250*, Berkeley, 1974.

Provisioning War in the Twelfth Century

M.T. Clanchy, *From Memory to Written Record: England 1066–1307*, 2nd edn, Oxford, 1993.

A.J. Otway-Ruthven, *A History of Medieval Ireland*, 2nd edn, 1980.

R.L. Poole, *The Exchequer in the Twelfth Century*, Oxford, 1912.

Representative Assemblies

A. Marongiu, *Medieval Parliaments*, London, 1968.

A.R. Myers, *Parliaments and Estates in Europe*, London, 1975.

E.S. Procter, *Curia and Cortes in Leon and Castile*, Cambridge, 1980.

Fairs, Passes and Towns

R.H. Britnell, *The Commercialization of English Society, 1000–1500*, Cambridge, 1993.

B.M.S. Campbell *et al.*, *A Medieval Capital and its Grain Supply*, London, 1993.

E. Ennen, *The Medieval Town*, Amsterdam, New York and Oxford, 1979.

N. Ohler, *The Medieval Traveller*, Woodbridge, 1989.

N.J.G. Pounds, *An Economic History of Medieval Europe*, 2nd edn, Harlow 1994.

J.E. Tyler, *The Alpine Passes*, Oxford, 1930.

Town Laws

M. Bateson, 'The laws of Breteuil', *English Historical Review*, 15 (1900); 16 (1901).

W. Ebel, 'Lübisches Recht im Ostseeraum', in C. Haase (ed.), *Die Stadt des Mittelalters*, rev. edn, 3 vols, Darmstadt, 1976–8.

R. Urena y Smenjaud, *Fuero de Cuenca*, Madrid, 1935.

The Contado of Lucca

V. Tirelli, 'Lucca nella seconda metà del secola XII: società e instituzioni', in *I ceti dirigenti dell'età comunale nei secoli XII e XIII*, Pisa, 1982.

D. Waley, *The Italian City Republics*, 3rd edn, London, 1988.

Communal Movements

A. MacKay, *Spain in the Middle Ages: From Frontier to Empire, 1000–1500*, London, 1977.

B. Tate and M. Tate, *The Pilgrim Route to Santiago*, Oxford, 1987.

Settlement

T.F. Glick, *Irrigation and Society in Medieval Valencia*, Cambridge, MA, 1970.

M.G. Jiménez, *En torno a los origenes de Andalucia*, 2nd edn, Seville, 1988.

M.G. Jiménez, 'Frontier and settlement in the kingdom of Castile (1085–1350)', in R. Bartlett and A. MacKay (eds), *Medieval Frontier Societies*, Oxford, 1989.

P. Toubert, *Les structures du Latium médiéval*, Rome, 1973.

C. Wickham, *The Mountains and the City*, Oxford, 1988.

C. Wickham, *Il problema dell' incastellamento nell' Italia centrale*, Florence, 1985.

Anti-Semitism 1096–1306

S.W. Baron, *A Social and Religious History of the Jews*, vols iv–xii, New York, 1957–67.

H.H. Ben-Sasson, *A History of the Jewish People*, London, 1976.

R.I. Moore, *The Formation of a Persecuting Society: Power and Deviance in Western Europe, 950–1250*, Oxford, 1987.

K.R. Stow, *Alienated Minority: The Jews of Medieval Latin Europe*, Cambridge MA, 1992.

The Twelfth-Century Renaissance

R.L. Benson and G. Constable (eds), *Renaissance and Renewal in the Twelfth Century*, Cambridge, MA, 1982.

C.H. Haskins, *The Renaissance of the Twelfth Century*, Cambridge, MA, 1927.

C. Morris, *The Discovery of the Individual, 1050–1200*, London, 1972.

Romanesque and Gothic Europe
Villard de Honnecourt

C.F. Barnes, *Villard de Honnecourt, the Artist and His Drawings: A Critical Bibliography*, Boston, MA, 1982.

J. Bony, *French Gothic Architecture of the 12th and 13th Centuries*, Berkeley and London, 1983.

T. Bowie, *The Sketchbook of Villard de Honnecourt*, Bloomington and London, 1959.

A. Erlande-Brandenburg, *The Cathedral Builders of the Middle Ages*, London, 1995.

F. Bucher, *Architector: The Lodge Books and Sketchbooks of Medieval Architects*, New York, 1979.

K.J. Conant, *Carolingian and Romanesque Architecture 800–1200*, 3rd edn, Harmondsworth, 1973.

L. Grodecki, *Gothic Architecture*, London, 1986.

H.R. Hahnloser, *Villard de Honnecourt*, 2nd edn, Graz, 1972.

Abbot Suger, *On the Abbey Church of St Denis and Its*

Art Treasures, ed. E. Panofsky, Princeton, 1946.
G. Zarnecki, *Art of the Medieval World*, Englewood Cliffs and New York, 1975.

French Epic
D.D.R. Owen, *The Legend of Roland: A Pageant of the Middle Ages*, London, 1973.
D.L. Sawyers (ed.), *The Song of Roland*, Harmondsworth, 1957.
F. Whitehead (ed.), *La chanson de Roland*, Oxford, 1942.

Troubadours
M. Egan (ed.), *Les vies des troubadours*, Paris, 1985.
L. Paterson, *The World of the Troubadours: Medieval Occitan Society, c. 1100–c.1300*, Cambridge, 1993.

The Hundred Years War
C.T. Allmand, *The Hundred Years War*, Cambridge, 1988.
M. Barber, *The Angevin Legacy and the Hundred Years War, 1250–1340*, Oxford, 1990.
A. Curry, *The Hundred Years War*, Basingstoke, 1993.
P. Contamine, *War in the Middle Ages*, Oxford, 1984.
K.A. Fowler, *The Age of Plantagenet and Valois*, London, 1980.
J. Sumption, *The Hundred Years War*, London, 1990.

The Growth of the Burgundian State
Burgundian Administration
D. Nicholas, *Medieval Flanders*, Harlow, 1992.
W. Prevenier and W. Blockmans, *The Burgundian Netherlands*, Cambridge, 1986.
R. Vaughan, *Philip the Bold*, London, 1962.
R. Vaughan, *John the Fearless*, London, 1966.
R. Vaughan, *Philip the Good*, London, 1970.
R. Vaughan, *Charles the Bold*, London, 1973.
R. Vaughan, *Valois Burgundy*, London, 1975.

The Scottish Wars of Independence
Late Medieval Scotland
G.W.S. Barrow, *Robert Bruce and the Community of the Realm of Scotland*, 3rd edn, Edinburgh, 1988.

G.W.S. Barrow, *Kingship and Unity: Scotland, 1000–1306*, London, 1981.
A. Grant, *Independence and Nationhood: Scotland, 1306–1469*, London, 1984.
R. Nicholson, *Scotland: The Later Middle Ages*, Edinburgh, 1975.

Wales
A.D. Carr, *Medieval Wales*, Basingstoke, 1995.
R.R. Davies, *Conquest, Co-existence and Compromise: Wales, 1063–1415*, Oxford, 1987.
A.J. Taylor, *The Welsh Castles of Edward I*, London, 1986.
D. Walker, *Medieval Wales*, Cambridge, 1990.

Ireland
A. Cosgrove (ed.), *Medieval Ireland, 1169–1534: A New History of Ireland*, vol. 2, Oxford, 1987.
S. Duffy, *Ireland in the Middle Ages*, Basingstoke, 1997.
R. Frame, 'Power and society in the lordship of Ireland, 1272–1377', *Past and Present*, 76 (1977).
K. Nichols, *Gaelic and Gaelicized Ireland in the Middle Ages*, Dublin, 1972.

Switzerland
E. Bonjour, H.S. Offler and G.R. Potter, *A Short History of Switzerland*, Oxford, 1952.
A. Dado *et al.*, *Ticino medievale: Storia di una terra lombarda*, Locarno, 1990.
H. Heibling *et al.*, *Handbuch der Schweizer Geschichte*, 2 vols, Zurich, 1980.

Scandinavia
B. Sawyer and P. Sawyer, *Medieval Scandinavia: From Conversion to Reformation, c. 800–1500*, Minneapolis and London, 1993.

Emperors and Princes: Germany in the Later Middle Ages
The Government of Later Medieval Germany
G. Benneke, *Maximilian I (1459–1519): An Analytical Biography*, London, 1982.
F.R.H. Du Boulay, *Germany in the Later Middle Ages*, London, 1983.
H. Cohn, *The Government of the Rhine Palatine in the Fifteenth Century*, London, 1965.
H.S. Offler, 'Aspects of government in the late

medieval empire', in J.R. Hale *et al.* (eds), *Europe in the Later Middle Ages*, London, 1962.

Italy
D. Hay and J. Law, *Italy in the Age of the Renaissance, 1380–1530*, Harlow, 1989.

J. Larner, *Italy in the Age of Dante and Petrarch, 1216–1380*, Harlow, 1980.

The Expansion of the Crown of Aragon
Late Medieval Iberia
T.N. Bisson, *The Medieval Crown of Aragon*, Oxford, 1986.

S. Haliczer, *The Comuneros of Castile: The Forging of a Revolution, 1475–1521*, Wisconsin, 1981.

A. MacKay, *Spain in the Middle Ages: From Frontier to Empire*, London, 1977.

B.F. Reilly, *The Medieval Spains*, Cambridge, 1993.

The Wars of the Roses
J. Gillingham, *The Wars of the Roses*, London, 1981.

A. Goodman, *The Wars of the Roses*, London, 1981.

A.J. Pollard (ed.), *The Wars of the Roses*, Basingstoke, 1995.

Late Medieval Scotland
see Scottish Wars of Independence, *above*

The Advance of Turkey and the Crusade
F. Babinger, *Mehmed the Conqueror and His Time*, Princeton, 1978.

J.V.A. Fine, *The Late Medieval Balkans*, Ann Arbor, 1987.

N. Housley, *The Later Crusades from Lyons to Alcazar, 1274–1580*, Oxford, 1992.

R.P. Lindner, *Nomads and Ottomans in Medieval Anatolia*, Bloomington, 1983.

E. Zachariadou, *Trade and Crusade*, Venice, 1983.

Muscovy, Lithuania and Poland
E. Christiansen, *The Northern Crusade*, London, 1988.

R.O. Crummey, *The Formation of Muscovy, 1304–1613*, London, 1987.

J. Fennell, *The Crisis of Medieval Russia, 1200–1304*, London, 1983.

J. Meyendorff, *Byzantium and the Rise of Russia*, Cambridge, 1981.

S.C. Rowell, *Lithuania Ascending: A Pagan Empire within East Central Europe, 1295–1345*, Cambridge, 1994.

The Avignon Papacy
The Great Schism and the Councils
The Papal States
E. Goeller (ed.), *Die Einnahmen der apostolischen Kammer unter Johan XXII*, Paderborn, 1910.

W.F. Lunt, *Papal Revenues in the Middle Ages*, 2 vols, New York, 1934.

G. Mollat, *The Popes at Avignon, 1305–1378*, Edinburgh, 1963.

J.B. Morrall, *Gerson and the Great Schism*, Manchester, 1960.

P. Partner, *The Papal State under Martin V*, London, 1958.

P. Partner, *The Lands of St Peter: The Papal State in the Middle Ages and the Early Renaissance*, London, 1972.

Y. Renouard, *The Avignon Papacy, 1305–1403*, London, 1970.

R.N. Swanson, *Universities, Academics and the Great Schism*, Cambridge, 1979.

W. Ullmann, *The Origins of the Great Schism*, London, 1948.

D. Waley, *The Papal State in the Thirteenth Century*, London, 1961.

Byzantine Cultural and Monastic Centres
R. Browning, *The Byzantine Empire*, London, 1980.

J.M. Hussey, *The Orthodox Church in the Byzantine Empire*, Oxford, 1986.

D.M. Nicol, *Meteora: The Rock Monasteries of Thessaly*, London, 1963.

L. Rodley, *Cave Monasteries of Byzantine Cappadocia*, Cambridge, 1985.

S. Runciman, *Mistra*, London, 1980.

C.M. Woodhouse, *Gemistos Plethon: The Last of the Hellenes*, Oxford, 1986.

Bohemian Lands and Hussite Wars
F.M. Bartos, *The Hussite Revolution (1424–37)*, Boulder, 1986.

H. Kaminsky, *A History of the Hussite Revolution*, Berkeley, 1967.

The Growth of Fiscality in France

J.B. Henneman, *Royal Taxation in Fourteenth Century France*, 2 vols, Princeton and Philadelphia, 1971–6.

J.R. Major, *Representative Government in Early Modern France*, New Haven and London, 1980.

M. Wolfe, *The Fiscal System of Renaissance France*, New Haven, 1972.

Burgundian Administration

see The Growth of the Burgundian State, *above*

Castilian *Corregidores*

A. Bermúdez Aznar, *El corregidor en Castilla durante la baja edad media (1348–1474)*, Murcia, 1974.

S. Haliczer, *The Comuneros of Castile: The Forging of a Revolution, 1475–1521*, Wisconsin, 1981.

Representation at the Castilian *Cortes*

W. Piskorski, *Las cortes de Castilla en el periodo de tránsito de la edad media a la edad moderna (1188–1520)*, Barcelona, 1930.

C.O. Serrano, *Las cortes de Castilla y León y la crisis del reino (1445–1474): El registro de cortes*, Burgos, 1986.

Parliamentary Representation in England

G. Holmes, *The Good Parliament*, Oxford, 1975.

M. McKisack, *The Parliamentary Representation of the English Boroughs during the Middle Ages*, Oxford, 1932.

J.S. Roskell, *The Commons in the Parliament of 1422*, Manchester, 1954.

J.S. Roskell *et al.* (eds), *The History of Parliament: The House of Commons, 1386–1421*, Stroud, 1993.

The Government of Later Medieval Germany

see Emperors and Princes: Germany in the Later Middle Ages, *above*

The Spread of the Black Death

E. Carpentier, 'Autour de la Peste Noire: Famines et epidémies dans l'histoire du XIVe siècle', *Annales: Économies, Sociétés, Civilisations*, 17 (1962), pp. 1062–92.

R. Horrox, *The Black Death*, Manchester, 1994.

P. Ziegler, *The Black Death*, London, 1969.

The German Hanse

P. Dollinger, *The German Hansa*, London, 1970.

K. Friedland, *Die Hanse*, Stuttgart, 1991.

T.R. Lloyd, *England and the German Hanse, 1157–1611*, Cambridge, 1991.

M.M. Postan, *Medieval Trade and Finance*, Cambridge, 1973.

Financial Centres in Western Europe

A. MacKay, *Money and Prices in Fifteenth-Century Castile*, London, 1981.

H.A. Miskimin, *Money and Power in Fifteenth-Century France*, New Haven and London, 1984.

R. De Roover, *The Rise and Decline of the Medici Bank*, Cambridge, MA, 1963.

P. Spufford, *Handbook of Medieval Exchange*, London, 1986.

P. Spufford, *Money and its Uses in Medieval Europe*, Cambridge, 1988.

Towns in the Later Middle Ages

E. Ennen, *The Medieval Town*, Amsterdam, New York and Oxford, 1979.

H. Inalcik, 'The policy of Mehmed II toward the Greek population of Istanbul and the Byzantine buildings of the city', *Dumbarton Oaks Papers*, 23–4 (1969–70).

B. Lewis, *Istanbul and the Civilization of the Ottoman Empire*, Norman, 1963.

H. Planitz, *Die Deutsche Stadt im Mittelalter*, Graz, 1954.

A. Collantes de Terán Sánchez, *Sevilla en la baja edad media: la ciudad y sus hombres*, Seville, 1977.

W. Vischer, 'Geschichte des schwäbishen Städtebundes der Jahre 1376–1389', *Forschungen zur deutschen Geschichte*, 2 (1862).

Late Medieval Transhumance in Western Europe

C.J. Bishko, 'The Castilian as plainsman: the medieval ranching frontier in La Mancha and Extremadura', in A.R. Lewis and T.F. McGann (eds), *The New World Looks at its History*, Austin, 1963.

E.H. Carrier, *Water and Grass: A Study in the Pastoral Economy of Southern Europe*, London, 1932.

J. Klein, *The Mesta: A Study of Spanish Economic History, 1273–1836*, Cambridge, MA, 1920.

E. Le Roy Ladurie, *Montaillou: Cathars and Catholics in a French Village, 1294–1324*, London, 1978.

M.L. Ryder, *Sheep and Man*, London, 1983.

C.D. Smith, *Western Mediterranean Europe: A Historical Geography of Italy, Spain and Southern France since the Neolithic*, London, 1979.

European Expansion

F. Fernandez-Armesto, *Before Columbus: Exploration and Colonisation from the Mediterranean to the Atlantic, 1229–1492*, London, 1987.

F. Fernandez-Armesto, *Columbus*, Oxford, 1991.

J.S.R. Phillips, *The Medieval Expansion of Europe*, Oxford, 1988.

P.E. Russell, *Prince Henry the Navigator: The Rise and Fall of a Cultural Hero*, Oxford, 1984.

G.V. Scammell, *The First Imperial Age: European Overseas Expansion, c. 1400–1715*, London, 1989.

The Jacquerie
The Peasants' Revolt

R.B. Dobson (ed.), *The Peasants' Revolt of 1381*, 2nd edn, London, 1983.

G. Fourquin, *The Anatomy of Popular Rebellion in the Middle Ages*, New York, 1978.

E.B. Fryde, *The Great Revolt of 1381*, London, 1981.

R.H. Hilton, *Bond Men Made Free: Medieval Peasant Movements and the English Rising of 1381*, London, 1973.

R.H. Hilton and T.H. Aston (eds), *The English Rising of 1381*, Cambridge, 1984.

M. Mollat and P. Wolff, *The Popular Revolutions of the Later Middle Ages*, London, 1973.

Jews

M.R. Cohen, *Under Crescent and Cross: The Jews in the Middle Ages*, Princeton, 1994.

J. Edwards, *The Jews in Christian Europe*, London, 1991.

J. Edwards, *The Jews in Western Europe, 1400–1600*, Manchester, 1994.

A. Haverkamp (ed.), *Zur Geschichte der Juden im deutschland des Späten Mittelalters und der Frühen Neuzeit*, Stuttgart, 1981.

Margery Kempe

A. Goodman, 'The piety of John Brunham's daughter', in D. Baker (ed.), *Medieval Women*, Oxford, 1978.

Julian of Norwich, *Relevations of Divine Love*, ed. C. Wolters, Harmondsworth, 1966.

B.A. Windeatt (ed.), *The Book of Margery Kempe*, Harmondsworth, 1985.

Printing

E. Eisenstein, *The Printing Revolution in Early Modern Europe*, Cambridge, 1983.

L. Febvre and H.-J. Martin, *The Coming of the Book: The Impact of Printing, 1450–1800*, London and New York, 1990.

Journeys of Major Italian Artists

J. Pope-Hennessey, *Italian Gothic Sculpture*, London, 1965.

A. Smart, *The Dawn of Italian Painting*, Oxford, 1978.

J. White, *Art and Architecture in Italy, 1250–1400*, Harmondsworth, 1966.

Rediscovery of Classical Texts

G. Billanovich, 'Petrarch and the textual tradition of Livy', *Journal of the Warburg and Courtauld Institutes*, 14 (1951), pp. 137–203.

L.D. Reynolds (ed.), *Texts and Transmissions: A Survey of the Latin Classics*, Oxford, 1983.

L.D. Reynolds and N.G. Wilson (eds), *Scribes and Scholars: A Guide to the Transmission of Greek and Latin Literature*, Oxford, 1968.

R. Sabbadini, *Le scoperte dei codici latini e greci ne' secoli XIV e XV*, 2 vols, Florence, 1905–14.

The Rise of Universities

A.B. Cobban, *The Medieval Universities: Their Development and Organisation*, London, 1975.

S.C. Ferruolo, *The Origins of the University: The Schools of Paris and their Critics, 1100–1215*, Stanford, 1985.

J. Le Goff, *Intellectuals in the Middle Ages*, Oxford and Cambridge, MA, 1993.

A. Piltz, *The World of Medieval Learning*, Oxford, 1981.

H. de Ridder-Symoens (ed.), *A History of the University in Europe*, vol. 1: *Universities in the Middle Ages*, Cambridge, 1992.

INDEX

Entries in this index relate only to references in the text. Place-names in the index and text are usually identified on the corresponding map. Modern states or continents are used in the index to identify the location of place names.

Dol, France 53, 111
Dôle, France 201
Domažlice, battle of (1431) 196
Domesday Book 55
Dominicans, mendicant order 117, 122, 124
Don, river (Russia) 24
Dorestad, Netherlands 57, 61
Dorylaion, Turkey 75, 87; battle of (1097) 86
Douai, France 106
Douglas, Scottish family 179
dowries 213
Dristria, battle of (1087) 75
Drogheda, Ireland 133
Dublin, Ireland 25, 110, 125, 168
Dubrovnik, Croatia 153, 220
Duccio, artist 239
Duero, river 33, 35
Dunstan, monk 45
Durham, England 149, 205
Dürnkrut, battle of (1278) 102
Durrow, Ireland 42
Dyrrachion/Durrës, Albania 75, 86

Eadred, king of Wessex 32
East Anglia, England 32, 61, 226, 227
Ebles II, count of Ventadour 154
Ebro, river 33
Echternach, Luxembourg 44, 65–6
Ecija, Spain 229
Edessa/Urfa, Turkey 12, 14, 86–7, 89
Edgar, king of Wessex 53
Edinburgh, Scotland 179, 208
Edington, battle of (878) 32
Edmund, king of Wessex 32
education 117, 192, 193, 216, 241
Edward I, king of England 86, 110, 164, 168, 205
Edward II, king of England 205
Edward III, king of England 159, 164
Edward IV, king of England 177
Edward V, king of England 177
Edward the Confessor, king of England 53, 55
Edward the Elder, king of Wessex 32
Eger, pacification of (1389) 217
Eginhard, Carolongian author 152
Egypt; Egyptians 12, 14, 23, 40, 61, 88–9, 91, 104, 122, 184, 192
Elbe, river 46, 87, 97, 99, 211
electoral princes 172, 205, 208
Ellendun, battle of (825) 32
emigration 168
Emilia, Italy 174
Engelbrechtson, Engelbrecht, Swedish leader 172
England; English 19, 24, 30, 32, 40, 42, 45, 50, 52, 55, 66, 71, 77, 85, 87, 110, 111, 114, 117, 119, 125, 127, 129, 132–4, 138, 143, 145, 149, 152, 154, 156, 159, 160, 161, 164, 168, 177, 179, 182, 189, 191, 200, 205, 209, 211, 213, 218, 226, 227, 232
English Channel 61, 154
episcopal sees 38, 46–50, 79, 99, 110, 111

Era, river 135
Erasmus, scholar 236
Eric Bloodaxe, Norwegian king of Northumbria 32
Espina, Alonso de, Franciscan friar 229
Essex, England 226, 227
Esslingen, Germany 208
estates, Burgundian 162, 201; French 197, 200, 201; German 174, 208
Estella, Spain 153
Estonia; Estonians 99, 154
Esztergom, Hungary 28, 47, 110
Ethelwold, monk 45
Euclid, Greek scholar 147
Eugenius IV, pope 192
Euphrates, river 12, 16, 21, 89, 104
Euric, Visigoth king 9
Euclid, Greek scholar 147
Evora, Portugal 107
Evreux, Louis, count of 106
Extremadura, Spain 204

fairs 129, 131, 213
famine 168, 209
Faremoutiers, France 42
Faro, Portugal 107
Faroe Islands 25, 156
Fatimid dynasty 23
Fécamp, France 42
Feltre, Italy 176
Ferdinand III, king of Castile 107, 142
Ferdinand V, king of Aragon 107
Ferrara, Italy 96, 241
feudalism 30, 71, 79, 194, 197, 200
Ficino, Marsilio, scholar 241
Fidenza, Italy 153
Field of Blood, battle of (1119) 89
Fife, Scotland 79, 179
Finland: Finns 97, 154
Fiore, Joachim of, abbot 188
fishing 218
Flagellants, religious sect 122, 230
Flanders, Belgium/France 30, 45, 77, 79, 86, 99, 119, 129, 131–2, 137, 156, 160, 162, 164, 191, 197, 201, 211; Robert II, count of 86
Fleury, France 42, 45
Flint, Wales 168
Florence/Firenze, Italy 96, 111, 132, 156, 176, 209, 213, 238–9, 241
Florentino, Italy 94
Foggia, Italy 220
Foix, France 226
Fondi, Italy 189
Fonte Avellana, Italy 45
Fontenoy, battle of (841) 21
Fontevrault, France 114
Forest of Dean, England 125
Forth, river 156, 164
Fossanova, Italy 150
Fournier, Jacques, bishop 221

Urban V, pope 189
Urban VI, pope 189, 191
Urbino, Italy 191
Uri, Switzerland 170
usury 145, 213
Utraquists, Hussite sect 194, 196

Vaillant, Jean, Jacquerie leader 226
Valdemar IV (Atterdag), king of Denmark 171
Val Demone, Italy 84
Valencia, Spain 33, 107, 111, 141–3, 176–7, 239
Valenciennes, France 106
Valens, Emperor 7–8
Vallombrosa, Italy 45
Valois, Catherine of, daughter of Charles VI, 161;
    Charles of, brother of Philip IV 96, 106; dynasty
    159, 162, 164, 172; *see also* individual French kings
    and Burgundian dukes
Vandals, tribe 9–10, 12, 38, 59
Varna, battle of (1444) 184
Vaspurakan, Turkey 23
Vastergarn, Sweden 61
Vaucelles, France 151
Vejer de la Frontera, Spain 143
Velay, France 106
Vendôme, France 71
Veneto, Italy 132, 152
Venezuela, America 222
Venice, Italy 18, 45, 75, 86, 96, 132, 176, 184,
    232
Ventadour, Bernart of, troubadour 154; Maria de,
    troubadour 154
Vercelli, Italy 96, 241
Verdun, France 21; treaty of (843) 106
Vermandois, Herbert II, count of 30; Hugh, count of
    86
Verona, Italy 96, 132, 174, 176, 239
Via Amerina, road 18
Via Egnatia, road 86
Vicenza, Italy 96, 174, 176
Vico da, Roman family 191
Vidal, Peire, troubadour 154
Vienne, France 9, 154; council of (1311–12) 118;
    Girart de, author 152
Vikings, warriors 21, 23–5, 28, 30, 32, 35, 46, 50, 57, 61
vineyards 51, 134
Visby, Sweden 99, 211
Visconti, Milanese family 96, 174, 176
Visigoths, tribe 7–10, 12, 14, 16, 33, 38, 59
Vistula, river 99
Viterbo, Italy 238
Vitry, Jacques de, archbishop of Acre 118
Vivarium, Italy 42
Viviers, France 106
Vladimir, prince of Kiev 23, 26, 28, 45
Vladimir, Russia 104
Vladimir-Suzdal, principality of 186
Volga, river 24
Volkov, river 216

Volturno, river 63
Vordingborg, peace of (1435) 171
Vouillé, battle of (507) 9

Waiblingen, Germany 96
Wales; Welsh 32, 50, 71, 77, 110, 125, 152, 156, 164,
    168, 179
Walsingham, England 232
Waltbraht, Saxon noble 50
War of Independence, Scottish 164, 168, 179
War of the Roses 177, 179
War of the Vespers 96
Waterford, Ireland 79
Welf dynasty 72, 96
Wells, England 142
Welser, German family 222
Wenceslas, duke of Bohemia 28
Wenceslas II, king of Bohemia 102
Wenceslas IV/Wenzel, king of Bohemia 194, 217
Wends, tribe 87
Werla, Germany 35
Wessex, kingdom of 32–3, 45, 57
Westminster, England 168
Westphalia, Germany 99
wheat 221
Whitby, England 42; synod of (664) 42
Whithorn, Scotland 42, 110
Widukind, Saxon leader 50
Wijk bij Duurstede, Netherlands 57
Wildeshausen, Germany 50
William, duke of Aquitaine 45
William I, king of England and duke of Normandy 30,
    55, 77
William I (the Lion), king of Scots 71, 79
Willibrord, missionary 40, 44, 65–6
Wimpfen, Germany 149
Winchester, England 53, 57
wine 51, 129, 132, 213, 235
Witgis, Ostrogoth leader 10
wool 129, 132, 159
Worms, Germany 208, 217
Wurtemberg, Germany 217
Würzburg, Germany 65

Xanten, Norbert of, preacher 114

Yarmuk, Syria 14
York, England 32, 40, 50, 53, 61, 66, 110, 232; English
    dynasty 177; Richard, duke of 177
Yorkshire, England 227
Ypres/Ieper, Belgium 129

Zamora, Spain 33, 204
Žatec, Czech Republic 194
Zeeland, Netherlands 162, 179, 201
Žižka, Jan, Taborite leader 194, 196
Zorita, Spain 107
Zug, Switzerland 170
Zürich, Switzerland 170